Baseball's
Best
1,000

D1509880

Base
Best

Rankings of the Skills, the Achievements and the

ball's

1,000

Performance of the Greatest Players of All Time

Derek Gentile

Timothy Cebula, Jack Passetto and Brian Sullivan, contributors

BLACK DOG
& LEVENTHAL
PUBLISHERS
NEW YORK

Copyright © 2004, 2008, 2012 Derek Gentile

All rights reserved. No part of this book, either text or illustration, may be used or reproduced in any form without the prior written permission from the publisher.

Published by
Black Dog & Leventhal Publishers, Inc.
151 West 19th Street
New York, NY 10011

Distributed by
Workman Publishing Company
225 Varick Street
New York, NY 10025

Manufactured in the United States of America

Cover and interior design by Elizabeth Driesbach
Photographs courtesy of Transcendental Graphics, AP Wide World Photos, Baseball Hall of Fame Library, Cooperstown, NY, Newscom, LLC, NoirTech Research.

ISBN-13: 978-1-57912-908-8

h g f e d c b a

Library of Congress Cataloging-in-Publication Data available on file.

Contents

Dedication

For my father, Joseph Gentile, 1927-2012

Introduction

This is an updated version of *Baseball's Best 1,000*, which I wrote in 2004. It was an attempt to list, in some kind of order, the top 1,000 baseball players of all time. Many people liked it; some didn't. But I had a good time writing it. This new edition gives me a chance to make a few changes and update the profiles that appear on these pages

I don't want to beat the proverbial dead horse, so I won't go into an extended explanation of how these rankings were put together. The way I compiled the list, as I explained in the previous introduction, was kind of backward. Instead of starting from Player Number One and moving on toward 1,000, I took every player in organized baseball and the Negro Leagues, and whittled the list down. There were about 20,000 players total with which to work, and after several weeks I got down to 2,800, then 1,500, then 1,000.

I tried to base the formula on a combination of real and comparative statistics. By that, I mean that Babe Ruth's 714 home runs are factored in, as are his 2,213 RBI. But I also gave weight to the number of times he led the league in these categories, or finished second, or third, or whatever. This gave me a yardstick to, at least as I see it, measure players from different eras. In other words, if a guy won the home run crown five times between 1880 and 1900, as the Phillies' Harry Stovey did, well, that had weight, regardless of how many he hit, which was about 10 a year.

In addition, I decided that players had to play at least 10 years. That enabled me to set some kind of guideline based on player durability.

The hardest things to factor in were awards. Yes, Don Mattingly won nine Gold Glove awards for his fine fielding at first base. Did he deserve all nine? Yankees fans will say yes. Non-Yankees fans may say no. I think he was a darn good defensive first baseman, and all those Gold Gloves meant other people did too.

In 1927, the MVP of the American League was Lou Gehrig. Not because he was better than Babe Ruth; he wasn't. But at the time, the league's sportswriters, who voted for MVP, had a silly rule that a ballplayer could win the award only once. That rule is no longer in force, but for my purposes, I had to give Gehrig's MVP less weight than, say, Carl Yastrzemski's award in 1967.

Similarly, selections to the midseason All Star teams have always been somewhat suspect. Major League Baseball specifies that every team in the league be represented at the All Star game. Certainly we all know of one or more players every year who are excluded from an All Star team because they are the third or fourth All Star on a team already sending two or three. That was a factor as well.

But these awards meant something. They meant that the individual had performed at a higher level than his peers, so they absolutely could not be ignored. And they were not. I have taken them all on a case-by-case basis.

The major exception in all this is the list of players from the Negro Leagues. In many cases, we are dealing with players with very incomplete stats. In a few cases, despite a lot of research, I sort of throw up my hands and indicate that the lifetime stats of a certain player just aren't available. But I don't want to give the impression that I based my ranking on guesswork in these cases. There are some great reference books out there on the Negro Leagues, and I have just about every one of them.

Anyway, because of that, while these stats are incomplete, they are not barren. We have a better-than-decent idea of the abilities of the Negro League players I list. So I did what I could.

That, in a nutshell, is how the list was compiled. If this sounds like a ponderous, tedious, difficult thing to do, I admit that parts of it were. But it's kind of like eating one of those big, chocolate Easter bunnies: Once you start, you have to finish, sooner or later.

The interesting thing about lists is that everybody has one. And in the case of baseball, everyone seems to have three or four or five. I received a lot of feedback on this book, more than from any other baseball book I've written. Most people gave me credit for even trying to do what I did. Some people had suggestions. What I decided to do was list the suggestions—the reasonable ones—and let you, the reader, know what I did about them.

1. There are two Kid Gleasons.

Not anymore. That was a mistake, which we fixed. And, frankly, a list that was 99.8-percent correct ain't too bad.

2. Where is Hall of Famer Goose Goslin?

Right there, at Number 210. He was not, however, in the last index, which generated a call from a Tigers fan.

3. Why are some Hall of Famers so far down on the list? Doesn't the Hall of Fame induct the greatest players in baseball?

This is my list, not the Hall of Fame's. That's the easiest way to explain it. The Hall of Fame is run by some of the nicest, most professional people I have encountered in book-writing land. That said, I don't agree with all their selections. Nor do you, dear reader, if I'm not mistaken. So some of these guys aren't in the upper echelon of this book because, while they may have fit the guidelines of the Hall of Fame, they didn't fit mine. That's about it.

4. I can't believe Pete Rose is at Number 28. Is this because of his gambling problems?

No. Pete Rose is where he is for a lot of reasons, but his penchant for betting on baseball was not a factor. To the folks who sent me reasoned letters and e-mails as to why their guy should be in or higher, or why someone who's not their guy should be out or lower, I'm sorry. It's not that I can't defend this list, it's that, again, this is my list. If you want to come to town and buy me lunch and argue it, that's fine. If lunch is good enough, I may concede you have a point. But I doubt I'll change my decision much.

5. Why is Barry Bonds in here? He's a cheater, a steroid-abusing fool that spits in the eye of baseball and its fans. Cheaters should not be honored.

Ah, Barry Bonds. This was something of a toughie. Bonds was recently indicted for allegedly lying to a grand jury about his use of steroids. We have a sense that certain steroids are performance-enhancing drugs. That is, science has told us that steroid users are stronger and their recovery time from injury is shorter. That is an advantage. And, as my father pointed out, Bonds's added strength means that balls he hit that were long outs, say, 10 years ago, are now home runs.

That said, we don't know how long Bonds was on these steroids. And without some documentation, we don't know what he actually ingested. (We think we know, based on published reports, but conjecture and proof are two different things. Take it from an old court reporter.)

I had no choice but to go by the numbers, which, as we all know, are considerable. Barry Bonds is the greatest player of our generation, drugs or no drugs, and this fact is reflected in his positioning. I don't see how I can do anything else.

We also have a very interesting point brought up by Jose Canseco, a steroid user and proud of it. Canseco says that, by his estimation, 90 to 95 percent of the guys in baseball in the 1990s were on some kind of performance-enhancing steroid. Thus, he posited, Bonds accomplished all that he accomplished on a relatively level playing field. I don't necessarily agree with that position, but it's something to consider.

So here we are. The list you will read reflects who I think are the top 1,000 ballplayers today, in 2012. It is not the same list as the one in 2004, or the same one I updated in 2008. Just remember one thing: I had fun writing this book (as opposed to researching it!), so please have fun reading it.

#**1** George Herman "Babe" Ruth

P-OF-1B, Red Sox, Yankees, Braves, 1914–35.
Hall of Fame, 1936

It's been almost 100 years since the world first heard of George Herman Ruth. In that time, there have been a lot of great players. But over that 100-year span, it's hard to argue that the man his teammates called "Jidge" isn't still the greatest.

He started his baseball career as a left-handed catcher for the St. Mary's Industrial School for Boys. He was, in the words of one of his later teammates, Harry Hooper, a "green pea," fresh off the streets of Baltimore. At St. Mary's, Ruth was introduced to baseball, which gave him focus and structure. Since he was a big kid, he was a catcher at first and, on occasion, he pitched. Eventually, his coach at St. Mary's decided the big fellow was better on the mound than behind the plate.

Ruth was eventually signed by the Baltimore Orioles at the time a successful minor league club. On one of his first days with the team, one of the veterans asked another who the new kid was. Oh, said the other vet, that's [manager] Jack Dunn's "baby." A nickname was born.

He was a great pitcher for the Orioles. Signed by the Red Sox in 1914, he became a star in his second season. By 1915, he was arguably the best left-handed pitcher in the American League. His duels with the Senators' Walter Johnson are considered classics.

That 1915 season was the first time he ever hit a home run, a mighty blast off New York pitcher Jack Warhop on May 5. He found he enjoyed it.

In 1920, the Red Sox sold Ruth to the New York Yankees. That trade may have been the most significant in baseball history. It marked the end of the Boston dynasty (four World Series wins in the decade) and the beginning of Yankee greatness.

The Yankees converted one of the best pitchers in baseball to an outfielder, a ridiculous concept even now. But of course, it worked. In 1921, he hit 59 home runs, more than every other team in the league. In 1927, he hit 60, still one of the top seasons in baseball history.

He was stylish, he was colorful. In 1930, Ruth signed for $80,000 per year, a figure that brought his annual salary to $5,000 more than President Herbert Hoover. A reporter asked Ruth how he could justify making more than the president of the United States of America.

"Well," said Ruth, "I had a better year than he did."

His pitching and hitting records have, for the most part, been broken over the last few decades. But his legacy as baseball's star of stars endures.

LIFETIME STATS: BA: .342, HR: 714, RBI: 2,213, H: 2,873, SB: 123. W: 95, L: 46, SV: 4, ERA: 2.28, SO: 488, CG: 107

#2 Willie Howard "Say Hey Kid" Mays

OF-1B, Giants, Mets, 1951–73. Hall of Fame, 1979

Speed (led the NL in stolen bases four consecutive years). Power (second player in baseball history to hit 600 home runs, ending up with 660). Durability (20 consecutive All-Star Game appearances).

In Willie Mays' case the numbers shout for themselves: This is an all-time great.

Mays was a star in the Negro Leagues for a few years, before being signed by the New York Giants. His first year in the Big Apple was 1951, the year the Giants edged the Dodgers for the National League crown. Mays, in fact, was in the on-deck circle when the Giants' Bobby Thomson hit his historic home run.

Mays won 11 Gold Glove Awards. His most famous defensive play came in the 1954 World Series, off Cleveland's Vic Wertz. Wertz ripped a deep fly ball to center field. Mays turned and ran full speed to the center field wall, and caught the ball over his shoulder, a feat that is still seen on replays.

When appraised of the play, Mays was always quick to point out that the reason the catch was so vital was that he also had to make a throw afterwards, as there were less than two outs, with men on base.

Mays won MVP awards in 1954 and 1965. There are at least three other years in which his statistics are comparable to or better than those years, but the fact is, baseball writers were always uneasy awarding to many MVP awards to one player.

LIFETIME STATS: BA: .302, HR: 660, RBI: 1,903, H: 3,283, SB: 338

#3 Johannes Peter "Honus" Wagner
SS-OF-1B-3B, Louisville, Pirates, 1897–1917. Hall of Fame, 1936

The story goes that one day in Pittsburgh, Wagner was manning his shortstop position when he reached around with his glove hand to pull out a chaw of tobacco from his back pocket. (In the early days of baseball, players wore gloves that more closely resembled golf gloves.) The batter hit a sharp grounder his way. Wagner calmly barehanded the ball and gunned it over to first, thus throwing out a man with one hand behind his back.

Wagner was stocky, barrel-chested and had shovels for hands. Legend has it that when he dug balls out of the infield dirt and zipped them over to first base, a small load of stones and dirt would travel with the ball.

He played virtually every position except catcher. He was a tremendous hitter, winning eight batting titles and six slugging average titles. He hit over

.300 16 times, led the league in doubles seven times and triples three times. He stole 722 bases, and led the league in that category five times.

In 1902, Wagner played 61 games in the outfield, 44 at shortstop, 32 games at first base, one at second base and pitched once. He didn't make an error at any of those positions. From 1913 to 1916, he led the league's shortstops in fielding position.

Wagner was a terrific athlete: He may well have been the first baseball player to lift weights, and he was a fanatic about a new game that had recently been invented in Springfield called basketball. He played baseball until he was 43 and was perhaps the best 40-year-old player in baseball history.

LIFETIME STATS: BA: .327, HR: 101, RBI: 1,732, H: 3,415, SB: 722

#4 Tyrus Raymond "Ty" Cobb

OF-1B, Tigers, A's, 1905–28. Hall of Fame, 1936

Seventy-five years after he retired from baseball, Ty Cobb still owns the best career batting average of all time: .366. And he still holds the distinction of being the nastiest SOB of all time. There are no stats for that; Cobb has retired the trait.

Be that as it may, the man could hit: a total of 12 batting championships, including five in a row from 1911 to 1915. He had back-to-back .400 seasons in 1911 and 1912, with another .400 season in 1922, and more than 4,100 career hits, a record that stood for 50 years.

Cobb wasn't a slugger in the present sense of the word, but he still had a career slugging percentage of .512, and led the league in that category eight times.

And he could run: 892 stolen bases, leading the league six times. He was the all-time leader until Lou Brock passed him in 1978.

Was he mean? Yeah, he was mean. He used to sharpen his spikes in the dugout as opposing teams took batting practice, and he wasn't afraid to jab a slow-footed infielder when sliding into second or third base. He had more than his share of fights, and in 1912, went into the stands after a heckling fan.

He's known to have cheated. According to pitcher Dutch Leonard, he paid off Cleveland's Tris Speaker and Joe Wood to throw a game to the Tigers so Detroit could finish third. He may have tried to fix other games, but it was impossible to determine.

Cobb, were he alive today, would probably say that he played to win, at any cost. He did. And it paid off. In 1936, he was the top vote-getter for the first class of the Baseball Hall of Fame, topping Babe Ruth, Cy Young and Honus Wagner.

LIFETIME STATS: BA: .366, HR: 117, RBI: 1,937, H: 4,189, SB: 892

#5 Walter "The Big Train," "Barney" Johnson

RHP, Senators, 1907–27. Hall of Fame, 1936

Johnson was a 6'1" strikeout machine, an affable soul who could buzz a baseball from the mound to home plate as fast as anyone in history.

It was, at least partly, the arms. Johnson had long, limber arms, and he threw the ball with an easy sidearm motion that arrived in his catcher's mitt with a sound like a rifle shot.

Johnson played his entire career with the Washington Senators, an organization not particularly known for its acumen. With Johnson leading the way, the Senators did manage a pair of World Series appearances, and in 1924, he was a world champion.

The story of that final game is one of the fine yarns of World Series play. Johnson pitched four innings of scoreless relief in Game Seven after pitching a complete game two days earlier. Teammate Early McNeely's 12th-inning seeing-eye single scored the winning run.

Johnson was the Sultan of Strikeouts, to borrow a nickname from his contemporary, Babe Ruth. The Big Train (so named for the locomotive-like velocity of his pitches) led the league in strikeouts 12 times, in shutouts seven times, in wins and complete games six times and in ERA five times.

Johnson won 417 games and saved 34 more for the Senators.

He was as affable as Ty Cobb was rambunctious. Old-timers swore that when Johnson was far ahead in a game, he would ease up on a rookie or former teammate and let them get a hit. It's probably true.

LIFETIME STATS: W: 417, L: 279, SV: 34, ERA: 2.17, SO: 3,509, CG: 531

#6 Barry Lamar Bonds
OF, Pirates, Giants, 1986–2007

The new home run king, Bonds is one of the greatest offensive performers in baseball history. The 14-time All Star has been the Most Valuable Player of the National League seven times, in 1990, 1992, 1993, 2001, 2002, 2003 and 2004. In three of those years, he was voted the Player of the Year in the Major Leagues.

Throughout most of his career, Bonds has never been far from the top. He was the runner-up to the National League MVP award twice, in 1991 and 2000. In 1994, he was fourth in the voting, and in 1996 and 1997, he was fifth.

Bonds is the all-time leader in walks, with 2,515; second in career extra-base hits, with 1,425; third in career runs scored, with 2,198; fourth in career total bases, with 5,906; and third in RBI, with 1,996. Heck, he's even 32nd on the stolen-base list, with 514. In the field, Bonds has won eight Gold Gloves.

If there is a knock on Bonds, statistically, it's that his postseason work has not been as stellar. His teams, the Pirates and the Giants, have made it to the postseason nine times, winning only two series, in 2002, when San Francisco defeated Atlanta and St. Louis before falling to the Angels in the World Series.

Bonds has batted .245 in postseason play, with nine homers and 24 RBI. His best three series were in 2002, when he hit .294 with three home runs against the Braves in the Divisional Series, .273 with six RBI against the Cardinals in the Championship Series and a stellar .471 in his only trip to the World Series.

On Nov. 15, 2007, Bonds was indicted by a federal grand jury for allegedly lying to another grand jury in 2003 about his use of performance-enhancing steroids. Bonds pled not guilty to four counts of perjury and one count of obstruction of justice. His trial is expected to start sometime in late 2008. His adherents will say, this is a player who stands above all others of his generation. His detractors will say the numbers are artificial. But Bonds is clearly the greatest player of his time, steroids or no steroids.

LIFETIME STATS: BA: .298, HR: 762, RBI: 1,996, H: 2,935, SB: 514

#7 Mickey "The Commerce Comet" Mantle

OF-1B-SS, Yankees, 1951–68. Hall of Fame, 1974

Mantle was a man blessed with thunderous home run power and blazing speed. He was named after Hall of Fame catcher Mickey Cochrane, and he was even better than Cochrane.

Where to start? He was a switch-hitter who hit 536 home runs: 373 from the left side of the plate, 163 from the right. With his great upper body strength, some of those home runs were monster shots, like the one on May 22, 1963, which almost carried out of Yankee Stadium.

But he was also a tremendous bunter and base stealer. Mantle stole 153 bases, including 21 in 1959. He was only caught stealing three times that year. With his speed, he also hit 72 career triples, leading the league with 11 in 1955.

Mantle, a 16-time All Star, won the Triple Crown in 1956, with 52 home runs, 130 RBI and a .353 batting average. He won the MVP award that year, as well as in 1957 and 1962. He also won a Gold Glove in 1962. He was as fast afield as he was on the base paths, and had a rocket arm.

He was a clutch player, who regularly played in pain. He was also a great teammate who befriended rookies and marginal players throughout his career. He was a leader on the Yankees and a huge fan favorite throughout his career.

He may have hung in with the Yankees a few years too long, at least by some folks' standards. But let's face it: The Mick loved the game, and it was hard to let go.

LIFETIME STATS: BA: .298, HR: 536, RBI: 1,509, H: 2,415, SB: 153

#8 Theodore Samuel "Ted," "Teddy Ballgame," "The Kid," "The Splendid Splinter," "The Thumper" Williams

OF, Red Sox, 1939–42, 1946–60. Hall of Fame, 1966

It is hard to believe that Ted Williams, a man who was so much larger than life, is no longer with us. We want him to be like those actors on the silver screen: undaunted, immortal, unconquerable.

He wanted to be known as the greatest hitter who ever lived. He might have been. He didn't hit for as much power as Babe Ruth (although he lost four years to two wars, and still hit 521 homers). He didn't make as many hits as Ty Cobb (although his career on-base percentage is almost 50 points higher: .482 to .433).

Five times in his career, in fact, Williams had an on-base percentage of .500 or better. The year he hit .406, it was .553, a record at the time. That meant that 55 percent of the time, when Williams came to bat, he at least made it to first base. He was as nearly unstoppable as a player could be.

He played hard every game. He played on great Red Sox teams in the late 1940s, and he played on awful Red Sox teams in the 1950s. He hit .406 in 1941, two numbers every baseball fan worth his salt knows. He hit .400 two other times, albeit in shortened seasons: In 1952 he hit .400 in the first six games of the season and went back into the service to fight in the Korean War. He came back from that war late in 1953 and hit .407.

He was an authentic American hero who fought in World War II and the Korean conflict. His plane was shot down in the Korean War and he almost died. But Williams didn't want to sit on an Army base and play on a club team: He wanted to be where the action was.

He won six batting titles, two MVP awards, four home run crowns, a Triple Crown in 1942 and was a 17-time All Star. He was a great player. When he was elected to the Hall of Fame, he used his acceptance speech to lobby for the great players of the Negro Leagues to be inducted. And soon, of course, they were.

LIFETIME STATS: BA: .344, HR: 521, RBI: 1,839, H: 2,654, SB: 24

#9 Joshua "Josh" Gibson

C, Homestead Grays, Pittsburgh Crawfords (Negro Leagues), 1929–46. Hall of Fame, 1972

He was a stellar player in a legendary league. He was Josh Gibson, "the Black Babe Ruth," the greatest catcher of all time, the best position player in Negro League history.

His numbers are stratospheric. He is credited with 962 home runs over his long career, although there were several years in which he played a Negro League season and then headed south and played in either the Dominican League or the Mexican League. Still, 962 home runs are 962 home runs. Author John Holway's statistical analysis of the Negro Leagues credits Gibson with 224 in Negro League play.

He is credited with 84 homers in 170 games in 1936, which includes non–Negro League contests. He hit 75 homers in 1931 and 69 in 1934. He is credited with hitting a ball nearly out of Yankee Stadium when the Grays played an exhibition game there one year.

His .351 batting average in Negro League play is the third-highest of all time. Gibson would routinely hit .400 or better in winter league play. In 1937, Gibson hit .479 in the Puerto Rican League. He was elected to nine Negro League All Star teams, where he hit an amazing .483 in All Star contests.

Defensively, Gibson was extremely quick, with a rifle arm. He was also a good base runner, and exceptionally fast for a catcher.

Gibson was a big man, at 6'1", 210 pounds. His easygoing nature was often interpreted as ignorance or low intelligence by writers and even fellow Negro League players. But it's hard to believe a dumb guy could be such a great player.

In 1943, Gibson suffered a nervous breakdown, and his skills eroded quickly after that. He had begun to drink and probably also took drugs. He was still a good player for the next few years, but he was no longer the greatest. Early in 1947, he suffered a fatal stroke.

LIFETIME STATS: BA: .351, HR: 224, H: 1,010

#**10** Stanley Frank "Stan the Man" Musial

OF-1B, Cardinals, 1941–63. Hall of Fame, 1969

Consistency, durability and affability were the hallmarks of this man, the greatest player in a storied St. Louis Cardinal history.

In fact, the consistency of Stan the Man was taken to an amazing extreme: Musial had 1,815 hits at home and 1,815 on the road. He scored 1,949 runs and drove in 1,951.

His nickname, "Stan the Man" was a token of respect, bestowed on him by awed Dodger fans in the 1940s, as Musial led the Cardinals to four pennants in five years from 1942 to 1946. Musial, like the vast majority of his fellow ballplayers, didn't play in 1945, as he was in the Navy.

Dodger hurler Preacher Roe summed up his pitching strategy against Musial succinctly: "Throw him four wide ones and try to pick him off first base." Roe was only half kidding.

Musial was a hittin' fool. He won seven batting titles, and led the league in hits six times, doubles eight times, triples five times, RBI twice, slugging percentage six times and walks once. In 1948, he missed the Triple Crown by a single home run. He was MVP three times and finished second four other times.

He was a 20-time All Star, and he probably should have made the All Star team in 1942, when he hit .315 with 32 doubles and led the Cardinals to a stunning five-game upset of the New York Yankees in the World Series.

He was a man who understood the gift he had, and appreciated it deeply. He never questioned umpires' decisions and always seemed to enjoy the game.

He played in St. Louis for 22 years, and following his stint as a player, worked in the Card front office for another 25. After his career, the city erected a statue of Musial outside Busch Stadium. It was the least they could do.

LIFETIME STATS: BA: .331, HR: 475, RBI: 1,951, H: 3,630, SB: 78

#11 Joseph Paul "The Yankee Clipper," "Joltin' Joe" DiMaggio

OF, Yankees, 1936–51. Hall of Fame, 1955

Joe DiMaggio might have been the best ballplayer ever, and the reason he isn't farther up the list has more to do with the era than the man.

There is no way to measure what might be called the "woulda, shoulda, coulda" factor in sports. In this case, there is no way to determine how much his three-year participation in World War II affected Joe DiMaggio's stats.

Put it this way: It didn't help. Joltin' Joe went into the service at 28 and came out when he was 31. He was an MVP twice before he went into the service, in 1939 and 1941, and once after, in 1947. He won two batting titles, both prior to 1942, in 1939 and 1940. In short, before Hitler shouldered his way into the equation, DiMaggio had a heck of a run.

And let's face it, he still put up numbers. His 56-game hitting streak in 1941 is the one record that we'd be hard-pressed to see exceeded in the modern era. His .325 lifetime batting average is 41st all-time. Four times in his career, in 1937, 1939, 1940 and 1948, he had more RBI than games played.

He almost never struck out. For his career, DiMaggio whiffed 369 times, which is 2,228 times fewer than Reggie Jackson.

In the field, he saved the Yankees a lot of money in dry-cleaning bills. He was almost never out of position, so rare is the old-time Yankee fan who can recall DiMaggio ever having to make a diving catch or a lunging grab. He was always right there when the ball was hit to him.

DiMaggio didn't really glide; former teammates recall a guy who ran like a buffalo in the outfield, with a thundering step and a good amount of huffing and puffing. But that was only close up. Watching from the stands, Joe made it look easy.

LIFETIME STATS: BA: .325, HR: 361, RBI: 1,537, H: 2,214, SB: 30

#12 Tristam E. "Tris," "The Grey Eagle," "Spoke" Speaker

OF-1B, Red Sox, Indians, Senators, A's, 1907–28.
Hall of Fame, 1937

Tris Speaker was the best two-way player of his generation. He was not as great a hitter as Ty Cobb, but was a better defensive player by miles and miles and a better teammate by a greater margin than that.

Speaker lived a legendary life. He broke his right arm as a youngster, so he learned to hit and throw left-handed. He started out as a pitcher. Scouts were interested, but his mother refused to sign his contract (Speaker was only 17), believing that buying and selling players was an insult. She eventually came around.

After he signed his first professional contract, Speaker hopped a freight car to the minor league town he signed with to save money. Speaker arrived literally an hour before the game and was told by his manager he was the starting pitcher. He lost the game, 2–1.

He was eventually converted into an outfielder but the Red Sox thought so little of him, they didn't send him a contract the year after he signed. He reported anyway. The Sox still didn't want him and left him behind in spring training, as payment to the Little Rock minor league team for the use of their ball field. He stuck around and dominated the Southern League. The Sox finally decided they liked him and brought him up in 1907.

He was a great hitter, winning the batting crown in 1916, and hitting .345 lifetime.

But he was an unearthly fielder. Blessed with great speed, he played the shallowest center field anyone could remember. Several times in his career, he completed unassisted double plays—that is, he would catch a line drive and run over second base to double up the runner. Amazing. He remains,

66 years after his retirement, the all-time baseball leader in double plays by an outfielder (139), as well as assists (449).

And he was a winner, with two world championships in Boston and the first-ever title in Cleveland in 1920.

LIFETIME STATS: BA: .345, HR: 117, RBI: 1,529, H: 3,514, SB: 432

#**13** Louis Henry "The Iron Horse" Gehrig

1B, Yankees, 1923–39. Hall of Fame, 1939

Lou Gehrig was the best first baseman, ever. A couple players come close, including Jimmie Foxx and, in the modern era, Mark McGwire. But neither can really match Gehrig's tremendous production, year after year after year.

The story of how Gehrig began his amazing longevity streak of 2,130 consecutive games has, in the 21st century, undergone several permutations. He did replace Wally Pipp on May 31, 1925, and Pipp did indeed have a headache. But manager Miller Huggins didn't exactly hand the position to Gehrig after Pipp sat out. Huggins pinch-hit for Lou several times in June and, in fact, Gehrig did not start at first base for New York on July 5 of that year (Pipp did), but got in for a couple of innings late in the game.

But Lou was hitting well and Pipp wasn't, so Huggins left him in the rest of the year. And, of course, the year after that and the year after that, and, you get the idea.

Gehrig hit for average and he hit for power. He won three home run crowns, in 1931, 1934, and 1936. In that 1934 season, he won the Triple Crown with a .363 batting average, 49 homers and 165 RBI. He was MVP in 1927 and 1936.

Huggins used to say he thought Gehrig was actually a more dangerous hitter than Babe Ruth because he could use more of the field than Ruth. Gehrig also tended to hit line drives, which scared the hell out of his opponents.

In 1939, his health began to fail. Rumors abounded, and he finally traveled west to the Mayo Clinic. The diagnosis was almost too cruel to believe: amyotrophic lateral sclerosis, to be known forever after as Lou Gehrig's disease.

Gehrig was fading so fast, that Lou Gehrig Day was held on July 4, 1939. It is the most famous ceremony in baseball history, with Gehrig declaring, "Today, I consider myself the luckiest man on the face of the earth." Maybe he was. He died two years later.

LIFETIME STATS: BA: .340, HR: 493, RBI: 1,995, H: 2,721, SB: 102

#14 Henry Louis "The Hammer" Aaron

OF-1B-DH, Braves, Brewers, 1954–76. Hall of Fame, 1982

The first name in baseball, literally. Aaron's name is the opening entry in the baseball encyclopedia, and that is somehow fitting.

A self-effacing star who was, except for perhaps Lou Gehrig, the most stunningly consistent player ever, Aaron showed emotion only once on the field: when he cried after he broke Babe Ruth's home run record. On April 8, 1974, against the Los Angeles Dodgers in Atlanta, Aaron belted a pitch from Al Downing over the left-field fence into the Braves' bullpen to give him 715 career home runs, one more than Ruth.

Those tears were probably at least partly of relief. It may have been 1974, but this was still Atlanta, the heartland of the South, and Henry Aaron was a black man trying to outdo a white man, who was the all-time baseball legend, to boot.

Aaron's performance under such conditions—he and his family received an incredible amount of hate mail—was remarkable. After hitting number 715, Aaron continued to play for two more years after 1974, and finally ended up with 755 for his career.

His consistency was numbing. Twenty-three consecutive years hitting 10 or more home runs, leading the league four times. Twenty-two consecutive years with 10 or more doubles, leading the league four times. Twenty-one years with more than 100 hits, twice leading the league. He was named to the All Star team 21 consecutive times. He went 14 years hitting over .300, winning batting crowns in 1956 and 1959. He garnered three consecutive Gold Gloves. And how about this? He went nine straight years stealing 15 or more bases. Not too shabby.

Aaron remains baseball's top home run hitter, and the top man in RBI, total bases and extra base hits.

LIFETIME STATS: BA: .305, HR: 755, RBI: 2,297, H: 3,771, SB: 240

#**15** Robert Moses "Lefty" Grove
LHP, A's, Red Sox, 1925–41. Hall of Fame, 1947

For most of his career, Lefty Grove was a surly SOB. He had a sizzling fastball and a temper to match it.

Maybe it was because the big left-hander didn't get a chance to pitch in the big leagues until he was 25. He starred for the Baltimore Orioles, then a minor league squad, in the early 1920s, helping them win several International League championships.

Grove was finally sold to the Philadelphia A's for

$100,600 in 1920. That was more than the $100,000 fee the Yankees paid for Babe Ruth.

Grove was worth every penny—eventually. He was a tremendous pitcher as a rookie, leading the league in both strikeouts (116) and walks (131) in 1925. He ended up 10–12 that year, his only losing record in the major leagues.

By 1927, Grove was still blowing fastballs by hitters, and his placement was improving, as well. He struck out a league-high 174 batters and walked only 79. Grove would lead the league in strikeouts seven consecutive years while with Philadelphia.

In 1931, Grove went 31–4, with 27 complete games and four shutouts, both league highs. He also struck out a league-best 175 batters and won the ERA crown with a 2.06 mark. It was his best year.

Grove won nine ERA titles in his career. No other pitcher to date has won more than six.

For whatever reason, Grove didn't hesitate to brush back, or hit, batters. He often scowled at teammates who made a bad play behind him.

In 1934, Grove was traded to the Boston Red Sox, who hoped Lefty could anchor a staff that would win a World Series. That didn't happen, mostly because Grove sustained an injury to his left shoulder that dropped him to 8–8 that year.

But Grove was smart as well as talented. He was no longer a power pitcher, but he relied on guile and a good slider to win games now. He won 17 or more games three times with Boston, including a 20–12 mark in 1935.

Grove staggered to the finish line in 1941, going 7–7 and winning his 300th and last game. He retired to his home town of Lonaconing, Maryland, and opened a bowling alley.

LIFETIME STATS: W: 300, L: 141, SV: 55, ERA: 3.06, SO: 2,266, CG: 298

#16 Grover Cleveland "Pete" Alexander

RHP, Phillies, Cubs, Cardinals, 1911–30. Hall of Fame, 1938

Grover Cleveland Alexander is remembered, when he is remembered at all, as the guy who pitched drunk in the 1926 World Series. It's an unfortunate distinction, because Alexander was one of the greatest pitchers in the history of the game.

He had an amazing rookie season, leading the league in wins (28), complete games (31), shutouts (seven) and innings pitched (367). Four of those shutouts were consecutive, including a 1–0 win over Cy Young, then in his final season.

He was a workhorse for the Phillies, leading them to the National League championship in 1915. That season, Alexander led the National League in wins (31), complete games (36), shutouts (12), innings pitched (376 1/3), strikeouts (241) and ERA (1.22).

That was a great year for "Old Pete," as he was called then, but it was about routine for Alexander, who led the league in wins, strikeouts and complete games six times each, shutouts and innings pitched seven times each and ERA five times. From 1915 to 1920, six years in a row, Alexander's ERA was below 2.00.

He did it with a rising fastball that he could throw at several different velocities, and a great, looping curveball that he could throw for strikes at any point in the count. He almost never walked anyone and he usually pitched very well in big games.

That was why the St. Louis Cardinals picked him up in midseason in 1926. Alexander won nine games down the stretch for St. Louis, propelling the National Leaguers into the World Series against the powerful Yankees.

Alexander had pitched a masterful Game Six in Yankee Stadium that year, winning 10–2, and figured he wouldn't have to worry about appearing in Game Seven. Which is why he was in Billy LaHiff's tavern in Manhattan the night before that final game. He closed LaHiff's and missed batting practice the next afternoon.

In the bottom of the seventh, the Cardinals were ahead, 3–2, but the bases were loaded. So was Alexander, but he got future Hall of Famer Tony Lazzeri on knee-high fastballs to get him out and pitched two more scoreless innings for the win.

LIFETIME STATS: W: 373, L: 208, SV: 32, ERA: 2.56, SO: 2,198, CG: 437

#17 Robert LeRoy "Satchel" Paige

RHP, Birmingham Barons, Baltimore Black Sox, Cleveland Cubs, Pittsburgh Crawfords, Kansas City Monarchs, New York Black Yankees, Satchel Paige's All Stars, Memphis Red Sox, Philadelphia Stars (Negro Leagues), Cleveland Indians, St. Louis Browns, Kansas City Royals, 1926–65. Hall of Fame, 1971

Satchel Paige was one of the few legends who might have been better than some of the stories told about him. A Negro League mainstay from 1926 until 1946, Paige was a gangly man who threw a blistering fastball for most of his career.

And the stories are true. He once walked the bases loaded with no outs and struck out the side (although it was in a semipro tournament). Several times, he would call in his outfielders and pitch to an opponent, again always in exhibitions or semipro games.

Once, in a tournament in Denver in the 1930s, Paige called in his outfielders and struck out the first two batters. The third batter slapped a soft fly ball to center field that would have easily been caught had there been anyone out there to catch it. The batter raced around the bases for an inside-the-park home run.

Paige estimated that in his total career, which often included playing exhibitions and playing in several leagues in one year, he pitched in 2,600 games, won 1,800, and threw 300 shutouts and 55 no-hitters.

Paige didn't like his nickname much. He earned it when, as a young boy, he tried to steal a satchel from a man at a train station. He was caught and cuffed in front of his friends, who gleefully gave him the name. Over the years, he made up several more colorful stories that better fit his status as a great pitcher.

His frequent pay disputes with the various managers of teams in the Negro Leagues caused Paige to jump teams on an almost annual basis. In 1938, he was banned from the Negro National League, so he formed his own independent team, Satchel Paige's All Stars, which easily outdrew other Negro League franchises. Paige was readmitted the next year.

In addition to his fastball, Paige had tremendous control and, like former Red Sox great Luis Tiant, possessed a variety of windups to deliver the baseball. In 1948, he was signed by the Cleveland Indians and went 6–1 as Cleveland won the world championship. He played for several more years before retiring to semipro teams and exhibitions. In 1965, he returned to the bigs, pitching three scoreless innings for the Kansas City Royals to become, at age 59, the oldest pitcher ever in the majors. It was one last story for the legend.

LIFETIME STATS: (MAJOR LEAGUES) W: 28, L: 31, SV: 32, ERA: 3.29, SO: 288, CG: 7. (NEGRO LEAGUES) W: 142, L: 92

#18 Edward Trowbridge "Cocky" Collins Sr.

2B, A's, White Sox, 1906–30. Hall of Fame, 1939

At 5'9", 175 pounds, Collins wasn't much to look at, but he was the most durable and consistent second base-man in baseball history.

Collins began with the Philadelphia A's, and was the lynchpin of A's manager Connie Mack's "$100,000 infield" along with Stuffy McInnis at first base, Jack Barry at shortstop and Frank "Home Run" Baker at third. The $100,000 figure was the combined salaries of the four men in 1910. That is a little less than Alex Rodriguez makes a game, these days.

Collins was an excellent hitter who hit better than .300 a total of 19 times in a 25-year career. He led the league in runs scored three times and had 160 or more hits in 17 seasons.

He was also a great base runner, leading the league in stolen bases four times. As a fielder, Collins led American League second basemen in fielding nine times. Collins remains baseball's all-time leader in assists with 7,630 and is second all-time in putouts with 6,526. There was simply nothing he did not do well.

Collins loved playing with the A's, but his trade to the Chicago White Sox was, initially, something he looked forward to too. Mack was disman-tling the A's to reduce his payroll, and Collins did not want to be a part of a losing franchise.

He led the White Sox to the 1917 world championship, hitting .409 in the World Series. After a stint in the Marines during World War I, Collins returned to the White Sox to find a group of very talented players who hated skinflint owner Charles Comisky.

That White Sox team was, according to Collins, the most talented he played on. But their desire to make money "on the side" by throwing the

World Series and betting against themselves horrified Collins. He did not participate and was one of the few starters of that infamous "Black Sox" team not banned from baseball.

Collins survived the scandal, and went on to manage Chicago and later become general manager of the Boston Red Sox.

LIFETIME STATS: BA: .333, HR: 47, RBI: 1,300, H: 3,315, SB: 744

#19 Joe Leonard Morgan

2B, Astros, Reds, Giants, Phillies, A's, 1963–84. Hall of Fame, 1990

Compact and powerful, Joe Morgan was the National League's greatest second baseman.

Morgan broke in with the Houston Astros and played nine years in the Astrodome, making two All Star teams. He was traded to Cincinnati and developed into a superstar. Morgan was one of the keys to the Cincinnati "Big Red Machine" of 1972–76. The Reds won three National League pennants in that span, and back-to-back World Series in 1975 and 1976.

Not coincidentally, Morgan picked up a pair of MVP awards in that span, as well. Morgan is the only second baseman in baseball history to win consecutive MVPs.

An extremely patient hitter, Morgan led the National League in walks four times, and eight times in his career walked more than 100 times a year. He also led the league in on-base percentage four times.

Known for the distinctive flapping motion of his back elbow in the batter's box, Morgan had very good power for a second baseman, hitting 27 home runs in 1976 and becoming that year only the fifth second baseman in major league history to drive in more than 100 runs with 111 RBI.

He was also an exceptional base stealer, swiping 20 or more bases 14 times in his career.

But beyond his stats, Morgan was a winner. He hit the game-winning single in the 10th inning in Game Three against the Red Sox in the 1975 World Series. And in Game Seven, he struck again, dropping in an RBI single in the top of the ninth to give the Reds the championship. Against the Yankees in the 1976 World Series, he hit .333 in a four-game sweep.

In 1980, Morgan was traded back to Houston, and helped the Astros win the division title. After a two-year stint with the Giants, he signed with the Phillies in 1983 and helped that team get into the World Series. Morgan led the team with five hits and two home runs, but the Phillies lost to the Baltimore Orioles in five games.

LIFETIME STATS: BA: .271, HR: 268, RBI: 1,133, H: 2,517, SB: 689

#20 William Roger "The Rocket" Clemens

RHP, Red Sox, Blue Jays, Yankees, Astros, 1984–present

Think about this: There are only seven other hurlers in baseball history who have won more than 350 games in their careers, as Clemens has. All of them, except Walter Johnson and Warren Spahn, began their careers in the 19th century, an era in which pitchers pitched two or three or four times a week. It was a completely different era with a completely different philosophy of pitching.

Now think about this: In 1986, playing with the Boston Red Sox, Clemens set a Major League record by striking out 20 batters in a game against Seattle. Pretty good, eh? But 10 years later, in 1996, he tied that record while playing for Toronto. Set an all-time record once, that makes a guy an all-time player. Set it again a decade later, well, what does that make him?

The question becomes, in the latter part of his career, how much of these stats are abetted by performance-enhancing drugs? That we don't know. But the numbers are terrific, either way.

And the man is still pitching, 23 years after he broke in. And he is not just hanging on. He dominated the Minnesota Twins to win his 350th game in June 2007, and he would have a better record had he gotten more run support from his team, the Yankees.

So is Clemens the greatest pitcher in baseball history? Well, put it this way: He's 20th on my list, but it's my opinion that there is a thin line between Roger Clemens and Walter Johnson, Lefty Grove, Grover Alexander, and Satchel Paige, the four pitchers ahead of him on the list. Seventh Game, World Series, on the road, I would gladly take any one of these guys.

In terms of other records, Clemens has won six Cy Young awards, in 1986, 1987, 1991, 1997, 1998, 2001 and 2004. He was also the American League MVP in 1986, the year the Red Sox almost won the World Series.

LIFETIME STATS: W: 350, L: 118, SV: 0, ERA: 3.11, SO: 4,633, CG: 118

#**21** Rogers "Rajah" Hornsby

2B-SS-3B-1B-OF, Cardinals, Giants, Braves, Cubs, Browns, 1915–37. Hall of Fame, 1942

The greatest right-handed hitter in baseball history was also one of its biggest curmudgeons.

On the field, Hornsby was a joy to watch. Hornsby stood at the back of the batter's box and executed a perfectly level swing that delivered the baseball to all corners of the field. In the early part of his career, Hornsby had some speed; he was quick out of the batter's box, and would always take the extra base against an unwary outfielder.

Hornsby led the league in doubles four times, in triples twice, in home runs twice, and in RBI four times. His Triple Crown year in 1922 was one of the greatest seasons any player has ever had in baseball history: His .401 batting average, 42 homers, 152 RBI, 46 doubles, 250 hits, 141 runs scored, .459 on-base percentage and .722 slugging average were all league leaders. And his .967 fielding percentage was the best in either league for a second baseman. He also had a 33-game hitting streak that year.

His .424 batting average in 1924 was the highest average in baseball history after 1900 (four players before that year did post better averages). Only Ty Cobb's lifetime batting average tops Hornsby's .358.

But Hornsby could be, well, difficult. He was very confident of his ability and had no problem reminding teammates or his manager of it. Hornsby had a major issue when dealing with authority, and often quarreled with managers and front-office types. As good as he was, that was not a good idea, and he was traded four times in his career.

He also had a whopper of a gambling problem. It didn't seem to affect him much in his early career, but it got worse as he got older. He managed the Cubs from 1925 to 1926, and was known to hit up his players for loans to cover his gambling losses. Again, not a good idea.

He ended his career with the St. Louis Browns, and, as he got older, he coached for several organizations, and seemed to mellow a bit. Still, Chicago Cub great Billy Williams will always remember his first tryout with the Cubs. The Rajah was overseeing it, and, when the tryout was over, Hornsby pointed to Williams and budding third baseman Ron Santo. Those two, Hornsby, said, will play in the big leagues. The rest of you, Hornsby said, might as well go home. And of course, Williams conceded, Hornsby was right. Except for Santo and him, none of the other players made it.

LIFETIME STATS: BA: .358, HR: 301, RBI: 1,584, H: 2,930, SB: 135

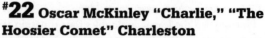

#22 Oscar McKinley "Charlie," "The Hoosier Comet" Charleston

CF-1B, Indianapolis ABCs, New York Lincoln Stars, Chicago American Giants, Harrisburg Giants, Homestead Grays, Pittsburgh Crawfords, Philadelphia Stars, Indianapolis Clowns (Negro Leagues), 1915–41. Hall of Fame, 1976

Charleston had a barrel chest and spindly legs, and played the outfield, which drew comparisons to white slugger Babe Ruth. But he was closer to Ty Cobb as a hitter and to Tris Speaker as a defensive player. What it all meant was that Charleston is believed by some to be the greatest all-around player in Negro League history.

Charleston was born in Indianapolis in 1896. After a stint in the Army, Charleston joined the Indianapolis ABCs as a pitcher-outfielder. Eventually, he was moved to the outfield permanently, and he soon became a star.

Charleston was an exceptional hitter with good power. Available records show him putting together back-to-back .400 seasons in 1924 and 1925, while playing for the Harrisburg Giants of the Eastern Colored League.

He was also an aggressive base runner. Several times, playing for several leagues over the years, Charleston would lead the circuit in stolen bases and home runs. Tales of Charleston's baserunning never fail to emphasize that he was not afraid to slide into opponents with his spikes high, much like his white contemporary, Ty Cobb.

Defensively, Charleston's exceptional speed enabled him, like Speaker, to play a very shallow center field. He, like Speaker, would often snag a line drive and run over to second base to double up the runner.

In 1931, Charleston was the best player on one of the best, if not the best, Negro League teams of all time, the Homestead Grays. Charleston played center field and hit .351. In a nine-game "world championship" series against another all-time great team, the Kansas City Monarchs, the Grays won the series, five games to four, and Charleston hit .511.

As he grew older and his legs began to bother him, Charleston moved from center field to first base. But he could still hit. Playing for another all-time great team, the 1935 Pittsburgh Crawfords, Charleston hit .294 and led the team to another Negro League World Series win over the New York Cuban Stars.

Charleston was coveted by white big-league managers and owners, and no wonder: He holds the all-time record with 18 home runs in games between Negro League teams and white major league teams. But he came along a little too early to break into the major leagues.

LIFETIME STATS: BA: .330, HR: 169

#**23** Denton True "Cy" Young
RHP, Cleveland Spiders, Cardinals, Red Sox, Indians, Braves, 1890–1911. Hall of Fame, 1937

Cy Young not only set the world record for winning base-ball games by the end of his amazing career, he truly sparked the evolution of baseball itself. When Young started, pitchers threw out of a box 50 feet from home plate. By the time he retired, pitchers stood on a mound 60 feet, six inches from the plate and fired the ball in.

Young was effective either way. He won 30 or more games five times in his career, and 10 other times won 20 or more. He led the league in wins five times, in shutouts seven times and in saves twice. He won more games (511), lost more (316), pitched more innings (7,354 2/3) and completed more games (749) than any pitcher, ever. He was durable, versatile and tough as nails.

His nickname was reportedly earned when he was being warmed up by a young catcher in his minor league days, and several of his pitches got past the young man and damaged a fence behind the fellow. The catcher remarked that the fence looked like a "cyclone" had hit it, and thus was born the tag.

Young became a canny veteran only two or three years into his professional career. He threw a fastball and curve, and he threw those pitches from various angles at various speeds. He also understood that many major league teams of the 19th century didn't like to use up too many balls during a game, as the balls cost money. So those balls tended to get softer and more lopsided as games went on. Young rarely asked an umpire for a new ball, because he could make lopsided or scuffed balls dance like an ant on a hot stove.

But Young's greatest secret was that he was as limber as an Indian yogi. He rarely warmed up by throwing more than a handful of pitches, and was usually ready to pitch again on a day's rest. This advantage appeared to be a natural one, as Young clearly wasn't an exercise buff, particularly at the end of his career. By 1911, Young had to retire, because at 44, he was so rotund that batters would bunt on him and make him field the ball.

No matter, Young was a great, great pitcher for many years, and he is now annually honored by the most valuable pitcher's award that carries his name. No one deserves it more.

LIFETIME STATS: W: 511, L: 316, SV: 17, ERA: 2.63, SO: 2,803, CG: 749

#**24** Michael Jack Schmidt
3B, Phillies, 1972–89. Hall of Fame, 1995

Great hitting always overshadows great defense. That's a fact, and that's why it's so important to emphasize that while Mike Schmidt might not be as acrobatic a third baseman as Brooks Robinson or Graig Nettles, he was probably a better overall fielder.

But let's talk about hitting first, because first and foremost, Mike Schmidt was an offensive machine. He led the National League in home runs eight times, in RBI four times and in slugging percentage five times.

He had an early problem with strikeouts, whiffing a league-high 180 times in 1975. But Schmidt eventually became more selective at the plate, and four times in his career, led the league in walks.

On July 17, 1986, Schmidt hit four home runs in one game, as the Phillies rallied from a 13–2 deficit to defeat the Cubs 18–16 in 10 innings. He hit his first home run off Cub starter Rick Reuschel and his fourth off Cub reliever (and Rick's brother) Paul Reuschel.

He was also a smart base runner. He stole 174 bases in his career, and twice swiped 20 or more. He won MVP awards in 1980, 1981 and 1986. He was also the MVP of the World Series in 1980, hitting .381 with two home runs and seven RBI in Philadelphia's win over the Royals.

In the field, Schmidt was a 10-time Gold Glove winner. In 1974, he set a National League record for third basemen with 404 assists. Three years later, his 396 assists were the second-highest single season total in major league history.

He was also tough to keep out of the lineup. Until a season-ending rotator-cuff injury in 1988, Schmidt played in 145 or more games in 13 of his 16 full seasons in the league.

LIFETIME STATS: BA: .267, HR: 548, RBI: 1,595, H: 2,234, SB: 174

#25 Rickey Henley Henderson

OF-DH, A's, Yankees, Blue Jays, Padres, Angels, Mets, Mariners, Red Sox, Dodgers, 1979–2003. Hall of Fame, 2009

Henderson was the greatest leadoff hitter in baseball history, and one of the best outfielders, ever, as well.

His numbers are prodigious. Henderson is the all-time leader in walks with 2,190, breaking Babe Ruth's record on April, 25, 2001. (Henderson led the league in walks four times in his career, and was in the top five eight other times.)

Later that season, on September 28, 2001, Henderson broke Ty Cobb's all-time record for runs scored when he crossed home plate for the 2,247th time. Henderson now has 2,295 career runs scored. When you break records by Babe Ruth and Ty Cobb in the same year, you are good.

Henderson is also the all-time leader in stolen bases, a record he broke more than a decade ago, in 1992. Henderson ended his career with 1,406 stolen bases. Lou Brock, in second place, has 938.

Henderson is the only player to steal more than 100 bases more than twice, doing it three times in his career. In 1982, he stole 130 bases, setting the modern major league record. (Hugh Nicol of the Cincinnati Red Stockings of the defunct American Association stole 138 bases in 1887.)

Henderson stole 108 bases in 1983 and 100 bases in 1980. He led the league in stolen bases 12 times, including seven times in a row from 1980 to 1986.

He has hit 79 leadoff home runs, another record. That sum is more than the next two players combined, Brady Anderson (44) and Bobby Bonds (34).

Henderson is also one of the most adept players in major league history at getting hit by a pitch, doing so 98 times in his career, which places him 56th on the all-time roster.

His speed enabled him to be a very good defensive outfielder. Henderson won only one Gold Glove in his career, but he is sixth all-time in putouts in the outfield with 6,466.

Henderson may have lost a few points with purists with his "snap" catches in the outfield. This was a move where he whipped his glove across his head to grab a fly out.

Henderson was a clutch player in the postseason. He hit .339 in 14 World Series games.

LIFETIME STATS: BA: .279, HR: 297, RBI: 1,115, H: 3,055, SB: 1,406

#26 Jack Roosevelt "Jackie" Robinson

2B-3B-1B-OF, Dodgers, 1947–56. Hall of Fame, 1962

Yes, yes, yes, Jackie Robinson broke the color barrier in 1947, became an icon and a hero to every African-American boy of the next generation and paved the way for baseball as we know it now.

But what sometimes gets lost in all this is that Robinson was a really, really good baseball player.

Robinson was, in fact, one of the greatest athletes in the history of sport, any sport. Jim Thorpe may have been slightly better, but not by much.

For example, Robinson averaged a hard-to-fathom 11 yards per carry as a running back in his junior year at UCLA. He was the leading scorer in the Pacific 10 in basketball for three years running. He won the 1940 NCAA long jump championship, and was slated to go to the Olympics, had they not been canceled that year. He also won both the singles and doubles titles in the Western Tennis Club championships.

He was recruited by Dodgers general manager Branch Rickey to spearhead the long-overdue integration of baseball in 1946 and began playing in major league ballparks in 1947. Robinson endured extraordinary abuse from fans and opponents, yet held his emotions in check. He retaliated with a superb rookie season and was named Rookie of the Year. The rest, as they say, is history—American history, not baseball history.

Robinson was a superior base runner, perhaps the best ever. He stole home 19 times in his career. In 1955, he became one of only 12 players in baseball history to steal home in a World Series game. In 1954, he became the first National League player in 26 years to steal his way around the base paths. He was probably the best player in history at finding a way to return to base safely after being caught in a rundown.

Robinson was a good hitter, winning a batting title in 1949 and topping

.300 six times in his career. He didn't strike out much and averaged about 75 walks a season.

Defensively, he led the National League three times in fielding average at second base, and was also a very good defensive third baseman and left fielder. Robinson wasn't flashy; he didn't make the diving stab. Rather, he played very intelligently, and was usually in the right place at the right time.

At his death in 1972, his former teammate Joe Page spoke for all the black players then in the league, and in fact all the black players to come in the history of baseball, when he said, "When I look at my house, I say, 'Thank God for Jackie Robinson.'"

LIFETIME STATS: BA: .311, HR: 137, RBI: 734, H: 1,518, SB: 197

#27 James Emory "Jimmie," "Double X," "The Beast" Foxx
1B-3B-C, A's, Red Sox, Cubs, Phillies, 1925–45. Hall of Fame, 1951

The prototypical slugger of the 1920s and 1930s, Jimmie Foxx was called "the right-handed Babe Ruth" when he toiled for the A's.

Foxx didn't actually get his career started until 1929, four years after he was signed by the A's. That's because Connie Mack's A's were so deep that Foxx, who started out as a catcher, was sitting behind future Hall of Famer Mickey Cochrane for several years. When Mack finally moved Foxx to first base, he displaced veteran Jimmy Dykes.

But it was worth it. In Foxx's first full season as a starter, he led the American League in on-base percentage, and batted .354 with 33 home runs and 118 RBI. To top it off, the A's displaced the mighty New York Yankees as American League champions, and won the 1929 World Series over the Cubs. Foxx hit .350 in that Fall Classic, and added a pair of home runs.

In 1932, Foxx smacked 58 home runs, two short of Ruth's record. A's fans like to point out that Foxx hit two home runs in games that were eventually rained out. Foxx won back-to-back MVP awards in 1932 and 1933. The latter season, he won the Triple Crown, with 48 home runs, 163 RBI and a .356 batting average.

In 1938, after he was traded to the Red Sox, Foxx had another sensational season, leading the league with a .349 batting average, 175 RBI, 119 walks, a .462 on-base percentage and a .704 slugging percentage. His 50 home runs were second in the league to Hank Greenberg's 58. But Foxx won the MVP.

He was a big dude. At six feet and 195 pounds, Foxx had huge upper arms and a powerful chest. Foxx would cut back the sleeves on his uniform so pitchers could see those biceps. He also had a great throwing arm and in fact pitched in 10 games in the majors, including two starts with the Phillies in 1945. His career record is 1–0 with a 1.52 ERA.

Foxx was also a very good teammate. He was especially kind to rookies, and Red Sox great Ted Williams recalled fondly how Foxx encouraged him and helped him when he was starting out in Boston.

LIFETIME STATS: BA: .325, HR: 534, RBI: 1,922, H: 2,646, SB: 87

#28 Peter Edward "Charlie Hustle" Rose Sr.

OF-1B-2B-3B, Reds, Phillies, Expos, 1963–86

Versatile, tough and durable, the accomplishments of Pete Rose ensure him a place in the highest pantheon of baseball immortals. But his wrong-thinking attitude toward his gambling problem makes it difficult to envision him in the baseball Hall of Fame anytime soon.

Rose is the most prolific switch-hitter ever. He is the all-time leader in base hits with 4,256, singles with 3,215, at bats with 14,053 and games played with 3,562. He is second all-time in doubles with 746 and collected more than 200 hits in a season 10 times, which is a record. He made 100 or more hits 23 consecutive years, which is also a record.

Rose is the only player in baseball history to play more than 500 games at five positions: first base, second base, third base, right field and left field, and was named the Player of the Decade by the *Sporting News* for the 1970s. He won two Gold Gloves playing in right field for the Reds.

Fans loved Rose's hustle, even those whose teams were beaten by him. He began running to first base after being issued a walk after he saw Enos Slaughter, another hustling guy, do it. Rose popularized the head-first slide, although baseball purists insist that the slide is not as effective as a feet-first attempt. Still, it was another example of a guy who was trying to squeeze every ounce of talent out of his body. Rose clearly did.

On September 11, 1985, batting left-handed for the Reds, Rose hit a single to left field off the Padres' Eric Show to record his 4,193rd hit, passing Ty Cobb and breaking a record many thought unbreakable.

That said, he has admitted to gambling on baseball games. In 2004, he released a book that detailed some of those gambling exploits, and went on a national tour to publicly apologize. But sportswriters, stung by Rose's previous adamant stance that he did not bet on the game, have so far been largely unforgiving. Baseball fans have been a little easier on Rose, and acknowledge his greatness. But it may be a long while before Rose is elected to the Hall of Fame, which is his last goal in baseball.

LIFETIME STATS: BA: .303, HR: 160, RBI: 1,314, H: 4,256, SB: 198

#29 Frank Robinson

OF-DH, Reds, Orioles, Dodgers, Angels, Indians,
1956–76. Hall of Fame, 1982

Frank Robinson was one of the great power hitters of the
1960s. He was also a leader in the clubhouse, which was
a rarity for a black man in the late 1950s and early 1960s.

Robinson made an immediate impact on the National
League with the Cincinnati Reds in his first year, hitting 38 home runs, then
a record for a rookie player. He also led the National League with 122 runs
scored and was hit by pitches 20 times, another rookie record. For the next
10 seasons, Robinson was "the Man" in Cincinnati.

In 1961, Robinson led the Reds to the team's first pennant in 21 years,
although Cincinnati had the misfortune of playing the Roger Maris–Mickey
Mantle Yankees in the World Series. Robinson won the first of two MVP
awards that year, hitting .323, slugging a league-leading .611 with 37 home
runs and 124 RBI.

Robinson's aggressive play often led to nagging injuries, although he rarely
sat down for any long stretch. Still, Reds officials believed he was losing his
effectiveness in the mid-1960s. This led to a trade to the Baltimore Orioles
in 1966 in one of the more lopsided deals in baseball history.

Robinson led the Orioles to the 1966 American League pennant, and a
surprising upset of a powerful Los Angeles Dodger team in the World Series.
Robinson that season won the Triple Crown and his second MVP award
with a .316 batting average, 49 home runs and 122 RBI. He became the first
player in baseball history to win MVP awards in both leagues.

He was the cornerstone of a late 1960s Orioles team that was dubbed "the
best damn team in baseball" by Orioles manager Earl Weaver. They were,
winning three consecutive American League pennants and beating the Cincinnati Reds in the 1971 World Series in five games, surely a sweet win for
Robinson.

In 1975, Robinson became the player-manager of the Cleveland Indians, the first black man to be a big-league manager. In 1976, Robinson led the Indians to their first winning record (81–78) since 1968 and only their third winning record in 26 years. He would eventually manage the Indians, Giants and Orioles in an 11-year managing career.

LIFETIME STATS: BA: .294, HR: 586, RBI: 1,812, H: 2,943, SB: 204

#**30** Edwin Lee "Eddie" Mathews

3B-1B-OF, Braves, Astros, Tigers, 1952–68. Hall of Fame, 1978

No less an authority than Ty Cobb once remarked that Eddie Mathews's swing was the most perfect he had ever seen.

Mathews was the best third baseman of his era, a powerful, agile man with a cannon for an arm and tremendous pop in his bat. His 486 home runs as a third baseman (he has 512 overall) was a record until Mike Schmidt broke it.

Mathews was one of the best high school baseball players of any era, and he signed with the Boston Braves on the night of his high school graduation in 1949. He spent only a couple of years in the minors before being brought up to Boston in 1952.

Mathews played well in 1952, but in 1953, he blossomed. He had one of the best seasons a 21-year-old player ever had, hitting .302 with 135 RBI and a league-leading 47 home runs.

Mathews's improvement coincided with the ascension of the Braves. After several moribund decades in Boston, the Braves moved out to the Midwest. They were embraced by the city of Milwaukee, and were strong pennant contenders throughout the 1950s, reaching the World Series in 1957 and 1958.

Mathews, along with Hank Aaron, Lew Burdette and other stars, was one of the keys of the team. After losing a heartbreaking pennant race to the Dodgers in 1956, the Braves came back in 1957 and won the world championship over the Yankees in a stirring seven-game Series.

Mathews was one of the stars of the Series. His 10th-inning home run off Bob Grim won Game Four, and his backhanded grab of a Bill Skowron line drive in Game Seven was the final out of the Series. He only hit .227 in the seven-game matchup, but four of his hits were for extra bases.

Mathews was still a fixture at third base for Milwaukee into the mid-1960s, but his power numbers declined after 1961. In 1966, the Braves moved from Milwaukee to Atlanta, making Mathews the only player to play in three cities with one franchise.

LIFETIME STATS: BA: .271, HR: 512, RBI: 1,453, H: 2,315, SB: 68

#31 John Henry "Pop," "El Cuchara" Lloyd

SS-2B-1B-C, Cuban X-Giants, Philadelphia Giants, Leland Giants, New York Lincoln Giants, Chicago American Giants, New York Lincoln Stars, Brooklyn Royal Giants, New York Bacharach Giants, Atlantic City Bacharachs, Columbus Buckeyes, Hilldale Daisies, Harlem Stars (Negro Leagues), 1906–32. Hall of Fame, 1977

Lloyd was the best Negro League shortstop ever, and one of the best players, black or white, in the first part of the 20th century. Honus Wagner, the great shortstop for the Pittsburgh Pirates and a contemporary of Lloyd's, said it was an honor to be compared with him.

Lloyd began his career as a catcher with the Macon Acmes of Georgia, an impoverished semipro black team. In fact, the Acmes were so impoverished that they couldn't provide Lloyd with a catcher's mask. He had to run a rope through a wire basket and tie it around his head for protection. Needless to say, when Ed LeMarc, owner of the Cuban X-Giants, offered him a contract, Lloyd jumped at the chance. He also decided to become an infielder.

Lloyd was a lanky man, 5'11" and about 180 pounds. He had a powerful throwing arm and ran the bases with long, smooth strides. He seemed to glide along the base paths, and that gait had the advantage of making it seem as though Lloyd was slower than he really was.

Lloyd was a left-handed, line-drive hitter who batted in a closed stance. In the batter's box, Lloyd cradled the bat almost in the crook of his left elbow. As the pitch came in, the bat would whip off his arm like a coiled snake and lash the ball to all fields.

He was as fundamentally sound a player as there was in those days. Lloyd had superior bat control, and could execute the hit-and-run on command, as well as drop a bunt down either base line.

Lloyd was a popular teammate who didn't smoke, drink or curse. But while he was a gentleman on and off the field, he was a man who was well aware of his worth. He played for a number of teams in his career because he drove a hard bargain, and if he did not get it, he would look around for another employer. And up until the early 1930s, he was always able to find one.

One of his nicknames came from his years in the Cuban Leagues. His large hands would often scoop up dirt and pebbles when he grabbed for the ball, and teammates and opponents alike began calling him "el Cuchara," or the Shovel.

His other nickname came from his later years as a manager. As intense a competitor as Lloyd was, he was an easygoing manager who was particularly patient with rookies. His players called him "Pop," a term of endearment.

LIFETIME STATS: BA: .337, H: 970

#32 Melvin Thomas "Master Melvin," "Mel" Ott

OF-3B-2B, Giants, 1926–47. Hall of Fame, 1951

Mel Ott was a coach's nightmare at the plate. He had a "foot in the bucket" batting stance, in which he raised his right leg just as he swung the bat, and then hooked upward as he completed his swing.

But Ott was a heck of a lot more effective than a lot of guys who had better-looking swings. He was the first National League player to hit 500 home runs, and held the record until fellow Giant Willie Mays broke it in 1967. Ott led the league in homers six times in his career.

He also had an excellent eye in the batter's box, leading the league six times in walks, and holding that record, as well, until Joe Morgan broke it in 1982.

Ott was signed by the Giants as a 15-year-old and by the time he was 16, he was sitting on the Giants' bench. New York coach John McGraw loved Ott's athleticism, and initially wasn't quite sure where to play the kid. So he had Ott working out at third base, second base and in the outfield. Eventually, the outfield was where Ott would see a majority of action throughout his career.

Ott was a wet-behind-the-ears 19-year-old when he became a regular in the Giants' outfield. The New York papers joshingly called him "Master Melvin" in reference to his age and schoolboyish looks.

There was nothing boyish about the way Ott played, however. He hit .322, with 26 doubles and 18 home runs in his first full season. The next year, he socked 42 home runs and had 151 RBI, both career highs.

McGraw didn't really like the leg kick, but he never tried to change Ott, because it was clear that the leg kick gave Ott that much more power. At 5'9", and between 170 and 180 pounds during his career, Master Melvin needed a little help.

Born in Louisiana, Ott was the classic Southerner. He was a gentleman in a game where gentlemen were the exception rather than the rule. In fact, Ott was the player to whom famed Dodger coach Leo Durocher referred when he uttered his famous quote, "Nice guys finish last." It was untrue in Ott's case: He played in three World Series, and hit .389 with two home runs as the Giants won the 1933 world championship.

LIFETIME STATS: BA: .304, HR: 511, RBI: 1,860, H: 2,876, SB: 89

#**33** Carl Michael "Yaz" Yastrzemski
OF-1B-DH, Red Sox, 1961–83. Hall of Fame, 1989

Yastrzemski did everything well, and he did it well for a long time. The 5'11" Yastrzemski was a baseball and basketball standout from Long Island who signed with Notre Dame to do both, but left the university when he signed a baseball contract after his freshman year.

Yaz was being groomed to be Ted Williams's replacement in left field, a hefty load for anyone's shoulders. And when Williams retired after the 1960 season, Yastrzemski moved right into his left-field slot. He didn't overpower anyone in 1961, hitting .266 with 11 home runs, 80 RBI and 155 hits. But he did lead the team in total bases with 231 and extra base hits with 48.

Yastrzemski improved considerably in 1962, hitting .296 with 19 homers, 191 hits and 94 RBI. And in 1963, Yaz arrived, winning his first batting title with a .321 average and leading the league in hits with 183 and an on-base percentage of .418.

By the 1963 season, Yastrzemski was a fixture in left field. And the Red Sox, mired in mediocrity, were beginning to climb back toward respectability over the next few seasons.

In 1967, Yastrzemski put it all together, winning the Triple Crown with a .326 batting average, 44 home runs and 121 RBI, which also earned him an MVP award. Not coincidentally, the Red Sox also put it all together, winning their first American League championship since 1948. Boston lost a thrilling seven-game World Series to the St. Louis Cardinals, but Yastrzemski hit .400 with three home runs to lead the Sox. The 1967 season remains the most exciting season in Red Sox history, and one of the most exciting in baseball history.

With all his offensive numbers, it is easy to overlook the fact that Yastrzemski was also a great defensive player. He won seven Gold Gloves over his career, and led American League outfielders in assists in 1962, 1963, 1964 and 1966. He owned the Green Monster, which is the term Boston fans use for the left-field wall in Fenway Park. Yastrzemski knew every rivet, every dent and every nuance of the Wall, and his presence in left was a huge advantage for Boston.

In 1979, Yastrzemski became the first American League player to make 400 home runs and 3,000 hits. Three other players, Hank Aaron, Willie Mays and Stan Musial, did it in the National League.

LIFETIME STATS: BA: .285, HR: 452, RBI: 1,844, H: 3,419, SB: 168

#34 Warren Edward Spahn

LHP, Braves, Mets, Giants, 1942–65. Hall of Fame, 1973

Spahn was the winningest left-handed pitcher of all time, and one of the greatest hurlers, left-handed or right-handed, in baseball history.

Because of his military service in World War II, Spahn didn't really get a chance to show his stuff until 1946. He had a brief stint with the Braves in 1942, but didn't come away with any decisions that year.

But when he returned from the war, "Spahnie," as some of his teammates called him, began to display the kind of pitching that would make him a star in the late 1940s and throughout the 1950s. He went only 8–5, but his 2.94 ERA led the team.

By 1947, Spahn went 21–10, the first of a major league record-tying 13 seasons with 20 or more wins. Eight times he would lead the National League in wins, including five years in a row, from 1957 to 1961. His 63 shutouts place him sixth all-time in the National League record books.

He was the mainstay of a Braves staff that, most years, wasn't very deep. In the late 1940s, Boston fans rested their hopes on Spahn and fellow pitcher Johnny Sain most years. It was, as most Braves fans knew, "Spahn and Sain and pray for rain."

Spahn began his career as a fastball pitcher who also could throw his curve for strikes. And from 1949 to 1952, he led the league in strikeouts. But as he got older, Spahn got smarter. He added a screwball and a slider, and he was the best of his generation in changing speeds on all those pitches.

In 1960, at the age of 39, Spahn pitched his first no-hitter. The next season, five days past his 40th birthday, he pitched his second.

The Braves won the National League crown in 1957 and again in 1958, and Spahn was at the top of his game. He won the Cy Young award in 1957, with a league-leading 21 wins, as well as 111 strikeouts and a 2.69 ERA. In 1958, he might have been even better, with 22 wins, a .667 winning percentage, 23 complete games and 290 innings pitched, all tops in the National League.

Spahn began to slow down in the early 1960s, and the Braves sold him to the Mets in 1965. He spent part of his season in New York and later was shipped to the Giants. He was released after the season, but continued to pitch in the minors for two more years before retiring at age 46.

LIFETIME STATS: W: 363, L: 245, SV: 29, ERA: 3.09, SO: 2,583, CG: 382

#35 Napoleon "Larry" Lajoie

2B-1B-SS-3B, Phillies, A's, Indians, A's, 1896–1916.
Hall of Fame, 1937

Lajoie was the greatest second baseman of the so-called "dead ball" era of the late 19th and early 20th centuries.

The muscular 6'1", 195-pound Lajoie would not be considered a "power hitter" in this era, as he rarely cracked double figures in home runs during his career. But he was a very strong right-handed pull hitter who regularly cowed third basemen with his searing line shots down the left field line. He led the league in doubles five times, and hit 40 or more two-baggers seven times in his career. He also stroked 10 or more triples in a season six times.

He was a graceful and fundamentally sound second baseman, six times leading his league in fielding percentage at that position.

Lajoie began his career with the Philadelphia Phillies, but when Ban Johnson started up the American League in 1901, Lajoie jumped across town to the A's. Lajoie, along with several other ex–National League stars, gave the new league instant credibility. In that first year with the A's, Lajoie won the Triple Crown, with 14 home runs, 125 RBI and a .426 batting average. The latter figure remains the American League record.

Lajoie's A's easily outdrew the Phillies that year, so the National Leaguers obtained an injunction preventing him from playing in Philadelphia during the 1902 season.

Not to be outdone, Johnson ordered Lajoie's contract transferred to Cleveland. Lajoie quickly became a star with his new club, as well, winning back-to-back batting titles in 1903 and 1904.

In 1910, Lajoie and Detroit star Ty Cobb were locked in a race for that year's batting crown. The league would award a Chalmers automobile to the best hitter. On the last day of the season, Lajoie bunted for seven infield hits and slapped a triple in a doubleheader at St. Louis. He still fell short by a point to Cobb, with his .384 average.

But later, St. Louis manager Jack O'Connor revealed he had ordered his third baseman to play deep against Lajoie, thus enabling Lajoie to bunt down the third-base line successfully. O'Connor was fired. The league gave both Cobb and Lajoie automobiles.

LIFETIME STATS: BA: .338, HR: 83, RBI: 1,599, H: 3,242, SB: 380

#**36** Lawrence Peter "Yogi" Berra
C-OF, Yankees, 1946–65. Hall of Fame, 1972

Maybe it's because he doesn't look like a great athlete. Maybe it's because of all those odd sayings he is credited with uttering. But there are still baseball fans who are reluctant to regard Berra as the greatest catcher in baseball history. He is.

The hitting speaks for itself. Berra hit 10 or more home runs 16 years in a row, and 20 or more home runs 11 times, including 10 years in a row. He hit over .300 four times. He had over 90 RBI nine times. He hit 20 or more doubles eight times. In short, Berra's offensive prowess gave the Yankees a huge advantage over just about every other team in baseball in the 1950s.

Between 1949 and 1955, Berra led the Yankees in RBI every season and won MVP awards in 1951, 1954 and 1955.

He was, by far, the best bad-ball hitter ever in the American League. Berra's hand-eye coordination enabled him to golf low pitches right out of the ballpark, or slash at eyebrow-high offerings for base hits. And, according to most of the ballplayers who played with and against him, Berra was the toughest out in the last three innings in baseball for most of his career.

Yet for all that aggression at the plate, Berra was very tough to strike out.

He never whiffed more than 38 times in a season, and averaged only 22 strikeouts per year.

But he was also an excellent fielder. He became one of four catchers to record a 1.000 fielding average in a season when he did it in 1958. He led the league in games caught and chances accepted by a catcher eight times, and led the league in double plays six times

Finally, Berra was an excellent handler of pitchers. That is said of most great catchers, but that's the point. Yogi was a great catcher. He caught Allie Reynolds's two no-hitters in 1949 and, of course, also caught Don Larsen's perfect game in the 1956 World Series.

LIFETIME STATS: BA: .285, HR: 358, RBI: 1,430, H: 2,150, SB: 30

#37 George Thomas "Tom Terrific" Seaver
RHP, Mets, Reds, White Sox, Red Sox, 1967–86. Hall of Fame, 1991

Seaver is fondly recalled by Mets fans as the first true star the franchise ever had.

Seaver was a star at the University of Southern California when he signed a contract with the Braves for $40,000. The contract was voided on a technicality, so the NCAA and baseball commissioner William Eckert offered Seaver's services to any team who would match the Braves' offer. The Phillies, Indians and Mets did so, and the names of all three teams were placed in a hat in the commissioner's office. The Mets won when Eckert pulled their name out of the hat.

The whole thing obviously paid off handsomely. A year after the drawing, Seaver went 16–13 for a truly horrible Mets team that finished last, 40 1/2 games behind St. Louis. Not surprisingly, Seaver made the All Star team.

Seaver went 16–12 for another bad Mets team the next season and had his breakout year in 1969, going 25–7 and winning the Cy Young award. The Mets, of course, won the World Series over the Orioles.

Baseball historian Bill James suggests that, given Seaver's amazingly consistent performance with teams that, for the most part, didn't score a lot of runs for him, he may have been the greatest pitcher of all time. It's not an unreasonable point. Seaver was good when his teams were bad, and when he had a little help in terms of better run production and more consistent relief, he was very, very good. He won three Cy Young awards, in 1969, 1973 and 1975, won 20 or more games five times and led the league in wins three times.

He was the consummate professional, a fanatic about conditioning and a perfectionist on the field. He fired three one-hitters and one no-hitter. That came on June 16, 1968, shutting down the Cardinals. Seaver won his 300th game with the White Sox in 1984, firing a complete game, six-hitter to beat the Yankees, 4–1.

LIFETIME STATS: W: 311, L: 205, SV: 1, ERA: 2.86, SO: 3,640, CG: 231

#38 Robert William Andrew "Rapid Robert" Feller

RHP, Indians, 1936–56. Hall of Fame, 1962

Interestingly, although Bob Feller was clearly the fastest pitcher of his era, he always credited his numerous strikeout records to his curveball and slider.

Feller was something of a prodigy when he got to the big leagues. He was signed by Cleveland as a 17-year-old and brought up to the big club immediately. In his major league debut against the St. Louis Browns near the end of the 1936 season, he struck out 15 batters. Later in the year, Feller struck out 17 men in a game against the A's.

Curveball and slider notwithstanding, it was Feller's fastball that was doing all the damage initially. Feller threw an extremely "live" ball, which meant that it jumped around as it neared the plate.

And with this velocity came a certain degree of wildness, at first. In 1937, Feller's first full year with Cleveland, he struck out 150 and walked 106. In 1938, the year he led the league in strikeouts with 240, he also walked 208, which was a major league record at the time.

But Feller was already learning to nick the edge of the plate with his fastball. The 1938 season was the first of seven years he would lead the league in strikeouts. He won 20 or more games six times, and also led the league in complete games six times.

Feller fired three no-hitters, including an opening-day gem against the White Sox in 1940. Feller also threw 12 one-hitters.

Feller lost four years to World War II, but when he returned to baseball in 1946, he had clearly lost nothing off his fastball. His 348 strikeouts broke Rube Waddell's league record, and in 1948, he led the Indians to their first World Series championship in 28 years.

But after that season, the Feller fastball lost a little speed, and Rapid Robert became a little more canny on the mound. He had one more solid season in 1951, leading the league in wins with 22. But in his final five years with the Indians, Feller was 36–31. He was a very effective spot starter with the Indians in 1954, when Cleveland once again won the pennant, but didn't pitch in the World Series against the Giants.

LIFETIME STATS: W: 266, L: 162, SV: 21, ERA: 3.25, SO: 2,581, CG: 279

#39 Roy "Campy" Campenella

C-3B-OF, Baltimore Elite Giants (Negro Leagues), Brooklyn Dodgers, 1937–57. Hall of Fame, 1969

Campenella would rate much higher had his career not been shortened by an auto accident in 1958 that paralyzed him. Does he move ahead of Berra? Possibly. But that's all speculation.

Campenella's 20-year pro career began when he signed a contract to play with the Baltimore Elite Giants at age 15. He learned from one of the all-time greats: catcher Biz Mackey. He played behind Mackey for several years, but by 1941, Campenella was an all star, hitting .344 and inviting comparisons to Josh Gibson.

Campenella was a star in the Negro Leagues, and major league owners salivated at the chance of getting him. He eventually signed with the Dodgers, and was an All Star eight years in a row, from 1949 to 1956.

He was a great player, strong, yet surprisingly agile. He hit .300 or better three times, 20 or more home runs seven times, and won three MVP awards, in 1951, 1953 and 1955. From 1949 to 1956, the Dodgers won five National League pennants and defeated the New York Yankees in a memorable seven-game World Series in 1955. In that Series, Campenella hit .259 with three doubles and two home runs.

Campenella was a durable player, but like most catchers, he endured nagging injuries throughout his career, which, at times, affected his production at the plate. But he rarely begged off in a game, catching more than 100 contests for the Dodgers every season but his first.

Campenella's 242 lifetime home runs were a record for a catcher at the time of his retirement in 1957, and he would have surely added to that total had he not been injured. But although he was in a wheelchair the rest of his life, Campanella spent most of the rest of his life working in community relations for the Dodgers until his death in 1993.

LIFETIME STATS: BA: 276, HR: 242, RBI: 865, H: 1,161, SB: 25

#40 George Harold "Gorgeous George" Sisler

1B-OF-P, Browns, Senators, Braves, 1915–30. Hall of Fame, 1939

The beginnings of Sisler's career had an odd parallel with that of Babe Ruth's. He began his professional career as a pitcher, and when he was eventually brought up to play for the St. Louis Browns, he was 4–4 in 1915 and 1–2 in 1916. He also played first base and in the outfield.

In 1916, in part-time duty, Sisler hit .305. It was time to make a decision, and Browns manager Fielder Jones didn't have to think about it much. First base had been a problem for St. Louis for several years, so Sisler found a home there pretty quickly.

His hitting improved dramatically when he became a regular. In 1920, he hit .407 with 257 hits; the latter figure is a mark that still stands today. That year, he also smacked 49 doubles, 18 triples and 19 home runs. He hit safely in 131 of 154 games and closed out the season hitting .442 in August and .448 in September.

In 1922, he led the league with 246 hits and a .420 batting average, as well as a league-leading 51 stolen bases. In all, Sisler stole 30 or more bases six times in his career.

Sisler's fielding ability is sometimes overshadowed by his hitting, but Sisler led the American League in assists seven times, and remains third on the all-time career leader list in assists by a first baseman with 1,529.

His career took a downswing in 1923, when he suffered from severe sinus problems, which in turn affected his eyesight. Sisler sat out the entire 1923 season. When he returned, his batting eye was not as acute as it had been previously, although he hit .300 six more seasons after his affliction. In 1929, at age 36, Sisler still managed to hit .326 with 205 hits.

LIFETIME STATS: BA: .340, HR: 102, RBI: 1,175, H: 2,812, SB: 375

#41 Christopher "Christy," "Big Six," "Matty" Mathewson

RHP, Giants, Reds, 1900–16. Hall of Fame, 1936

Mathewson was probably not the clean-cut golden boy that newsmen of the day made him seem, but he was probably pretty close. And his pitching abilities were certainly not exaggerated.

"Big Six" (named after a famous fire engine in New York City) was a masterful control pitcher who possessed pinpoint accuracy and could vary the speed of his fastball, curveball and change-up so well that he appeared to have six or seven different pitches to call on.

Mathewson also was one of the early masters of what was then called the "fadeaway" pitch, which modern players call a screwball, because it broke in on right-handed hitters. The whole package was impressive.

Mathewson started his career slowly, going 34–37 from 1900 to 1902. But the 1902 season record was misleading: although he was 14–17 that year, Mathewson led the league in shutouts with eight. In 1903, he turned the corner, going 30–13, and never won fewer than 22 games for the next 12 years.

From 1903 to 1905, Matty was awe-inspiring. He won 30, 33 and 31 games, with a total of 18 shutouts and 685 strikeouts. He averaged about two walks per nine innings in that span, and in fact was always a very, very good control pitcher.

Eleven times in his career, Mathewson pitched 300 innings or more in a season. In the 1908 season, when he won a career-high 37 games, he led the league with a minuscule 1.43 ERA to go along with 259 strikeouts and threw 390 2/3 innings. He started 44 games and completed 34, while also saving five games.

He was John McGraw's unofficial adopted son, and the McGraws and Mathewsons often spent time together in the off-season. In 1936, he was one of the five original players elected to the Hall of Fame.

LIFETIME STATS: W: 373, L: 188, SV: 28, ERA: 2.13, SO: 2,502, CG: 434

#42 Norman Thomas "Turkey" Stearnes

OF-1B, Detroit Stars, New York Lincoln Giants, Kansas City Monarchs, Cole's American Giants, Philadelphia Stars, Chicago American Giants (Negro Leagues), 1923–42. Hall of Fame, 2000

At six feet, 175 pounds, the left-handed Stearnes had slim hips and a powerful upper body that enabled him to punch round-trippers out of Mack Park in Detroit for the Negro League Detroit Stars for several seasons.

In his first four seasons in the league, Stearnes belted 17, 10, 18 and 20 home runs for Detroit in a 70-game season, leading the league three times. In 1923, his rookie year, Stearnes made an auspicious debut against white big leaguers, as the Stars bested the St. Louis Browns of the American League, two games to one in an exhibition series. Stearnes hit .462 with two home runs in the three tilts.

In 1928, Stearnes led the Negro National League in home runs with 24, was second in triples with seven, third in doubles with 18 and hit .324 to win the unofficial MVP award.

In 1931, the Stars had trouble making their payroll, and Stearnes jumped to the Chicago American Giants. The team won two pennants in two years. In a playoff series in 1941 against the Nashville Elite Giants, Stearnes hit .700 in five games as Chicago won easily.

In 1940, Stearnes jumped to the Kansas City Monarchs, and, along with stars Buck O'Neil, Newt Allen and Satchel Paige, won back-to-back championships in the Negro American League.

A free-swinger, Stearnes reportedly never learned to bunt until Chicago manager Dave Malarcher taught him. Malarcher also batted Stearnes in the leadoff spot, making him one of the few home run kings to hit in that position. In all, Stearnes won seven home run titles in the Negro Leagues.

LIFETIME STATS: BA: .332, HR: 197, H: 1,308

#43 George Howard Brett
3B-DH, Royals, 1973–93. Hall of Fame, 1999

Hard work and a laser-like focus were the principal reasons George Brett became one of the greatest third basemen of all time.

Brett did not set the world on fire his first couple of years with the Royals. In his first full season, he hit two home runs and managed only 47 RBI. But Brett listened to his pitching coach, Charlie Lau, who taught him to wait on pitches and hit to all fields. In his second full season, 1975, Brett batted .308 and led the league with 13 triples and 195 hits.

In 1976, Brett led the league with 215 hits and 14 triples and earned his first batting championship with a .333 average. He became, over the next decade and a half, one of the most consistent players in the game.

From 1975 to 1990, Brett hit over .300 11 times. Three other times, he hit .290 or better. He had more than 100 RBI four times in that span and scored more than 100 runs four times as well.

In 1979, Brett became the sixth player in major league history to hit 20 or more doubles, triples and home runs in the same year. He also hit .329 and led the league in hits with 212.

But his best year was 1980, when he won the MVP award. Brett flirted with .400 through most of the season, and ended up hitting .390. He also had a 37-game hitting streak and led the league with a .664 on-base percentage. Ironically, it was a year in which Brett battled various nagging injuries all season, and ended up playing in only 117 games.

Brett was not a one-dimensional guy, though. He won a Gold Glove in 1985 for his play at third base, and was one of the more fundamentally sound defensive players of his era.

In 1987, after 14 years at third base, Brett was switched to first base to make way for rookie Kevin Seitzer. He made the transition work, hitting .290 with 22 homers that season. In 1990, at age 37, Brett won his final batting title, hitting .329 with a league-leading 45 doubles.

LIFETIME STATS: BA: .305, HR: 317, RBI: 1,595, H: 3,154, SB: 201

#44 Johnny Lee Bench
C-3B, Reds, 1967–83. Hall of Fame, 1989

The greatest catcher in National League history, Bench was a certified star almost as soon as he donned a catcher's mask for the Cincinnati Reds in 1967. At 18, after being named the MVP of the Carolina League, his uniform number was retired. A year later, he was playing in the major leagues, and by 1968, Bench was an All Star, hitting .275, with 15 home runs and 82 RBI. He set a rookie record by catching in 154 games, as well as hitting 40 doubles.

Bench was clearly a star, and he dominated the catcher's position for the next 15 years. He batted either fourth or fifth for the Cincinnati "Big Red Machine" of the late 1960s and early 1970s.

He was a fearful weapon for the Reds, hitting 20 or more home runs 11 times in his career, driving in 100 or more runs six times and hitting 30 or more doubles five times. He had very good power for a catcher, hitting 45 home runs in 1970, a record for a catcher, and driving in 148 runs that same year, which was also a record for that position.

Bench was an MVP in 1970 and again in 1972, but those seasons were only marginally better than most of his career: He was always a very good player, consistent and productive.

That kind of production alone would have made Bench a star. But he was also, by far, the best defensive catcher in the National League for a large part of his career. He won 10 consecutive Gold Glove awards, from 1968 to 1977, and set a National League record by catching in at least 100 games in his first 13 full seasons. He had a tremendous throwing arm, among the best of all time.

Bench played in four World Series, hitting .279 with five home runs and 14 RBI. He also hit .370 in 12 All Star games.

LIFETIME STATS: BA: .267, HR: 389, RBI: 1,376, H: 2,048, SB: 68

#45 Charles Leonard
"The Mechanical Man" Gehringer
2B-1B-3B, Detroit, 1924–42. Hall of Fame, 1949

Gehringer was legendary for two things: His incredible consistency and his stoic demeanor. The latter contributed to a story that when he was being scouted by, among many clubs, the Tigers, Detroit player-manager Ty Cobb didn't think much of Gehringer because of his lack of fire. Not true. Cobb later said, in what was also a bit of hyperbole, that after he saw Gehringer play at a tryout, Cobb was so eager to sign him that Cobb rushed off the field to the Tiger's front office to meet with Gehringer without taking off his uniform.

Cobb probably took his time changing, but he knew what he had seen: a smooth-hitting, smooth-fielding second baseman who would be among the league's elite a few years after he came up to the majors.

That was all correct. Gehringer signed with the Tigers out of the University of Michigan in 1924. By 1926, he was a regular, and by 1927, he was a star. The Senators' Bucky Harris was slightly better afield, and the Yankees' Tony Lazzeri was tougher out at the plate, but overall, Gehringer was the top man at second base.

He stayed there for more than a decade. Over the next 14 years, he topped .300 a total of 13 times. He hit 24 or more doubles 14 seasons in a row. He scored 100 or more runs 12 times and collected 200 or more hits seven times. In 1937, he won the batting title with a .371 average; had 96 RBI, 40 doubles and 14 home runs; and was MVP.

His nickname, "the Mechanical Man," was bestowed upon Gehringer as a sign of respect for his abilities.

In the field, he was equally consistent. From 1929 to 1941, Gehringer led the league's second basemen in fielding average seven times and was second three other times. He led the league's second basemen in assists seven times and in putouts three times. He was so smooth at the position that he very rarely made spectacular plays: He was always in position, and the ball always seemed to come right toward him.

Gehringer was equally tough in the postseason, hitting .321 in three World Series, including a .375 average for the world championship team of 1935.

LIFETIME STATS: BA: .320, HR: 184, RBI: 1,427, H: 2,839, SB: 181

#46 Charles Augustus "Kid" Nichols

RHP, Braves, Cardinals, Phillies, 1890–1906. Hall of Fame, 1949

Nichols was the best pitcher of the 19th century, and the cornerstone of the Boston Braves dynasty of the 1890s, leading that team to five National League championships.

Nichols was a rarity among pitchers, then or now: He had a blistering fastball and pinpoint control even as a rookie. He went 27–19 as a rookie for the Braves, and led the league with seven shutouts. He completed all 47 games he started that year, and also appeared in relief in another contest.

Nichols was not a big man at 5'10", 175 pounds, but he threw very hard. He had a live fastball, a good curve and a decent changeup. He was, like the best pitchers of his day, extremely durable. Nichols pitched 400 or more innings a season five times and 300 or more innings a year seven other times.

In addition, he was not afraid to pitch in relief on the days he didn't start. Nichols led the league in saves four times in his career, although the league leader rarely had more than three or four saves in those days.

Most impressively, Nichols won 30 or more games seven times in his career, including four years in a row, 1891–94. In fact, although Cy Young was playing in the same league for the Cleveland Spiders, Nichols won more games in the 1890s and had a lower ERA. Young, who was actually two years older than Nichols, clearly was a dominant pitcher well into the 20th century. But in the 19th, the Kid was better.

Nichols never pitched a no-hitter, but came close several times. He had 48 shutouts. He started 561 games and completed 531, still fourth all-time. He remains the youngest player, at 30 years and nine months, ever to win his 300th game.

From 1891 to 1893, the Boston Braves won three consecutive National League championships. Nichols was 99-47 in that span, with 137 complete games, 11 shutouts and four saves.

LIFETIME STATS: W: 361, L: 208, SV: 17, ERA: 2.95, SO: 1,868, CG: 531

#**47** Sanford "Sandy" Koufax
LHP, Dodgers, 1955–66. Hall of Fame, 1972

Koufax may not have possessed, technically speaking, the fastest fastball in major league history. But as countless former opponents would swear, it was the liveliest—a ball that rivaled the legendary heater of Jack Armstrong, the comic-strip all-American. A ball, which, like Armstrong's, dropped down and then rose up on a batter in the same path to the plate, like a ping-pong ball in a wind tunnel.

Koufax was a slow starter as a big leaguer. He was a rookie on the 1955 Brooklyn World Series champs, cobbling together a 2–2 mark with a 3.02 ERA. But in his first major league start on August 27 against the Reds, he struck out 14 in a 7–0 win. Clearly, he had something.

But there were also afternoons when Koufax didn't have it. In his first two years with the Dodgers, he was 4–6, striking out 60 and walking 57.

He became a regular in 1958, after the Dodgers moved to Los Angeles. In the more spacious confines of Dodger Stadium, Koufax felt he had a little more room for error. He was 11–11, with 131 strikeouts. Hitters batted a league low .223 against him.

As he cut down on his walks, Koufax got better and better. He added a sweeping curveball to go with the fastball. In 1961, he was 18–13 and led the league in strikeouts with 269. Koufax would lead the National League in strikeouts four times, including an amazing year in which he struck out 382 men, a league record, in only 335 innings.

In 1962, he pitched his first no-hitter. He would follow it up with a no-hitter every year until 1965. That final no-hitter was also a perfect game against the Cubs on September 7. He led the league in ERA five consecutive years, from 1962 to 1966. He won Cy Young awards in 1963, 1965 and 1966. Not coincidentally, those were also years in which the Dodgers won the National League crown.

In 1965, he won Game Five of the World Series against the Minnesota Twins on a four-hit shutout. He then came back three days later to win the Series by throwing a three-hit shutout.

Koufax retired after the 1966 season, nursing various arm troubles. But five years later, he became the youngest man ever to be elected to the Hall of Fame, at age 36.

LIFETIME STATS: W: 165, L: 87, SV: 9, ERA: 2.76, SO: 2,396, CG: 137

#48 Eddie Clarence Murray
1B-DH-3B, Orioles, Dodgers, Mets, Indians, Angels, 1977–97. Hall of Fame, 2003

Murray was a player who almost never had a bad year. And this was a guy who played for 21 seasons.

Murray had 110 or more hits and 20 or more doubles for 19 consecutive seasons. He hit 20 or more home runs in 16 seasons and had 90 or more RBI in 12 seasons. His 5,397 total bases are fifth all-time.

Murray never won a batting title, but hit over .300 seven times. In fact, Murray was such an overpowering hitter that he won the 1977 Rookie of the Year award as a designated hitter, the first player ever to accomplish that. He became a regular at first base the next season.

Murray won three Gold Gloves with the Orioles at first base, from 1982 to 1984. In 1981 and 1982, he led the league's first basemen in fielding percentage, a feat he accomplished again in 1989, his first year with the Dodgers.

Murray's low-key demeanor never seemed to bother a vast majority of his teammates, but fans and the Orioles ownership, specifically former owner Edward Bennett Williams, had a problem with it.

Ignoring Murray's amazing consistency, Williams was often critical of his first baseman's apparent lack of desire. Murray rarely endeared himself to the media, refusing to talk to the press for many years. The situation eventually became untenable, and Murray was eventually shipped to the Dodgers.

But after a slow start in 1989, Murray rebounded to hit a career-high .330 with Los Angeles. He was traded back to the East Coast in 1992 and responded by hitting .285, with 27 homers and 100 RBI for the Mets in 1993.

In 1996, after a stint in Cleveland, Murray returned briefly to the Orioles for the second half of the season, and helped his old team to the American League playoffs. He hit .400 in the first round of the playoffs against the Indians.

LIFETIME STATS: BA: .287, HR: 504, RBI: 1,917, H: 3,255, SB: 110

#49 Harry Edwin "Slug" Heilmann

OF-1B-2B, Tigers, Reds, 1914–32. Hall of Fame, 1952

But for a grand total of 17 more hits, Heilmann would have hit better than .400 in four separate seasons. As it was, he hit .403 in 1923, .394 in 1921, .393 in 1925 and .398 in 1927, all league bests.

But, 11 more hits in 1921, five more hits in 1925 and one more hit in 1927, and Heilmann would have topped the .400 mark those other three times, as well. As it was, he hit .300 or better 11 other times in addition to his .403 in 1923.

Heilmann was a big man, 6'1", 200 pounds, with a choppy swing, who rarely saw a pitch he didn't like. He wasn't particularly patient at the plate, averaging about 65 walks per season. But he was equally difficult to strike out, whiffing 50 or fewer times 16 of the 17 years he played in the majors.

In short, Heilmann inevitably made contact. It was rarely pretty, but very effective.

Heilmann was one of those players who floated just under the radar screen. Yet he was a star in the league for most of his tenure. In addition to his four batting titles, Heilmann was in the top 10 league hitters six other times. He was in the top 10 in slugging percentage and in RBI 12 times in his career, in the top 10 in home runs in 11 seasons, in batting average and doubles in 10 seasons, in on-base percentage and hits in seven seasons and in triples six seasons.

Defensively, he is remembered as a mediocre fielder. But that's based largely on a disastrous two-year switch to first base for the Tigers in 1919 and 1920, when he led the league in errors both years. When he returned to the outfield, Heilmann was a very good fielder. He led the league's right fielders in assists in 1923, was second in 1926 and 1930, and third in 1928. He also led right fielders in putouts in 1925.

LIFETIME STATS: BA: .342, HR: 183, RBI: 1,539, H: 2,660, SB: 113

#50 Ernest "Mr. Cub" Banks
1B-SS, Chicago, 1953–71. Hall of Fame, 1977

The greatest player in Cubs' history, Ernie Banks was a consistent breath of fresh air for a franchise that didn't have a lot of good years in the 1950s or 1960s.

Banks was a terrific athlete who, initially, wasn't particularly interested in baseball. He was a football, track and basketball star in high school, and he enjoyed playing softball more than baseball as a youngster.

But in the early 1950s, baseball was where the money was. Banks played briefly in the Negro Leagues, which included a stint with the Kansas City Monarchs. But Jackie Robinson had broken the color line a few years prior, and the good black players were beginning to be snapped up by big league teams.

It wasn't long before the Cubs discovered Banks. He was signed by Chicago in 1953 and brought up to the majors immediately. He played 10 games at the end of the season and hit .314. The next season, he was a regular and by 1955, Banks was a star.

His sunny demeanor and perpetual enthusiasm were legendary. When he would say, "It's a great day for baseball. Let's play two!" it was not an act. Banks had a fine appreciation for the game and where he would be if he were not playing it.

And he was a heck of a player. He started his career as the Cubs' shortstop, and won MVP awards in 1958 and 1959. He led the league in home runs in 1958 (47) and 1960 (41). In fact, from 1955 to 1960, nobody in the majors, including Mickey Mantle and Henry Aaron, hit more home runs.

Defensively, he led National League shortstops in fielding percentage three times, and won a Gold Glove in 1960. He was switched to first base in 1962, but handled that change pretty well, leading the league in fielding percentage at that position in 1969 and leading first basemen in assists five times.

Banks retired in 1971, and the next year he became the first Cub to have his number retired.

LIFETIME STATS: BA: .274, HR: 512, RBI: 1,636, H: 2,583, SB: 50

#51 Joseph Floyd "Arky" Vaughn

SS-3B, Pirates, Dodgers, 1932–43, 1947–48. Hall of Fame, 1985

Vaughn won the batting championship in 1935 while with Pittsburgh, hitting .385. He also led the league in walks for three years in a row, from 1934–36. He was one of the more accomplished shortstops, offensively, in baseball history.

Vaughn wasn't considered a speedster, but, playing half his games in huge Forbes Field in Pittsburgh, he hit 10 or more triples eight times in his career, leading the league three times. He also hit 15 or more doubles 12 times in his career.

Vaughn's nickname came from his state of birth, Arkansas, and he was generally considered a gentleman both on and off the field. But after he was traded to the Brooklyn Dodgers, he had a dispute with manager Leo Durocher that kept him away from the game for three years. He returned in 1947 and was a bit player for two years before retiring for good.

LIFETIME STATS: BA: .318, HR: 96, RBI: 926, H: 2,103, SB: 118

#52 William Harold "Memphis Bill" Terry

1B-OF, Giants, 1923–36. Hall of Fame, 1954

Terry hit .401 in 1930, which makes him the last National Leaguer to exceed .400. (Ted Williams did it 11 years later in the American League, batting .406.) His 250 hits that year are the second-best single-season total ever.

Terry was a great hitter in an era of very good batsmen. Three other times in his career, he hit .350 or better, and six times in his career, Terry had 200 hits or more. He also scored 100 or more runs seven different times.

He was an excellent defensive player, leading National League first basemen in putouts and double plays five times each, in assists three times and in fielding percentage twice.

He accomplished all this despite a relatively late start: Terry didn't make the big leagues until he was 25 and didn't become a regular with the Giants until he was 27. Terry was a productive player until the end of his career, hitting .310 as a part-time player-manager with the Giants in 1936.

LIFETIME STATS: BA: .341, HR: 154, RBI: 1,078, H: 2,193, SB: 56

#53 Calvin Edwin "Cal," "Iron Man" Ripken Jr.

SS-3B, Orioles, 1981–2001. Hall of Fame, 2007

The man who broke the "unbreakable" record, Ripken began his amazing streak in 1983 and didn't miss a game until 18 years later. He played in 2,632 consecutive games, smashing Lou Gehrig's record of 2,131. And, it's fair to point out, Ripken played a vast majority of those games at shortstop, which, defensively, is a tougher position to play than first base.

But let's not forget that the guy was also really good. He hit .300 or better five times in his career. He won the MVP award in 1983 and again in 1991. Twelve times in his career, Ripken belted 20 or more home runs, and he had 100 or more RBI four times.

On defense, Ripken won two Gold Gloves, in 1991 and 1992. In 1990, Ripken's .996 fielding average was the best for a shortstop in baseball history. In fact, Ripken's .990 fielding average in 1989 is fourth best all time and his .989 in 1995 is tied for eighth best all time. His career lifetime fielding average of .979 is fifth-best.

LIFETIME STATS: BA: .276, HR: 431, RBI: 1,695, H: 3,184, SB: 36

#54 Edward Charles "Whitey," "The Chairman of the Board," "Slick" Ford
LHP, Yankees, 1950–67. Hall of Fame, 1974

Whitey Ford pitched with a confident efficiency that made him one of the best "Big Game" pitchers in baseball history.

True, he played for a Yankee franchise that won 11 American League pennants and six World Championships in his tenure, but Ford's forte was taking the ball in big games and winning those games. Easier said than done.

He remains the leader in World Series wins with 10, games started with 22, as well as innings pitched, strikeouts and losses. Over the span of the 1961, 1962 and 1963 World Series, he pitched 33 consecutive shutout innings, breaking Babe Ruth's record of 29 2/3 innings with the Red Sox.

Ford's ERA during the regular season with New York was under 3.00 a total of 11 times, and he was the league leader twice, in 1956 and 1958. In 1961, he went 25–4 with 209 strikeouts to win the Cy Young award.

Ford only won 20 or more games twice in his career, but was a player unimpressed by stats anyway. Winning was the stat he cared more about.

LIFETIME STATS: W: 236, L: 106, SV: 10, ERA: 2.75, SO: 1,956, CG: 156

#**55** Edwin Donald "Duke," "The Silver Fox" Snider

OF, Dodgers, Mets, Giants, 1947–64. Hall of Fame, 1980

Looking back, Duke Snider was probably considered the third-best of the three stellar center fielders who played in New York, after the Giants' Willie Mays and the Yankees' Mickey Mantle. But Dodger fans of the day will gladly point out that the Duke of Flatbush, as he was called, hit more home runs than Mays or Mantle in the four years (1954–57) that all three men were manning center field in the Big Apple for their respective teams.

Snider was a part-time player for the first two years of his existence as a Dodger, but apt tutoring by George Sisler enabled Snider to adjust his stance slightly to better enable him to drive balls up and out of tiny Ebbets Field. He hit 40 or more home runs five consecutive years, from 1953 to 1957, leading the league in 1956 with 43.

Snider was a strong defensive player, with a powerful throwing arm and excellent speed.

Snider was one of the best postseason players ever, setting National League records for home runs (11) and RBI (26). In the 1952 and again in the 1955 Fall Classic, Snider hit four home runs. He is the only man to do so twice in World Series history.

LIFETIME STATS: BA: .295, HR: 407, RBI: 1,333, H: 2,116, SB: 99

#56 Steven Norman "Steve," "Lefty" Carlton

LHP, Cardinals, Phillies, Giants, White Sox, Indians, Twins, 1965–88. Hall of Fame, 1994

Carlton is the number two lefthander of all time, in terms of wins, behind Warren Spahn, and the number two all-time in strikeouts, behind Nolan Ryan.

Interestingly, when Carlton first began trying out for big league teams, there was some question as to his arm strength. In response, Carlton became almost a fitness fanatic, and within a few years was one of the hardest throwers in the game.

He became a solid, dependable starter with the Cardinals in 1967 to 1968, going 27–20 as St. Louis won back-to-back National League pennants. But his persistent salary demands were wearing out the Cardinal front office, and he was traded to the Phillies.

That trade was the turning point in Carlton's career. He became an instant star in Philadelphia, winning the Cy Young award four times while there: in 1972, 1977, 1980 and 1982. Carlton was the first pitcher to win four awards, although he has since been eclipsed by Roger Clemens, who has six.

That first Cy Young might have been the best. Carlton won 27 games for a team that won only 59 total. He led the league in complete games (30), innings pitched (346 1/3) and strikeouts (310), becoming only the second National League pitcher to amass more than 300 strikeouts in a season. (Sandy Koufax was the first.)

Carlton developed a devastating slider to go with his fastball and won the strikeout crown five times in all.

LIFETIME STATS: W: 329, L: 244, SV: 2, ERA: 3.22, SO: 4,136, CG: 254

#57 Walter Fenner "Buck" Leonard

1B-OF, Homestead Grays (Negro Leagues), 1934–50.
Hall of Fame, 1972

Leonard was a left-handed pull hitter who was the anchor for the legendary Homestead Grays in the 1930s and 1940s.

He was born in North Carolina, the oldest of six children. His parents called him "Buddy," but one of his younger brothers couldn't pronounce that name very well, instead calling his older sibling "Buck." The name stuck.

Leonard began his pro career playing in semipro Negro Leagues in North Carolina. But his fearsome hitting drew the attention of Cumberland "Cum" Posey, the manager-owner of the Grays. Leonard signed a contract to play for the Grays in the summer of 1933. For the next 17 years, he was the team's starting first baseman.

Leonard was a very good hitter, recording team-leading batting averages of .356 in 1936, .396 in 1937, .397 in 1938, .394 in 1939 and .378 in 1940, as the Grays won the Negro National League five consecutive years. His .397 in 1938 also led the Negro National League.

In 1942, when catcher Josh Gibson joined Leonard and the Grays, the two men became known as the "Thunder Twins," and led the Homesteads to three more NL titles, and Negro League World Series championships in 1943 and 1944.

Leonard was a solid defensive first baseman, described by observers at the time as being as agile as the legendary Hal Chase.

LIFETIME STATS: BA: .335, HR: 79, H: 779,

#58 Louis Clark "Lou" Brock
OF, Cubs, Cardinals, 1961–79. Hall of Fame, 1985

Brock was a weak-hitting but explosively fast outfielder with the Cubs when, in 1964, he was traded to the St. Louis Cardinals for pitcher Ernie Broglio. Broglio was a decent pitcher, but at the time, Brock was deemed a lousy outfielder. The conventional wisdom of the time was the Cardinals got snookered.

They didn't. The trade galvanized Brock. He hit .348 with 33 stolen bases and 81 runs scored in 103 games for the Cardinals as St. Louis surged to the pennant and beat the Yankees in a stirring seven-game World Series. It is regarded as one of the worst trades ever, possibly the worst ever in the National League, and not far from the Ruth trade all-time.

Brock went on to become a feared leadoff hitter, even though his strike-outs were exceptionally high for a leadoff man. Still, he led the league in stolen bases eight times, including a National League record 118 in 1974, when Brock was 35.

He was sensational in the postseason, hitting .391 in three World Series, which is second all-time for players who played in two or more Fall Classics. In the 1967 and the 1968 Series, Brock hit over .400 both times.

LIFETIME STATS: BA: .293, HR: 149, RBI: 900, H: 3,023, SB: 938

#59 William Malcolm "Bill" Dickey

C, Yankees, 1928–46. Hall of Fame, 1954

Dickey was the backbone of the Yankee powerhouses of the 1930s and early 1940s, a tough, durable, great-hitting catcher who hated to sit out games.

Dickey joined the Yankees in August of 1928 and played a handful of games. But by the next season, he was New York's starting catcher. He hit .324 with 10 homers and 65 RBI. He struck out only 16 times in 447 at bats.

Dickey was a durable backstopper, catching 100 or more games in 13 consecutive seasons. He led the league's catchers in fielding percentage four times and was second four other times.

He was also an excellent handler of pitchers. The Yankee pitching staff in those days ran the gamut from the eccentric Lefty Gomez to the ultra-competitive Red Ruffing, and Dickey commanded the respect of all of them.

He was a fearsome weapon for New York at the plate, as well. Dickey hit .300 or better 11 times in his career, and was a solid postseason batsman, twice hitting over .400 in the World Series, in 1932 and again in 1938.

LIFETIME STATS: BA: .313, HR: 202, RBI: 1,209, H: 1,969, SB: 36

#60 Adrian Constantine "Cap," "Pop" Anson

1B-3B-C-2B-OF, Rockford (NA), Philadelphia (NA), Cubs, 1871–97. Hall of Fame, 1939

Cap Anson might not have been the best baseball player of the 19th century, but he was the National League's first real star, and its most visible presence for almost three decades.

Anson began his career in the old National Association, the forerunner of the National League. He hit .415 for the Philadelphia Athletics in 1872, and the next season, fell one hit short of that magic number, batting .398.

After he signed with the Chicago White Stockings (the forerunners of the Cubs) in 1876, Anson continued his superior batting, hitting .300 or better in 19 of his 22 National League seasons, including 15 years in a row. Anson won batting titles in 1881 and 1888.

Anson was as good a manager as a player. In 1879, he became player-manager in Chicago. Anson was one of the first managers to rotate his pitchers, devise hit-and-run plays and encourage base stealing. He was one of the first, if not the first, manager to require his players to report to their team early for preseason training.

The White Stockings won five pennants under Anson's tenure in the 1880s, including three straight from 1880 to 1882.

The one mark against Anson was that he was clearly a racist. He once pulled his team off the field rather than play a team of blacks. But it may be a stretch to say that his influence kept blacks out of the majors until 1947.

LIFETIME STATS: BA: .329, HR: 97, RBI: 1,879, H: 2,995, SB: 247

#61 James Thomas "Cool Papa" Bell

OF-1B, St. Louis Stars, Homestead Grays, Pittsburgh Crawfords, Memphis Red Sox (Negro Leagues), 1922–42. Hall of Fame, 1974

The fastest man, probably, in baseball history. Some of the stories about Bell were almost certainly exaggerations, such as the time he slapped a single up the middle and was hit by his own batted ball, and the Satchel Paige–generated tale of Bell turning a light switch and scooting under the covers before the lights went out.

But others were not. He regularly took two bases on bunts down the first base line. Against a team of major league All Stars, onlookers watched in awe as Bell scored from second base on a sacrifice fly to right field.

Bell's superior speed enabled him to hit high averages for most of his Negro League career. His teammates noticed how calm he was under even the most pressure-packed situation, and one of his first coaches commented that the 19-year-old Bell was "one cool papa."

Bell was regularly among the league leaders in batting average, extra bases, stolen bases and runs scored. At least once he topped .400 during a Negro League season. That was in 1946; Bell, by then 43 years old, was hitting .402. But he sat out the last week of the season so that Monte Irvin would win the batting title and have a shot at the major leagues. Bell's decision to sit also cost him a $200 bonus.

It's no wonder Bell was so revered by his teammates. In 1951, Bell was approached by the St. Louis Browns of the American League to play for them. But Bell, at 48, turned them down, not wanting to possibly take a roster spot from another, younger, black hopeful.

LIFETIME STATS: BA: .328, HR: 73, H: 1,561

#**62** Gordon Stanley "Mickey," "Black Mike" Cochrane

C, Athletics, Tigers, 1925–37. Hall of Fame, 1947

Cochrane's "Black Mike" nickname came from when he was a multisport star (football, baseball) at Boston University. His extreme competitiveness rushed to the forefront if his team lost a close game and he would fall into an angry funk. He was, recalled one of his former college teammates, the wrong man to be around after a 1–0 loss. That competitiveness didn't disappear when he got to the big leagues.

Cochrane was a great hitter, a great defensive catcher and a leader on every team on which he played.

Cochrane hit better than .300 in nine of the 13 years he was a major league player. He did not have overwhelming power and wasn't an explosive runner, but he almost always put the ball in play and was nearly impossible to strike out. In 1929, he hit .331, with 170 hits in 514 at bats, and whiffed only eight times all year.

Cochrane twice hit for the cycle, in 1932 and again in 1933 with Philadelphia. In 1925, Cochrane hit three home runs in one game. He was named MVP in 1928 with Philadelphia and in 1933 with the Tigers.

Defensively, he led the league's catchers in fielding percentage twice and assists six times, although he also led the league's backstoppers in errors two other seasons.

He was a winner. Cochrane played in five World Series for two teams, winning three. He hit .400 in the 1929 Series against the Cubs.

Cochrane's career was ended prematurely when he was beaned by Yankee pitcher Bump Hadley. But he went on to a solid career as a manager, scout and executive. Mutt Mantle named his oldest son, Mickey, after Cochrane.

LIFETIME STATS: BA: .320, HR: 119, RBI: 832, H: 1,652, SB: 64

#63 Reginald Martinez "Reggie," "Mr. October" Jackson
OF-DH, Athletics, Orioles, Yankees, Angels, 1967–87. Hall of Fame, 1993

Jackson's outspoken behavior sometimes (well, actually most of the time) overshadowed a prodigious talent. He remains one of the better "big game" players in the history of the game.

Jackson played on 10 divisional championship teams, six pennant winners and five World Champions. Jackson's batting average in five World Series is .357, almost 100 points better than his career average. His career World Series slugging average of .755 is still a record.

In 1977, he hit three home runs in the deciding game of the World Series, off three different pitchers on three consecutive pitches, perhaps one of the most dramatic performances in World Series history.

He wasn't a slouch during the regular season, either. Jackson was MVP in 1973, when he led the American League in home runs (32), runs scored (99), RBI (117) and slugging percentage (.531). He led the league in round-trippers four times, in 1973, 1975, 1980 and 1982.

Jackson could also run the bases, stealing 20 or more four times in his career and averaging about 24 doubles per year for his career.

He struck out an awful lot, though, and his 2,597 whiffs are still the most ever.

He also had a big mouth. In 1977, when he was acquired by New York, he told a writer he was "the straw that stirred the drink," which alienated teammate Thurman Munson and manager Billy Martin. He was, but there was no reason to trumpet the fact. Basically, Jackson's philosophy was: It ain't bragging if you can do it. And he could.

LIFETIME STATS: BA: .262, HR: 563, RBI: 1,702, H: 2,584, SB: 228

#**64** Roberto Walker "Arriba" Clemente

OF, Pirates, 1955–72. Hall of Fame, 1973

Clemente was an outstanding defensive outfielder who was also one of the most consistent hitters of the 1950s and 1960s.

Clemente was noted more for his defensive abilities in the early part of his career. He had a strong, accurate throwing arm from the outfield, and his speed and athleticism enabled him to track down balls that would have eluded most defenders. He would go on to win 12 Gold Glove awards for his fielding and lead National League outfielders in assists five times.

Gradually, Clemente's offensive abilities began to catch up with his defensive prowess, but it wasn't until he won the first of four batting titles in 1961 (with a .351 average) that people began noticing that facet of his game.

In the 1960s, Roberto Clemente became a bona fide star, winning three more batting championships in 1964, 1965 and 1967, and the MVP award in 1966. Gradually, the Pirates were getting better, too.

Clemente's showcase came in the 1971 World Series. He had played well in the 1960 Fall Classic with Pittsburgh, hitting .310 as the Pirates upset the Yankees. But in 1971, Clemente was amazing, hitting .414 and slugging .759 to become MVP of the Series as the Pirates defeated the Orioles in seven games.

On New Year's Eve 1972, Clemente was on board a plane flying to Managua, Nicaragua, with relief supplies for earthquake victims there. His plane encountered turbulence, and crashed about a mile off the Puerto Rican coast. There were no survivors. The five-year waiting period for induction into the Hall of Fame was waived and Clemente was immediately inducted.

LIFETIME STATS: BA: .317, HR: 240, RBI: 1,305, H: 3,000, SB: 83

#65 Henry Benjamin "Hammerin' Hank" Greenberg

1B-OF, Tigers, 1930–41, 1945–47. Hall of Fame, 1956

A native New Yorker, Greenberg was initially deemed too big and clumsy to be a professional baseball player. But his hard work and persistence eventually paid off in spectacular fashion.

Greenberg was born in the Bronx, and while New York Giants manager John McGraw was always on the lookout for native New Yorkers who were also Jewish to expand his teams' fan base, Greenberg was so uncoordinated as a teen that McGraw didn't think he would make the cut.

Greenberg eventually signed with the Tigers in 1930, but it wasn't until 1933 that he actually became a regular. Greenberg hit .301 in that first full season, with 12 home runs and 87 RBI. He belted line drives all over Tiger Stadium, and while he was still a little awkward, he was clearly going to be a good one.

Greenberg led the Tigers to back-to-back American League pennants in 1934 and 1935, which, in the New York Yankee–dominated 1930s, was a great accomplishment indeed. He hit .321 in a loss to the Cardinals in 1934. In 1935, Greenberg had an MVP year, with 36 home runs, 170 RBI and a .328 batting average.

His 1938 assault on Babe Ruth's home run record in 1958 electrified Tiger fans, although Hank fell just short with 58. In 1940, he won another MVP award, this time after switching to the outfield.

He served four distinguished years in the military during World War II and upon his return in 1945, led the Tigers to another pennant. He hit .304 in Detroit's World Series win over the Cubs.

LIFETIME STATS: BA: .313, HR: 331, RBI: 1,276, H: 1,628, SB: 58

#66 Robin R. Yount
SS-OF, Brewers, 1974–93. Hall of Fame, 1999

Yount was only 18 when he started for the Brewers at shortstop in 1974. He learned quickly, cracking 28 doubles and 149 hits his second year in the bigs. By 1980, Yount was a star, leading the league with 49 doubles and 82 extra-base hits.

An aggressive weight-training regimen paid off in 1982, when his power numbers jumped. Yount hit 29 homers, 12 triples, a league-leading 46 doubles and scored 129 runs to earn the MVP award as the Brewers won the American League championship that year. Yount hit .414 in his only World Series appearance, a loss to the St. Louis Cardinals.

A shoulder injury forced the Brewers to move Yount to the outfield. He adapted well, hitting over .300 from 1986 to 1989. He won his second MVP award in 1989, hitting .318 with 195 hits, 21 home runs, 38 doubles and nine triples.

Yount was not particularly fast, but he was a smart base runner, stealing 15 or more bases nine times in his career.

Yount got his 3,000th hit at age 37, one of the youngest players ever to accomplish that feat.

LIFETIME STATS: BA: .285, HR: 251, RBI: 1,406, H: 3,142, SB: 271

#67 Anthony Keith "Tony" Gwynn
OF-DH, Padres, 1982–2000. Hall of Fame, 2007

Gwynn parlayed a tremendous work ethic into becoming one of the great National League hitters of modern times. And he was no slouch in the outfield, either.

Gwynn was a third-round pick by the Padres in 1981, and came up to the big club a year later. He was also a first-round pick of the NBA's San Diego Clippers. Gwynn hit .289 in limited action with San Diego, but his work ethic impressed his coaches.

In 1984, he became the first Padre to make more than 200 hits (he had 213) as well as the first San Diego player to win a batting title, with a .351 average. It was the first of eight batting titles for Gwynn. Only Ty Cobb has more crowns.

For several seasons in the late 1980s and early 1990s, Gwynn would get off to an explosive start, and sportswriters would speculate about his chances of hitting .400. Gwynn never made it, but in 1994, his .394 average was the best in the National League since Bill Terry's .401 in 1930. It was the first of four consecutive batting championships for Gwynn.

Never much of a power hitter, Gwynn was an excellent base runner. He hit 21 or more doubles 16 consecutive years, and tied a record in 1986 with five stolen bases in one game. In 1987, he stole 56 bases, good for second in the league.

Originally a fair to poor fielder, Gwynn's work ethic eventually earned him five Gold Gloves in the outfield.

LIFETIME STATS: BA: .338, HR: 134, RBI: 1,121, H: 3,108, SB: 318

#68 Charles Leo "Gabby" Hartnett
C, Cubs, Giants, 1922–41. Hall of Fame, 1955

As a first-year player with the Cubs in 1922, Hartnett was shy around his new teammates, which led to his ironic nickname. But until Johnny Bench came along, Hartnett was considered the best catcher in the history of the National League.

His strength was fielding, and he led National League catchers in fielding percentage six times in his career, including a record-tying four consecutive times from 1934 to 1937. Hartnett also led the league in assists six times, in putouts four times and in double plays six times.

But Hartnett's most famous moment came while at bat. On September 28, 1938, Hartnett was at bat against the Pirates in the bottom of the ninth, with the score 5–5 and two strikes on him. Hartnett had taken over management of the team at midseason, and the Cubs were charging toward a pennant, trailing Pittsburgh by a half-game at that point.

As darkness began to fall, Hartnett slammed a game-winning home run to put his team in first place. Three games later, the Cubs were National League champs, and the "Homer in the Gloamin' " was a part of baseball lore.

Hartnett was actually a pretty good hitter, so the home run was not a complete surprise. He hit .300 or better six times in his career, and won the MVP award in 1930 with a .339 batting average, 37 home runs and 122 RBI. The latter two stats were career highs.

LIFETIME STATS: BA: .297, HR: 236, RBI: 1,179, H: 1,912, SB: 28

#**69** Harmon Clayton "Killer," "The Fat Kid" Killebrew

1B-3B-OF-DH, Senators, Twins, Royals, 1954–75. Hall of Fame, 1984

A tremendous power hitter, Harmon Killebrew played several positions with the Senators and Twins over his career, and always seemed to handle them pretty well. His forte was obviously at the plate, but Killebrew was fundamentally sound enough to play well wherever he had to.

He actually didn't become a starter until his sixth year in the majors, and only then after an injury to infielder Pete Runnels. But that season, the Killer bashed 42 home runs to lead the league, the first of eight years he would hit 40 or more dingers.

His power was awesome. In 1962, he hit a ball completely out of vast Tiger Stadium. In 1967, his three-run blast shattered two seats in the upper deck of Minnesota's Metropolitan Stadium. The seats were painted orange and never sold again.

Killebrew, for a while, seemed poised to break some of Babe Ruth's home run records in the mid-1960s. But the muscular Minnesotan began suffering nagging injuries that usually didn't sit him down, but did hamper his production.

Killebrew had his best season in 1969, and won the MVP award while hitting 49 home runs, with a 140 RBI, 145 walks and a .430 slugging percentage, all league bests. He also had 153 hits and stole a career-high eight bases.

He probably should have ended his career in Minnesota, but after a contract squabble, Killebrew found himself in Kansas City in 1975.

LIFETIME STATS: BA: .256, HR: 573, RBI: 1,584, H: 2,086, SB: 19

#**70** Pack Robert "Bob," "Hoot" Gibson

RHP, Cardinals, 1959–75. Hall of Fame, 1981

One of the best "money" pitchers ever, Gibson combined a fierce competitiveness with tremendous athleticism to become one of the premiere pitchers of the 1960s.

Gibson was a great pitcher in the regular season: He won 20 or more games five times in his career, and seven times he completed 20 or more games in a season.

But his World Series pitching was even more impressive. He won seven World Series games in a row, and those seven career victories are second only to the Yankees' Whitey Ford. His World Series ERA is a minuscule 1.89 and he completed eight of his nine starts.

In 1968, he set a World Series record with 17 strikeouts in Game One of the series. He won the seventh game in both the 1964 and 1967 World Series.

Gibson's 1968 season was one of the greatest seasons of all time. He went 22–9, with a league-leading 13 shutouts, completed 28 of his 34 starts, struck out a league-leading 268 batters and turned in an incredible 1.12 ERA, still the lowest of the 20th century for a pitcher throwing 300 innings or more.

At one point, he allowed two runs in 92 innings. That effort earned him the Cy Young and Most Valuable Player awards. He would also win another Cy Young in 1970.

He was a great athlete, and fielded his position very well, earning nine Gold Gloves. A fierce competitor, he hated to come out of games. His catchers usually weren't too thrilled to visit him on the mound during games, either.

LIFETIME STATS: W: 251, L: 174, SV: 6, ERA: 2.91, SO: 3,117, CG: 255

#71 Ryne Dee "Ryno" Sandberg
2B-3B-22, Phillies, Cubs, 1981–97. Hall of Fame, 2005

Sandberg, a benchwarmer for the Phillies at the time, was a throw-in in the deal that sent Ivan DeJesus from the Cubs. It turned out to be a stunning deal for Chicago, who acquired the best second baseman of the 1980s.

Sandberg was a tremendous all-around player. He was a great fielder, winning a record nine consecutive Gold Gloves at second base. In 1986, he set a record for the fewest errors (five) and highest fielding percentage ever, with a .994 mark. In all, Sandberg had the best fielding percentage for a second baseman four times in his career. In 1989, he went 91 games without an error at second base, another record.

As good as he was in the field, Sandberg was also quite accomplished at the plate. He hit .300 or better five times in his career, and had 20 or more doubles 13 times, 19 or more home runs eight times, scored 100 or more runs seven times and racked up 100 RBI twice. In 1984, his MVP season, he was a triple and a home run short of being the first player ever to have 200 hits and 20 or more doubles, triples, home runs and stolen bases.

In 1990, Sandberg had another top-shelf season, leading the league in home runs with 40, in runs scored with a league-leading 116, and hitting .306 with 30 doubles, 100 RBI and 25 stolen bases.

Sandberg was also one of the best-hitting Cubs in the postseason, hitting .385 in two League Championship series.

LIFETIME STATS: BA: .285, HR: 282, RBI: 1,061, H: 2,386, SB: 344

#**72** Rodney Cline "Rod" Carew
1B-2B-DH, Twins, Angels, 1967–85. Hall of Fame, 1991

Carew was a hitting machine, turning in 15 consecutive .300 seasons in his 19-year career. Only Ty Cobb, Stan Musial and Honus Wagner ever exceeded that number.

In addition, Carew won seven batting titles, and won them by consistently larger margins than anyone in history except Rogers Hornsby. In 1977, the year he won the MVP Award, Carew hit .388. The next best average was Dave Parker's .338, which won the National League batting title. That 50-point margin is the greatest gap between the best and second-best hitters in major league history.

In 1972, he became the first player in history to win a batting crown without hitting a home run. Carew hit for the cycle in 1970 and, in five separate games over his career, got five base hits.

Besides hitting, Carew was one of the best base runners ever. He stole home seven times in 1969, and on May 18 of that year, stole three bases in one inning. In addition, he was probably one of the best players ever at taking the extra base on a single or a double.

Carew was not an outstanding defensive player, but he was solid. A misconception that has persisted after his retirement was that he was moved from second base to first base in 1976 because of his defensive liabilities.

Actually, he was moved there to prolong his career. He was named to 18 consecutive All Star games, although he missed two with injuries.

LIFETIME STATS: BA: .328, HR: 92, RBI: 1,015, H: 3,053, SB: 353

#**73** Joseph Jefferson "Shoeless Joe" Jackson

OF, Athletics, Indians, White Sox, 1908–20

Did he? Didn't he? We may never know for sure if Shoeless Joe Jackson conspired, with seven other members of the Chicago Black Sox, to throw the 1919 World Series. From most of the evidence, it seems as though Jackson may have tried to have the best of both worlds, accepting money to fix the series, but playing as hard as he could to win it.

At any rate, Jackson, with his ebony bat, "Black Betsy," was a superior hitter, making a career-high .408 in 1911, and following that up with a .395 average in 1912 and .373 in 1913. Babe Ruth reportedly patterned his swing after Jackson's.

Jackson was also a good base runner—fast, with excellent instincts. He stole 20 or more bases five times in his career and led the league in triples three times and doubles once.

Jackson played all three outfield positions in his career. He was second in assists and putouts in 1912 and assists in 1913 while playing right field for the Indians. While playing left field for the White Sox, he was second in putouts in 1917 and third in assists in 1919.

After a superior season in 1920 (218 hits, 42 doubles, a league-leading 20 triples, 12 home runs, 121 RBI and a .382 average), the betting scandal hit, and Jackson was banned from baseball for life.

LIFETIME STATS: BA: .356, HR: 54, RBI: 785, H: 1,772, SB: 202

#74 George "Mule" Suttles

1B-OF, Birmingham Black Barons, St. Louis Stars, Baltimore Black Sox, Detroit Wolves, Washington Pilots, Cole's American Giants, Newark Eagles, Indianapolis ABCs, New York Black Yankees (Negro Leagues), 1918–44. Hall of Fame, 2006

Suttles, at 6' 3", 215 pounds, was one of the great power hitters in Negro League history. Called "The Mule" because of his strength and penchant for carrying teams when he went on one of his typical hot streaks, Suttles played professionally for 26 seasons.

For most of his career, Suttles wielded a huge 50-ounce bat, with which he belted long home runs to all fields. He hit several legendary home runs, including a blast in an exhibition game in Cuba in 1930 that carried more than 600 feet, startling a squad of cavalrymen on horseback who were at the field to prevent trespassers coming in from that part of the ballpark.

Suttles often hit home runs in bunches. Reportedly, in 1929, while playing with the St. Louis Stars against the Memphis Red Sox, Suttles hit three home runs in one inning in a 26–4 rout. His best season was 1926, when he batted .413, with 26 home runs and a hard-to-believe 1.000 slugging average. Records are incomplete, but Suttles is believed to be the career home run leader in the Negro Leagues with 237.

Suttles was a fan favorite in St. Louis, with whom he won league championships in 1928, 1930 and 1931. When he came to bat, fans in the stands would yell, "Kick, Mule!" exhorting Suttles to hit a home run.

Suttles was often at his best in All Star games against white big leaguers. He hit .374 in 10 such contests, including a game against the Chicago Cubs in 1934 in which he hit a single, double and a triple in four at bats.

LIFETIME STATS: BA: .341, HR: 237, H: 1,103

#75 Brooks Calbert "Brooksie," "The Human Vacuum Cleaner" Robinson

3B-2B-SS, Orioles, 1955–77. Hall of Fame, 1983

Robinson was called "Brooksie" by his teammates and Oriole fans, but his unofficial nickname was "The Human Vacuum Cleaner" for his uncanny fielding abilities.

Robinson's play has set the standard to which all third basemen aspire. He won 16 consecutive Gold Gloves in his 23 years at third base. He led American League third basemen in fielding 11 times, including nine of 10 years from 1960–69 (the Tigers' immortal Don Wert beat him out in 1965). He led the league's third basemen in assists eight times and was a 15-time All Star.

Robinson didn't play baseball in high school, and was discovered by the Orioles playing in a church league. He sat on the bench for three years before becoming a regular in 1958. He was not an outstanding hitter, but he hit 20 or more home runs six times, batted .280 or better seven times and stroked 25 or more doubles 11 times in his career. In 1964, he hit .317, drove in a league-leading 118 runs and had 194 hits to win the MVP award.

His postseason performances have been legendary. Twice in League Championship Series in 1969 and 1970, he hit over .500. In the 1970 World Series, Robinson hit .429 and slugged .810 to win the MVP award (which included a late-model sedan) as Baltimore dominated a very good Cincinnati Reds team. "If we knew he wanted a car that badly," said Reds catcher Johnny Bench, "we'd have bought him one."

Robinson is the all-time leader at third base in games played with 2,870, fielding average with a .971 mark, putouts with 2,697, double plays with 618 and assists with 6,205.

LIFETIME STATS: BA: .267, HR: 268, RBI: 1,357, H: 2,848, SB: 28

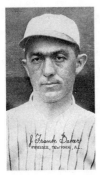

J. Frank Baker
INFIELDER, NEW YORK, A.L.

#76 John Franklin "Home Run" Baker

3B, A's, Yankees, 1908–14, 1916–19, 1921–22. Hall of Fame, 1955

Baker was not the fence-buster that players like Babe Ruth and Lou Gehrig would be less than a decade after his retirement, but he did lead the American League in home runs four years running, from 1911 to 1914. His highest total for a season in that span was 12.

But actually, Baker earned his nickname when he hit two key home runs in successive games in the 1911 World Series. The first homer was a two-run shot of future Hall of Famer Rube Marquard in the sixth inning of Game Two to give Baker's Athletics a 3–1 win. The next day, Baker's ninth-inning home run off another future Hall of Fame pitcher, Christy Mathewson, tied the game 1–1, and Philadelphia won in extra innings.

Baker was much more than a home run hitter. He was the third baseman in the Athletics' "$100,000" infield, along with shortstop Stuffy McInnins, second baseman Eddie Collin and first sacker Jack Barry. Baker led American League third basemen in fielding percentage twice in 1911 and again in 1918. He also led the league in assists and putouts twice, and in double plays three times.

He was a very good base runner, stealing 20 or more bases five times in his career, and also hit 10 or more triples five times in his career. In 1909, his 19 triples led the majors.

Baker was a great clutch player. His career average in World Series games is .363, fifth best of players who played in two or more Series.

LIFETIME STATS: BA: .307, HR: 96, RBI: 987, H: 1,838, SB: 235

#77 George Kenneth "The Kid" Griffey Jr.

OF-DH, Mariners, Reds, 1989–present

For a majority of his 11 years with the Seattle Mariners, "Junior" was almost surely the best player in the game. But in 2000, after signing with the Reds, he had one injury-plagued season after another for the next several years.

Griffey broke in with Seattle as a baby-faced 19-year-old in 1989 and had a solid season, with 120 hits in 127 games, 23 doubles and 16 home runs. By the next year, he was a star, winning the first of 10 Gold Gloves in the outfield, hitting .300, with 22 home runs and 80 RBI.

He became the cornerstone of the Mariner franchise. Griffey has hit 40 or more home runs seven times, and in 1997 and 1998, he had back-to-back seasons of 56 homers. He was the American League MVP in 1997, combining the aforementioned 56 dingers with a .304 average, 34 doubles and a league-leading 125 runs scored on top of 147 RBI and 393 total bases.

Griffey has scored 100 or more runs six times, hit .300 or better, and had 100 or more RBI eight times. He was a consistent MVP candidate in the 1990s.

The 21st century hasn't yet treated Griffey as well. From 2002 to 2004, he averaged about 72 games a year. The next two years were a little better, but 2007 has been his healthiest year by far. He had 23 homers and 59 RBI by the All Star break, and baseball fans hope this is a sign of future things to come.

LIFETIME STATS: BA: .291, HR: 586, RBI: 1,667, H: 2,494, SB: 181

#78 Willie Lee "Mac," "Big Mac," "Stretch" McCovey

1B-OF-DH, Giants, Padres, Athletics, 1959–80. Hall of Fame, 1986

McCovey's major league debut with the San Francisco Giants in 1959 was an impressive one: 4-for-4 with two singles and two triples against future Hall of Famer Robin Roberts. McCovey didn't actually get into a game until the end of July, but despite playing only 52 games, he was still named Rookie of the Year, with a .354 average, and 13 home runs and nine triples in 52 games.

McCovey became a regular in the outfield, as the Giants already had a great first baseman in Orlando Cepeda. But in 1965, when Cepeda was felled by an injury, McCovey moved over to first and remained there for the rest of his time with the Giants.

McCovey, at 6'4", 210 pounds, was a tremendous physical specimen, and his home runs were usually explosive shots that got out of the park in a hurry. He won three home run crowns, in 1963 with 44, 1968 with 36 and 1969 with 45. The latter year, McCovey won the MVP award, with a league-leading 126 RBI, 26 doubles, 121 walks, 101 runs scored and a league-leading .656 slugging percentage.

McCovey is the only man to hit two homers in one inning twice in his career, in 1973 and again in 1977, but he is best known for a ball he hit that made an out. In the 1961 World Series, in the bottom of the ninth inning, with two outs, runners on second and third and trailing 1–0, McCovey hit a line drive that Yankee second baseman Bobby Richardson speared to end the game. It was, said McCovey, the hardest-hit ball he had ever struck.

LIFETIME STATS: BA: .270, HR: 521, RBI: 1,555, H: 2,211, SB: 26

#79 Ronald Edward "Ron" Santo

3B-DH, Cubs, White Sox, 1960–74. Hall of Fame, 2012

Overshadowed by Brooks Robinson in the National League, Santo was nonetheless the best all-around third baseman in the National League throughout the 1960s. He won five consecutive Gold Gloves, from 1964 to 1968. Santo also led National League third basemen in putouts seven times, in double plays six times and in assists seven times. In 1964, he set a record (since broken) of assists by a third baseman with 367.

But Santo could also hit. He was not thought to be a power hitter, but Santo hit 25 or more home runs and drove in 90 or more runs in eight consecutive seasons, some of those years on Cubs teams that were notorious for their lack of hitting ability.

Santo led the league in bases on balls four times, but paradoxically, also struck out more than 100 times a season four times.

He was an intense guy, and was often very emotional after a big win or a tough loss. But Cub fans loved him for that and forgave some of his outbursts against umpires whom Santo thought might have given Chicago short shrift.

Oddly, Santo is best known for a quirky mannerism he displayed in 1969. As the Cubs began to make their ill-fated run toward a pennant, Santo would jump up and click his heels after every win.

Initially, it was simply a manifestation of his enthusiasm for finally being on a winning team. But of course, after a while, the fans demanded it, and other teams began to resent the move. It was all moot, of course, as Chicago fell short that year.

Santo died a few months after his election to the Hall of Fame. His election, in the eyes of many, was long overdue.

LIFETIME STATS: BA: .277, HR: 342, RBI: 1,331, H: 2,254, SB: 35

#80 Dennis Joseph "Big Dan" Brouthers

1B-OF, Troy Trojans (NL), Buffalo Bisons (NL), Detroit Wolverines (NL), Boston Braves (NL), Boston Red Stockings (PL), Boston (AA), Baltimore Orioles (NL), Louisville Grays (NL), Phillies, Giants, 1879–1904. Hall of Fame, 1945

Brouthers was a big fellow for his era, at 6'2", 207 pounds, and his big left-handed swing produced lots of hard hits and home runs for 10 teams over his long career.

Brouthers began his career with Troy, and was actually tried at pitcher for a few unsuccessful starts (0–2, 7.53 ERA) before being switched to first base, where he played most of his career.

Brouthers was traded to Buffalo in 1881, and led the league with eight home runs and a .541 slugging average. It was the first of seven years that Brouthers would lead the league in slugging percentage.

Brouthers won his first batting title, with a .368 mark, the next year. He would go on to win five batting titles, two home run crowns, top the league in hits three times, doubles three times and triples once.

In that 1882 season, he also led the league in slugging percentage with a .547 mark, on-base percentage with a .403 mark, hits with 129 and also was the top fielding first baseman in the league with a .974 percentage.

Brouthers was a strong defensive player, but he made his money at the plate. He went 6-for-6 in a game in 1883, and in 1886, he hit three home runs, a double and a single for 15 total bases.

LIFETIME STATS: BA: .342, HR: 106, RBI: 1,296, H: 2,367, SB: 256

#81 Joseph Edward "Joe" Cronin

SS-3B-1B, Pirates, Senators, Red Sox, 1926–45. Hall of Fame, 1956

The Washington Senators seemed to have unusually good luck with "boy wonder" managers. First it was a young Bucky Harris who piloted the Senators to the 1924 pennant and in 1933, it was 26-year-old player-manager Joe Cronin.

Cronin was a better player than Harris, though. He was a hard-hitting shortstop who came up through the Pittsburgh organization before being sold to Washington in 1928. There, Cronin blossomed. In 1930, he hit .346 and had 126 RBI, both career highs.

Cronin was tough and smart, and in 1933, Senators' owner Clark Griffith made him manager. He responded by leading Washington to its last American League pennant. They lost the World Series to the Giants in five games, but Cronin played well, hitting .318.

Cronin met Griffith's niece (not his daughter, as is often reported) Mildred Robertson, who was a club secretary, at the beginning of the 1934 season. They fell in love and were married later that year. Griffith did sell Cronin to the Red Sox after the season, but Joe was his nephew-in-law, not his son-in-law.

Regardless, Cronin thrived in Fenway Park, hitting .300 or better seven times, slugging .500 or better four times and driving in 90 or more runs six times. He eventually sat himself down in 1942 to make room for budding Sox star Johnny Pesky, but he was still a fearsome pinch hitter for Boston for years.

LIFETIME STATS: BA: .301, HR: 170, RBI: 1,424, H: 2,285, SB: 87

#82 Wade Anthony "Chicken Man" Boggs

3B-DH, Red Sox, Yankees, Devil Rays, 1982–99. Hall of Fame, 2005

Wade Boggs was a hitting machine for the Boston Red Sox in the 1980s and early 1990s. He had a beautiful, level swing, a superior eye for pitches in the strike zone and the patience to wait for the pitch he wanted to hit.

Boggs was mired for six years in the Red Sox minor league system, apparently because he was an indifferent fielder. But when he finally made it to Boston in 1982, Boggs was an immediate star, hitting a rookie record .349 with 118 hits in just 104 games.

In 1983, Boggs won his first batting title, hitting .361 with 210 hits, 100 runs scored, 44 doubles and 74 RBI. It was the first of seven consecutive years that he would go on to record 200 or more hits and 100 or more runs.

From 1983 to 1988, Boggs won the American League batting championship five of six years. In 1985, he led the league with 240 hits and a .368 batting average. He reached base 340 times that year, a feat only Babe Ruth, Ted Williams and Lou Gehrig have accomplished.

And his fielding improved, as well. In 1993 and 1995, while playing third base for the Yankees, he was the top fielding third baseman in the league. Boggs won back-to-back Gold Glove awards in 1994 and 1995.

Much was made of his metronome-like habits. His diet during the season was almost exclusively chicken, he took batting practice at 7:17 every night, and he walked to and from the dugout along exactly the same route. That intense concentration was clearly a key factor in Boggs' success.

LIFETIME STATS: BA: .328, HR: 118, RBI: 1,014, H: 3,010, SB: 24

#83 Carl Owen "King Carl," "The Meal Ticket" Hubbell

LHP, Giants, 1928–43. Hall of Fame, 1947

The nicknames alone give you a hint of how good this guy was. Hubbell, an affable Oklahoman, won 20 games or more five years in a row for the Giants between 1933 and 1937. He was the National League MVP in both 1933 and 1936, the only non-wartime pitcher to do that in baseball history (Hal Newhouser did it with Detroit in 1944 and 1945).

Hubbell was a seven-time All Star, and the game for which he is best known was the 1934 All Star Game. After giving up a single to Charley Gehringer in the first inning, Hubbell then walked Heinie Manush. He then proceeded to strike out Babe Ruth (looking), Lou Gehrig (swinging) and Jimmie Foxx (swinging). He came back in the second inning and punched out Joe Cronin (swinging) and Al Simmons (swinging). That's five Hall of Famers in a row, which has got to be some kind of record.

Hubbell's left arm, by the end of his career, was twisted almost completely around by the action of throwing tens of thousands of screwballs.

LIFETIME STATS: W: 253, L: 154, SV: 33, ERA: 2.98, SO: 1,677

#84 Aloysius Harry "Bucketfoot Al" Simmons

OF, Athletics, White Sox, Tigers, Senators, Braves, Reds, Red Sox, 1924–44. Hall of Fame, 1953

Simmons was born Aloys Szymanski in the Polish section of Milwaukee. He Americanized his name when he began to play baseball, but was always proud of his Eastern European heritage.

Simmons was nicknamed "Bucketfoot Al" because he strode into the plate as he swung, his mannerism apparently resembling a man placing his foot in a bucket. It was fundamentally unsound, but his first manager, Connie Mack of the Athletics, wouldn't allow any of his coaches to change it, because Simmons was clearly a very effective hitter.

Simmons's secret may have been that his long arms and longer than usual bat enabled him to reach pitches at the other side of the plate easier than most.

Simmons had several great years with the star-studded Athletics, winning batting titles in 1930 and 1931, with averages of .381 and .390, respectively. He also led the league's outfielders in fielding percentage in 1936.

When Mack began selling off his stars to pay the bills, Simmons was sent to the White Sox. The Polish Simmons was adopted by Chicago fans, and played in three All Star games while in the Windy City. He played for eight more teams in the next seven years, and ended his career back in Philadelphia in 1944.

LIFETIME STATS: BA: .334, HR: 307, RBI: 1,827, H: 2,927, SB: 88

#85 Gregory Alan "Greg" Maddux
RHP, Cubs, Braves, Dodgers, Padres, 1986–2008

Arguably the best pitcher of the 1990s and one of the best in this century, Maddux was a 16-time Gold Glove winner and the only man in baseball history to win four consecutive Cy Young awards, from 1992 to 1995. He earned his first "Cy" while toiling for Chicago, and the next three were won while pitching for the Braves.

Maddux is called "The Thinking Man's Pitcher," because he does not have an overpowering fastball. Yet he has found success by changing speeds well and pitching with exceptional control. He led the Braves to the 1995 World Championship over the Indians.

Maddux is also durable, known as an "inning eater" because, even now, he often pitches into the seventh and eighth innings. He has thrown for 200 or more innings 18 times in his career.

LIFETIME STATS: W: 355, L: 227, SV: 0, ERA: 3.09, SO: 3,371, CG: 109

#86 James Alvin "Jim," "Jockstrap Jim," "Cakes" Palmer

RHP, Orioles, 1965–67, 1969–84. Hall of Fame, 1990

Palmer played his entire career with the Orioles, and is Baltimore's greatest pitcher. But for the first four years of his career, he battled arm and back injuries that threatened to end that career.

Palmer was 23–15 in his first three years, but injuries forced him back to the minor leagues in 1968. Surgery and rehabilitation in the Instructional League helped him regain his form. Less than a week after he was called up in 1969, Palmer no-hit the Oakland A's.

For the next decade, except for an injury-filled 1974, Palmer was one of the most consistent hurlers in baseball. He won 20 or more games eight times. Only Walter Johnson had more 20-win seasons in the American League, with 12. Twelve times, Palmer struck out more than 100 batters and he pitched 300 or more innings four times.

Palmer won three Cy Young awards, in 1973, 1975 and 1976. He was also an excellent fielder, winning four Gold Gloves from 1976 to 1979.

Palmer was a legitimate big game pitcher. He participated in six American League Championship Series, and had a 4–1 mark with a 1.96 ERA. He also pitched in six World Series, and was 4–2 with 44 strikeouts in 64 innings.

LIFETIME STATS: W: 268, L: 152, SV: 4, ERA: 2.86, SO: 2,212, CG: 211

#87 Joseph "Smokey Joe" Williams

RHP, Chicago Giants, New York Lincoln Giants, Chicago American Giants, Atlantic City Bacharach Giants, Hilldale Daisies, Homestead Grays, Detroit Wolves (Negro Leagues), 1905–32. Hall of Fame, 1999

Williams, a lanky 6'4" fireballer from Texas, was the first real pitching star in the Negro Leagues. Armed with a hellacious fastball, Williams set all kinds of strikeout records for the various teams on which he played.

Williams had at least a dozen 20-strikeout games over his career, including a classic battle against the Kansas City Monarchs' Chet Brewer in 1930, when, as the starter for the Homestead Grays, William struck out 25 men in a 12-inning game in a 1–0 win. Brewer didn't do too bad either, striking out 19 men.

Prior to that, his most famous game was in 1917, when he no-hit the New York Giants of the National League in an exhibition game, although he lost the game 1–0 on an error. But it was reportedly that day that Giant star Ross Youngs dubbed Williams "Smokey Joe."

Williams reportedly had his best game against white major leaguers; his record against big-league clubs is 8-4. He also shut out the Giants in 1912, 6–0, on three hits, a few weeks after they lost the World Series to the Boston Red Sox, and, coincidentally, another "Smokey Joe," this pitcher being Boston's "Smokey Joe" Wood.

Wood was also an excellent batter, and at least twice hit better than .300 in a season.

LIFETIME STATS: W: 107, L: 57

#88 John Robert "Johnny," "The Big Cat" Mize

1B-OF, Cardinals, Giants, Yankees, 1936–53. Hall of Fame, 1981

Mize, called "The Big Cat" because he was, well, a pretty big cat, was a rarity in pro baseball: a slugger who was also a great contact hitter.

Twice in his career, Mize led the league in home runs, but had fewer strikeouts than dingers, a remarkable feat. In 1947, Mize led the league with 51 homers and struck out only 42 times in 586 at bats. In 1948, Mize struck a league-leading 40 home runs and struck out only 37 times. In all, Mize would claim four home run crowns and a batting title in 1939, and lead the league in RBI three times.

Mize is the only man to hit three home runs in a game six times. He also hit two home runs in 30 games. Mize had seven pinch-hit home runs in his career.

Mize was a four-time All Star for the Cardinals and a five-time All Star for the Giants, but in 1949, he was traded to the Yankees. From 1949 to 1953, Mize was a part-time first baseman and pinch hitter for the Bronx Bombers, and all five of those teams won pennants and subsequently won World Series.

He hit .286 in the five championship series, and was the World Series MVP in 1952, hitting three home runs and batting .400 as the Yankees beat the Dodgers.

Considered awkward, Mize was actually a graceful fielder, leading the league's first basemen in fielding twice, in 1942 and 1947.

LIFETIME STATS: BA: .312, HR: 359, RBI: 1,337, H: 2,011, SB: 28

#**89** Alexander Emmanuel "A-Rod" Rodriguez

SS-3B, Mariners, Rangers, Yankees, 1994–present

Expectations. They have been a part of Alex Rodriguez's career since he signed that blockbuster, quarter-of-a-billion-dollar contract with the Texas Rangers in 2001.

The funny thing is, A-Rod generally lives up to these expectations, at least statistically. He was one of the top players in the majors two years after he broke into the league in 1994. By 1996, at age 20, he won the batting championship with a .358 average, to go with 36 home runs, 123 RBI and a league-best 54 doubles and 141 runs scored.

From 2001 to 2003, Rodriguez led the American League in home runs. In 2003, he was league MVP, hitting .298 with 47 homers and 118 RBI. He also won his second Gold Glove.

He was traded to the Yankees before the start of the 2004 season, and many pundits predicted the trade would put New York back on top of baseball. Rodriguez gracefully switched from shortstop to third base to allow his pal, Derek Jeter, to remain at that position.

Rodriguez hit .286 that year, with 36 homers and 101 RBI. Not bad, but not A-Rod. In the 2004 postseason, the Yankees were at the edge of the World Series, leading their archrivals, The Red Sox, three games to none. Then, somehow managing to snatch defeat from the maw of victory, Boston swept the Yankees four consecutive games.

Since then, Rodriguez has been his usual dominant self in the regular season, winning the MVP award in 2005 and having a solid 2006 season. In 2010, the Yankees won the World Series, and A-Rod may have shed the "can't win the big one" mantle.

LIFETIME STATS: BA: .302, HR: 629, RBI: 1,893, H: 2,775, SB: 305

#90 Timothy "Tim," "Rock" Raines

OF-DH, Expos, White Sox, Yankees, Athletics, Orioles, Marlins, 1979–99, 2001–02

When the lighting-fast Raines came up with the Montreal Expos, he was an explosive base-stealer who could change games without getting a hit. He led the league in stolen bases from 1981 to 1984 and was second in 1985 and third in 1986, averaging an eye-popping 76 thefts a year in that span.

The switch-hitting Raines was an excellent leadoff hitter, scoring 90 or more runs eight times and leading the league in that department twice. His 808 steals are fifth all-time. Raines won the batting championship in 1986. He hit .300 or better eight times in his career.

Raines was also a pretty patient man at the plate. He drew 80 or more walks seven times in his career. His 1,330 walks are 29th all-time.

Following a 12-year stint with the Expos, Raines was signed by the White Sox in 1991. By 1994, he was a part-time player for Chicago, but he was still a good hitter, if not as effective a base-stealer as he had been. Raines became a part-time player with the Yankees from 1996–1998 and seemingly finished up his career with the Oakland Athletics in 1999. But he made a comeback in 2001 with the Expos and did pretty well, hitting .308 in part-time play. He was traded to the Orioles that year and finally retired in 2002 after a year with the Florida Marlins.

LIFETIME STATS: BA: .294, HR: 170, RBI: 980, H: 2,605, SB: 808

#91 Jay Hanna "Dizzy" Dean

RHP, Cardinals, Cubs, 1930, 1932–41, 1947. Hall of Fame, 1953

Dean was given his nickname by an unsympathetic sergeant in the U.S. Army, who had little patience for Private Dean's shenanigans. Dean came up to the Cardinals on the last day of the season in 1930 and tossed a complete-game three-hitter.

Despite that performance, Dean didn't get another chance with St. Louis until 1932, when he made the Opening Day roster. But he showed the Cardinals he was worth it, winning 18 games and leading the league in innings pitched, strikeouts and shutouts.

For the next four years, Dean was the best pitcher in baseball, by a country mile. He averaged 27 wins, 25 complete games, 311 innings pitched, 197 strikeouts, four shutouts, 50 starts and even seven saves a season over that span. Batters hit .252 against him and he walked a little fewer than two batters a game over that span. It is one of the most overpowering four-year stretches in baseball history.

In 1933, Dean struck out 17 batters in a game against the Cubs, a major league record at the time. Dean won the MVP award in 1934, and came in second the next two years.

In 1937, Dean, the starter for the National League in the All Star game, was hit in the foot by a line drive off the bat of Earl Averill. Dean sat out the first few weeks of the second half of the season but tried to come back too early. To compensate for his injured foot, Dean changed his delivery and suffered bursitis in his pitching arm.

The following year, Dean was traded to the Cubs, and became a spot starter, winning seven of eight games and helping Chicago to the National League pennant. But he would win only nine more games in his career.

LIFETIME STATS: W: 150, L: 83, SV: 30, ERA: 3.02, SO: 1,163, CG: 154

#92 Mark David "Big Mac," "Sack" McGwire

1B-3B, Athletics, Cardinals, 1986–2000

McGwire became a home run hitting machine in the latter part of his career, hitting 135 dingers in a two-year span, from 1998 to 1999.

There is some speculation that the 6'5", 225-pound McGwire may have enhanced his already hefty frame with steroid use, but frankly, that's all it is: speculation.

Regardless of whether or not his performances were "juiced," McGwire was a most gracious home run champion. In 1998, when he was on track to best the 37-year-old record of 61 home runs by former great Roger Maris, McGwire invited the Maris family to be his guests (Maris died in 1985) for the several days it took to hit his 62nd, and when that moment finally came, McGwire dutifully acknowledged Maris. McGwire went on, of course, to hit 70 homers that year.

It's also easy to forget that McGwire won two home run crowns before his 70 homers in 1998 and 65 in 1999. He cracked 49 homers in his second year with the Athletics in 1987 and hit 52 with Oakland in 1996.

McGwire came up with the Athletics, and was always a big swinger. He had 100 or more strikeouts in eight seasons, including a whopping 155 the year he hit 70 home runs. But he also led the league in bases on balls twice, and had more than 100 walks four times in his career.

McGwire was relatively slow afoot, with only six career triples and 12 career stolen bases. But his supporters will argue that he was not paid to steal bases, McGwire was paid to hit the ball out of the park, which he did with regularity.

LIFETIME STATS: BA: .263, HR: 583, RBI: 1,414, H: 1,626, SB: 12

#93 Wilver Dornel "Willie" Stargell

OF-1B, Pirates, 1962–82. Hall of Fame, 1988

Slugger Stargell was a fearsome opponent at the plate, looming over the batter's box, whipping his bat forward and back, forward and back, waiting almost eagerly for the next pitch.

Stargell was a big, powerful man at 6'2", 225 pounds. He belted some tape-measure home runs, including seven that carried over the right-field roof at Forbes Field, and the only two home runs ever hit out of Dodger Stadium.

A quiet, classy ballplayer, Stargell played, willingly, in the shadow of Pirate star Roberto Clemente for 10 years. But he became the Pirates' team leader after Clemente's sudden, stunning death in 1971. In 1979, Stargell won the MVP award in leading Pittsburgh to another World Series triumph over the Orioles.

Stargell's numbers that year were not overpowering: 32 home runs, 82 RBI, a .281 batting average. But he seemed to clock a majority of the key hits for Pittsburgh in the regular season. And in the World Series, Stargell killed Baltimore, with a .400 batting average, four doubles, three home runs and seven RBI. He was the leader of the Pirates' family, and the team song was "We Are Family" by Sister Sledge.

Thus, in addition to his MVP in the regular season, Stargell was the MVP of the National League Playoff Series against the Reds, the MVP of the World Series, The *Sporting News* Man of the Year and *Sports Illustrated*'s co-sportsman of the year with the Steelers' Terry Bradshaw.

LIFETIME STATS: BA: .282, HR: 475, RBI: 1,540, H: 2,232, SB: 17

#94 Paul Glee "Big Poison" Waner

OF, Pirates, Dodgers, Braves, Yankees, 1926–45. Hall of Fame, 1952

Waner was one of the original party boys, a man who went out and painted the town red at night, and then got up and slapped a few extra base hits the next day to win the ball game. One story has it that Waner, late in his career, announced he was going on the wagon. He started the season hitting .250, and one of his coaches personally brought him over to a speakeasy to get him back on track.

As a rookie in 1926, Waner hit .336 and led the league with 22 triples. The next season, he was signed by Pittsburgh. Paul Waner won the first of three batting crowns with a career-high .380 average, and won the MVP award as Pittsburgh won the National League crown. The Pirates were creamed by the Yankees that year in four games, but Paul hit .333, as he and his brother Lloyd outhit Babe Ruth and Lou Gehrig 11–10 over the four games.

The brothers' nicknames reportedly came from a Brooklyn fan, during an exceptionally productive day by the brothers at Ebbets Field. Reportedly, the fan's comment was, "Them Waners! It's always the little poison on thoid and the big poison on foist!"

An aggressive base runner, Waner was never afraid to take the extra base. He led the league in triples twice and doubles twice. His 62 doubles in 1932 is second best all-time in the National League.

LIFETIME STATS: BA: .333, HR: 113, RBI: 1,309, H: 3,152, SB: 104

#95 Willie James "The Devil" Wells

SS-2B-3B, St. Louis Stars, Detroit Wolves, Homestead Grays, Kansas City Monarchs, Cole's American Giants, Newark Eagles, Chicago American Giants, New York Black Yankees, Baltimore Elite Giants, Indianapolis Clowns, Memphis Red Sox, Birmingham Black Barons (Negro Leagues), 1924–49. Hall of Fame, 1997

Wells was the best shortstop in the Negro Leagues from the mid-1930s to the late 1940s. He was an excellent hitter and a very fundamentally sound infielder, who made up for a relatively weak throwing arm by studying hitters and trying to anticipate where they would hit the ball.

Wells rarely made acrobatic catches. Rather, he was usually right in front of the ball when it was hit. There are no fielding averages or records for assists or putouts for much of the history of the Negro Leagues. But Wells would likely be at the top or near the top of most of those lists.

Wells is credited with being one of the first professional players to wear a batting helmet. Because he often leaned over the plate while at bat, he was a frequent target of pitchers trying to "brush" him back.

One year, probably 1936, he was struck on the temple by a pitched ball. Advised by a doctor to refrain from playing for a time, Wells instead returned to the lineup the next day, wearing a modified construction helmet. He would wear it the rest of his career, and many other players began following suit.

Wells spent many years in the Mexican Leagues, where he was affectionately called "El Diablo" for his seemingly magical anticipation in the field.

Wells was happy to impart his wisdom to younger players, and throughout the late 1940s and early 1950s, he was a player-manager in various minor leagues.

LIFETIME STATS: BA: .328, HR: 138, H:1,306

#96 Albert William "Al" Kaline

OF-DH, Tigers, 1953–74. Hall of Fame, 1980

Kaline is also nicknamed "Mr. Tiger," in part because he holds the team record for games played with 2,834 and home runs with 399, and in part because he represented Detroit so well for his entire 22-season career.

Kaline was, initially, a small, shy kid who worked for virtually everything he earned on a baseball field. He was signed right out of a Baltimore sandlot league in 1953 and didn't play a game in the minors.

In 1954, Kaline's first full season in the majors, it was clear that he would be a solid defensive outfielder: He had a good arm and excellent instincts. But he built up his wrists and arms, reportedly from exercises suggested by Boston's Ted Williams, and by 1955, Kaline was a bona fide star. He won his only batting title that year, hitting .340, and stroked 200 hits, also tops in the league.

Kaline also smacked three home runs in one game at Kansas City that year, the only time in his career he would do so.

Kaline would hit .300 or better nine times in his career, and belt 20 or more home runs nine times.

He was one of the most graceful fielders of his era, and one of the best all time. Kaline earned 10 Gold Gloves in the outfield, and twice led the league in fielding percentage. In 1971, he played 133 games in the field without an error.

LIFETIME STATS: BA: .297, HR: 399, RBI: 1,583, H: 3,007, SB: 137

#97 Juan Antonio "The Dominican Dandy" Marichal

RHP, Giants, Red Sox, Dodgers, 1960–75. Hall of Fame, 1983

Marichal was signed by the Giants in 1960, and was already a polished pitcher at age 19. Still, San Francisco brought the Dominican Republic native along slowly, as a sport starter. He went 6–2 with a solid 2.66 ERA.

In 1962, Marichal was a key performer in the Giants' National League championship team with an 18–11 mark, although he injured his foot and lost his last three decisions. But from 1962 to 1969, Marichal won 172 games and lost 76. That comes out to an average 21–9 record.

He led the league in wins, innings pitched, shutouts and complete games twice in that span, and in ERA once. The sturdy Marichal three times threw more than 300 innings in a season, leading the league in that category twice.

Marichal's high kick before his pitch was legendary, and also effective. It was distracting to hitters, and it made his fastball, slider and curve that much tougher to hit.

In August of 1965, in the heat of a tense pennant race with the Dodgers, Marichal got into a brawl with Dodger catcher John Roseboro, hitting Roseboro with his bat. A wild brawl ensued and when the smoke cleared, Roseboro was hospitalized with a concussion.

Roseboro subsequently sued Marichal for assault, but eventually dropped the suit.

Marichal retired in 1975, and after he was passed over for induction into the Hall of Fame, the classy Roseboro led a letter-writing campaign to install Marichal. It worked, and Marichal made it a point to thank Roseboro at his induction in 1983.

LIFETIME STATS: W: 243, L: 142, SV: 2, ERA: 2.89, SO: 2,303, CG: 244

#98 Frank Francis "Frankie," "The Fordham Flash" Frisch

2B-3B-SS, Giants, Cardinals, 1919–37. Hall of Fame, 1947

The New York Giants signed Frisch straight out of Fordham University, where he was one of the greatest athletes in the history of the school, excelling in football, basketball, baseball and track. Frisch never played a day in the minors, although he was basically a utility infielder in his first season with the Giants.

By 1920, Frisch was a regular, hitting .280 with 34 stolen bases, 10 doubles and 10 triples.

But while his offensive numbers were always solid, Frisch never blew anyone away with his stats. His principal weapons were his prodigious speed, heady decision-making ability and coolness under pressure. Still, he hit .300 or better in 13 seasons and led the league in stolen bases three times. He was nearly impossible to strike out. Only twice in 19 years did Frisch whiff more than 20 times a season.

From 1921 to 1924, he helped the Giants to four consecutive National League pennants and two world championship. In four World Series with the Giants, Frisch hit .300 in 1921, .471 in 1922, .400 in 1923 and .333 in 1924, with 37 hits that included five doubles and three triples.

In 1927, Frisch was traded to the Cardinals, and his slashing, aggressive style helped Cardinal fans forget the departed Rogers Hornsby. And once again, Frisch was one of the keys in helping St. Louis to four National League crowns and another two wins in the World Series. He was MVP in 1931 and finished second in the voting in 1937.

LIFETIME STATS: BA: .316, HR: 105, RBI: 1,244, H: 2,880, SB: 419

#99 Samuel Earl "Sam," "Wahoo Sam" Crawford

OF-1B, Reds, Tigers, 1899–1917. Hall of Fame, 1957

Like many of his Tiger teammates, Crawford did not get along with Ty Cobb. But while Cobb and Crawford were never friends, Cobb had no choice but to respect the speedy, resilient, hard-hitting Crawford in the years they shared outfield duties.

Crawford began his career with the Reds, and jumped to the Tigers in 1903. Crawford, nicknamed after his hometown of Wahoo, Nebraska, was almost as intimidating on the base paths as Cobb. He didn't spike opponents as often, but he always took the extra base.

He led the league in triples six times, and his lifetime total of 309 is still the best all-time. Crawford also led the league in doubles once and home runs twice. In fact, in 1901, he led the National League with 16 home runs and, in 1908, led the American League with seven. He became the only man to lead both leagues in homers.

Crawford and Cobb worked closely together. They frequently pulled a double steal, usually with Crawford going from first to second and Cobb going from third to home.

With Cobb batting ahead of him, Crawford led the league in RBI three times, and six times drove in 100 or more runs.

LIFETIME STATS: BA: .309, HR: 97, RBI: 1,525, H: 2,961, SB: 366

#100 Mordecai Peter Centennial "Three-Finger," "Miner" Brown

RHP, Cardinals, Cubs, St. Louis (FL), Brooklyn (FL), Chicago Whales (FL), 1903–16. Hall of Fame, 1949

Brown is the ultimate lemons-to-lemonade ballplayer. As a 7-year-old, he caught his right hand in his father's corn grinder. That cost him his forefinger, which was amputated. His middle finger was permanently mangled. His little finger was cut to a stub.

But Brown learned to pitch by spinning the ball off his twisted middle finger, which, coupled with the velocity with which Brown threw, gave it a twisting, darting motion that was difficult for hitters to pick up.

Brown was signed by the Cardinals, but struggled to a 9–13 record. But Cub manager Frank Chance liked Brown's toughness, and got him for Chicago in 1904. It was a fortuitous pickup. For six seasons, from 1906 to 1911, Brown won 20 or more games. His ERA from 1904 to 1908 was under 2.00 four of those five years. He also wasn't afraid to pitch in relief between starts. He led the league in saves from 1908 to 1911. Brown was the ace of those dominant Cub teams, which won four pennants and two World Series in five years.

He was the Cubs' "money pitcher." Four of his five World Series wins were shutouts. His duels with Giant ace Christy Mathewson were electrifying. At one point, he owned Matty, beating him nine consecutive times.

The media, jumping on his handicap, called him "Three-Finger" Brown. His teammates called him "Miner," as he had worked in the coal mines before he became a big leaguer.

Brown was probably the best pitcher in the short history of the Federal League, going 31–19 in two years, and helping the Chicago Whales to the 1914 Federal League pennant.

LIFETIME STATS: W: 239, L: 130, SV: 49, ERA: 2.06, SO: 1,375, CG: 271

#101 Carlton Fisk

C, Red Sox, White Sox, 1969, 1971–93. Hall of Fame, 2000

Fisk remains the best offensive catcher in baseball, with 1,276 runs scored, more than 100 more than any other backstopper, 3,999 total bases, far ahead of any other catcher, and more stolen bases (128) than Johnny Bench, Yogi Berra and Mike Piazza combined.

The first player to be voted Rookie of the Year unanimously, Fisk was a tremendous weapon for the Red Sox in the 1970s, hitting .290 or better five times and getting 100 or more hits six times. And how many catchers ever led the league in triples, as Fisk did in 1972, with nine? Fisk has more career triples (47) than Bench, Piazza and Roy Campanella combined. In 1972, he won a Gold Glove for his catching and led the AL in triples (9).

Fisk was injured for part of the 1975 season, but rebounded to hit .331 and lead Boston into the World Series against the Cincinnati Reds. He was the center of two of the key plays in the Series. The first came in the 10th inning of Game Three, when he collided with Ed Armbrister while trying to field a bunt. No interference was called on Armbrister, even though it was clear Fisk's ability to field the ball was impeded. The Sox lost that contest.

But in Game Six, he hit the most dramatic home run in Series history. He blasted a pitch by Red hurler Pat Darcy into the night in the 12th inning, and there probably aren't too many people who haven't seen Fisk jumping into the air, hands upraised, as the ball leaves Fenway Park.

He wasn't as effective with the White Sox. But no matter where he was, Fisk was a clubhouse leader and a masterful handler of pitchers.

LIFETIME STATS: BA: .269, HR: 376, RBI: 1,330, H: 2,356, SB: 128

#**102** William "Judy" Johnson

3B, Hilldale Daisies, Homestead Greys, Darby Daises, Pittsburgh Crawfords (Negro Leagues), 1918–38. Hall of Fame, 1988

A solid, unspectacular, but fundamentally sound third baseman who toiled in the Negro Leagues for 20 years, Johnson joined the famous Philadelphia Hilldales in 1921 and was the anchor of the infield for eight years. He hit .364 in the 1924 black World Series in a losing cause.

Johnson was a "scientific hitter," which meant he didn't hit for much power. He was perennially a .300-plus hitter throughout his years in the Negro Leagues, however, and was renowned for his clutch hitting. In 1930, he joined the Pittsburgh Crawfords as a player-manager, making him a part of perhaps the greatest dynasty in Negro League history. The 1935 Crawfords are considered the greatest Negro League team of all time.

Following his retirement in 1938, Johnson worked as a scout for several major league teams.

LIFETIME STATS: BA: .285, H: 1,100

#**103** Frank "The Big Hurt" Thomas

1B-DH, White Sox, A's, Blue Jays, 1991–2007

Here's a guy who, for the first eight years of his career, was on fire. From 1990 to 1997, "The Big Hurt" was a five-time All Star, and he was the American League MVP in 1993 and 1994. His numbers in the years before and after those seasons were not appreciably different.

In fact, in that 1990 to 1997 span, he hit .300 or better every year, had 109 or more walks every year, and was consistently among the league leaders in on-base and slugging percentages.

Since 2000, plagued by injuries, Thomas' numbers began to dip, although he bounced back after going to the Oakland A's in 2005, hitting .270, with 39 homers.

His best postseason year was 1993, when he hit .393 for the Sox in the American League Championship Series.

LIFETIME STATS: BA: .303, HR: 501, RBI: 1,622, H: 2,332, SB: 32

#104 William Frederick Bill "Bad Bill" Dahlen

SS, White Stockings, Dodgers, Giants, Braves, 1891–1911

Nicknamed "Bad Bill" because of his altercations with umpires, Dahlen was a good-hitting, sure-handed short-stop for National League teams for a record 20 years. He broke in with Chicago, and played third base, outfield and second base as well as shortstop his first few years there. Player-manager Adrian "Cap" Anson was asked why he kept moving Dahlen around so much. Cap replied that he didn't really give a damn where Dahlen played, as long as he was in the lineup.

In nine years with Chicago, Dahlen his .290 or better six times. He was an excellent runner, as well. Dahlen stole 60 bases in 1892 and 51 in 1896. He is still in the top 30 in stolen bases all-time. He was also a superb fielder, and is still second all-time in putouts for a second baseman with 4,850 and third in assists with 7,500.

Dahlen had a 42-game hitting streak in 1894, which was a record for two years, until Wee Willie Keeler broke it. After going hitless in Game 43, Dahlen embarked on a 28-game streak, meaning he hit safely in 70 of 71 games.

LIFETIME STATS: BA: .272, HR: 84, RBI: 1,233, H: 2,457, SB: 547

#105 Saturnino Orestes Arrieta "Minnie," "The Cuban Comet" Minoso
OF, Cleveland, White Sox, Cardinals, Senators, 1949–1964, 1976, 1980

In his first game with the White Sox in 1951, Minnie Minoso became the first black player to don a Chicago uniform in the history of the team. In the first inning of the game, he homered off Yankee pitcher Vic Raschi.

Minoso was a three-time Gold Glove winner who had consistently good numbers throughout his career. He led the league in stolen bases three times: in 1951, 1952 and 1953. In 1954, he led the league in triples, with 18, and a .535 slugging percentage. In 1957, Minoso led the league in doubles with 36. He also had no problems leaning into a pitch: He was hit by pitchers 192 times in his career, a league record.

Minoso is one of only two players (along with Nick Altrock) to have played in five decades. The record is something of a gimmick; he was activated for three games in 1976 (he went 1–8) and two more in 1980 (0–2).

LIFETIME STATS: BA: .298, HR: 186, RBI: 1,023, H: 1,963, SB: 205

#106 Barry Louis Larkin
SS, Cincinnati, 1986–2004. Hall of Fame, 2011

Larkin was one of the best all-around players in the 1990s, and, at 39, continues to play at a high level into the 21st century.

You want hitting? Between 1988 and 2000, 11-time All Star Larkin hit better than .300 nine times. Three other years, he hit .293 or better. You want baserunning? Larkin stole 40 bases in 1988 and 51 in 1995. His lifetime success ratio is 83 percent.

He is an excellent fielder, leading the league in 1994 with a .980 average, and only once dropping below .975. Larkin is a three-time Gold Glove winner. He was the league MVP in 1995, the year the Reds won the World Series. In 1996, he became the first shortstop ever to hit more than 30 home runs and steal 30 bases in the same season.

In the 1996 All Star game, Ozzie Smith, the best shortstop in the league, presented Larkin with an autographed bat and told him, "The torch is now officially passed."

LIFETIME STATS: BA: .295, HR: 198, RBI: 960, H: 2,340, SB: 379

#107 Jeff Robert "Jeff" Bagwell
1B, Astros, 1991–2005

Pittsburgh won the National League crown. The Pirates were creamed by the Yankees that year in four games, but Paul hit .333, as he and his brother Lloyd outhit Babe Ruth and Lou Gehrig 11–10 over the four games.

The brothers' nicknames reportedly came from a Brooklyn fan, during an exceptionally productive day by the brothers at Ebbets Field. Reportedly, the fan's comment was, "Them Waners! It's always the little poison on thoid and the big poison on foist!"

An aggressive base runner, Waner was never afraid to take the extra base. He led the league in triples twice and doubles twice. His 62 doubles in 1932 is second best all-time in the National League.

LIFETIME STATS: BA: .297, HR: 449, RBI: 1,529, H: 2,314, SB: 202

#108 Paul Leo "The Igniter," "Molly" Molitor

DH-3B-2B-1B-SS-OF, Brewers, Blue Jays, Twins, 1978–98. Hall of Fame, 2004

Molitor was one of the most versatile players in the majors during his first decade as a player. For the first three years of his career with the Brewers, Molitor was the team's starting second baseman, and also played shortstop and third base. He was switched to third base in 1982, and played there, for the most part, over the next seven years, but also played shortstop, second base and the outfield.

Molitor was moved to the designated hitter slot more or less permanently in 1991, but was also used at first base for as many as 40 games a season. This was less because of any defensive liability, and more to protect Molitor from injury.

At the plate, he was Mr. Consistency. He hit .300 or better 12 times, scored 90 or more runs eight times, topped 190 hits six times and five times scored 100 runs or more. A total of 13 times in his career, Molitor stole 20 or more bases. In 1987, Molitor had a 39-game hitting streak.

Molitor is 10th lifetime in doubles with 605, ninth lifetime in hits with 3,319, 11th lifetime in sacrifice flies with 109 and 17th lifetime in runs scored with 1,782.

Molitor has been outstanding in the postseason. He has hit .368 in five series, including .418 in two World Series. In 1993, in the Blue Jays' win over the Phillies, Molitor was 12 for 24 with two home runs, two doubles and 10 runs scored to win the MVP award.

LIFETIME STATS: BA: .306, HR: 234, RBI: 1,307, H: 3,319, SB: 504

#109 Lynn Nolan "The Ryan Express" Ryan

RHP, Mets, Angels, Astros, Rangers, 1966–93. Hall of Fame, 1999

The strikeout king, with 5,714. Nobody else is even close. A model of consistency and durability, Nolan Ryan pitched for 27 years in the big leagues, finally retiring at age 46.

Somehow, people have the impression that Ryan's numbers are misleading. Until late in his career, when he punched out a league-leading 301 batters at age 42 in 1989, the "book" on Ryan was that he wasn't a winner. (He was a World Series winner: the 1969 Mets.) Certainly many of his teams weren't successful, but Ryan, an eight-time All Star, won 324 games in his career. He struck out 300 or more batters in six separate seasons and has thrown a major league record seven no-hitters. He broke Sandy Koufax's single-season record of 382 strikeouts, getting 383 in 1973.

LIFETIME STATS: W: 324, L: 292, SV: 3, ERA: 3.19, SO: 5,714, CG: 222

#110 Timothy John "Smiling Tim," "Sir Timothy" Keefe

RHP, Troy (NL), New York (AA), Giants, New York (PL), Phillies, 1880–93. Hall of Fame, 1964

Keefe was one of the best pitchers of the 1880s, twice winning 40 or more games in a season and winning 30 or more four times.

This was the era of mounds that were only 50 feet from home plate, and Keefe's fastball was a devastating weapon. He struck out 300 or more batters three times in his career, leading the league in 1883 and 1888. He lead his league in ERA three times, including a minuscule .086 his rookie season.

The 1883 season was Keefe's best. Keefe struck out a league-leading 359 batters, worked 619 innings, and started 68 and completed 68 games, all league bests. His ERA was 2.41.

That year, he won both ends of a doubleheader against Columbus, throwing a one-hitter in the morning game and a two-hitter in the afternoon.

In 1888, pitching for the Giants, Keefe won 35 games, had eight shutouts, 335 strikeouts and a 1.74 ERA, all league bests. He won four more contests in a postseason championship series against American Association champion St. Louis. Keefe had 30 strikeouts and allowed only two earned runs, as the Giants won the series.

LIFETIME STATS: W: 342, L: 225, SV: 2, ERA: 2.62, SO: 2,562, CG: 554

#**111** Robin Evan Roberts
RHP, Phillies, Orioles, Astros, Cubs, 1948–66. Hall of Fame, 1976

Robin Roberts in 10 words or less: "Hated to come out; let 'em hit the ball."

The seven-time All Star remains the winningest right-hander in the history of the Philadelphia Phillies. He won 20 games or more six years in a row, from 1950 to 1955 and from 1952 to 1955, led the league in wins. He also led the league in complete games from 1952 to 1956 and pitched 300 or more innings for six seasons in a row, from 1950 to 1955.

A lanky righty with a smooth motion, Roberts also gave up a lot of home run balls, although it often seemed that most of them occurred with the bases empty. Still, he gave up a major-league record 46 dingers in 1956. Roberts wasn't quite as dominant after the early to mid-1950s, and struggled with arm trouble for a while. But he bounced back in 1962 to 1964, winning 37 games for Baltimore.

LIFETIME STATS: W: 286, L: 245, SV; 25, ERA: 3.41, SO: 2,357, CG: 305

#112 Edward James "Big Ed" Delahanty

OF-1B, Phillies, Cleveland (PL), Senators, 1888–1903. Hall of Fame, 1945

One of a long string of 19th-century baseball players who fought a losing battle with the bottle, the most enduring story about Delahanty is that, in June of 1903, he was put off a train at International Bridge, near Niagara Falls, for being drunk and disorderly. Unfortunately, Big Ed, unable to see in the dark, began walking the tracks and fell through an open drawbridge into Niagara Falls, which killed him.

Delahanty was a fearsome slugger, who hit .400 or better three times in his career and led the league in doubles five times, triples once and home runs twice. In 1896, he just missed the Triple Crown, with 13 home runs, 126 RBI and a .397 batting average, which was third in the league, behind Jesse Burkett's .410 and Hughie Jennings' .401. He was also pretty fleet afoot, stealing 30 or more bases six times in his career. In 1898, he stole a league-leading 58 bases.

LIFETIME STATS: BA: .346, HR: 101, RBI: 1,464, H: 2,596, SB: 455

#113 Lucius Benjamin "Luke," "Old Aches and Pains" Appling

SS, White Sox, 1930–50. Hall of Fame, 1964

Despite his one-of-a-kind nickname, Appling held down the shortstop's job for the Chicago White Sox for 20 years, and usually played most of his team's games at that position every year.

Appling was a sweet-hitting, good-fielding shortstop for most of his career. The eight-time All Star won two batting championships, in 1936 with a .388 average and in 1943, when he hit .328. He hit .300 or better 16 times and his lifetime average is .310.

He was one of the most frustrating leadoff batters in baseball history. With his sharp batting eye, Appling would patiently foul off ball after ball until he got a good pitch to hit. He once reportedly fouled off 17 pitches in one at bat before hitting a triple. Appling was voted the Greatest White Sox Player Ever in 1969.

Appling's batting title in 1936 was the first ever such title for a White Sox player.

LIFETIME STATS: BA: .310, HR: 45, RBI: 1,116, H: 2,749, SB: 179

#114 Harold Joseph "Pie" Traynor

3B-SS, Pirates, 1920–36. Hall of Fame, 1948

There was a point in the 1950s and 1960s when Pie Traynor was dubbed the greatest third baseman in baseball history. Mike Schmidt, George Brett, Ron Santo and Eddie Mathews have since disabused that claim, but Traynor remains one of the all-time greats.

An excellent fielder of bunts and slow rollers down the line, Traynor also batted .300 or better 10 times. A two-time All Star, Traynor almost never struck out, ending up with only 278 career whiffs, or about 16 a season.

Traynor did not have a lot of power in cavernous Forbes Field, but he hit 20 or more doubles in 11 consecutive seasons and 10 or more triples 11 times in his career.

Traynor's nickname has a number of possible origins, but the most common one is that he was said to have been fond of pies as a youth in Framingham, Massachusetts.

LIFETIME STATS: BA: .320, HR: 58, RBI: 1,273, H: 2,416, SB: 158

#**115** Gary Edmund "The Kid" Carter

C, Expos, Mets, Giants, Dodgers, 1974–92. Hall of Fame, 2003

The ebullient Carter was one of the most popular players in the 1970s and 1980s, and one of the best catchers in that span, as well.

The 11-time All Star was the anchor of the Montreal Expos in the 1970s and early 1980s. Between 1977 and 1982, Carter led National League catchers in most chances six times, putouts six times, assists five times and double plays four times.

He was traded to the Mets in 1984, and led New York to the 1986 World Championship. His single in the 10th inning of Game Six of that World Series was one of the key blows in that amazing three-run rally.

Carter won three Gold Gloves during his career, but many believe his fielding was vastly underrated, probably because he was such a good hitter. Carter was also well known for being a good handler of younger pitchers.

LIFETIME STATS: BA: .262, HR: 324, RBI: 1,225, H: 2,092, SB: 39

#116 Billy Leo Williams

OF-DH-1B, Cubs, Athletics, 1959–76. Hall of Fame, 1987

Billy Williams was the quiet assassin for the Chicago Cubs for 17 years. Often overshadowed by teammate Ernie Banks, Williams was nonetheless one of the most durable players in National League history, playing in a record 1,117 consecutive games, a National League mark later broken by Steve Garvey in 1983.

Williams had a lovely swing that Hall of Famer Rogers Hornsby recognized immediately. At Williams' first tryout with the Cubs, Hornsby deemed the soft-spoken Williams as major league material immediately.

The six-time All Star won a batting crown in 1972, at age 34. He hit 20 or more home runs 13 years in a row and 14 out of 15 seasons.

LIFETIME STATS: BA: .290, HR: 426, RBI: 1,475, H: 2,711, SB: 90

#117 Robert Pershing "Bobby" Doerr

2B, Red Sox, 1937–43, 1946–51. Hall of Fame, 1986

Bobby Doerr was the gem of the Red Sox infield in the 1940s: a steady hitter and sure-handed fielder who simply never seemed to make a mistake at the plate or in the field.

Doerr was a veteran when he was signed by the Red Sox in 1937 as a 19-year-old rookie; by then, he had been playing pro ball for three years in the Pacific Coast League. When he came to Boston, he was a Sea of Tranquility in the roiling Red Sox clubhouse.

Doerr led league second basemen in fielding percentage four times during his career, but he was also a steady hitter, topping .300 three times, driving in more than 100 runs six times and leading the league in slugging (.528) in 1944. Like many of his contemporaries, he lost two years to World War II, but in 1946, came back to lead Boston to its first pennant since 1918. Doerr hit .409 in the 1946 World Series against the Cardinals.

LIFETIME STATS: BA: .288, HR: 223, RBI: 1,247, H: 2,042, SB: 54

#**118** Richard Anthony "Dick" Allen
1B-3B, Phillies, Dodgers, Cardinals, White Sox, Athletics, 1963–77

Dick Allen was one of the greatest athletes in the history of the game. He was also, hands down, one of its greatest enigmas.

Immensely talented, often incredibly, amazingly contradictory, Allen generated as much newsprint for his eccentric behavior as for his ball-playing abilities.

He was a seven-time All Star. He hit better than .300 seven times, socked 20 or more home runs 10 times, and was the American League MVP in 1972. But in 1974, he was on his way to another big year when he "retired" for no good reason—or at least for no reason he would tell anyone about.

Allen feuded with coaches and with fans. Interestingly, he got along, for the most part, with his teammates, who knew enough to let him alone. It adds up to a very good career, but one that probably could have been much better.

LIFETIME STATS: BA: .292, HR: 351, RBI: 1,119, H: 1,848, SB: 133

#**119** Raymond Emmitt "Ray" Dandridge

3B-2B-SS, Detroit Stars, Nashville Elite Giants, Newark Dodgers, Newark Eagles, New York Cubans (Negro Leagues), 1933–49. Hall of Fame, 1987

The good-hitting, smooth-fielding Dandridge was the greatest third baseman in the history of the Negro Leagues.

Accounts of Dandridge's prowess emphasize his smooth fielding and rocket arm from the hot corner. But he was also an excellent hitter, compiling a lifetime .355 in the Negro National League. He was even better in All Star games, hitting .545 in three such contests.

Dandridge was clearly one of the best players, black, white or otherwise, of the 1940s. In fact, he was probably better than Jackie Robinson, the man chosen by the Dodgers to break the color barrier.

But Dandridge never made it to the big leagues. He was signed by the New York Giants in 1949 and assigned to their AAA team. He won the MVP award in 1950 and led the Giants' Minneapolis farm team to the league championship. It wasn't enough at the time.

LIFETIME STATS: BA: .350, H: 408

#**120** Ferguson Arthur "Fergie" Jenkins

RHP, Phillies, Cubs, Rangers, Red Sox, 1965–83. Hall of Fame, 1991

As a pitcher, Jenkins was durable, athletic and consistent. Yet during his playing years, he rarely got the credit he deserved.

Jenkins won 20 games or more six years in a row and

seven years out of eight between 1967 and 1974. From 1967 to 1972, he won 127 games for the Cubs. In that span, Chicago had seven 20-game winners: Jenkins (six times) and Bill Hands. In other words, it was Ferguson Jenkins and a cast of dozens. Five times, he pitched more than 300 innings in a season.

Yet Jenkins was named to only three All Star teams. He won the Cy Young Award in 1971, but he won more games in 1974, struck out more men in 1969 and 1970 and held opponents to lower batting averages in 1968, 1969 and 1970.

Jenkins won 284 games in his career and struck out 3,192.

In 1991, Jenkins became the first Canadian-born player to be inducted into the Hall of Fame.

LIFETIME STATS: W: 284, L: 226, SV: 7, ERA: 3.34, SO: 3,192, CG: 267

#121 William "Buck" Ewing

C-1B, Troy Trojans, Giants, Cleveland Spiders, Reds, 1880–97. Hall of Fame, 1939

Buck Ewing was clearly the greatest catcher of the 19th century, a solid hitter and terrific receiver.

Ewing was a great hitter, averaging .300 or better in 11 of his 18 years. He was a daring base runner, with more than 354 steals from 1886–97. Prior to that, statistics on steals were not kept. And he was an outstanding defensive catcher. Ewing pioneered the practice of throwing base runners out from a crouch. No one had ever seen catchers do that before.

Actually, Ewing was a great all-around player who could have played anywhere and sometimes did. In 1882, playing for Troy, he played all four infield positions, pitched, caught and played the outfield in various games during the year.

He was fast enough to be the leadoff hitter for many years for Troy and the Giants, and was also a home run threat in the "dead ball" era, leading the league in dingers in 1883.

LIFETIME STATS: BA: .303, HR: 71, RBI: 883, H: 1,625, SB: 354

#**122** Michael Joseph "Mike" Piazza
C-DH-1B, Dodgers, Mets, Marlins, Padres, A's, 1992–2007

In 2004, Piazza became the all-time leader in home runs by a catcher. On May 5, 2004, he blasted his 352nd dinger, leaving him one ahead of Carleton Fisk. A superior athlete, Piazza has hit 30 or more home runs nine times in his career, and has hit 40 homers twice.

Piazza was drafted by the Dodgers, and brought up at the tail end of 1992. He played his first full season in 1993, and was named Rookie of the Year, on the basis of a .318 batting average, 35 home runs, 112 RBI, 24 doubles and 174 hits.

Piazza is a great all-around hitter. In addition to socking home runs, he has hit .300 or better nine consecutive seasons, from 1993 to 2001. A 10-time All Star, Piazza's .319 career batting average is fourth among active players and 55th all-time.

In 1996, he won the league MVP award, hitting .336 with 36 home runs, 105 RBI, 184 hits and 87 runs scored.

He was traded to the Mets in 1998, and, in 2000, was a key to New York's National League championship. Piazza batted .324 with 38 home runs, 113 RBI and 90 runs scored that season.

Piazza, when healthy, has been amazingly consistent. He generally hits between 35 and 40 homers a year, scores 80 to 100 runs, makes 150 to 200 hits and drives in 90 to 120 runs. He is generally a tough out in the postseason, and hit four home runs and five doubles in 10 games in the National League Championship Series win over the Cardinals and the World Series loss to the Yankees in 2000.

LIFETIME STATS: BA: .309, HR: 420, RBI: 1,299, H: 2,071, SB: 17

#123 Donald Arthur "Don," "Donnie Baseball" Mattingly

1B, Yankees, 1982–95

Unlike many superstars who play a year or two (or three) beyond their time, Mattingly is the one guy who should not have retired when he did.

Donnie Baseball was playing pretty well at the end of the 1995 season, but he felt he could not perform up to the standards that he had set, and left baseball. The next season, the Yankees won their first World Championship in 18 years. There is not a Yankee fan alive who doesn't wish the classy Mattingly had hung around.

He was great. He won nine Gold Gloves, a record for first basemen. He was a six-time All Star. He was MVP of the league in 1985 and probably should have won it again in 1986 (Boston's Roger Clemens beat him out).

But by 1992, his back was bothering him and it began to get tough to play. Still, he hung in there for three more years, and always played hard. In his only postseason series, a loss to the Seattle Mariners, Mattingly acquitted himself well, hitting .417 with six RBI.

LIFETIME STATS: BA: .307, HR: 222, RBI: 1,099, H: 2,153, SB: 14

#124 Amos Wilson "The Hoosier Thunderbolt" Rusie

RHP, Indianapolis, Giants, Reds, 1889–1901. Hall of Fame, 1977

Amos Rusie is the original power pitcher and one of the principal reasons the mound had to be moved back from 50 feet to 60 feet, six inches, in 1893.

At 6'1", 200 pounds, Rusie was a scary guy. He had a good curve ball and a nice change of pace, but most of the time, he just reared back and fired the ball in.

His first few years in the league, Rusie was a terror. He struck out 341, 337 and 304 batters from 1890 to 1892. But in that same span, he also walked 289, 262 and 267 batters. He was all over the place. When the mound was moved back prior to the 1893 season, Rusie, like every other pitcher, threw fewer games and had fewer strikeouts and walks, but he was still very effective.

Rusie won 30 or more games five years in a row and 20 or more eight years in a row. But like many 19th-century pitchers, all that work burned up his arm. He retired in 1901.

LIFETIME STATS: W: 245, L: 174, SV: 5, ERA: 3.07, SO: 1,950 CG: 393

#125 Osborne Earl "Ozzie," "The Wizard of Oz" Smith

SS, Padres, Cardinals, 1978–96. Hall of Fame, 2001

It's almost impossible, on a statistical basis, to judge which individual might have been the greatest defensive player at his position. Fielding averages don't measure range, or arm accuracy. But it's very hard to dismiss Smith as at least the best defensive shortstop ever.

He was a 15-time All Star and a 13-time Gold Glove winner. Smith was not an overpowering hitter. But he made 100 hits or more 17 consecutive years and stole 580 bases for his career. His postseason numbers are good, but not great, except for 1982, when he hit .556 in the National League Championship Series against the Braves.

LIFETIME STATS: BA: .262, HR: 28, RBI: 793, H: 2,460, SB: 580

#126 Wilbur "Bullet," "Bullet Joe" Rogan

RHP, Kansas City Colored Giants, Kansas City Monarchs (Negro Leagues), 1917–38. Hall of Fame, 1998

Bullet Joe Rogan got his nickname not so much for his fireballing delivery, but for his pinpoint accuracy on the mound.

Rogan was an outstanding pitcher for the Kansas City Monarchs, boasting a variety of pitches and deliveries. He threw sidearm, and could throw a fastball, curve, forkball, palmball and spitball for strikes.

But Rogan was also an exceptional hitter. In 1922, he hit 13 home runs in 47 league games for the Monarchs. In 1924, he hit .411 and led the Negro American League in victories with 16.

Rogan started out as a catcher, but began his pitching career with the 25th Infantry Wreckers Army team in 1911.

Rogan's career winning percentage of .699 is the best ever in the Negro American League.

LIFETIME STATS: W: 151, L: 65

#127 Joseph Michael "Ducky-Wucky," "Muscles" Medwick

OF, Cardinals, Dodgers, Giants, Braves, 1932–48.
Hall of Fame, 1968

Joe Medwick is known for two things: winning the last Triple Crown in the National League in 1937 and inciting a near-brawl in 1934.

The Triple Crown (.374 batting average, 31 homers, 154 RBI) also got Medwick the MVP Award that year. It was one of those years where everything dropped in for Ducky-Wucky: he also led the league in runs scored (111), hits (237), doubles (56), slugging percentage (.641) and even fielding percentage for an outfielder (.988).

The brawl was not really his fault. The Cardinals were pounding Detroit 9–0 in Game Seven of the World Series. Medwick tripled and slid hard into third baseman Marv Owen, even though the throw hadn't come in yet. This incensed the already annoyed Tiger fans, and when Medwick took the field in the bottom of the inning, he was pelted with bottles and garbage.

Commissioner Kenesaw Landis, who was in attendance, and fearing for Medwick's safety, ordered him into the dugout so the game could resume. One has to wonder what would have happened if Medwick had refused.

Medwick picked up his nickname in the minor leagues because of his unusual, duck-like gait.

LIFETIME STATS: BA: .324, HR: 205, RBI: 1,383, H: 2,471, SB: 42

#128 Orlando "The Baby Bull," "Cha Cha" Cepeda

1B-OF, Giants, Cardinals, Braves, Athletics, Red Sox, Royals, 1958–74

Cepeda was one of the greatest pure hitters in the history of the league. In his first big-league game, he socked a game-winning home run. A seven-time All Star, Cepeda topped .300 nine times in his career and topped .295 one other seasons.

A knee injury in 1965 slowed Cepeda down in the field, but he was still a tremendous hitter. In 1973, he was traded to the Red Sox, where he became a designated hitter, hitting .289 with 20 homers and 25 doubles. Sox pitcher Bill Lee, in his autobiography, recalled that a nearly immobile Cepeda would drill pitches to all corners of Fenway Park that year.

Cepeda's father, Orlando Sr., was a star in the Cuban Leagues. His nickname was "The Bull." Thus, his son became "The Baby Bull."

LIFETIME STATS: BA: .297, HR: 379, RBI: 1,365, H: 2,351, SB: 142

#129 Carl Reginald "Reggie" Smith

OF-1B, Red Sox, Cardinals, Dodgers, Giants, 1966–82

An outstanding athlete, Reggie Smith had a tremendous career that was often overshadowed by more illustrious teammates. In Boston, he was a two-time All Star performing in the shadow of Carl Yastrzemski. He was traded to the Cardinals and was a two-time All Star there, also, but all anyone talked about in St. Louis was Lou Brock and Al Hrabosky. With the Dodgers it was Steve Garvey and Dusty Baker.

Still, the switch-hitting Smith went about his business, hitting .300 or better five times and 20 or more homers seven times. He hit 314 home runs; second only to Mickey Mantle as a switch-hitting power hitter. He remains the only switch-hitter to hit 100 or more round-trippers in both the American and National Leagues and the only player to hit a home run from each side of the plate at least twice in both leagues.

LIFETIME STATS: BA: .287, HR: 314, RBI: 1,092, H: 2,020, SB: 137

#**130** Luis Ernesto "Little Louie" Aparicio

SS, White Sox, Orioles, Red Sox, 1956–73. Hall of Fame, 1984

Luis Aparicio began playing professionally when he was just a teen, in his native Venezuela. His personal coach was perhaps the greatest shortstop in the history of the Venezuelan Leagues, Luis Aparicio Sr.

Luis Jr. was signed by the White Sox, who were so confident he would make it, they traded the incumbent, Chico Carrasquel. Chicago's confidence was not misplaced. Aparicio became a nine-time Gold Glove winner at shortstop and led the American League in stolen bases for nine consecutive seasons, from 1956–64.

He teamed with second baseman Nellie Fox to give the White Sox a tremendous double-play combination. They led Chicago to the team's first pennant since the 1919 "Black Sox."

Aparicio was a steady but not overpowering hitter. He hit over .300 only once, in 1970. But he had 20 or more doubles 14 times in his career.

LIFETIME STATS: BA: .262, HR: 83, RBI: 791, H: 2,677, SB: 506

#131 John Gibson Clarkson

RHP, Worcester, White Stockings, Braves, Spiders, 1882–94. Hall of Fame, 1963

Clarkson pitched in the era of two-man staffs, and his statistics reflect that. In 1885 he completed 68 of 70 starts in winning 53 games. That's a tidy 623 innings. In the next four years he won 36, 38, 33 and 49 games, for an average of 40 wins per season.

Although the perception these days is that workhorse pitchers like Clarkson relied on guile to win games, in reality, Clarkson was primarily a fastball pitcher with an excellent curve. The year he won 53 games, his ERA was 1.85 and he posted a league-leading 10 shutouts.

But like most 19th-century pitchers, Clarkson's peak years were few: 1885–92. And his fall was precipitous. He developed arm trouble in 1892, and hung on for only two more years before retiring.

LIFETIME STATS: W: 328, L: 128, SV: 5, ERA: 2.81, SO: 1,978, SB: 485

#132 William Jennings Bryant "Billy" Herman

2B-3B, Cubs, Dodgers, Braves, Pirates, 1931–47. Hall of Fame, 1975

One of the great all-around second baseman of his era, Herman was an expert at the hit-and-run play. Many observers say he was the best practitioner of the hit-and-run in baseball history, which is saying something.

He was a 10-time All Star, and he anchored the infield of the last great Cub dynasty of the 1930s, those heady days when the Cubs won National League pennants in 1932, 1935 and 1938.

He was a great defensive player, leading the league in fielding percentage in 1935, 1936 and 1938. But he was also an excellent hitter, topping .300 eight times in his career. He was, Leo Durocher once said, "the absolute master at hitting behind the runner."

Herman hit .433 in 10 All Star games (13 for 30).

LIFETIME STATS: BA: .304, HR: 47, RBI: 839, H: 2,345, SB: 67

#**133** Leon Day

P-2B-OF, Baltimore Black Sox, Brooklyn Eagles, Newark Eagles, Baltimore Elite Giants (Negro Leagues), 1934–50. Hall of Fame, 1995

The best pitcher in the Negro Leagues in the late 1930s and 1940s, Day was a strikeout king who was also an excellent fielder and solid hitter.

Day had an outstanding fastball and excellent control. He set strikeout records in three venues. Pitching for the Newark Eagles, Day fanned 18 Baltimore Elite Giants in 1942, allowing only a bloop hit. A year earlier, playing in the Venezuelan League, he had struck out 19 batters to set another league record. And in seven Negro League All Star games, he set a career strikeout record with 14.

Day also was a regular .300 hitters with most of the teams on which he played, and was often used in the field when he wasn't pitching.

Following his retirement from the Negro Leagues, Day played for years for various minor leagues.

LIFETIME STATS: W: 68, L: 30

#**134** Monford Merrill "Monte" Irvin

OF-1B, Newark Eagles (NL), Giants, Cubs, 1938–56. Hall of Fame, 1973

Monte Irvin began his pro career in the shadows of the Negro Leagues and finished it in the bright lights of pro baseball.

Irvin was a fleet-footed shortstop for the Newark Eagles and led that team to the Negro League World Series championship over Satchel Paige's Kansas City Monarchs.

He was drafted by the New York Giants in 1949 and, in 1951, hit .312 and led the league in RBI with 121 as the Giants won the pennant. In the World Series against the Yankees, Irvin led both teams with 11 hits, a .458 average and two stolen bases, including a steal of home.

Irvin played seven years in New York before finishing up his career in Chicago, hitting a very respectable .271.

LIFETIME STATS: BA: .293, HR: 99, RBI: 443, H: 731, SB: 28 (Note: MLB totals only)

#**135** Edward Augustine "Big Ed" Walsh

RHP, White Sox, Braves, 1904–17. Hall of Fame, 1946

Almost a century ago, the Chicago White Sox engineered one of the greatest upsets in baseball history, winning the 1906 World Series. And Big Ed Walsh was the main reason, winning both his starts and posting a minuscule .60 ERA and 17 strikeouts.

Walsh was the Catfish Hunter of the early part of the 20th century: A tough, smart durable pitcher who wanted the ball in big games.

In 1908, Walsh went 40–15, starting 66 games and finishing 42. He had 11 shutouts, six saves and struck out 269, all league highs. He also pitched 464 innings, still an American League record. The White Sox finished third that year, 1 1/2 games behind Ty Cobb's Detroit Tigers. Walsh pitched in seven games in the final nine days of the season in an attempt to get the White Sox back to the World Series.

In addition to being one of the top starters for the White Sox at the turn of the 20th century, Walsh was also a top reliever, leading the league in saves five times.

LIFETIME STATS: W: 195, L: 126, SV: 34, ERA: 1.82, SO: 1,736, SB: 315

#136 Roger Phillip "The Duke of Tralee" Bresnahan

C, Washington, Cubs, Orioles, Giants, Cardinals, 1897–1915. Hall of Fame, 1945

In his time, Bresnahan was deemed the greatest catcher ever. He was a good hitter (three seasons over .300), an excellent base runner (he stole 212 bases in his career) and a canny receiver.

Contrary to legend, Bresnahan did not invent the batting helmet in 1903; the A.G. Spalding Co. were already marketing them. But he legitimized it. He did not invent shin guards, either. Many infielders were using them long before he donned them in 1905. But again, because Roger Bresnahan, star catcher for the Giants used them, it meant everyone else could, too.

And he didn't invent the catcher's mask. That was already in use. He did improve on it after he donned one for good in 1908. Basically, he was trying to find ways to protect himself from injury and catch more games.

In 1945, Bresnahan became the first catcher to be inducted into the Hall of Fame.

Bresnahan's nickname is "The Duke of Tralee," after a town in Ireland that was supposedly Bresnahan's birthplace. Actually, he was born in Toledo.

LIFETIME STATS: BA: .279, HR: 26, RBI: 530, H: 1,252, SB: 212

#**137** Stanley Camfield "Smiling Stan" Hack
3B, Cubs, 1932–47

A vastly underrated third baseman during the 1930s and 1940s, Hack was an excellent leadoff hitter for the Chicago Cubs, seven times scoring 100 runs or more. He led the National League in hits twice, in 1940 and 1941.

A four-time All Star, Hack also led the league in stolen bases in 1938 and 1939. In four World Series, his batting average was .348. His lifetime average was .301.

Despite leading the league's third basemen in fielding percentage twice and finishing second or third five other times, Hack was never recognized as the stellar fielder that he was.

Fast fact: Hack actually retired near the end of 1943 because he couldn't get along with Cub manager Jimmy Wilson. Wilson was fired in early 1944 and Charlie Grimm was hired. Grimm coaxed Hack out of retirement, and in 1945, Hack hit .323 to lead the Cubs to the National League pennant.

LIFETIME STATS: BA: .301, HR: 57, RBI: 642, H: 2,193, SB: 165

#**138** Dale Bryan Murphy

OF-1B, Braves, Phillies, Rockies, 1976–93

Murphy was one of the best players in the game in the 1980s, becoming the youngest player ever to win back-to-back MVP awards in 1982 and 1983.

Murphy started his major league career as a catcher, but was eventually moved to the outfield with the Braves. He was low-key, likeable and a great hitter. A seven-time All Star, he twice led the league in home runs, in 1984 and 1985.

Murphy was primarily a slugger, but he was patient, leading the league in walks in 1985 and three other times topping 90 bases on balls.

He was a five-time Gold Glove winner in the outfield. He also could run a little, and in 1983 stole 30 bases and hit 36 home runs, placing him in the elite "30–30" category.

Murphy played in 740 consecutive games from September of 1981 to July of 1986.

LIFETIME STATS: BA: .265, HR: 398, RBI: 1,266, H: 2,111, SB: 161

#**139** Alan Stuart Trammell

SS-DH, Tigers, 1977–96

One of the great all-around players of the 1980s. The six-time All Star hit .300 or better seven times and won four Gold Gloves while holding down the shortstop position for Detroit for most of his 20 seasons in a Tiger uniform.

Trammell was a self-made superstar. He was not a good hitter initially, but his tireless work ethic in the off-season paid off. His anemic home run totals in the first six years of his career steadily improved until he popped a career-high 28 in 1987.

He was a good base runner. His 30 steals in 1983 were the most by a Tiger shortstop since a fellow named Cobb stole 34 in 1917.

Trammell was MVP of the 1984 World Series with a .450 average and nine hits in five games.

LIFETIME STATS: BA: .285, HR: 185, RBI: 1,003, H: 2,365, SB: 236

#**140** David Mark "Dave" Winfield

OF-DH, Padres, Yankees, Angels, Blue Jays, Twins, Indians, 1973–95. Hall of Fame, 2001

At 6'2", 220 pounds, big Dave Winfield looked like an All Star. Which he was, having been named to the All Star team 12 times.

Winfield didn't put up explosive numbers most of his career, but he was, when healthy, incredibly consistent. He never won a home run crown, but socked 465 in his career. He never had more than 193 hits in a season, but ended up with 3,110.

Winfield was also a stellar fielder, winning seven Gold Glove awards. His outfield arm was one of the most accurate in the game, although ironically, that arm gained most of its notoriety when Winfield accidentally killed a seagull with a throw in Toronto.

However well he played, though, team success eluded Winfield until he was traded to Toronto in 1992. In his one year with the Blue Jays, Winfield played in the outfield and was a DH for the World Champions.

LIFETIME STATS: BA: .283, HR: 465, RBI: 1,833, H: 3,110, SB: 1,686

#141 Thurman Lee "Tugboat," "Squatty Body," "The Wall" Munson

C-OF, Yankees, 1969–79

Munson, despite what Reggie Jackson may claim, was the anchor of those late 1970s Yankee teams that won three AL titles in a row.

Munson was squat and looked a little dumpy in uniform, but that hid an athlete's body. He was one of the fastest catchers of all time and was very quick. He was one of the best in the league at covering bunts.

Munson, a seven-time All Star, hit over .300 in five seasons, and won three Gold Glove awards. He was league MVP in 1976, when he hit .302 with 105 RBI and 17 home runs as the Yankees won their first pennant of the 1970s.

Munson was still a fine ballplayer in 1979, but on August 2 of that year, the plane he was piloting crashed near Cleveland, killing him. Munson hit .373 in World Series play.

LIFETIME STATS: BA: .292, HR: 113, RBI: 701, H: 1,558, SB: 48

#142 Tony (Pedro) Oliva

OF-DH, Twins, 1962–76

Oliva remains the only player in major league history to win batting championships in his first two full years in the major leagues. Oliva had two brief stints with the Twins in 1962 and 1963. He hit .444 in nine games in 1962 and .429 in seven games the next year.

Finally, he came up for good in 1964, and just exploded. He had 217 hits, scored 109 runs, smacked 43 doubles and hit .323, all of which led the league. Not surprisingly, he was Rookie of the Year. But sportswriters of the 1960s didn't give MVP awards to rookies, even ones as good as Oliva. In fact, Oliva finished fourth behind Brooks Robinson, Mickey Mantle and Elston Howard.

No matter. Oliva proved it wasn't a fluke, hitting .321 to win the batting title again. He also led the league with 185 hits.

An eight-time All Star, Oliva would win one more batting title, but the smooth-swinging Cuban would hit .300 or better seven times in his career, make 190 or more hits four times in his career and lead the league in doubles four times. He won a Gold Glove award in 1966.

Injuries hampered his career in the 1970s, but Oliva still hit well enough to finish with a career average above .300.

Oliva's real name is Pedro, but he arrived in the United States on his brother's passport, in 1961, and has been known as Tony ever since.

LIFETIME STATS: BA: .304, HR: 220, RBI: 947, H: 1,917, SB: 86

#143 Andre Nolan "The Hawk" Dawson

OF-DH, Expos, Cubs, Red Sox, Marlins, 1976–96. Hall of Fame, 2010

Dawson was a solid performer while with the Expos: a three-time All Star who hit .300 or better three times with Montreal, possessing excellent power.

He was also an excellent fielder, winning six consecutive Gold Gloves with the Expos, from 1980 to 1985. The Hawk could run, too, stealing 20 or more bases seven times while in Montreal.

But Dawson was traded to the Cubs in 1987 and took things up a notch. That first year, Dawson smacked a league-leading 49 home runs and added a league-best 137 RBI. Dawson also hit .287 with 24 doubles.

The numbers won him the MVP award, even though there were some grumblings that Dawson was playing with a last-place team. He remains the only MVP winner to play for a cellar-dweller.

Dawson was named to the All Star team five times in Chicago, and hit .300 or better twice more. He also won two more Gold Gloves, in 1987 and 1988. In 1993, it was on to the Red Sox, where he had two more good years, primarily as a designated hitter.

LIFETIME STATS: BA: .279, HR: 438, RBI: 1,591, H: 2,774, SB: 314

#**144** Keith "Mex" Hernandez
1B-OF, Cardinals, Mets, Indians, 1974–90

Hernandez won 11 consecutive Gold Gloves at first base, from 1978 to 1982 with the Cardinals and from 1983 to 1988 with the Mets. He was one of the best-fielding first basemen of all time.

His strength in the field was his amazing range. The agile six-footer led the league's first basemen in assists five times, putouts four times and fielding percentage twice. He is second to Eddie Murray in assists all-time with 1,682.

But Hernandez could also hit pretty well. In his 17-year career, Hernandez hit .290 or better 11 seasons. In 1979, he won the batting title, hitting .344 with St. Louis. That same year, his on-base percentage was .417, second-best in the league, and his 116 runs scored topped the circuit. Those stats, plus his stellar fielding, earned him the MVP award that year.

Hernandez was a key contributor to the Mets' championship drive in 1986, hitting .310 during the regular season and leading the league in walks. In fact, his on-base percentage was above .400 six times in his career.

LIFETIME STATS: BA: .296, HR: 162, RBI: 1,071, H: 2,182, SB: 98

#145 William Nuschler "Will the Thrill" Clark

1B-DH, Giants, Rangers, Orioles, Cardinals, 1986–2000

The rangy Clark hit .300 or better four times for the San Francisco Giants. He hit a career-high 35 home runs for San Francisco in 1987, and drove in a career-high 116 runs in 1991.

In the late 1980s, Clark was one of the best players in the National League. He finished in the top five in the MVP voting three years in a row, from 1987 to 1989. He led the league in RBI in 1988 with 109 and led the league in runs scored in 1989 with 104.

In the 1989 National League Championship Series against the Cubs, Clark was phenomenal, hitting .650 in five game, with 13 hits, eight RBI, three doubles, a triple and two home runs.

In 1991, Clark hit .301 with 116 RBI, 29 home runs and 32 doubles. He also won his only Gold Glove at first base.

A trade to Texas saw Clark continue his solid hitting. Clark spent five years with the Rangers and hit .300 or better four times, although his power numbers dropped.

LIFETIME STATS: BA: .303, HR: 284, RBI: 1,205, H: 2,176, SB: 67

#146 Kirby Puckett

OF-DH, Twins, 1984–95. Hall of Fame, 2001

Puckett was built like a fireplug with legs, and generated tremendous power from that relatively small frame. As a 23-year-old rookie with the Twins in 1984, Puckett hit .296 with 165 hits in 128 games.

He became the ninth player in major league history

to debut with four hits in a nine-inning game, and his 16 assists from the outfield led the league.

Puckett had a little trouble figuring out big league pitching, and didn't hit a home run in his first season, and only socked four in 1985. But he clearly figured things out by 1986, and belted 31. After that, Puckett hit 12 or more home runs eight of the next nine years.

In 1989, he won his only batting title, hitting .339. But Puckett hit .300 or better eight times in his career, and in fact hit .325 or better five times. Five times, he made 200 or more hits, leading the league four times.

Puckett didn't look particularly graceful when he ran, but he still managed to collect six Gold Glove awards. He was also a better base-stealer than he gets credit for, swiping 10 or more bases seven times.

LIFETIME STATS: BA: .318, HR: 207, RBI: 1,085, H: 2,304, SB: 134

#**147** Theodore Amar "Ted," "Tex," "The Baylor Bearcat" Lyons
RHP, White Sox, 1923–46. Hall of Fame, 1955

Lyons, who never spent a day in the minors, was a 20-game winner only three times in his 21-year career. But he was a consistent pitcher for a Chicago team that was, for the most part, not very good during his tenure. Lyons in fact never made it to a World Series.

He was durable, though, pitching 200 or more innings 10 times in his career, and leading the league twice, in 1927 and 1930.

Lyons was always a control pitcher, rarely walking more than 70 batters a season. He walked only 1,121 batters in 4,161 innings in his career, and in 1939, Lyons threw 42 consecutive innings without walking a batter.

In 1931, he battled arm miseries, and for the next two years, his effectiveness decreased. But he learned to throw a knuckleball, and was 15–8 in 1935, his first winning season in four years.

Lyons was a tremendously popular pitcher, so much so that in his later years, Sox managers would pitch him exclusively on Sundays, to take advantage of his drawing power with the fans. In 1942, on just 20 starts, Lyons was 14–6 with a league-leading 2.10 ERA.

LIFETIME STATS: W: 260, L: 230, SV: 23, ERA: 3.67, SO: 1,073, CG: 356

#**148** Albert Jojuan "Joey" Belle

OF-DH, Indians, White Sox, Orioles, 1989–2000

Belle was one of the best players in baseball in the mid- to late-1990s, a power hitter with speed who consistently drove in runs.

After two desultory seasons in Cleveland, Belle broke out, hitting .282 in 1991, with 31 doubles, 28 home runs and 95 RBI. From 1993 to 1996, he was a holy terror, leading the league in RBI three years and hitting over .300 three consecutive seasons.

He was third in the MVP balloting in 1994 and 1996 and second in 1995.

The 1995 season was Belle's best, statistically. He led the American League with 50 home runs, 52 doubles, 121 runs scored, 126 RBI and a .690 slugging percentage. Belle, a surly cuss for the most part, lost the award to Boston's Mo Vaughn, a more affable man who had good numbers of his own, but not as good as Belle's that year. Interestingly, the two teams met in the playoffs. Belle hit .235; Vaughn was hitless in 14 at bats as the Indians swept the series.

After another solid season in Cleveland, Belle went over to the White Sox in 1997. He had a strong season in 1998, leading the league in slugging percentage with a .655 mark, total bases with 399 and sacrifice flies with 15.

He was second in home runs with 49, second in doubles with 48 and third in batting average with a .328 mark. Yet again, his surliness cost him many MVP votes, and Belle was eighth.

LIFETIME STATS: BA: .295, HR: 381, RBI: 1,239, H: 1,726, SB: 88

#**149** William Ashley "Bill" Freehan
C-1B-DH, Tigers, 1961–76

Freehan was one of the best defensive catchers of his era, winning five Gold Gloves and leading American League catchers in fielding percentage three times.

Freehan, a Detroit native, was playing football at the University of Michigan when he signed with the Tigers in 1961. By 1964, he was the team's regular catcher. He hit .300 that year, the only season he would attain that mark. Freehan also had a career-high 80 RBI.

In 1968, Freehan hit 25 homers and had a .263 batting average, as the Tigers won their first World Series over the Cardinals. Freehan ended the series by catching Tim McCarver's pop-up in Game Seven.

Freehan was a tough cookie who crowded the plate and was frequently hit by pitchers. In 1968, he was hit by a record 24 pitches, including three plunks in a game in August.

Freehan's real strength was his work behind the plate, handling pitchers, throwing out base-stealers and fielding bunts. In 1965, he tied a major league record for catchers with 69 putouts.

Freehan remains the career leader in fielding percentage by a catcher, with a .993 mark. He is also fifth in career putouts with 9,941.

LIFETIME STATS: BA: .262, HR: 200, RBI: 758, H: 1,591, SB: 24

#150 James Edward "Jim" Rice

OF-DH, Red Sox, 1974–89. Hall of Fame, 2009

Rice, in the late 1970s, was a one-man wrecking ball for the Red Sox. He came up in 1975, along with fellow rookie Fred Lynn. That season, Lynn got all the headlines, winning the Rookie of the Year and the MVP award. But while Lynn had a hard time duplicating his first season, Rice, who was no slouch himself in 1975, just seemed to get better and better.

In 1978, he was MVP, and deservedly so. Although this was also the year that the Yankees' Ron Guidry was 25–3, Rice was, day in and day out, the best player in either league. He hit .315, with a league-leading 46 home runs, 139 RBI, 15 triples and 213 hits. His 406 total bases were the highest in the league since Joe DiMaggio's 418 in 1937.

Rice hit .300 or better seven times in his career, had 20 or more homers 11 times, 100 or more RBI eight times and 200 or more hits four times.

He hit .333 in his only World Series in 1986 (he broke his wrist just before the 1975 playoffs), with six runs scored.

Rice was relatively slow afoot, and had a penchant for grounding into double plays. He grounded into 36 doubles in 1984, a major league record at the time.

LIFETIME STATS: BA: .298, HR: 382, RBI: 1,451, H: 2,452, SB: 58

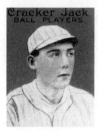

#**151** Edd J. Roush

OF-1B, White Sox, Indianapolis (FL), Newark (FL), Giants, Reds, 1913–31. Hall of Fame, 1986

Roush was one of the best hitters of the 1910s and '20s, a strong guy who was not afraid to spike opposing players on the base paths, and then dare them to retaliate.

Roush bounced around the major leagues for the first four years of his career, playing for five teams in that span. But when he came to Cincinnati, he found a home. Roush was installed at center field, and became a star, hitting .300 or better 10 times in his 11 years with the Reds.

Roush would hit .300 or better 13 times overall. He would win batting titles in 1917, when he hit .341, and in 1919, when he hit .321.

Roush also led the league in doubles with 41 in 1923, and in triples with 21 in 1924. He would hit 20 or more doubles eight times in his career and 10 or more triples 11 times. He was also a pretty good base-stealer, swiping 10 or more bases 12 times.

The 1919 season was the year Roush led the Reds into the World Series against the White Sox. Cincinnati won the series, five games to three (in those days it was a best-of-nine series), and Roush never believed the Sox were lying down against him.

Roush used a big, thick bat, and most opponents believed it was to enable Roush to sock homers. They were wrong. The canny Roush was a tremendous bunter and slap hitter. Reportedly, Roush owns the record for most hits on a pitchout, making seven one year.

LIFETIME STATS: BA: .323, HR: 68, RBI: 981, H: 2,376, SB: 268

#152 Donald Scott "Don" Drysdale
RHP, Dodgers, 1956–69. Hall of Fame, 1984

The towering (6'6") Drysdale was an intimidating presence on the mound, for several reasons. First, he was a sidearm pitcher with excellent control. His delivery meant the ball came at batters from a difficult angle. Second, Drysdale was not afraid, and in fact was happy, to pitch inside on batters.

Drysdale set a 20th-century record by hitting 154 batters, and led the league in that department a record five times. He would often refer to his knockdown pitches as "kisses."

But Drysdale was much more than a knockdown artist. He led the league in strikeouts three times, and had 200 or more strikeouts in a season six times. A workhorse who hated to come out of games, he pitched 300 or more innings in a season four times.

He also led the league in shutouts in 1959. In 1968, he threw six consecutive shutouts, and a since-broken 58 2/3 shutout innings.

An excellent hitter, Drysdale twice tied the major league record for home runs by a pitcher, with seven. His career total of 29 is second all-time. In 1965, he hit .300 and was one of the best pinch hitters on the Dodgers.

Drysdale was a terrific pitcher in the All Star game, with a 2–1 mark overall, and a record 1.40 ERA with 19 strikeouts.

LIFETIME STATS: W: 209, L: 166, SV: 6, ERA: 2.95, SO: 2,486, CG: 167

#153 William Robert "Sliding Billy" Hamilton

OF, Kansas City (AA), Phillies, Braves, 1888–1901.
Hall of Fame, 1961

Hamilton combined speed, smarts and aggressiveness on the base paths to become one of the premiere players of the 19th century.

Hamilton started out in the old American Association, where he hit .301 for Kansas City in 1889. That began a string of hitting .300 or better for 12 consecutive years. Hamilton signed with the Phillies in 1890 and won the National League batting title with a .340 average the following year. Ironically, Hamilton would top that mark six more times (in fact, his career batting average is .344, sixth best all-time) but never won another batting crown.

In addition to being a solid hitter, Hamilton had an excellent eye at the plate. He led the league in walks five times.

He was a run-scoring machine, four times topping the league in that category. In 1894, Hamilton scored a record 192 runs in 129 games, hitting .404 and walking a league-best 126 times.

Hamilton stole 100 or more bases three times in his career, and led the league in thefts five times. He was called "Sliding Billy" for his baserunning feats. He also had 20 or more doubles seven times in his career.

Hamilton ended his 14-year career as one of only three men to have more runs (1,690) than games played (1,591).

LIFETIME STATS: BA: .344, HR: 40, RBI: 736, H: 2,158, SB: 912

#**154** Lawrence Eugene "Larry" Doby

OF, Indians, Tigers, White Sox, 1947–59. Hall of Fame, 1998

Doby is now a historical asterisk, which is unfortunate. The first black player to play in the American League (Jackie Robinson integrated baseball in the National League), Doby was also a very good player: an excellent hitter and a sure-handed outfielder with great range.

He was signed by the Cleveland Indians in 1947, just four months after the Dodgers signed Robinson. Doby was surely subjected to as many racial indignities as Robinson, but his low-key demeanor did not attract as much media attention.

Prior to his signing, Doby was a budding star in the Negro Leagues, hitting .341 and .414 in his first two years with the Newark Eagles.

Doby, like Robinson, preferred to let his playing talk for him. He hit .301 to lead the Indians to the World Championship in 1948 and picked up the pace in the World Series, hitting .318.

Doby led the AL in home runs (32) and RBI (126) in 1954, and finished a close second to Yogi Berra in the MVP voting. In Cleveland's pennant-winning year of 1954, Doby again led the league in homers with 32 and in RBI with 126. Five times in his career, Doby had 100 or more RBI.

Doby's big swing left him vulnerable to strikeouts, and in fact, he fanned 100 or more times four times in his career.

LIFETIME STATS: BA: .283, HR: 253, RBI: 970, H: 1,515, SB: 47 (MLB stats only)

#155 George Stacey Davis

SS-3B-OF, Cleveland (NL), Giants, White Sox, 1890–1909. Hall of Fame, 1998

Davis began his career as a third baseman for the Cleveland Naps and then the Giants of the National League, but then was switched to shortstop. He was a solid performer at both positions, but was clearly a better fielder as a shortstop than a third baseman.

He was also a switch-hitter, and one of the best in the 19th century. He hit 27 triples in 1893, still a record for a switch-hitter.

Davis hit .300 or better for nine consecutive years, including a career-high .353 in 1897. That same year, Davis led the National League in RBI with 136.

An excellent base runner, Davis stole 20 or more bases 17 times in his career. His career high was 65, also accomplished in 1897.

Davis led the league's shortstops in fielding percentage twice in the National League and twice in the American League, after he had been traded to the White Sox. In 1906, he led the White Sox's "Hitless Wonders" to the World Championship, upsetting the heavily favored Chicago Cubs. Davis was definitely not a hitless wonder: He hit .308 with three doubles, four runs scored and six RBI in the series.

LIFETIME STATS: BA: .295, HR: 73, RBI: 1,437, H: 2,660, SB: 616

#156 Roberto "Robby," "Bobby" Alomar

2B-DH, Padres, Blue Jays, Orioles, Indians, Mets, White Sox, Diamondbacks, 1988–2004. Hall of Fame, 2011

Bobby Alomar is a 12-time All Star with 10 Gold Glove awards on his resume. In addition he is an excellent hitter, with nine seasons hitting .300 or better.

Orlando Cepeda once compared Alomar favorably to Joe Morgan, Rod Carew and Cool Papa Bell.

Truthfully, he doesn't hit as well as Morgan or Carew, but he's close. And he doesn't run as well as Bell, but maybe nobody ever did. Suffice to say that Alomar has played at a high level from the 1990s into this century.

His biggest problem is that when people think of Robby Alomar, they don't think of Gold Gloves or .300 seasons. They remember the last weekend of the 1996 season, when a frustrated Alomar spat on umpire John Hirschbeck. It's sort of the curse of ESPN, if you will. But Alomar is a good one who could be a great one if he keeps it up.

Alomar hit .400 or better in three postseason series: the 1991 ALCS, the 1992 ALCS and the 1993 World Series.

LIFETIME STATS: BA: .300, HR: 210, RBI: 1,134, H: 2,734, SB: 474

#157 Jacob Nelson "Nellie," "Little Nel" Fox

2B-3B, Athletics, White Sox, Astros, 1947–65. Hall of Fame, 1997

Fox was a part-time player for three years with the Athletics, and had a relatively unremarkable career there. But he was traded to the White Sox, and his career took off. Fox became Chicago's regular second baseman, and was hard to dislodge, playing in 798 consecutive games there from August 7, 1956, to September 3, 1960.

But more than his durability, Fox was a tremendous defensive second baseman. Six times, he led second basemen in fielding percentage, and he won three Gold Gloves. He teamed up with Chico Carrasquel and later Luis Aparacio to give Chicago a strong defensive presence in their middle infield.

Fox had six seasons where he hit .300 or better, and he also led the league in hits four times. Six times, he made 190 or more base hits.

Not necessarily a threat to steal bases, Fox was nonetheless aggressive on the base paths. He stroked 20 or more doubles 11 times and 10 or more triples four times. He led the league in triples with 10 in 1960.

Fox was very tough to strike out. He never had more than 18 strikeouts in a full season, and ended up with only 216 on his career.

LIFETIME STATS: BA: .288, HR: 35, RBI: 790, H: 2,663, SB: 76

#**158** Philip Henry "Phil" Niekro
RHP, Braves, Yankees, Indians, Blue Jays, 1964–87. Hall of Fame, 1997

When the 48-year-old Niekro finally retired, he was the oldest player to perform regularly in the major leagues. Niekro rode his mastery of the quirky knuckleball into the Hall of Fame.

The 300-game winner was consistent and durable throughout his 24-year career. He won 20 games only three times, and led the league in that department only once, in 1974 when he was 20–13.

Because the knuckler didn't take a lot out of his arm, Niekro was durable. He threw over 300 innings four times, and tossed more than 250 seven other times. He led the league in complete games four times, with a career-high of 23 in 1979.

Niekro also has a lot of success striking out batters with the knuckler. He led the league with 262 punchouts in 1977, and had 190 or more strikeouts four other times.

Yet his prowess, perhaps because it was with the knuckler, was often taken for granted. He was chosen for only five All Star games, and only pitched in two, throwing a total of 1 1/3 innings.

Yet he pitched well, for good teams and not-so-good teams. At age 43, he was 17–4 for the Braves and led the league with an .810 winning percentage. In 1985 and 1985, he was a solid 32–20 for the Yankees.

LIFETIME STATS: W: 318, L: 274, SV: 29, ERA: 3.35, SO: 3,342, CG: 245

#**159** Fredric Michael "Fred" Lynn
OF-DH, Red Sox, Angels, Orioles, Tigers, Padres, 1974–90

Wow. How about that first season, huh?

Fred Lynn burst into the limelight in Boston with a stunning season in which he won the Rookie of the Year award and MVP, a feat never accomplished before or since.

And he deserved it. Lynn hit .331 and slugged a league-leading .556, with 47 doubles and 103 runs scored, also league bests. He also had 21 homers and 105 RBI.

Lynn's swing was tailor-made for the left-field wall in Fenway Park, but he was no slouch on the road, either. On June 18 of his rookie season, he drilled three homers and had 10 RBI and 16 total bases against the Tigers.

In his six years in a Boston uniform, Lynn hit .300 or better four times (and hit .298 in 1978), won a batting title in 1979 with a .333 mark, hit 124 home runs and made the All Star team every year.

His failure to keep up that standard was actually a tribute to his hustle. Lynn was also an amazing defensive outfielder, but his all-out play often had him slamming into walls. He was frequently injured his last few years with the Sox, and when he was finally signed by the Angels, he wasn't the Fred Lynn of old.

He was certainly pretty decent, however. Lynn hit .299 with 21 home runs for the Angels in 1982, and .287 in 1986 with the Orioles. He made the All Star team three times with California.

LIFETIME STATS: BA: .283, HR: 306, RBI: 1,111, H: 1,960, SB: 72

#**160** Martin DiHugo

2B-RHP-OF-SS-3B-1B-C, Cuban Stars, New York Cubans, Homestead Grays, Hilldale Daisies, Darby Daisies (Negro Leagues), 1923–36. Hall of Fame, 1977

DiHugo was an exceptional athlete who may have been the most versatile baseball player ever. He was a man who could—and did—play every position on the diamond at some point in his career, including pitcher.

DiHugo had a very strong arm, was very fast on the base paths and in the outfield, and had a natural confidence in his abilities, enabling him to excel wherever he played.

He began as an infielder in his native Cuba, but as was often the case in semipro teams of the 1920s in Cuba, he was also asked to play first and third base, and take a turn in the outfield. DiHugo would do so, and usually turn in an outstanding performance.

He was signed by the Cuban Stars of the Eastern Colored League in 1923, and began his pitching career. The Cubans were not a strong team, but DiHugo played the infield, hitting .299 in 1925, and pitching. In 1927, he led the league in home runs and was 2–2 on the mound.

He was also going back to Cuba and playing winter ball. He hit .413 and .415 in consecutive seasons for the Havana Sugar Kings in 1927 and 1928.

DiHugo began pitching more as he got older, preferring to let younger players toil in the field. By 1937, he was 32, and a veteran of 10 seasons in the Negro Leagues and eight in the Cuban Leagues. That year, he went 11–5 for Havana, and the next year, was 18–2. He had a good, but not overpowering fastball, and a very good curveball. He pitched the first no-hitter in the Mexican League in 1939.

DiHugo was elected to the Halls of Fame in Mexico and Cuba as well as the United States Hall of Fame.

LIFETIME STATS: BA: .299, HR: 69, H: 1,609

#**161** Lewis Robert "Hack" Wilson

OF, Giants, Cubs, Dodgers, Phillies, 1923–34. Hall of Fame, 1979

For many years, Hack Wilson was a trivia question, as in, Who holds the single-season National League record for most home runs (56) and Who still holds the major league record for RBI (191)?

Wilson was 5'6", and weighed 190 pounds. But he was all muscle. He had an enormous upper body, huge, Popeye-like forearms and a barrel chest. His body tapered down to spindly ankles and a size-six cleat.

But he could hit. His nickname actually came from his resemblance to journeyman Hack Miller, who played for the Giants before Wilson came on the scene. He was a better hitter than Miller; he was a better hitter than almost anyone. Wilson led the league in home runs four times, including the aforementioned 56 dingers in 1930, a record that was not broken until Mark McGwire and Sammy Sosa each bested it in 1998.

His 191 RBI mark, also set in 1930, is still untouched, and there have not been a lot of challengers in the ensuing 74 seasons.

But he was not just a slugger. He had a 27-game hitting streak in 1931, and hit for the cycle in 1930.

In the outfield, he was better than most thought. He led the league in

1927 with 400 putouts and had enough speed to make a lot of plays.

But his battles with the bottle were legendary. Several mangers tried to wean him of it; none succeeded. Wilson died nearly broke at age 48.

LIFETIME STATS: BA: .307, HR: 244, RBI: 1,063, H: 1,461, SB: 52

#**162** Joseph Lowell "Joe," "Flash" Gordon

2B, Yankees, Indians, 1938–43, 1946–50. Hall of Fame, 2009

Gordon was a great athlete, and had excellent range at second base. He tried to get every ball hit close to him, and was a hustler both at bat and in the field.

As a rookie, he displaced future Hall of Famer Tony Lazzeri at second base, and there was little doubt that he had earned it. He was a better defensive player than Lazzeri, and hit .255 with 25 home runs and 97 RBI that year.

Gordon hit .300 or better only once, but he had over 100 RBI four seasons, 20 or more home runs seven times, 20 or more doubles eight times and scored 100 or more runs twice.

Gordon was the MVP of the league in 1942, hitting .322 with 18 home runs, 103 RBI and 88 runs scored. He hit for the cycle in 1940.

His postseason work was also mostly successful. Gordon played in five World Series with the Yankees and one with Cleveland. He had two doubles and a home run to go along with a .400 batting average for New York in 1939, and hit .500 with a home run and seven RBI in the 1941 series.

Traded to the Indians in 1947, Gordon hit .280 with 32 home runs and 124 RBI in 1948 to lead Cleveland to the pennant and world championship over the Boston Braves.

#163 Louis Rodman "Lou," "Sweet Lou" Whitaker

2B-DH, Tigers, 1977-95

In the field, Whitaker made defensive plays that were seemingly effortless, leading critics to decide he wasn't trying. Well, he had to be doing something right: He ranks ninth all-time among second basemen in runs scored (1,386) and RBI (1,084).

Whitaker was the Rookie of the Year in 1978, hitting .285 with 58 RBI and 71 runs scored. A down year in 1980, in which he hit only .233 with one home run, led many Tiger fans to conclude that he was something of a fluke. But Whitaker erased all that criticism over the next decade, making the All Star team five consecutive times and, in 1983, hitting .320 and becoming the first Tiger to make 200 or more hits since 1943.

His power numbers steadily increased, and in 1985, Whitaker set a team record for second basemen with 21 home runs. He later shattered that mark with 28 in 1989. In all, Whitaker hit 20 or more home runs four times for the Tigers.

Defensively, Whitaker led the league's second basemen in fielding average twice, in 1982 and again in 1991. He was usually among the leaders in most defensive categories throughout the 1980s.

In the World Series of 1984, which the Tigers won over the Padres, Whitaker led the team with six runs scored and two doubles.

As the 1990s dawned, Whitaker was used as a part-time player more and more. But he was still effective, hitting .290, .301 and .293 in his last three seasons.

LIFETIME STATS: BA: .276, HR: 244, RBI: 1,084, H: 2,369, SB: 143

#**164** Frank Leroy "Husk," "The Peerless Leader" Chance

1B-C-OF, Cubs, Yankees, 1898–1914. Hall of Fame, 1946

Chance was, of course, the first baseman in the famed "Tinker to Evers to Chance" double-play combination of legend. He was nicknamed "The Peerless Leader" because he was a team leader on the Cubs who later became a manager. He was nicknamed "Husk" because he was big (six feet), husky, and took no guff from players—or managers, or fans, or anyone, for that matter.

Chance began his career as a catcher, but when Johnny Kling came along he was moved to first base. He was fast for a first baseman: In 1903 he stole 67 bases to lead the league, and in 1906, swiped a league-best 57.

His best years were from 1903 to 1908. He hit .300 or better four years in a row, from 1903 to 1906; stole between 27 and 67 bases each year; and led the National League in runs scored in 1906. In 1907, Chance led all National League first basemen in fielding percentage.

He was a clutch player. He batted .421 in the 1908 World Series against the Tigers, with five stolen bases and four runs scored. In that tumultuous 1908 season, Chance made what may still be considered the biggest hit in franchise history: a bases-loaded double that scored three runs that defeated the Giants and propelled Chicago to the World Series.

Chance took over the managerial reins of the Cubs in 1905, and by 1908, began to play less and less. He hit .298 in 1910, which was the last season he was a semi-regular.

LIFETIME STATS: BA: .296, HR: 20, RBI: 596, H: 1,273, SB: 401

#**165** Louis "Lou" Boudreau

SS-3B-1B, Indians, Red Sox, 1938–52. Hall of Fame, 1970

Boudreau came up with the Indians in 1938, and played sparingly. But by 1940, he was the team's starting shortstop, hitting .295, with 46 doubles, 10 triples and 101 RBI. He made the All Star team and also led American League shortstops in fielding percentage.

By 1942, Boudreau was, at 24, the team leader. He also became the team manager, the youngest man ever to take charge of a team at the onset of a season.

Boudreau was a hustler who took full advantage of his limited gifts. Never afraid to take the extra base, he led the league in doubles three times. A smart player in the field who studied hitters, he led the league in fielding percentage by a shortstop eight times. In 1944, he won the batting title with a .327 average.

In 1948, Boudreau had an amazing season: He hit .355, second best in the league, with 199 hits, 106 RBI, 34 doubles, 18 home runs and 98 walks. He struck out only nine times all year. That season, the Indians and Red Sox tied for first place in the American League, Boudreau went four-for-four with two homers to lead the Indians to the championship.

LIFETIME STATS: BA: .295, HR: 68, RBI: 789, H: 1,779, SB: 51

#**166** Darrell Wayne Evans

3B-1B-DH, Braves, Giants, Tigers, 1969–89

The power-hitting Evans was one of the best third basemen of his era, and was the first player to hit 40 home runs in both leagues.

Evans came up with Atlanta in 1969, becoming the Braves' regular third baseman by the 1971 season. That was the season he first wore contact lenses, and Evans credits that adjustment with helping him improve.

By 1973, he was an All Star, hitting .281 with 41 homers, 104 RBI and a league-leading 124 walks. He and teammates Henry Aaron (40) and Davey Johnson (43) became the first teammates to hit 40 or more home runs in the same season.

Evans usually batted third, ahead of Aaron, and was on first base on April 8, 1974, the day Aaron belted home run Number 715 to break Babe Ruth's record. A patient hitter, Evans led the league in walks twice and five times had 100 or more.

He was traded to Detroit in 1984, and led the league in home runs with 40 the following year, his only home run crown. But he was one of the cornerstones of the Tigers' World Championship team of 1984.

LIFETIME STATS: BA: .248, HR: 414, RBI: 1,354, H: 2,223, SB: 98

#**167** Derek Sanderson Jeter

SS, Yankees, 1995–present

Derek Jeter is one of the great postseason performers, in any sport, of this generation.

The seven-time All-Star has played in 24 postseason series, including six World Series. Eight times in these individual series, Jeter hit .400 or better. Twice he hit .500. In 13 series, his on-base percentage was .400 or better. He has 150 hits in the postseason, 17 home runs and 48 RBI, with a .314 batting average.

In 2000, he was MVP of the World Series win over the crosstown Mets, with a gaudy .409 batting average and two home runs, a triple and a double.

He is by no means a one-man team, but Jeter is clearly the spark plug of the Yankees when the game is on the line in October.

He's not exactly a slouch during the regular season, either. Six times, he's finished in the top five in batting. He led the league in runs scored in 1998, with 127, and in base hits in 1999, with 219.

Jeter is a four-time Gold Glove winner, recognized throughout his career for his steady play at shortstop.

LIFETIME STATS: BA: .312, HR: 240, RBI: 1,196, H: 3,088, SB: 339

#**168** Salvatore Leonard "Sal" Bando
3B-DH, Athletics, Brewers, 1966–80

Bando was a power-hitting third baseman who was the team leader of the raucous, three-time World Champion Oakland Athletics.

Bando's stats were rarely overpowering. In fact, a look at his postseason numbers would lead the unsuspecting observer to think he had played poorly: Bando hit only .206 in three World Series, and .270 in five League Championship Series.

So much for stats. Bando knocked in the tying run in Game Seven of the 1972 World Series against the Reds and then scored the game-winner in a 3–2 win. In Game Two of the 1973 American League Championship Series, he belted two home runs to help the A's win the game and tie the series.

And in Game Four of the 1974 ALCS, Bando's solo shot in Game Three was the only run of the game. Bando scored the game-winning run the next day to close out the Orioles.

His regular season numbers were similar. Bando did lead the league in doubles in 1973 with 32, but that is really the only major statistical category he ever won. He was consistent, however. Bando hit 20 or more home runs six times in his career, 20 or more doubles 10 times and twice had over 100 RBI.

LIFETIME STATS: BA: .254, HR: 242, RBI: 1,039, H: 1,790, SB: 75

#**169** Hilton Lee Smith

RHP-OF, Monroe Monarchs, New Orleans Crescent
Stars, Kansas City Monarchs (Negro Leagues),
1932–48. Hall of Fame, 2001

Smith was known, for many years in the Negro Leagues,
as "Satchel Paige's relief," as Smith would inevitably come
in for Paige after Paige had made an appearance and pitched
for three innings. Smith would come in and finish the game.

There were many players, both teammates and opponents, who declared
that Smith might have been a better pitcher than Paige. But Smith was as
low-key as Paige was loquacious, and that demeanor worked against him.

Smith did have the uncanny control that Paige had, but he had an excellent curveball and a live fastball that hopped as it reached the plate. Smith
also threw both sidearm and overhand, which further befuddled batters.

Smith played for several teams in the south before signing with the Kansas
City Monarchs in 1936. He would remain one of the aces of the Monarch
staff for years to come.

Smith led the Negro American League in strikeouts in 1938, 1939, 1940
and was second in 1941. Smith pitched in six consecutive Negro League All
Star games, and his 13 strikeouts in those contests are second all-time.

LIFETIME STATS: W: 78, L: 28

#**170** Atanasio "Tony," "Doggie" Perez

1B-3B-DH, Reds, Expos, Red Sox, Phillies, 1964–86.
Hall of Fame, 2000

Perez was an RBI machine for most of his career. He only
hit .300 or better three times in a 23-year career, but
drove in 90 or more runs 12 times.

Perez was a first baseman for his initial three years with the Reds, from 1964 to 1966. He was moved over to third base from 1967 to 1971, to make room for Lee May. But he was moved back to first in 1972, where he remained for most of the rest of his career.

Perez was one of the cornerstones of the "Big Red Machine" of the 1970s. His job was to drive in runs, and nobody did it better in that span. He hit 20 or more home runs nine times, and his RBI totals from 1967 to 1976 never fell below 90.

Perez was a pretty good fielder, as well, leading National League first baseman in fielding percentage in 1974 with a .996 mark.

In the postseason, Perez usually shone, even if his numbers weren't always outstanding. He hit only .179 against the Red Sox in 1975, for example, but three of his five hits in the series were home runs, including a solo blast in Game Seven. He had 10 hits in the 1972 series loss to Oakland.

Following the 1976 season, Perez wandered around the big leagues, spending three years each in Montreal and Boston, and a year in Philadelphia before returning to Cincinnati to retire.

LIFETIME STATS: BA: .279, HR: 379, RBI: 1,652, H: 2,732, SB: 49

#171 Graig "Puff" Nettles

3B-OF, Twins, Indians, Yankees, Padres, Braves, Expos, 1967–88

Nettles was an acrobatic, power-hitting third baseman who showcased his talent with the New York Yankees from the mid-1970s to the mid-1980s.

Nettles started out as an outfielder for the Twins at the beginning of his career, but by the time he got to Cleveland, he was manning third. Nettles proved how wise that move was by leading the league's third basemen in fielding percentage. In 1971, he set an American League record with 412 assists and 54 double plays.

He was traded to the Yankees at the start of the 1973 season, and had problems adapting. His average fell to .234 and he fielded poorly. But he rebounded over the next few seasons, and was named to the All Star team in 1975.

Nettles was one of the leaders of the Yankees' three consecutive American League champions from 1976 to 1978. He led the league in home runs with 32 in 1976, and won Gold Gloves in 1977 and 1978.

His defensive play in 1977 was amazing. In Game Three of the World Series, Nettles made three diving stops of line drives that preserved a 5–1 Yankee win over the Dodgers. Los Angeles coach Tommy Lasorda said later that Nettles's defensive play that night was the greatest individual effort he had ever seen.

Nettles's production dropped off in the early 1980s, and he was traded to the Padres. But there, at age 40, he and ex-teammate Goose Gossage helped San Diego to the National League pennant.

LIFETIME STATS: BA: .248, HR: 390, RBI: 1,314, H: 2,225, SB: 32

#**172** Anthony Michael "Poosh 'Em Up" Lazzeri

2B-3B, Yankees, Cubs, Dodgers, Giants, 1926–39.
Hall of Fame, 1991

Lazzeri was part of the Yankees' "San Francisco connection" of the 1920s and 1930s, ballplayers like Lazzeri, Frankie Crosetti and Joe DiMaggio who were weaned in the ballyards of the City by the Bay.

Lazzeri came to the Yankees in 1926 and immediately

took over the second base chores. He hit .275 and drove in 114 runs that year. The next year, Lazzeri hit .309 and drove in 102 runs.

He was painfully shy, and an epileptic. Lazzeri never had a seizure on the field, but teammates recall that he would have one or two during the season. Roommate Mark Koenig carried a roll of pencils with him at all times, to shove between Lazzeri's jaws to prevent him from swallowing his tongue.

A fan favorite, Lazzeri's nickname came from his Italian countrymen urging Lazzeri to "Poosh 'Em Up!" or hit a home run, when he came to bat.

Playing with offensive powerhouses like Babe Ruth and Lou Gehrig, Lazzeri never led the league in any of the power categories. But he drove in 100 or more runs seven times, hit 10 or more homers 10 times and hit .300 or more five times. He became the first major leaguer to hit two grand slams in one game, in 1936, setting an AL single-game record with 11 RBI.

LIFETIME STATS: BA: .292, HR: 178, RBI: 1,191, H: 1,840, SB: 148

#**173** Gaylord Jackson Perry

RHP, Giants, Indians, Rangers, Padres, Yankees, Braves, Mariners, Royals, 1962–83. Hall of Fame, 1991

The (alleged) master of the spitball, and various other illegal pitches, Perry was the first player to win the Cy Young award in both leagues.

Perry was signed by the Giants, and spent four unremarkable seasons there as a spot starter. In 1966, Perry got off to an amazing start, at one point owning a 20–2 record, before tailing off to a very solid 21–8 mark. Still, he earned a berth in the All Star game, the first of five.

Perry won 20 or more games twice with the Giants, but slumped to 16–12 in 1971, and was traded to the Indians. But in 1972, Perry led the league with 24 wins, five shutouts and 342 2/3 innings pitched. It was good enough to win his first Cy Young award. After a stint with the Texas Rangers, Perry was traded again, this time to the San Diego Padres.

Perry had a masterful first season with San Diego, going 21–6, with a 2.73 ERA, 154 strikeouts and 260 2/3 innings pitched. He easily won his second Cy Young that year.

Perry had an assortment of pitches, including a good curve and a live slider. But over the years, allegations surfaced that he also doctored the ball, using spit, or Vaseline, or grease or something.

Perry was constantly moving on the mound, touching his cap, his uniform, his hair, and was often searched by umpires, who never found anything. All those shenanigans were, more often than not, used by Perry to distract the batter.

LIFETIME STATS: W: 314, L: 265, SV: 11, ERA: 3.11, SO: 3,534, CG: 303

#174 Sherwood Robert "Sherry" Magee

OF-1B, Phillies, Braves, Reds, 1904–19

Magee was a feared slugger at the turn of the 20th century, several times leading his league in RBI. But more than that, he was an excellent all-around ballplayer who could also run and field exceptionally well.

Magee spent his rookie year with the Philadelphia Phillies on the bench, for the most part. The next year, however, he got his chance, and made the most of it, hitting .299, scoring 100 runs and driving in 98. Two years later, he hit .328, with 28 doubles and a league-best 85 RBI.

In 1910, Magee won his only batting title with a .331 average, and also topped the league with 123 RBI, 110 runs scored, a .445 on-base percentage and a .507 slugging percentage.

Magee did not suffer fools well. He was critical of teammates who made mental errors, and was once suspended for five weeks after punching an umpire who Magee thought was doing a sloppy job.

He was an excellent fielder, leading the league's outfielders in fielding percentage in 1911. He was also an excellent base-stealer. Magee stole home 23 times in his career and seven times stole 30 or more bases in a season. On July 12, 1906, he stole second base, third base and home against St. Louis.

LIFETIME STATS: BA: .291, HR: 83, RBI: 1,176, H: 2,169, SB: 441

#175 Maurice Morning "Maury" Wills

SS-3B, Dodgers, Pirates, Expos, 1959–72

Wills was actually a pretty decent hitter who was also a pretty good infielder, but he is most remembered for his phenomenal success in stealing bases in the early 1960s.

Wills came to the Dodgers in 1959, and shared the shortstop duties with veteran Don Zimmer. Wills was pretty unspectacular, but Zimmer wasn't a heck of a lot better, so Wills became the regular second baseman for Los Angeles in 1960.

He took off, hitting .295 and leading the league in stolen bases with 50. In 1961, Wills scored 105 runs and stole 35 bases, again leading the league.

By now, Wills was a bona fide weapon for the Dodgers. In 1962, he stole a stunning 104 bases, hit .299, had 208 hits, scored 130 runs and had a league-leading 10 triples to edge Willie Mays and win the MVP award.

Wills's 104 stolen bases shattered Ty Cobb's old record of 96. More importantly, Wills was caught stealing only 13 times in 1962; Cobb was caught 38 times in 1915.

Wills led the league in stolen bases three more years after 1962, and stole 25 or more bases five more times, including 52 for the Pirates in 1968.

Wills, by the way, was a pretty good defensive shortstop. He won two Gold Gloves, in 1961 and again in 1962.

LIFETIME STATS: BA: .281, HR: 20, RBI: 458, H: 2,134, SB: 586

#**176** Willie Larry Randolph

2B, Pirates, Yankees, Dodgers, Athletics, Brewers, Mets, 1975–92

Randolph played a handful of games with the Pirates before being traded to the Yankees in 1976, which was technically his rookie year. He was so highly regarded that year that he was on the All Star ballot as a rookie and eventually made the team.

Randolph was the quiet member of the tumultuous New York Yankees teams of the late 1970s. He didn't feud with owner George Steinbrenner, he didn't snipe at teammates in the papers, he didn't pout when he was in a slump. He just played. And he played very well.

The Yankees won three consecutive pennants from 1976 to 1978 with Randolph at second base, including two World Championships. Randolph was a very consistent player for New York, hitting around .275, scoring 70 runs and stealing 30 bases in that span.

In the 1980s, when the Yankees began to flounder, Randolph continued to play well. He hit .294 in 1980, and led the league with 119 walks.

From 1982 to 1987, Randolph never hit below .276, averaged 20 doubles, 82 runs scored and 80 walks a season, and played well in the field. He made six All Star teams in his career.

After the 1988 season, Randolph was signed by the Dodgers. He was mostly a part-time player there, and finished up his career with three teams in his last two years, including 90 games with the Mets in 1992.

LIFETIME STATS: BA: .276, HR: 54, RBI: 687, H: 2,210, SB: 271

#177 Roger Connor

1B-3B-2B, Troy (NL), Giants, New York (PL),
Phillies, Cardinals, 1880–97. Hall of Fame, 1976

Connor was one of the greatest home run hitters of the
19th century: His 138 career home runs was the record
until broken by Babe Ruth.

At 6'3", 220 pounds, Connor was a very big man
in 19th-century baseball. He was a fast man also, and
he stole 20 or more bases seven times in his career
(maybe more, as stolen bases were not counted the first
six years Connor played). The sight of the muscular
Connor thundering down the base paths was not one opposing infielders
cared to see.

Connor also took the extra base. He hit 20 or more triples 14 times in
his career and 10 or more triples 11 times.

Connor won one batting title, in 1885 while with the Giants. But he also
hit .300 or better 11 times and topped 100 RBI four times. He went six-for-
six in a game in 1885.

The rangy Connor had long arms and big hands, and that enabled him
to dig balls out of the dirt and field his position very well. He topped the
league's first basemen in fielding percentage four times.

Connor retired from major league baseball in 1897, at age 40. But he
played in the minors for six more years.

LIFETIME STATS: BA: .317, HR: 138, RBI: 1,322, H: 2,467, SB: 244

#**178** Ivan "Pudge" Rodriguez

C-DH, Rangers, Marlins, Tigers, Yankees, Astros, Senators, 1991–present

Rodriguez is one of the best defensive catchers of all time and has established himself as a team leader in the clubhouse virtually everywhere he has gone. A 12-time Gold Glove winner as a catcher, the Puerto Rican native was the American League MVP in 1999, with a .332 batting average, 35 home runs, 113 RBI, 116 runs scored and 25 stolen bases.

From 1992 to 2002, Rodriguez was a 10-time All-Star with the Rangers. In that span, he hit .300 or better eight consecutive times, hit 20 or more home runs five times and had 20 or more doubles nine times. He's known as "Pudge"—not for his physical frame, but for his similarity to the original "Pudge," Boston and White Sox star Carlton Fisk.

When Rodriguez signed with the Florida Marlins in 2003, he became the anchor of the young pitching staff, a clubhouse leader and one of the team's best players. He hit .353 in the Divisional Championship Series win over the San Francisco Giants.

Rodriguez was similarly impressive in the National League Championship Series win over the Cubs, in which the Marlins rallied from a 1–3 deficit to win the series in seven games. Rodriguez hit .321 with two homers and 10 RBI, and he was named MVP of the series for his work. In the 2003 World Series, Rodriguez had several key hits in the Marlins' win over the Yankees.

Rodriguez was traded to the Tigers prior to the 2004 season. He has continued his solid play with Detroit, hitting .334 in 2004 and .300 in 2006. His hitting and defensive play helped propel the Tigers, a team that had slumped horribly in the early part of the decade, back to its first World Series in two decades.

LIFETIME STATS: BA: .296, HR: 311, RBI: 1,332, H: 2,814, SB: 127

#179 Albert Leonard "Al," "Flip" Rosen

3B-1B, Cleveland, 1947–56

Rosen got his nickname as an underhanded softball pitcher in the sandlots in the Depression. He was one of those kids who played all sorts of games, and was also an amateur boxer. But baseball was his first love, and he eventually signed a professional contract with the Indians.

Rosen came up with Cleveland in 1947, but was such a poor fielder he didn't land a starting position for three years. But the determined Rosen made himself into a good, if not great, third baseman in the field.

At bat, there was little doubt. In his first full season, he led the league with 37 home runs. He also had 116 RBI, 100 runs scored, 100 walks and a .287 batting average.

Rosen became a star in 1952, hitting .302, leading the league with 105 RBI, hitting 28 home runs and scoring 101 times. But he elevated his play to another level in 1953, with a .336 batting average, a league-leading .613 slugging percentage, 43 homers and 145 RBI and 115 runs scored. He missed a Triple Crown on the last day of the season, losing the batting championship to Mickey Vernon. The writers voted him the MVP award overwhelmingly.

In 1954, Rosen led the Indians to the American League pennant, and socked two home runs in the All Star game. But nagging injuries began to take their toll, and Rosen retired at the relatively young age of 32 to become a stockbroker.

LIFETIME STATS: BA: .285, HR: 192, RBI: 717, H: 1,063, SB: 39

#180 John Joseph "Johnny," "The Crab," "The Trojan" Evers

2B-3B-SS, Cubs, Braves, Phillies, White Sox, 1902–17, 1922, 1929. Hall of Fame, 1946

Evers (rhymes with "weavers") was the middleman in the "Tinker-to-Evers-to-Chance" double-play combination immortalized by sportswriter Franklin P. Adams's poem. He was a smart, tough, temperamental second baseman who was nicknamed "The Crab" because of the way he sidled up to ground balls. His other nickname, "Trojan," was derived from the city of his birth, Troy, New York.

Evers's most famous moment, and indeed one of the most famous moments in baseball, came on September 23, 1908. The Cubs and Giants were locked in a tight pennant race, and New York's Al Bridwell had singled in Mike McCormick in the bottom of the ninth with two outs to apparently win the game, 2–1.

But New York rookie Fred Merkle, who was on first base, joyously rushed to the Giants' clubhouse after seeing McCormick score. He didn't touch second, and Evers, standing on the bag, called for the ball and touched second himself for the force out. Umpire Hank O'Day called Merkle out, and the run didn't count.

After numerous protests from both teams, the game was replayed at the end of the season with the two teams tied for first place in the standings. The Cubs won, and went on to win their final World Series.

Evers was a great player, but a bad teammate. He and shortstop Joe Tinker feuded for years, and rarely talked off the field.

In 1914, Evers was traded to the Boston Braves, hit .279 and sparked the "Miracle Braves" to the pennant and the World Series. That season won him the MVP award.

LIFETIME STATS: BA: .270, HR: 12, RBI: 538, H: 1,659, SB: 324

#**181** Pedro Jaime Martinez

RHP, Dodgers, Expos, Red Sox, Mets, Phillies, 1992–2009

From 1997 to 2000, Martinez was, without a doubt, the best pitcher in baseball. From 2001 to 2004, he remained in the top two or three. Since then, he has struggled with a rotator-cuff injury, and only time will tell if Martinez can return to some semblance of his former self.

In that first four-year span, Martinez won three Cy Young awards, one with Montreal in 1997 and two with the Red Sox in 1999 and 2000.

Martinez, at 5'10" and 175 pounds, is not a big man. But up until his rotator-cuff injury, in 2006, he threw a blazing fastball that had tremendous movement. In 1997, his first Cy Young year, Martinez became the first right-handed pitcher since Walter Johnson in 1912 to strike out more than 300 batters and post an ERA under 2.00.

In 1999, his second Cy Young year, Martinez had eight 10-strikeout games. He became the first pitcher since Nolan Ryan to strike out 10 or more batters seven times in succession.

His next season was even more dominant. He broke one of the oldest records in baseball: Batters hit an average of only .167 against him.

Martinez was still a tough pitcher by 2004, when he helped the Boston Red Sox to its first World Championship in 86 years. He was masterful in Game Three of the World Series, shutting down the Cardinals in a 4–0 win. It was his swan song in Boston, and it was magnificent.

Traded to the Mets, Martinez posted a 15–8 record, but he began experiencing shoulder problems. That was a harbinger for 2006, when his record fell to 9–8 with an uncharacteristic 4.48 ERA, his worst ever.

LIFETIME STATS: W: 219, L: 100, SV: 3, ERA: 2.93, SO: 3,154, CG: 46

#182 Walter Antone "Wally" Berger
OF-1B, Braves, Giants, Reds, Phillies, 1930–40

The muscular Berger was the fulcrum of the Braves' offense throughout the early 1930s. He is all but forgotten these days, but in the 1930s, Wally Berger was a star.

Berger was actually in the Cubs farm system in 1929, but Chicago already had a solid outfield, so Berger was shipped to Boston prior to the 1930 season.

He had a great year, hitting .310 with 38 homers, 27 doubles, 14 triples and 119 RBI. In 1931, Berger hit career highs in batting, with a .323 average, and doubles, with 44. He hit .300 or better his first four seasons with the Braves.

Berger's power numbers were not augmented at spacious Braves Field in Boston, but he still hit 103 home runs there, which was the best all-time.

For several years, Berger played for mediocre Braves teams, and none of them won the pennant. In 1933, he had 27 home runs, which matched the total socked by the rest of the team. Still, Berger turned in a high level of play on a regular basis. He was the starting center fielder in the 1933 and 1934 All Star game, and in 1935, led the league with 34 home runs and 130 RBI.

Berger was a very good fielder, leading the league in fielding percentage in 1932.

LIFETIME STATS: BA: .300, HR: 242, RBI: 898, H: 1,550, SB: 36

#183 David Gene "Dave," "The Cobra" Parker
OF-DH, Pirates, Reds, Athletics, Brewers, Angels, Blue Jays, 1973–91

The imposing (6'5", 230 pounds) Parker was a part-time player for his first two seasons in Pittsburgh, but he moved into the starting lineup in 1975. That year, he belted 25 home runs, 35 doubles and 10 triples to go with 101 RBI.

Dubbed "The Cobra" because of his intimidating bat speed, Parker won back-to-back batting titles in 1977 and 1978, with averages of .338 and .334, respectively. He never won a home run crown, but twice led the league in doubles with 44 in 1977 and 42 in 1985.

He won the MVP award in 1978, with 30 homers, 117 RBI and 194 hits to go with the batting title.

Despite being a very large man, Parker was a pretty good base-stealer, swiping 20 bases twice and 10 or more five other times.

During his tenure with the Pirates, Parker was also an excellent defensive outfielder. He had a cannon arm from right field, and won three Gold Glove awards from 1977 to 1979.

But his size and weight caused leg and knee injuries, and Parker's effectiveness began to wane. He was traded to the Reds in 1984, and had two good years out of four there, and then bounced around with five teams in four years before retiring.

LIFETIME STATS: BA: .290, HR: 339, RBI: 1,493, H: 2,712, SB: 154

#184 Manuel Aristides Ramirez

OF-DH, Indians, Red Sox, Dodgers, Rays, Mariners, 1993–present

One of the greatest right-handed hitters of all time, Ramirez was one of the players who finally put the Boston Red Sox in the winner's circle after 86 years of futility.

The 11-time All Star was the World Series MVP in 2004, as Boston swept the St. Louis Cardinals. He hit safely in every postseason game that year.

A career .312 hitter, Ramirez has 555 career home runs, and has hit 30 or more homers 11 times in his career and 30 or more doubles 10 times. He has a deceptively strong throwing arm and is the latest in legendary Sox left fielders who have learned to play fly balls off the Green Monster to hold potential extra base hits to singles.

Ramirez is a free swinger and a free spirit. He swings a lot, in fact, having struck out 100 or more times 10 times in his career. And whether he's giving elaborate high and low fives to teammates or stepping off the field to check out the scorekeepers behind the scoreboard in left field, Ramirez clearly marches to his own drummer. But his Sox teammates find it hard to be critical; when push comes to shove, Manny usually comes to play in the big games.

LIFETIME STATS: BA: .312, HR: 555, RBI: 1,8231, H: 2,575, SB: 348

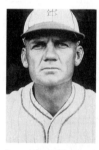

#185 Max "Scoops" Carey (real name: Maximillian Carnarius)
Pirates, Dodgers, 1910–29. Hall of Fame, 1961

Carey was the prototypical leadoff man of the early part of the 20th century. A switch hitter with good patience who stole bases, Carey scored 99 or more runs six times in his career. He led the league in stolen bases 10 times.

Six of those times, he stole 50 or more, and in 1922, he stole 51 bases in 53 attempts. The next year, Carey stole 51 bases in 59 attempts. He is ninth all-time on the career stolen-base list.

Carey was a solid hitter, topping .300 in six full seasons. But he had a good eye for pitches: He had 55 or more walks in a season 14 times, and led the league twice.

In cavernous Forbes Field, Carey did not strike a lot of home runs. But he could hit the ball: nine times, he had 10 or more triples, and twice, in 1914 and again in 1923, Carey led the league.

In the field, Carey may have been the best center fielder of his time. For nine of his 18 full seasons, he led the league in putouts and chances, and four times he led in assists. His lifetime total of 339 assists is the best of the modern major leaguers. His double-play totals are the best ever in the National League, trailing only Ty Cobb and Tris Speaker.

LIFETIME STATS: BA: .285, HR: 70, RBI: 800, H: 2,665, SB: 738

#**186** Craig Alan Biggio
2B-C-OF-DH, Astros, 1988–2007

Biggio is one of the most durable, smartest and most talented players in the league. He plays primarily second base, but for his first three years in Houston, he was primarily a catcher. In 1991, he was named to the All Star team, as he hit .295, scored 79 runs and had 23 doubles.

But the next season, Biggio was converted to second base, and hit 32 doubles, scored 96 runs and batted .277. He again made the All Star team, and would be an All Star a total of seven times.

Biggio has hit .290 or better seven times, stolen 20 or more bases nine times and hit 20 or more doubles 14 times, leading the league in 1994 (44 doubles), 1998 (51) and 1999 (56). Biggio does not have a lot of power, but he has socked 15 or more home runs nine times.

Biggio is tough to double up, having hit into an average of nine double plays a year. In 1997, he played all 162 games without hitting into a double play.

Biggio is also a tough cookie. He has been hit by a pitch 10 or more times a total of 10 years in his career. In 1997, the same year he didn't ground into a double play, he was hit a total of 34 times without missing a game.

LIFETIME STATS: BA: .282, HR: 286, RBI: 1,154, H: 3,013, SB: 413

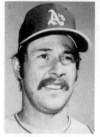

#**187** Fiore Gino "Gene" Tenace

C-1B-3B, Athletics, Padres, Cardinals, Pirates, 1969–83

Tenace is a greatly underappreciated player whose versatility and clutch abilities were one of the keys to the success of the Oakland Athletics in the early 1970s.

Tenace's numbers were never overpowering, but he was a tremendous clutch player. In 1972, in the League Championship Series against Detroit, his single drove in the winning run in Game Five. It was his only hit of the series.

In the World Series, Tenace hit .348 with eight hits, four of which were home runs. He became the first player ever to hit home runs in his first two World Series at bats. Tenace hit a two-run shot in the second inning and a solo blast in the fifth as the A's won the first game, 3–2.

In Game Four, Tenace hit another home run, and was part of the two-run rally in the ninth inning that gave the Athletics another 3–2 win and in Game Seven, Tenace had two more RBI as the A's won 3–2 again to capture their first World Championship in 41 years. Tenace never approached that marvelous postseason again, but he had several more key hits in the playoffs as Oakland won two more World Series.

Tenace never had a high batting average, which led some to overlook his pluses. He drew more than 100 walks six times in his career, leading the league twice, and his on-base percentage was above .390 seven times. Teance hit 20 or more home runs five times.

Defensively, Tenace led the league's catchers in fielding percentage once, in 1979.

LIFETIME STATS: BA: .241, HR: 201, RBI: 674, H: 1,060, SB: 36

#188 William Hendrick "Willie" Foster

LHP, Memphis Red Sox, Chicago American Giants, Birmingham Black Barons, Homestead Grays, Kansas City Monarchs, Cole's American Giants, Pittsburgh Crawfords (Negro Leagues), 1923–38. Hall of Fame, 1996

Foster was one of the best left-handed pitchers in Negro League history. The half brother of Rube Foster, who was the organizer of the Negro National League, Willie Foster possessed a smooth delivery that delivered blazing fastballs, baffling curve balls and masterful changeups.

Foster was born in Calvert, Texas. He was a college man, attending Alcorn College for a few years before signing a contract to play baseball. He signed with the Memphis Red Sox initially, but jumped to the Chicago American Giants. From 1924 to 1930, Foster was one of the stars of one of the most powerful teams of the 1920s.

The Chicago American Giants won pennants in 1926 and 1927. In 1926, Foster won 26 games in row against all competition and was 11–4 in the Negro National League.

In the Negro National League playoffs against the Kansas City Monarchs, the western champions, Chicago won the series, five games to four. With his team trailing, four games to three, Foster pitched the first game of a double-header against future Hall of Famer "Bullet Joe" Rogan. Each man allowed seven hits, but Chicago scored in the bottom of the 10th to win, 1–0.

In the second game, Giants manager Dave Malarcher heeded the advice of his players, and sent Foster out again. Chet Brewer was pitching for the Monarchs, but when Rogan saw Foster warming up, he told Monarch manager Jose Mendez he would pitch, as well. Foster won that game, 5–0. It remains one of the greatest playoff performances ever in baseball history.

LIFETIME STATS: W: 146, L: 66

#189 Elston Gene Howard

C-OF-1B, Yankees, Red Sox, 1955–68

Howard was the first black player in Yankees franchise history, and it probably hurt him, in the sense that he didn't get the call up to the major leagues until he was 26, and didn't get a chance to catch until he was 30.

But the Yankees, an acknowledged racist outfit in the 1950s, had a problem with Howard: He was too good to keep on the farm. Howard hit .300 or better three times with New York, and hit 20 or more home runs three times.

But his principal strength was defensive. Howard led American League catchers in fielding with a .998 mark in 1964, and was usually among the league leaders. His career .993 mark is tied for first place all-time with Bill Freehan and Jim Sundberg.

Howard also was a deft handler of pitchers, and he pioneered the use of the hinged catcher's mitt, which led to the modern one-handed catching technique.

He won the MVP award in 1963, hitting .287 with 28 home runs and 85 RBI. His stats weren't overwhelming, but he was the clear leader of the Yankees' pennant-winners, especially since both Mickey Mantle and Roger Maris battled injuries.

In 1967, he was traded to the Red Sox, and helped Boston win its first pennant in 29 years.

LIFETIME STATS: BA: .274, HR: 167, RBI: 762, H: 1,471, SB: 9

#190 Joseph Paul "Joe" Torre
C-1B-3B, Braves, Cardinals, Mets, 1960–77

Torre was one of the most versatile players of the 1960s. He started out as a catcher with the Braves, and finished second behind Billy Williams in the Rookie of the Year voting. In 1963, he became Milwaukee's regular catcher, and hit .293 with 14 homers and 71 RBI.

The next season, his stats improved, even though he split his time between catching and playing first base. Torre hit .321, with 20 homers and 109 RBI, led all catchers in fielding percentage and again made the All Star team. Torre won a Gold Glove in 1965, and hit 27 home runs. In 1968, he led the league's catchers in fielding with a .996 mark.

Torre was traded to St. Louis, and, after a year, became the Cardinals' starting third baseman. He responded with a tremendous season in 1971; leading the league with a .363 batting average, 137 RBI and 230 hits, Torre easily won the MVP Award. He also led the league's third basemen in putouts.

After two years at third, the Cardinals moved Torre back to first base, and he hit .280 or better for the next three years. He was traded to the Mets in 1975, and hit .306 while splitting time between first and third base.

LIFETIME STATS: BA: .297, HR: 252, RBI: 1,185, H: 2,342, SB: 23

#191 Donald Howard "Don" Sutton
RHP, Dodgers, Astros, Brewers, Athletics, Angels, 1966–88. Hall of Fame, 1998

Sutton was a smart, tough pitcher who knew his limitations and parlayed that knowledge into a Hall of Fame career.

Sutton began his career with the Dodgers, and was named Rookie of the Year in 1966, when his 209 strikeouts were the most by a first-year player since Grover Cleveland Alexander's 227 in 1911. Sutton struck out 200 or more batters five times in his career.

Sutton played in the shadow of other Dodger greats, such as Sandy Koufax and Don Drysdale, for several years. But by 1971, with a 17–12 record, 194 strikeouts and four shutouts, Sutton was the ace of the staff.

Sutton was always in tremendous condition, and it served him well. He played 23 years in the bigs, and never spent a day on the disabled list, and his durability enabled him to become the first pitcher ever to win 300 or more games while breaking the 20-game mark only once.

Sutton never pitched a no-hitter, but he did pitch five one-hitters and nine two-hitters. He was more of a control pitcher than a strikeout king, walking 80 or more batters only three in his career, and usually issuing around 50 to 60 free passes a season.

Sutton was tough in the postseason, although none of his teams ever won a World Series. He was 6–4 overall in postseason games, with 61 strikeouts in 100 innings.

LIFETIME STATS: W: 324, L: 256, SV: 5, ERA: 3.26, SO: 3,574, CG: 178

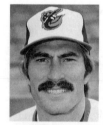

#192 Robert Anthony "Bobby" Grich
2B-SS, Orioles, Angels, 1970–86

Grich was a superb defensive second baseman with excellent home run power. At 6'2", Grich was considered big for a second baseman, but he was agile, with very good reflexes and hands, and performed well in the infield.

Grich had two brief stints with Baltimore in 1970–71, and became a regular in 1972, hitting .278, with 12 home runs and 21 doubles. He was the starter in the All Star team that year, the first of six All Star appearances for Grich.

In 1973, Grich set a major league record for fielding percentage (.995) at second base, and had 12 home runs and 29 doubles on the offense side of his ledger.

Grich, in fact, hit 12 or more home runs 12 times in his career, with a high of 30 in 1979 with California. He led the league with 22 home runs in strike-shortened 1981.

But he was perhaps more impressive in the field. Grich won four consecutive Gold Gloves from 1973–76, and in 1985, his next-to-last year in the league, he set another major league fielding record with a .997 percentage. His percentage is ninth all-time.

LIFETIME STATS: BA: .266, HR: 224, RBI: 864, H: 1,833, SB: 104

#193 Harold Henry "Pee Wee," "The Little Colonel" Reese

SS-3B, Dodgers, 1940–42, 1946–58. Hall of Fame, 1984

Reese, at 5'10", wasn't a small man, and in fact his name came from his prowess at marbles as a youngster. A "pee wee" is a kind of marble. But the name stuck with him throughout his life.

Reese was initially signed by the Red Sox, but incumbent Sox shortstop Joe Cronin was also the incumbent Sox manager, and manager Cronin wasn't planning on replacing player Cronin any time soon. So the Sox sold Reese to the Brooklyn Dodgers.

In 1940, Reese's rookie season, he was hampered by a heel injury and missed a good part of the season. But he healed by 1941, and his defensive presence in the infield sparked the Dodgers to their first pennant in 21 years.

Reese was the best shortstop in the National League in the mid-1940s to the early 1950s. Reese lost three years (1943–45) to World War II. But the

Dodgers won seven pennants and one World Champion with him in the lineup.

Reese was an exceptional leadoff hitter. He drew 90 or more walks four times in his career, leading the league with 104 in 1947. He scored 90 or more runs eight times, leading the league with 132 in 1949. And he stole 20 or more bases five times, leading the league with 30 in 1952.

Reese hit .272 in World Series play, including .345 in the 1952 series and .316 in 1949. In the 1955 World Series, which the Dodgers won, Reese hit .296 and scored five runs.

LIFETIME STATS: BA: .269, HR: 126, RBI: 885, H: 2,170, SB: 232

#**194** Zachary Davis "Zack," "Buck" Wheat

OF, Dodgers, Athletics, 1909–27. Hall of Fame, 1959

Wheat was one of the first great stars for the Dodgers: a graceful fielder, durable hitter and a leader in the clubhouse. Wheat manned left field for Brooklyn from 1910 until 1926, and almost never sat out a game.

Wheat was named Zachary after President Zachary Taylor. Similarly, his younger brother, McKinley, who also made the big leagues, was named after President William McKinley.

Wheat was Brooklyn's cleanup hitter for most of his tenure, and he performed his duties well. He hit .300 or better 13 times, including a league-leading .335 in 1918. He topped 20 or more doubles 13 times, as well, with a high of 42 in 1925. Wheat was also a pretty good base-stealer, and swiped 11 or more bases nine times in his career.

Wheat was one of the best curveball hitters of his era. He was, in fact, so good that Giant manager John McGraw forbade his pitchers to throw curves to Wheat.

Wheat was even-tempered and, in his later years, known to take rookies under his wing. Wheat took in a young Casey Stengel when Casey broke in with the Dodgers, a gesture which Casey always appreciated.

Wheat was released by the Dodgers in January of 1927, but was quickly signed by the Athletics, and hit .324 in his last year as a part-time player.

LIFETIME STATS: BA: .317, HR: 132, RBI: 1,248, H: 2,884, SB: 205

#**195** Roger Eugene Maris

OF, Indians, Athletics, Yankees, Cardinals, 1957–68

When Roger Maris his 61 home runs in 1961, it was, in many ways, an unfortunate thing. It was unfortunate because Maris was one of the best all-around players in the 1960s: a superb outfielder with a cannon arm, a very good base runner and, of course, an explosive offensive star.

All this was submerged in that 1961 season, and when Maris wasn't as graceful a player as teammate Mickey Mantle in dealing with the press, he was labeled a malcontent. His mistakes were magnified, his accomplishments downplayed.

This isn't an editorial in favor of Roger Maris; it is fact. Maris drove in 100 or more runs three times in his career, leading the league with 112 in 1960 and 142 in 1961. He scored 85 or more runs five times in his career, with a league-best 132 in 1961. He had 16 or more doubles seven times in his career, and 20 or more home runs six times.

It surprises some people that Maris was MVP of the league in 1960, a year before he hit 61 homers. He deserved it. He hit 39 homers, drove in 112 runs, batted .283 and scored 98 runs. He also collected a Gold Glove.

His 1961 MVP season was more of the same: the record-breaking 61 dingers, a league-leading 142 RBI, 132 runs scored (also a league best), 16 doubles and a .269 batting average. Maris won the Hickok Belt as the best professional athlete in the world.

It was rumored that Mantle and Maris didn't get along during the 1961 season. Ridiculous. They were roommates for most of the year, and the gracious Mantle was always encouraging of Rog.

In 1967, Maris was traded to St. Louis, and helped the Cardinals to a pair of World Series, including a win over the Red Sox that year.

LIFETIME STATS: BA: .260, HR: 275, RBI: 851, H: 1,325, SB: 21

#**196** Enos Bradsher "Country" Slaughter

OF, Cardinals, Yankees, Athletics, Braves, 1938–42, 1946–59. Hall of Fame, 1985

Slaughter was a hustling, talented country boy from North Carolina, who sparked the Cardinals of the 1940s to a pair of World Championships.

Slaughter was an exceptional player who was a starter his first year in the major leagues, which was 1938. He hit .276 with 20 doubles and 59 runs scored that first season. But the next year, Slaughter took off. He hit .320, led the league in doubles with 52 and had 193 hits.

Slaughter went on to hit .300 or better 10 times, scored 100 runs three times, drove in over 100 three times and had 10 or more triples seven times. He led the league in three-baggers with 17 in 1942 and 13 in 1949.

Slaughter had a good World Series in 1942 against the Yankees, but he tore up the Red Sox in 1946. He hit .320, scored five runs and had a double, triple and home run in the series. And it was Slaughter, of course, whose mad dash from first base in Game Seven scored the winning run and gave the Cardinals the championship.

Slaughter was a southerner, and something of a racist. He was one of the principals who were unhappy when Jackie Robinson was signed by the Dodgers. Slaughter tried to get other players to boycott Brooklyn, but he failed.

LIFETIME STATS: BA: .300, HR: 169, RBI: 1,304, H: 2,383, SB: 71

#197 Thomas William "Tommy" Leach

OF-3B-SS-2B, Louisville (NL), Pirates, Cubs, Reds, 1898–15, 1918

Leach was one of the fastest men of his era. He hit 63 home runs in his career, and 49 of them were inside-the-park homers. In 1903, he hit seven home runs, all inside the park. A year before, four of his league-leading six home runs were inside-the-park jobs.

Leach was one of the best leadoff men of the early 20th century. He scored 90 or more runs in a season seven times, leading the league in 1909 with 126 and in 1913 with 99. He hit .300 or better twice, and .298 one other time in his career.

As he got older, Leach's patience also improved. The early part of his career, he rarely walked more than 40 times a year. But as he got older, he took free passes to first base between 40 and 79 times a year.

Aggressive on the base paths, he stole 15 or more bases 16 times in his career, with a career-best 43 in 1907.

Leach also did pretty well in the World Series. He hit a series-record four triples in 1903 against Boston, and batted .273 in a losing cause. But he and the Pirates won it all in 1908, as Leach hit .360 with four doubles.

LIFETIME STATS: BA: .269, HR: 63, RBI: 810, H: 2,143, SB: 361

#198 Clarence Algernon "Cupid" Childs

2B, Phillies, Syracuse (AA), Cleveland (NL), Cardinals, Cubs, 1888, 1890–1901

Childs was the leadoff man for the Cleveland Spiders throughout the 1890s, and was one of the keys to their offense.

Childs hit .300 or better six times in his career, and scored 100 or more runs seven times. He led the National League in runs scored with 136 in 1892.

An explosive base runner, Childs stole 20 or more bases seven times in his career, with a high of 56 while he was with Syracuse in the old American Association in 1890. That was also the year he led the AA in doubles with 33. In all, Childs would hit 15 or more doubles seven times in his career.

He had a good batting eye. Childs was tough to strike out, and in 1893, he walked 120 times and struck out only 12 times.

Childs was also a better-than-average defensive player. He set a since-tied record with 18 chances accepted at second base in 1888, and was among the leader in the National League in assists and putouts while with Cleveland.

LIFETIME STATS: BA: .306, HR: 20, RBI: 743, H: 1,720, SB: 269

#199 Vladimir Alvino Guerrero

OF-DH, Expos, Angels, 1996–present

A fearsome combination of hitting ability and power, Guerrero has hit .300 or better (usually much better) every year he has played full-time in the majors. He was signed by the Expos as an amateur free agent in 1993, and made it to the big club for a cup of coffee in 1996.

He came up for good in 1997 and hit .302 with 11 homers in 90 games. It was his worst year as a regular. The eight-time All Star was the American League MVP in 2004, the year he was signed by the Angels. He hit .337 with 39 home runs and 126 RBI. He could have won the award a few other times, most notably in 2002, when he hit .336, with 39 homers and 111 runs batted in. Vladi, as Angel fans call him, has also hit 34 or more home runs eight times in his career. He is regularly among the league leaders in intentional walks, and has led the league from 2005 to 2007.

In the postseason, Guerrero's best year was 2005, when he hit .333 in a win over the Yankees in the first round of the playoffs.

LIFETIME STATS: BA: .318, HR: 449, RBI: 1,496, H: 2,590, SB: 184

#200 James Paul David "Jim" Bunning

RHP, Tigers, Phillies, Pirates, Dodgers, 1955–71. Hall of Fame, 1996

Bunning spent nine years in the American League and eight in the National League. At the end of his career, he became the first pitcher since Cy Young to win 100 games in each league.

Bunning began his career with the Tigers in 1955, but spent two years as a spot starter and went 8–6. Coaches were concerned about his odd delivery, an awkward-looking sidearm delivery that pulled him off balance after every pitch.

The delivery may have looked awkward, but so did the folks who batted against Bunning. The ball came in especially sharply against right-handed hitters, and was difficult for them to pick up.

Bunning was 20–8 for Detroit in 1957, but, ironically, never won 20 games again. He won 19 with Detroit in 1962 and then, after being traded, won 19 games three years in a row for the Phillies, but never cracked 20.

No matter. He struck out 200 or more batters six times in his career, including three years where he led the league. Bunning was also an "inning-eater," in that he rarely came out of games. He threw 300 or more innings twice in his career and led the league one other time with 267 1/3 innings pitched in 1957.

Bunning had excellent control, never walking more than 79 batters in a season. In 1966, he had 55 walks in 314 innings.

LIFETIME STATS: W: 224, L: 184, SV: 16, ERA: 3.27, SO: 2,855, CG: 151

#**201** Ted Lyle Simmons

C-DH-1B, Cardinals, Brewers, Braves, 1968–88

The consistent Simmons hit .300 or better seven times in his career and also drove in 90 or more runs in eight seasons. The eight-time All Star ranked among the league leaders in doubles eight times. Simmons hit two home runs in the 1982 World Series, though the Brewers ultimately lost to the Cardinals. He led AL catchers with a .995 fielding percentage for the Brewers in 1982.

LIFETIME STATS: BA: .285, HR: 248, RBI: 1,389, H: 2,472, SB: 21

#202 Ronald Charles "The Penguin" Cey

3B, Dodgers, Cubs, A's, 1971–87

Nicknamed "the Penguin" because of his stocky stature, Cey was named co-MVP of the 1981 World Series, along with Steve Yeager and Pedro Guerrero. He hit .350 with six RBI in the Series, helping lead the Dodgers over the Yankees. Cey hit 22 or more home runs a season 10 times and led National League third basemen in fielding percentage in 1979 and putouts in 1980.

LIFETIME STATS: BA: .261, HR: 316, RBI: 1,139, H: 1,868, SB: 24

#203 Clarence Arthur "Dazzy" Vance

RHP, Pirates, Yankees, Brooklyn Dodgers, Cardinals, Reds, 1915, 1918, 1922–35. Hall of Fame, 1955

Vance earned his nickname because he was something of a carouser. He was named National League MVP in 1924 with the Dodgers, and led league pitchers that year with a 2.16 ERA, 28 wins and 262 strikeouts. Vance topped the National League three times in ERA, twice in wins, and led the league seven consecutive seasons in strikeouts, from 1922 to 1928. Vance led the league in shutouts four times and collected 170 or more strikeouts six times.

LIFETIME STATS: W: 197, L: 140, SV: 11, ERA: 3.24, SO: 2,045, CG: 216

#204 Don Richard "Richie" Ashburn
OF, Phillies, Cubs, Mets, 1948–62. Hall of Fame, 1995

Ashburn was an excellent batsman, hitting .300 or better in nine seasons. He ranked among the National League batting average leaders nine times, topping the league in 1955 and 1958 with the Phillies. He led the league three times in hits and twice in triples. The ultimate leadoff man, Ashburn held the league's highest on-base percentage four times, and collected 180 or more hits eight times.

LIFETIME STATS: BA: .308, HR: 29, RBI: 586, H: 2,574, SB: 234

#205 Bobby Lee Bonds
OF, Giants, Yankees, Angels, White Sox, Rangers, Indians, Cardinals, Cubs, 1968–81

Now known as "Barry's dad," Bonds was a leadoff man with power. He stole 30 or more bases in a season 10 times, and hit 25 or more home runs nine times. He led the National League in runs scored twice with the Giants, and in fact scored 100 or more runs a season six times. Bonds set a major league record, hitting 30 or more home runs for five different teams, but he was also a solid defensive player, winning three Gold Gloves in the outfield.

LIFETIME STATS: BA: .268, HR: 332, RBI: 1,024, H: 1,886, SB: 461

#206 Frederick Stanley McGriff

1B-DH, Blue Jays, Padres, Braves, Devil Rays, Cubs, Dodgers, 1986–2003

McGriff was the epitome of power and consistency in the 1990s and into the 21st century. He hit 30 or more home runs in a season 10 times, and drove in 100 or more runs eight times. McGriff led his league twice in home runs. He was named MVP of the 1994 All Star game for a game-tying, ninth-inning home run. McGriff was also known as a clutch man in the postseason, batting .303 over 10 postseason series with 10 home runs and 37 RBI. He was a five-time All Star.

LIFETIME STATS: BA: .285, HR: 491, RBI: 1,543, H: 2,477, SB: 72

#207 Cesar Cedeno

OF-1B, Astros, Reds, Cardinals, Dodgers, 1970–86

Cedeno was the defensive keystone when he was with Houston, winning five Gold Gloves, from 1972 to 1976. In addition, the swift Cedeno averaged 44 stolen bases a year over his 17-season career. He stole 50 or more bases six times. Cedeno led the National League in doubles, 1971–72, and hit 35 or more doubles five times. He recorded his highest power numbers in 1974, hitting 26 home runs with 102 RBI for the Astros.

LIFETIME STATS: BA: .285, HR: 199, RBI: 976, H: 2,087, SB: 550

#208 Philip Francis "The Scooter" Rizzuto

SS, Yankees, 1941–42, 1946–56. Hall of Fame, 1994

"The Scooter," so named for his size (5'6", 160 pounds) and quickness, has been unfairly tagged as being just a good player on a series of great Yankees teams. Well, he was named 1950 American League MVP, with a .324 batting average, 200 hits, 125 runs and 36 doubles, and defensively, led AL shortstops in fielding percentage and putouts. He was clearly the glue of the Yankee champs of the early 1950s. He topped league shortstops three times in double plays and twice in fielding percentage and putouts.

LIFETIME STATS: BA: .273, HR: 38, RBI: 563, H: 1,588, SB: 149

#209 Jesse Cail "The Crab" Burkett

OF, New York Giants, Cleveland Spiders, Cardinals, St. Louis Browns, Red Sox, 1890–1905. Hall of Fame, 1946

Called "the Crab" because of his caustic remarks to teammates and foes alike, Burkett hit over .400 twice with Cleveland, in back-to-back years, 1895–96. Overall, he won three batting titles and led his league in hits three times. Burkett hit .300 or better 11 times in his 16-year career. A speedy runner on the base paths, Burkett topped the league twice in runs. He tallied 100 or more runs in eight consecutive seasons, 1892–99. His .338 career batting average ranks 19th-highest of all time.

LIFETIME STATS: BA: .338, HR: 75, RBI: 952, H: 2,850, SB: 389

#**210** Leon Allen "Goose" Goslin

OF, Senators, St. Louis Browns, Tigers, 1921–38. Hall of Fame, 1968

The "Goose" (so named because of his last name) hit .300 or better 11 times in his career. He drove in 100 or more runs 11 times, and scored 100 or more runs seven times. In 1928, the Goose led the American League with a .379 batting average for the Senators. A good man to have in the postseason, Goslin drove in the Series-clinching run in the 1935 World Series, helping the Tigers defeat the Cubs. He also hit .344 in the 1924 World Series, with three home runs and seven RBI for the Senators.

LIFETIME STATS: BA: .316, HR: 248, RBI: 1,609, H: 2,735, SB: 175

#**211** James Hoyt Wilhelm

RHP, New York Giants, Cardinals, Indians, Orioles, White Sox, Angels, Braves, Dodgers, 1952–72. Hall of Fame, 1985

The ageless Wilhelm became the first relief pitcher to be voted into the Hall of Fame. Durable, and with a rubber arm, Wilhelm ranked among league leaders in saves 14 times. Wilhelm was the master of the knuckleball, and led his league twice in ERA, in 1952 and 1959. He kept his ERA below 2.00 in five consecutive seasons, 1964–68. Wilhelm did sometimes start, and in 1958, he threw a no-hitter against the Yankees. His 651 games finished ranks sixth-most of all time.

LIFETIME STATS: W: 143, L: 122, SV: 227, ERA: 2.52, SO: 1,610, CG: 20

#212 Mark Eugene Grace
1B, Cubs, Diamondbacks, 1988–2003

The popular Grace was the anchor of the Cubs' infield from 1988 to 1999, winning four Gold Glove awards in that span. Grace hit .300 or better in nine seasons. His best postseason was 1989, when he batted .647 with eight RBI in the 1989 NLCS, though the Cubs lost to the Giants. Grace batted .329 over six postseason series. He led the NL with 51 doubles in 1995 and ranked among NL on-base percentage leaders seven times.

LIFETIME STATS: BA: .303, HR: 173, RBI: 1,146, H: 2,445, SB: 70

#213 Norman Dalton Cash
1B, White Sox, Tigers, 1958–74

Cash's best year was 1961, when he led the American League with a .361 batting average, a .487 on-base percentage and 193 hits. He also reached career highs that year of 132 RBI, 41 home runs, 119 runs and 124 walks. A powerful slugger, Cash ranked among the league's home-run leaders nine times. He batted .385 in the 1968 World Series, with a home run and five RBI, to help the Tigers beat the Cardinals in a thrilling seven-game Series.

LIFETIME STATS: BA: .271, HR: 377, RBI: 1,103, H: 1,820, SB: 43

#214 Ted "Double Duty" Radcliffe

C-RHP, Detroit Stars, St. Louis Stars, Homestead Grays, Pittsburgh Crawfords, Columbus Blue Birds, New York Black Yankees, Brooklyn Eagles, Cincinnati Tigers, Memphis Red Sox, Birmingham Black Barons, Chicago American Giants, Louisville Buckeyes (Negro Leagues),1928–50

Radcliffe was called "Double Duty" because he often pitched one end of a doubleheader, and then donned catcher's gear and caught the second game. His most famous "double duty" came in 1931, when, playing for the Homestead Grays, he caught Lefty Williams's five-hitter in the first game of a doubleheader during the Negro League World Series, then pitched in the second game, which he lost, 8–1, to the Kansas City Monarchs. A six-time All Star, Radcliff played three All Star games as a pitcher and three as a catcher.

LIFETIME STATS: BA: .313, W: 64, L: 42

#215 Steven Patrick "Steve" Garvey

1B-3B, Dodgers, Padres, 1969–87

The affable Garvey was also nicknamed "Popeye" because of his enormous forearms. He was named the 1974 National League MVP, batting .312 with 200 hits, 111 RBI and 21 home runs. Garvey was also voted the All Star game MVP twice, in 1974 and 1978. An excellent fielder, he won four Gold Gloves at first base, from 1974 to 1977. The National League Championship Series MVP twice, Garvey batted .338 over 11 postseason series, with 11 home runs and 31 RBI. He hit .300 or better seven times with the Dodgers, six times collecting 200 or more hits.

LIFETIME STATS: BA: .294, HR: 272, RBI: 1,308, H: 2,599, SB: 83

#**216** Kenneth Wayne "Ken" Singleton

OF-DH, Mets, Expos, Orioles, 1970–84

Singleton led the American League in 1973 with a .425 on-base percentage, which also set an Orioles franchise record. He has ranked among his league's on-base percentage leaders nine times. He has also hit 20 or more home runs five times in his career. In 1979, Singleton, who bats from both sides of the plate, became one of only three switch-hitters in history to hit 35 or more home runs in a season. He batted .300 or better four times.

LIFETIME STATS: BA: .282, HR: 246, RBI: 1,065, H: 2,029, SB: 21

#**217** Harold "Prince Hal" Newhouser

LHP, Tigers, Indians, 1939–55. Hall of Fame, 1992

Newhouser was the most dominant pitcher in baseball from 1944 to 1946, and remains the only American League pitcher to be MVP in consecutive seasons, 1944–45. Newhouser, with his explosive fastball and big roundhouse curve, led the AL in 1944 with 29 wins and 187 strikeouts, and posted a second-best 2.22 ERA. He topped the league in 1945 with a 1.81 ERA, 25 wins and 212 strikeouts. Overall, Newhouser led the AL in wins four times. He ranked among the league's top eight strikeout leaders in nine consecutive seasons, 1941–49.

LIFETIME STATS: W: 207, L: 150, SV: 26, ERA: 3.06, SO: 1,796, CG: 212

#**218** Gilbert Raymond "Gil" Hodges

1B, Brooklyn Dodgers, Los Angeles Dodgers, Mets, 1943, 1947–63

The affable, muscular Hodges was the best first baseman of his generation. A three-time Gold Glove winner, 1957–59, Hodges hit 20 or more home runs in 11 consecutive seasons with the Dodgers, from 1949 to 1959. He collected 100 or more RBI seven times, 1949–55. Hodges hit four home runs in one game against the Braves in 1950. His postseason work was also impressive. Hodges hit game-winning home runs for the Dodgers in the 1956 and 1959 World Series.

LIFETIME STATS: BA: .273, HR: 370, RBI: 1,274, H: 1,921, SB: 63

#**219** James Sherman "Jimmy," "The Toy Cannon" Wynn

OF, Astros, Dodgers, Braves, Yankees, Brewers, 1963–77

The muscular Wynn was 5'9"and 170 pounds. He hit 20 or more home runs eight times in his career, hence his nickname. Wynn was also fast, as he stole 43 bases in 1965, his first full season with the Astros, and scored 90 runs. He led his team that year with a .275 batting average and 73 RBI. Wynn twice hit three home runs in one game and led the National League in walks twice, in 1969 and 1976. In 1974, Wynn's hitting carried the slumping Dodgers during the first part of the season. Los Angeles would eventually win the National League pennant that year, with Wynn hitting .271 with 32 homers.

LIFETIME STATS: BA: .250, HR: 291, RBI: 964, H: 1,665, SB: 225

#220 David Ismael Concepcion
SS-2B-3B, Reds, 1970–88

The versatile Concepcion was the cornerstone of the defense for the infield of Cincinnati's "Big Red Machine" in the 1970s. A five-time Gold Glove winner at short-stop, Concepcion was named Reds MVP in 1981, batting .306 with 129 hits, 28 doubles and 67 RBI. He led the National League that year with 14 game-winning RBI. He had several great postseason series. He hit .455 in the 1975 National League Championship Series, leading the Reds over Pittsburgh with a home run and two stolen bases. Concepcion hit .429 in the 1979 NLCS, though the Reds lost to the Pirates.

LIFETIME STATS: BA: .267, HR: 101, RBI: 950, H: 2,326, SB: 321

#221 Anthony Nomar Garciaparra
SS-1B-2B-3B-DH, Red Sox, Cubs, Dodgers, 1996–2007

It's interesting that, despite a number of injuries in the past several years, Garciaparra has continued to play at a pretty high level, especially in terms of his offensive production. In 2004, he played only 81 games and still hit .308. He played 62 games in 2005 and still hit .283.

The Rookie of the Year for Boston in 1997, Garcia-parra had a very bright future. For awhile, he was everything Boston fans hoped for and more: He won back-to-back batting titles in 1999 (.357) and 2000 (.372). He was a five-time All Star as a Sox. And from 1997 to 2003, he was in the MVP voting top 10 every year except 2001, an injury year, and 2002, when he finished 11th.

But he was traded by Boston to the Cubs midway through the 2004 season, and the fortunes of both parties went in opposite directions. For Boston, the trade helped the team win the World Series. For Nomar, the trade began several years of struggling with physical problems.

Still, when healthy, which he has been for the last two seasons, Garciaparra is very, very good. He hit .303 in 2006, with 20 home runs and 90 RBI.

LIFETIME STATS: BA: .315, HR: 213, RBI: 874, H: 1,618, SB: 91

#222 Henry Emmett "Heinie" Manush

OF, Tigers, St. Louis Browns, Senators, Red Sox, Brooklyn Dodgers, Pirates, 1923–39. Hall of Fame, 1964

The left-handed, line-drive-hitting Manush hit .300 or better 11 times in his 17-season career, and ranked among league batting average leaders nine times. His one batting title came in 1926 with a .378 batting average for the Tigers, beating out Babe Ruth. Manush twice led the AL in hits and doubles. He collected 200 or more hits a season four times and scored 100 or more runs six times.

LIFETIME STATS: BA: .330, HR: 110, RBI: 1,183, H: 2,524, SB: 114

#223 Daniel Joseph "Rusty" Staub

OF-DH-1B, Astros, Expos, Mets, Tigers, Rangers, 1963–85

Staub led the American League with 44 doubles for the Astros in 1967, batting a career-high .333. He also topped his league four times in outfield assists. The husky (some said he was overweight) Staub was a fan favorite everywhere he played. He logged 500 or more hits for the Astros, Expos, Mets and Tigers. He batted .423 with a home run and six RBI in the 1973 World Series, though the Mets ultimately lost to the A's.

LIFETIME STATS: BA: .279, HR: 292, RBI: 1,466, H: 2,716, SB: 47

#**224** Vernon Decatur "Vern" Stephens

SS-3B, St. Louis Browns, Red Sox, White Sox, Orioles, 1941–55

Stephens showed unusual power for a shortstop, and led the American League in 1945 with 24 home runs for the Browns. His power stats peaked in 1949, as Stephens hit a career-high 39 home runs with 159 RBI for the Red Sox. An eight-time All Star, Stephens ranked seven times among league leaders in hits and home runs. He also led the AL three times in RBI. Defensively he led league shortstops three times in assists.

LIFETIME STATS: BA: .286, HR: 247, RBI: 1,174, H: 1,859, SB: 25

#**225** Richard Benjamin "Rick" Ferrell

C, St. Louis Browns, Red Sox, Senators, 1929–45, 1947. Hall of Fame, 1984

The durable Ferrell set an American League record, catching 1,806 games in his career, a mark that has since been broken. He also batted .290 or better in six consecutive seasons with St. Louis and Boston, 1931–36. An eight-time All Star, Ferrell hit .312 with a career-high eight home runs for Boston in 1936. He topped AL catchers in 1938 with 15 double plays for the Red Sox.

LIFETIME STATS: BA: .281, HR: 28, RBI: 734, H: 1,692, SB: 29

#**226** Richard Morrow "Dick" Groat
SS, Pirates, Cardinals, Phillies, Giants, 1952, 1955–67

The athletic Groat was an All-American basketball player at Duke and played briefly for the Fort Wayne Pistons of the NBA. But baseball was his love. He was named National League MVP in 1960, batting a league-high .325 with 186 hits and 85 runs for the Pirates. Groat also led the National League in 1963 with 43 doubles for the Cardinals. He hit .300 or better four times in his career. Groat led NL shortstops four times in double plays, and regularly ranked among leaders in putouts, assists and fielding percentage.

LIFETIME STATS: BA: .286, HR: 39, RBI: 707, H: 2,138, SB: 14

#**227** James Joseph "Jimmy" Collins
3B, Louisville Colonels, Boston Beaneaters (NL), Red Sox, Philadelphia A's, 1895–1908. Hall of Fame, 1945

Collins was a star in Boston, leading the National League with 15 home runs and 286 total bases for the Beaneaters in 1898. His 111 RBI were second-best in the league that year. But he jumped to the fledgeling Boston franchise of the newly formed American League, and helped them to the championship of the first World Series in 1903. The best defensive third sacker of his era, Collins led league third basemen in putouts five times and assists four times. His 2,372 career putouts at third base still stand, almost 100 years later, as second-most of all time.

LIFETIME STATS: BA: .294, HR: 65, RBI: 983, H: 1,999, SB: 194

#228 Lawrence Joseph "Larry" Doyle

2B, New York Giants, Cubs, 1907–20

Doyle was named National League MVP in 1912, batting .330 with 90 RBI, 98 runs and 36 stolen bases for the Giants. In 1915, he won the batting championship with a .320 batting average and a league-best 40 doubles. Doyle, who coined the phrase "It's great to be young and a Giant," led the league in hits twice, stole 30 or more bases five times in his career, and batted .300 or better five times.

LIFETIME STATS: BA: .290, HR: 74, RBI: 793, H: 1,887, SB: 298

#229 Charles Ernest "King Kong" Keller

OF, Yankees, Tigers, 1939–43, 1945–52

Keller, whose nickname came because of his tremendous strength, hit .438 with three home runs and six RBI in the 1939 World Series, helping the Yankees defeat the Reds. Keller was a terrific postseason player who batted .306 over four World Series with the Yankees. He hit a career-high 33 home runs with 122 RBI in 1941. Keller hit 20 or more home runs five times and collected 100 or more runs and RBI three times.

LIFETIME STATS: BA: .286, HR: 189, RBI: 760, H: 1,085, SB: 45

#230 John Kling

C, Cubs, Boston Braves, Reds, 1900–08, 1910–13

Kling, the National League's premier defensive catcher at the turn of the 20th century, led all backstoppers in putouts six times and fielding percentage four times. He dominated the 1907 World Series, throwing out half of the 14 Tigers trying to steal second. He ranked among NL leaders in slugging percentage from 1906 to 1908. Kling logged career-high numbers in 1903 with 68 RBI, 13 triples, 29 doubles, 146 hits and 67 runs for the Cubs.

LIFETIME STATS: BA: .271, HR: 20, RBI: 513, H: 1,151, SB: 123

#231 David Gus "Buddy" Bell

3B-OF, Indians, Rangers, Reds, Astros, 1972–89

Bell was the best defensive third baseman of the late 1970s and early 1980s, winning six consecutive Gold Gloves from 1979 to 1984 for Texas. He led AL third basemen three times in assists and putouts, and twice in fielding percentage and double plays. Bell was also a strong batter, hitting .292 or better six times in his career. He peaked offensively in 1979, his first year with Texas, hitting career highs of 101 RBI, 42 doubles, 200 hits and 89 runs.

LIFETIME STATS: BA: .279, HR: 201, RBI: 1,106, H: 2,514, SB: 55

#232 Dennis Lee "Eck" Eckersley

RHP, Indians, Red Sox, Cubs, A's, Cardinals, 1975–98. Hall of Fame, 2004

Eckersley began his career as a starter for the Indians, Red Sox and Cubs from 1975 to 1986, and was a two-time All Star and a 20-game winner for Boston in 1978. But "Eck" reinvented himself in 1987 and went to the bullpen. The result was basically a whole new career as a reliever, in which he was even more successful. He was named 1992 American League MVP and Cy Young award winner and led the AL with 51 saves that year, logging a 1.91 ERA for the A's. He recorded 40 or more saves four times and ranked among league leaders in saves from 1987 to 1997. Eckersley ranks third among all-time saves leaders.

LIFETIME STATS: W: 197, L: 171, SV: 390, ERA: 3.50, SO: 2,401, CG: 100

#233 Richard John "Dick" McAuliffe

2B-SS-3B, Tigers, Red Sox, 1960–75

McAuliffe ranked among American League leaders in triples eight times, from 1963 to 1969 and again in 1971. He also led the AL in 1968 with 95 runs scored. He helped the Tigers clinch a world championship that year over the Cardinals, hitting a home run and collecting three RBI in the Series. McAuliffe was one of the best leadoff men ever, tying a major league record by going the entire 1968 season without hitting into a double play.

LIFETIME STATS: BA: .247, HR: 197, RBI: 697, H: 1,530, SB: 63

#234 Theodore Bernard "Big Klu" Kluszewski

1B, Reds, Pirates, White Sox, Angels, 1947–61

The hulking (6'2", 225 pounds) Kluszewski led the National League in 1954 with 49 home runs and 141 RBI. The next season, he led the league with 192 hits. "Klu" hit 40 or more home runs over three consecutive seasons with the Reds, from 1953 to 1955, and batted .300 or better seven times in his career. He also logged 100 or more RBI five times. But Kluszewski was also graceful afield, and led NL first basemen in fielding percentage four consecutive years, from 1951 to 1955.

LIFETIME STATS: BA: .298, HR: 279, RBI: 1,028, H: 1,766, SB: 20

#235 John Alexander "King Bid" McPhee

2B, Cincinnati Red Stockings, Reds, 1882–99. Hall of Fame, 2000

In an era where great fielders were held in high regard, Bid McPhee was the best of the best. With 529 putouts in 1886, McPhee set a season record for a second baseman. His record still stands, 108 years later. McPhee is still the career leader in putouts with 6,549 and fourth in assists with 6,909. He led league second basemen in double plays 11 times in his career, and in fielding percentage nine times. McPhee was also a smart base runner, stealing 30 or more bases ten times.

LIFETIME STATS: BA: .271, HR: 53, RBI: 1,067, H: 2,250, SB: 568

#**236** Joseph Bert Tinker

SS, Cubs, Reds, Chicago Whales (FL), 1902–16. Hall of Fame, 1946

Tinker was, of course, best known as part of the Cubs' infield that included second baseman Johnny Evers and first baseman Frank Chance. He was a solid infielder, and led National League shortstops four times in fielding percentage, three times in total chances and twice in assists and putouts. Only an average hitter, Tinker stole 25 or more bases a season eight times in his career.

LIFETIME STATS: BA: .262, HR: 31, RBI: 782, H: 1,687, SB: 336

#**237** Carl William Mays

RHP, Red Sox, Yankees, Reds, New York Giants, 1915–29

Mays led the American League with 27 wins and seven saves for the Yankees in 1921, while also batting .343. He logged 20 or more wins a season five times in his career. He threw two complete-game victories in one 1918 doubleheader, holding Philadelphia to one run. Mays also threw two complete-game wins in the 1918 World Series, posting a 1.00 ERA. He threw almost underhand, a "submarine" delivery that may have contributed to the fatal beaning of Ray Chapman.

LIFETIME STATS: W: 207, L: 126, SV: 31, ERA: 2.92, SO: 862, CG: 231

#238 Earle Bryan Combs

OF, Yankees, 1924–35. Hall of Fame, 1970

The speedy Combs was the Yankees' leadoff man in the glory years of the mid- to late 1920s. He hit .300 or better in eight full seasons. Combs also collected 190 or more hits five times, and scored 100 or more runs in eight consecutive seasons, 1925–32. He led the American League in 1927 with 231 hits and 23 triples, both Yankee team records. He led the AL three times in triples. His postseason record was equally impressive, as Combs batted .350 over four World Series.

LIFETIME STATS: BA: .325, HR: 58, RBI: 632, H: 1,866, SB: 96

#239 Michael Joseph "King" Kelly

OF-C-3B-2B-1B-P, Reds, Chicago White Stockings, Boston Beaneaters, Cincinnati Kelly's Killers, Boston Reds, New York Giants, 1878–93. Hall of Fame, 1945

Kelly was not the greatest player of the 19th century, but he was the most colorful. A terrific athlete, Kelly played every infield and outfield position and even pitched on occasion. He was the best player in baseball in 1884, leading the National League with a .354 batting average, a .414 on-base percentage and 120 runs scored for Chicago. He won a second batting title in 1886, hitting .388 with a league-leading 155 runs. Kelly led his league three times in doubles and stole 50 or more bases a season five times.

LIFETIME STATS: BA: .308, HR: 69, RBI: 950, H: 1,813, SB: 368

#240 Wesley Cheek Ferrell

RHP, Indians, Red Sox, Senators, Brooklyn Dodgers, Boston Braves, 1927–41

The fiery Ferrell led the American League in 1935 with 25 wins for the Red Sox but is better known that year for walking off the mound during one game when he felt he wasn't getting enough run support. He notched 20 or more wins six times in his career, including four consecutive seasons with the Indians, 1929–32. Ferrell threw a no-hitter for the Indians against the St. Louis Browns in 1931. He led his league four times in complete games, and ranked among league leaders in wins and ERA for most of his career.

LIFETIME STATS: W: 193, L: 128, SV: 13, ERA: 4.04, SO: 985, CG: 227

#241 Samuel Peralta "Sammy" Sosa

OF, Rangers, White Sox, Cubs, 1989–present

Sosa was named the 1998 National League MVP, leading the league with 158 RBI and 134 runs scored, his 66 home runs second only to the 70 hit by Mark McGwire of the Cardinals in that amazing year when both men broke Roger Maris's home run record. A powerful slugger, Sosa logged 100 or more RBI in nine consecutive seasons, 1995–2003. He led the NL three times in runs and twice in home runs and RBI. Presently, Sosa is 10th on the career home run list.

LIFETIME STATS: BA: .278, HR: 539, RBI: 1,450, H: 2,099, SB: 233

#242 William Henry "Wee Willie" Keeler

OF, New York Giants, Orioles, Brooklyn Superbas, New York Highlanders, 1892–1910. Hall of Fame, 1939

When asked how he amassed his impressive batting averages, Keeler shrugged and told a sportswriter he "hit where they ain't." The fielders, that is. Keeler led the National League in 1897 with a .424 batting average—third highest in major league history—and 239 hits for Baltimore. He hit .300 or better in 16 of his 19 professional seasons. Keeler was a consistent hitter, leading his league three times in hits and twice in batting average. He collected 200 or more hits and 100 or more runs in eight consecutive seasons, 1894–1901.

LIFETIME STATS: BA: .341, HR: 33, RBI: 810, H: 2,932, SB: 495

#243 Edgar Charles "Sam" Rice

OF, Senators, Indians, 1915–34. Hall of Fame, 1963

One of the best outfielders of his generation, Rice hit .300 or better in 15 seasons. He led the American League twice in hits, including the 1924 season, in which he held a 31-game hitting streak. He made 200 or more hits in a season six times and scored 100 or more runs five times. Not a fast man, Rice nonetheless led the AL in 1920 with 63 stolen bases. His most famous play was when he robbed the Pirates of a home run in the 1925 World Series by leaping over the outfield fence to catch the ball. But no one really saw Rice catch the ball, and there was a considerable controversy. Rice left a sealed letter at the Hall of Fame to be opened after his death. In it, he wrote, "At no time did I lose control over the ball."

LIFETIME STATS: BA: .322, HR: 34, RBI: 1,078, H: 2,987, SB: 351

#244 Joseph Wheeler Sewell

SS-3B, Indians, Yankees, 1920–33. Hall of Fame, 1977

The diminutive (5'7") Sewell was a hitter his whole career. He hit .300 or better in 10 seasons, and led the American League in 1924 with 45 doubles for the Indians. A smart fielder with great range, Sewell led AL shortstops in putouts over four consecutive seasons, 1924–27. He also led the leagues shortstops in assists four times and twice in fielding percentage. Perhaps his most impressive achievement was setting a record by striking out just 114 times in 7,132 games. This was one guy who always seemed to put his bat on the ball.

LIFETIME STATS: BA: .312, HR: 49, RBI: 1,055, H: 2,226, SB: 74

#245 Randall David "The Big Unit" Johnson

LHP, Expos, Mariners, Astros, Diamondbacks, Yankees, Giants, 1988–2009

The 6'10" Johnson has been one of the most intimidating pitchers in baseball for almost two decades. A five-time Cy Young award winner, Johnson led the National League in 2002 with 24 wins, 334 strikeouts and a 2.32 ERA. He has topped his league four times in ERA and eight times in strikeouts, 1992–95 and 1999–2002. His 4,875 strikeouts are second all-time to Nolan Ryan. Possessing a powerful sidearm delivery, Johnson collected 300 or more strikeouts in six seasons. He was named co-MVP of the 2001 World Series, posting a 1.04 ERA for the Diamondbacks and going 3–0 with 19 strikeouts against the Yankees.

LIFETIME STATS: W: 303, L:166, SV: 3, ERA: 3.29, SO: 4,875, CG: 98

#246 Frank Oliver "Capitol Punishment" Howard

OF-1B, Dodgers, Senators, Rangers, Tigers, 1958–73

The supersized Howard (6'7", 255 pounds) was named 1960 National League Rookie of the Year, batting .268 with 23 home runs and 77 RBI for the Dodgers. Traded to Washington, Howard led the American League in 1968 with a .552 slugging average and 44 home runs. His nickname came from the way he smacked home runs, thus "punishing" pitchers. And, of course, he was doing it in Washington, the nation's capitol. Howard topped the league again in 1970 with 44 home runs and 126 RBI, and collected 100 or more RBI four times.

LIFETIME STATS: BA: .273, HR: 382, RBI: 1,119, H: 1,774, SB: 8

#247 David Earl "Davey" Lopes

2B-OF, Dodgers, A's, Cubs, Astros, 1972–87

Lopes was a fast, savvy base runner who led the National League in stolen bases in 1975 and 1976, swiping 140 over the two seasons for the Dodgers. He stole 35 or more bases a season eight times in his career. In a game in 1974, Lopes stole five bases. He set a record with eight career stolen bases in the National League Championship Series. Lopes won a Gold Glove as the Dodgers' second baseman in 1978.

LIFETIME STATS: BA: .263, HR: 155, RBI: 614, H: 1,671, SB: 557

#**248** John Wesley "Boog" Powell
1B-OF, Orioles, Indians, Dodgers, 1961–77

For a while there, Powell looked to be sure Hall of Fame material, but he battled too many injuries over his career and didn't quite put up the numbers he would have needed. He was named 1970 American League MVP, hitting 35 home runs with 114 RBI for the Orioles. Powell batted .294 with two home runs and five RBI in Baltimore's 1970 World Series win over the Reds. He was an excellent postseason player, hitting six home runs with 18 RBI over nine postseason series with the Orioles. Powell hit 25 or more home runs six times in his career and hit three homers in a game three times.

LIFETIME STATS: BA: .266, HR: 339, RBI: 1,187, H: 1,776, SB: 20

#**249** Edward Stewart Plank
LHP, Philadelphia A's, St. Louis Terriers, St. Louis Browns, 1901–17. Hall of Fame, 1946

The Pride of Gettysburg College won 20 or more games a season eight times. Because Plank went to college, he got a late start in the pros, but he still ranks 11th all-time in career wins and 16th in complete games. Until Warren Spahn came along, Plank was the greatest left-hander of all time. His 69 career shutouts ranks fifth all-time. Twice, he led the American League in shutouts. Plank posted a 1.32 ERA over four World Series with the A's. He ranked among league strikeout leaders through most of his career.

LIFETIME STATS: W: 326, L: 194, SV: 23, ERA: 2.35, SO: 2,246, CG: 410

#250 Thomas David "Ol' Reliable" Henrich

OF-1B, Yankees, 1937–42, 1946–50

In a more media-conscious era, Heinrich would have been called "Mr. Clutch" or "Captain October." He was an excellent hitter, leading the American League in triples for two consecutive seasons, 1947–48. He also topped the AL in 1948 with 138 runs and 81 extra-base hits and scored 100 or more runs four times. But it was in the postseason that Heinrich excelled. In the 1941 World Series against the Dodgers, Henrich was the player who scrambled to first after Brooklyn catcher Mickey Owen dropped a third strike. The hustle play ignited a game-winning rally. Eight years later, Henrich hit the game-winning home run in New York's World Series opener against the Dodgers. He hit a home run in each of four World Series with the Yankees.

LIFETIME STATS: BA: .282, HR: 183, RBI: 795, H: 1,297, SB: 37

#251 Ulysses F. "Frank" Grant

2B-SS, Meriden Cuban X-Giants, Colored Capital Giants (Negro Leagues), 1886–1903. Hall of Fame, 2006

Grant was considered the best black second baseman of the 19th century. He was called "the Colored Dunlap" because he was compared favorably to Fred Dunlap, a white major league star of the same era. A terrific hitter with a strong throwing arm, Grant played several years in the white International League, and is still considered the best professional player in Buffalo baseball history, where he hit .344 and .353 over two seasons. Eventually, however, the league banned black players. Grant is believed to be one of the pioneers of the use of shin guards, which he used to prevent being spiked on the base paths.

LIFETIME STATS (incomplete): BA: .316

The Pre-Historic Players

Although there is now evidence that baseball was played in the 18th century (documents on file in Pittsfield, Massachusetts, archives indicate that the city council passed an ordinance against playing baseball near the local church in 1792), the first stars of the game didn't emerge until the mid-1800s. Most of these fellows died in the 1800s and are all but forgotten. The dates in parentheses are birth and death years.

1. Asa "The Count" Brainard, RHP (1841–88)

Before John "The Count" Montefusco plied his trade in the 1970s, Asa "The Count" Brainard toiled as a pitcher a century earlier. Brainard, born in Albany, New York, was the best of the early pitchers.

Brainard was not a big man, at 5'8", 150 pounds, but he had a wicked fastball and delivered what was called a "twist ball," which appears to be something like a curve or a slider. Brainard played for several pro teams before being signed by the Cincinnati Red Stockings in 1868. In 1869, the Red Stockings went 59–0, with Brainard pitching most of those wins. In a lot of ways, Brainard was more valuable to the Red Stockings than George Wright, the acrobatic shortstop of that team. Brainard's career lasted 15 years, from 1860–74.

Brainard was a wild guy. He reportedly deserted his wife and their infant son in 1870. He liked the nightlife and, after he retired from baseball, operated a pool room in Denver. It is believed he is responsible for a well-known baseball term. Other successful teams used to say that they had their own "Asa" pitching for them. That term eventually became "Ace."

2. James Creighton, RHP (1841–62)

Creighton is believed to been the first pitcher to throw hard. Prior to his arrival on the scene, pitchers lobbed the ball in to let batters hit it. Creighton still threw the ball underhand, but he snapped his wrist, and the pitch came in considerably faster than batters were used to seeing.

There was much consternation when Creighton began this practice, around 1858 with the Niagaras of Brooklyn. Many baseball observers believed his delivery was illegal. But umpires could find nothing in the rule book that supported this. By 1860, more and more pitchers were throwing hard, and baseball had entered a new era.

Creighton died after hitting a home run. Reportedly, he struck the ball and heard a loud pop. Creighton told a teammate he thought he had broken his belt. But his belt was intact. Two days later, he died of what a newspaper account reported was "an internal rupture." He was 21.

3. William Arthur "Candy" Cummings, RHP (1848–1924)
Cummings is considered the inventor of the curve ball. Reportedly, he learned to throw it by skipping clamshells on a New England beach as a child. Maybe that's true, but the town in which he was born, Ware, Massachusetts, is about 60 miles inland from the beach.

Be that as it may, Cummings was a wisp of a guy, at 5'9", 120 pounds. He was not a strong man, and once broke his wrist throwing a curve. Still, Cummings earned his nickname because his curveball broke so "sweetly."

Cummings pitched for a number of professional teams, and was one of the stars of the National Association, winning 124 games in four years. He also played briefly in the National League. He was elected into the Hall of Fame in 1939.

4. Alexander "Mac" McKinnon, 1B (1856–87)
The oft-injured McKinnon was one of the best hitters of the mid-1880s, hitting .300 or better five times in a nine-year career. He began his career

with the Lowell Stars, and played for two other teams from 1875–79. But 1879 was the year he was afflicted by a paralysis of his left side that was most likely Bell's palsy. He took several years off to recover and returned in 1884, hitting .272 for New York. In 1885, he hit .294 for St. Louis of the National League and led all first basemen with a fielding percentage of .979.

But in 1887, midway through the season, "Mac" developed typhoid fever. About three weeks after he was sidelined, he died. He was 30.

5. "Long" Levi Mayerle, 3B-2B-SS-1B-P (1845–1921)

Meyerle, at 6'1", 177 pounds, was a tall drink of water. He was the original "good hit-no field" player in the National Association, the forerunner of the National League. In 1871, Mayerle hit .492 for the Athletics of Philadelphia, winning the first professional batting title. He played third base, and made 44 errors in 26 games. Mayerle, who played professionally from 1867–84, was moved around the infield and outfield, and never seemed to do very well. Reports indicate that Long Levi loved to hit, but was relatively indifferent about playing in the field. He died of heart trouble, and his death went unmentioned in the sports pages of his native Philadelphia newspapers.

6. Dickey Pearce, SS (1836–1908).

Pearce was the first player to play shortstop as we know it now. Prior to Pearce, most players rarely moved from their spot between second and third base.

Pearce, who was 5'3" and a hefty 162 pounds, changed all that. He was one of the first players to study hitters, and shift his positioning accordingly. He played deep, he played shallow, and soon players began to imitate him. He had a terrific throwing arm, very accurate and strong, so that he could afford to move around in the infield.

He was also an excellent contact hitter who developed a choppy style of hitting that was copied by fellow Brooklynite Wee Willie Keeler years later. After his retirement, he became an umpire, and was well-known for his fairness and cool-headed response to angry players.

7. Al Reach, 2B (1840–1928)

Al Reach is known these days for developing one of the first baseball guides, called, not surprisingly, The Reach Guide. But during his 16-year career, (1861–76) he was also a solid second baseman.

Reach was born in England, and came to America as a child. He grew up loving baseball, and playing in Brooklyn sandlots. He was a small guy, at 5'6", 155 pounds, but he was an excellent athlete, and quickly became a pro, earning as much as $25 or $30 a game, which was good money in the 1860s.

Reach was a so-so hitter, socking a career high .353 in 1871 and being named to the first professional league All Star team by a New York City newspaper.

After his retirement, he branched out into several lucrative businesses, including publishing, and, unlike many of his baseball contemporaries, died a rich man.

#252 Adolf Louis "Dolf" Camilli

1B, Cubs, Phillies, Brooklyn Dodgers, Red Sox,
1933–45

Camilli was named 1941 National League MVP, leading the league with 34 home runs and 120 RBI. Camilli scored 100 or more runs in four consecutive seasons, 1936–39, and had 100 or more RBI five times. He hit 23 or more home runs in eight consecutive seasons, 1935–42. A former boxer whose brother had been killed in the ring, Camilli was the calming influence in the Dodger clubhouse, and prevented teammates from picking on rookies Pee Wee Reese and Pete Reiser.

LIFETIME STATS: BA: .277, HR: 239, RBI: 950, H: 1,482, SB: 60

#253 Vada Edward Pinson Jr.

OF, Reds, Cardinals, Indians, Angels, Royals, 1958–75

Pinson led the National League in hits twice, and collected 200 or more hits four times with the Reds. He topped the NL with 131 runs in 1959 and scored 100 or more runs four times. The speedy Pinson stole at least 21 bases in nine seasons, and hit at least 20 home runs in seven seasons. Defensively, Pinson's speed helped him considerably, as he led NL outfielders in putouts three times and won a Gold Glove in 1961.

LIFETIME STATS: BA: .286, HR: 256, RBI: 1,170, H: 2,757, SB: 305

#254 Richard Michael "Goose" Gossage

RHP, White Sox, Pirates, Yankees, Padres, Cubs, Giants, Rangers, A's, Mariners, 1972–89, 1991–94. Hall of Fame, 2008

Opponents of the Pirates, and later the Yankees, often watched with respect as the muscular Gossage strode to the mound and burned in a half-dozen glove-popping fastballs before beckoning a batter into the box. The "Goose" earned the 13th-most career saves in major league history, and led the American League three times in saves. In 1978, he was one of the Yankees' best weapons, winning the AL Rolaids Relief Pitcher of the Year. He ranked among the top nine league leaders in saves for 10 consecutive seasons, 1977–86. More importantly, he posted a 2.87 ERA over eight postseason series, with a 2–1 record and eight saves.

LIFETIME STATS: W: 124, L: 107, SV: 310, ERA: 3.01, SO: 1,502, CG: 16

#255 Darrell Ray Porter

C-DH, Brewers, Royals, Cardinals, Rangers, 1971–87

The bespectacled Porter didn't look particularly imposing, but he was one of the best catchers of the late 1970s and early 1980s. He was named the 1982 National League Championship Series MVP, batting .556 to lead the Cardinals over the Braves in a three-game sweep. That same year, Porter was named the 1982 World Series MVP, batting .286 with two doubles, a home run and five RBI to help the Cardinals beat the Brewers. With the Royals in 1979, he became only the second catcher to log 100 runs, RBI and walks in one season.

LIFETIME STATS: BA: .247, HR: 188, RBI: 826, H: 1,369, SB: 39

#256 Bobby Murcer

OF-DH, Yankees, Giants, Cubs, 1965–66, 1969–83

Murcer was supposed to be the second coming of Mickey Mantle. He wasn't, but he wasn't bad in his own right. He led the American League in 1971 with a .427 on-base percentage, and his .331 batting average was second-best in the league. The next year, Murcer topped the AL with 102 runs, 70 extra-base hits and 314 total bases. He also won a Gold Glove for outfielding that year. Murcer also drove in 80 or more runs a season eight times and hit 20 or more home runs seven times.

LIFETIME STATS: BA: .277, HR: 252, RBI: 1,043, H: 1,862, SB: 127

#257 Charles Solomon "Buddy" Myer

2B-SS-3B, Senators, Red Sox, 1925–41

Myer won the American League batting champion in 1935 when he led the league with a .349 batting average for the Senators. He also reached career highs with 215 hits and 100 RBI that season. A good-hitting infielder for most of his career, Myer hit .300 or better nine times in his career. He also led the AL in 1928 with 30 stolen bases for the Red Sox. Myer topped AL second basemen twice in fielding percentage.

LIFETIME STATS: BA: .303, HR: 38, RBI: 850, H: 2,131, SB: 156

#258 John Joseph McGraw

3B-SS, Orioles, Cardinals, New York Giants, 1891–1906. Hall of Fame, 1937

Before there was John McGraw the pugnacious manager, there was John McGraw the superb infielder. McGraw hit .321 or better in nine consecutive seasons, from 1893 to 1901. He led the National League in runs scored for two consecutive seasons, 1898–99, and scored 100 or more runs a season five times. He was tough to keep off the base paths, as he led his league in on-base percentage three times and stole 38 or more bases in six seasons, with a career-high 78 in 1894 for the Orioles.

LIFETIME STATS: BA: .334, HR: 13, RBI: 462, H: 1,309, SB: 436

#259 James Barton "Mickey" Vernon

1B, Senators, Indians, Red Sox, Milwaukee Brewers, Pirates, 1939–43, 1946–60

Vernon was a two-time American League batting champion, in 1946 and 1953 with the Senators. He topped the league three times in doubles, and led with 67 extra-base hits in 1954. The soft-spoken left-hander collected 85 or more RBI eight times. Defensively, Vernon led AL first basemen in fielding percentage four times and set a major league record for first basemen in 1949 with 155 assists.

LIFETIME STATS: BA: .286, HR: 172, RBI: 1,311, H: 2,495, SB: 137

#260 Andre Thornton

DH-1B, Cubs, Expos, Indians, 1973–79, 1981–87

The low-key Thornton was a fierce competitor on the ball field. He led the Indians franchise in home runs in seven seasons and hit 26 or more home runs a season five times in his career. In 1982 Thornton became the second Indian to collect 100 walks and 100 RBI in the same season. He ranked among league home run leaders four times, and bases on balls leaders six times. Thornton hit a career-high .293 for the Cubs in 1975.

LIFETIME STATS: BA: .254, HR: 253, RBI: 895, H: 1,342, SB: 48

#261 Fred Clifford "Cap" Clarke

OF, Louisville Colonels, Pirates, 1894–1911, 1913–15. Hall of Fame, 1945

Clarke went five-for-five in his first major league game in 1894, still a major league record. One of the best players in the National League at the turn of the century, Clarke led the league in 1903 with a .532 slugging percentage and 32 doubles, while batting .351, second-best in the circuit. He batted .300 or better 11 times in his career, and scored 100 or more runs five times. The speedy Clarke also stole 30 or more bases in seven seasons. Clarke also led the NL with 13 triples in 1906 and ranked among league triples leaders for 11 seasons in his career.

LIFETIME STATS: BA: .312, HR: 67, RBI: 1,015, H: 2,672, SB: 506

#262 Dwight Michael "Dewey" Evans
OF-DH-1B, Red Sox, Orioles, 1972–91

Dwight Evans was a fixture in right field in Boston for 18 years. Known primarily for his cannon arm, Evans won eight American League Gold Gloves. But he was clearly much more than that. He led the AL in 1981 with 22 home runs, in 1982 with a .402 on-base percentage and in 1984 with 121 runs. Patient at the plate, he led the league three times in walks and collected 100 or more RBI and 100 or more runs four times. Evans hit .308 with two home runs and a team-high nine RBI in Boston's losing effort against the Mets in the 1986 World Series.

LIFETIME STATS: BA: .272, HR: 385, RBI: 1,384, H: 2,446, SB: 78

#263 Robert Granville "Bob" Lemon
RHP, Indians, 1941–42, 1946–58. Hall of Fame, 1976

The affable Lemon began his professional career as a third baseman. But his throws to first, while strong enough, had a tendency to sink, and one of his minor league managers convinced Lemon to convert to a pitcher. It worked out well. Lemon led the American League three times in wins, and collected 20 or more wins a season seven times. He ranked among league wins leaders for nine consecutive seasons, 1948–56. In addition, Lemon led the league five times in complete games. He topped AL pitchers in 1950 with 170 strikeouts. Lemon threw a no-hitter against the Tigers in 1948. He logged a 1.65 ERA with a 2–0 record in the 1948 World Series against the Braves.

LIFETIME STATS: W: 207, L: 128, SV: 22, ERA: 3.23, SO: 1,277, CG: 188

#264 George Arthur Foster

OF, Giants, Reds, Mets, White Sox, 1969–86

A superb all-around athlete who excelled in track and football as well as baseball at El Camino College in California, Foster eventually became a key cog in the Cincinnati "Big Red Machine" of the 1970s. He was named 1977 National League MVP, leading the league with 52 home runs, 149 RBI, 124 runs, a .631 slugging average, 388 total bases and 85 extra-base hits. Foster led the NL three consecutive seasons in RBI, 1976–78, still a National League record. He logged 90 or more RBI seven times and hit 25 or more home runs six times. Foster was named MVP of the 1976 All Star game.

LIFETIME STATS: BA: .274, HR: 348, RBI: 1,239, H: 1,925, SB: 51

#265 James Louis Fregosi

SS-1B-3B, Angels, Mets, Rangers, Pirates, 1961–78

Fregosi was the first real star of the California Angels, a power hitter who played shortstop. He led the AL in 1968 with 13 triples, and ranked among league triples leaders for seven consecutive seasons, 1963–69. Fregosi hit a career-high 22 home runs with 82 RBI for the Angels in 1970 and had five other years in which he hit 12 or more home runs. Fregosi collected 150 or more hits seven times. He won an American League Gold Glove for shortstops in 1967 with the Angels.

LIFETIME STATS: BA: .265, HR: 151, RBI: 706, H: 1,726, SB: 76

#**266** Henry Knight "Heinie" Groh

3B-2B, New York Giants, Reds, Pirates, 1912–27

Groh was famous for his "bottle bat," a bat with a fat barrel and thin handle. He used it well, leading the National League in on-base percentage and doubles, 1917–18. Groh, one of many players of German extraction in that era who were called "Heinie," topped the NL in 1917 with 182 hits and in 1918 with 86 runs. He hit .300 or better over three consecutive seasons with the Reds, 1917–19. Groh also batted .474 in the 1922 World Series, helping the Giants defeat the Yankees. Groh scored 80 or more runs a season six times.

LIFETIME STATS: BA: .292, HR: 26, RBI: 566, H: 1,774, SB: 180

#**267** Hazen Shirley "Kiki" Cuyler

OF, Pirates, Cubs, Reds, Brooklyn Dodgers, 1921–38. Hall of Fame, 1968

With a name like "Hazen Shirley," a nickname like "Kiki" wasn't too bad. Pronounced "Kie-Kie," it was actually a derivative of Cuyler's last name. When he called for the ball in the outfield, he would shout "Cuy! Cuy!" and a nickname was born, although sportswriters spelled it all wrong and eventually began pronouncing it differently. The gentlemanly Cuyler led the National League in runs, 1925–26. An excellent base runner, he topped the NL in stolen bases for three consecutive seasons with the Cubs, 1928–30, and four times over his career. Cuyler scored 100 or more runs in five seasons. He also collected 200 or more hits and 100 or more RBI three times and batted .300 or better in 10 seasons.

LIFETIME STATS: BA: .321, HR: 128, RBI: 1,065, H: 2,299, SB: 328

#268 Americo Peter "Rico" Petrocelli

SS-3B, Red Sox, 1963–76

Petrocelli was a rough-and-tumble infielder who could hit and always played well in the clutch. He set an American League record for shortstops by hitting 40 home runs in 1969. Petrocelli peaked offensively that year, hitting a career-high .297, with 159 hits, 32 doubles and 92 runs. He hit two home runs in Game Six of Boston's 1967 World Series against the Cardinals. Later Petrocelli hit .308 with four RBI in the 1975 World Series against the Reds.

LIFETIME STATS: BA: .251, HR: 210, RBI: 773, H: 1,352, SB: 10

#269 Rik Aalbert "Bert" Blyleven

RHP, Twins, Rangers, Pirates, Indians, Angels, 1970–90, 1992

The Netherlands-born Blyleven was the premier curveballer of the 1970s and 1980s. He recorded 200 or more strikeouts eight times in his career, including five consecutive seasons with the Twins, from 1971 to 1975. But 10 years later, he showed little signs of wear, as he led the American League in 1985 with 206 strikeouts and 24 complete games. Blyleven topped the league three times in shutouts, and threw a no-hitter for the Rangers against the Pirates in 1977. He still ranks fifth among all-time strikeouts leaders.

LIFETIME STATS: W: 287, L: 250, SV: 0, ERA: 3.31, SO: 3,701, CG: 242

#270 Jack Anthony Clark

OF-1B-DH, Giants, Cardinals, Yankees, Padres, Red Sox, 1975–92

Clark led the National League in 1987 with a .459 on-base percentage, a .597 slugging percentage and 136 walks for the Cardinals. He notched slugging percentages of .500 or better six times in his career and led his league in walks three times. In 1978, Clark topped the NL with 79 extra-base hits for the Giants. Not particularly known for his defense, Clark led NL outfielders in assists in 1981 with the Giants.

LIFETIME STATS: BA: .267, HR: 340, RBI: 1,180, H: 1,826, SB: 77

#271 Early Wynn Jr.

RHP, Senators, Indians, White Sox, 1939–44, 1946–63. Hall of Fame, 1972

Wynn was a tough son of a gun on the mound, where his take-no-prisoners attitude served him well. He won the 1959 Cy Young award with an American League–leading 22 wins for the White Sox. In 1950 he led the AL with a 3.20 ERA. Wynn led the AL in strikeouts for two consecutive seasons, 1957–58. He logged 20 or more wins a season five times. Wynn was not an easy man to coach, and hated to be removed from games. Thus he ranked among league leaders in complete games 14 times. He was also among the American League's best in wins 13 times and in strikeouts 11 times.

LIFETIME STATS: W: 300, L: 244, SV: 15, ERA: 3.54, SO: 2,334, CG: 290

#272 Harry Bartholomew Hooper

OF, Red Sox, White Sox, 1909–25. Hall of Fame, 1971

One of the early stars for the Red Sox, Hooper hit .350 for Boston in the 1915 World Series against Philadelphia, becoming the first player to hit two home runs in one World Series game. Hooper scored 100 or more runs three times in his career. He hit 10 or more triples in nine seasons, and set a Red Sox franchise record with 160 triples lifetime. He ranked among league leaders in walks 10 times.

LIFETIME STATS: BA: .281, HR: 75, RBI: 817, H: 2,466, SB: 375

#273 Amos Joseph Otis

OF-DH, Mets, Royals, Pirates, 1967, 1969–84

Otis was known for his bat, but he also won three American League Gold Glove awards. He led the AL twice in doubles. A good base runner, Otis topped the league in 1971 with 52 stolen bases, and tied an AL record in 1975 with seven stolen bases in back-to-back games. Otis batted .478 for the Royals in the 1980 World Series against the Phillies, leading all players with 11 hits, including three home runs.

LIFETIME STATS: BA: .277, HR: 193, RBI: 1,007, H: 2,020, SB: 341

#274 Gary Antonian Sheffield

OF-3B, Brewers, Padres, Marlins, Dodgers, Braves, Yankees, Tigers, Mets, 1988–2009

The well-traveled Sheffield has played on eight teams in his 21-year career. A solid hitter, he led the National League in 1992 with a .330 batting average and 323 total bases for the Padres. He topped the league in 1996 with a .465 slugging average.

"Sheff" is an all-star hitter and has ranked among the league's on-base-percentage leaders in eight consecutive seasons, from 1996 to 2003.

After three years with the Yankees, Sheffield signed with the Detroit Tigers. While some believed he might be washed up, Sheffield has enjoyed a resurgence in Detroit and has remained one of the league's feared hitters in 2007.

LIFETIME STATS: BA: .292, HR: 509, RBI: 1,626, H: 2,689, SB: 253

#275 Lance Michael Parrish

C-DH, Tigers, Phillies, Angels, Mariners, Indians, Pirates, Blue Jays, 1977–95

Parish, a three-time Gold Glove award winner, also briefly held the American League record for home runs by a catcher with 32 in 1982. He broke out offensively in 1983 with the Tigers, logging career highs with 114 RBI, 42 doubles, 163 hits and 80 runs. In 1990, playing with the Angels, he led AL catchers in double plays and assists.

LIFETIME STATS: BA: .252, HR: 324, RBI: 1,070, H: 1,782, SB: 28

#276 George Joseph Burns

OF, Giants, Reds, Phillies, 1911–25

One of two George Burns who played in the majors in the 1910s and 1920s, this George Burns was mostly an outfielder who played in the National League. He scored 100 or more runs six times in his career, leading the National League five times. Burns also ranked among league leaders in hits for eight consecutive seasons, 1913–20. He stole 30 or more bases seven times, leading the league twice, including a career-high 62 steals in 1914. Burns led the NL in 1919 with a .396 on-base percentage.

LIFETIME STATS: BA: .287, HR: 41, RBI: 611, H: 2,077, SB: 383

#277 Elmer Harrison Flick

OF, Phillies, Philadelphia A's, Cleveland Naps, 1898–1910. Hall of Fame, 1963

Flick was a solid all-around player at the turn of the 20th century. He captured the 1905 American League batting title with a .308 batting average for Cleveland, while also leading the league with a .462 slugging average and 18 triples. Flick hit career highs in 1900 with the Phillies, batting .367 with 200 hits, 11 home runs and a league-leading 110 RBI. He was excellent on the base paths, stealing 30 or more bases seven times, leading his league twice. Flick also batted .300 or better in eight seasons.

LIFETIME STATS: BA: .313, HR: 48, RBI: 756, H: 1,752, SB: 330

#**278** Robert Irving Elliott

3B-OF, Pirates, Boston Braves, New York Giants, St. Louis Browns, White Sox, 1939–53

Elliott's principal claim to baseball fame was when he was named National League MVP in 1947, batting .317 with 22 HR and 113 RBI for the Braves. But he had several solid years in the majors, logging 100 or more RBI in six seasons. He ranked among league leaders in triples for five consecutive seasons, 1940–44, and ranked among on-base percentage leaders for four consecutive seasons, 1947–50. Elliott was a seven-time All Star.

LIFETIME STATS: BA: .289, HR: 170, RBI: 1,195, H: 2,061, SB: 60

#**279** Samuel James Tilden "Jimmy" Sheckard

OF, Brooklyn Bridegrooms, Orioles, Cubs, Cardinals, Reds, 1897–13

Sheckard was one of only a handful of Pennsylvania Dutch to play major league baseball. He led the National League in 1901 with a .534 slugging percentage and 19 triples for Brooklyn. In 1903, he topped the NL with nine home runs and 67 stolen bases. Sheckard stole 30 or more bases in seven seasons, including a career-best 77 steals in 1899 for the Orioles. He led the NL in 1911 with a .434 on-base percentage, 147 walks and 121 runs for the Cubs.

LIFETIME STATS: BA: .274, HR: 56, RBI: 813, H: 2,084, SB: 465

#**280** Clifford Carlton "Gavvy," "Cactus" Cravath

OF, Red Sox, White Sox, Senators, Phillies, 1908–09, 1912–20

There are about a dozen stories as to how Cravath got the name "Gavvy." Essentially, "Gavvy" is short for gaviotas, which is Spanish for seagull, and it had something to do with his baseball days. Cravath led the National League in 1915 with 24 home runs, 115 RBI and 89 runs for the Phillies. He topped the NL in 1913 with 179 hits and 19 home runs. In fact, Cravath was the "Home Run King" before Babe Ruth annexed the crown, leading his league in home runs six times, and twice in RBI, slugging and on-base percentages. He collected 100 or more RBI in three seasons.

LIFETIME STATS: BA: .287, HR: 119, RBI: 719, H: 1,134, SB: 89

#**281** Edward Frederick Joseph "Eddie," "The Walking Man" Yost

3B, Senators, Tigers, Angels, 1944, 1946–62

True to his nickname, Yost led the American League six times in walks, drawing 100 or more walks in eight seasons. His career total of 1,614 walks ranks ninth-most of all time. Yost could also play a little defense, leading AL third basemen in putouts a major-league-record eight times. He also set career records for putouts and assists at third base. Yost topped the AL in 1959 with a .435 on-base percentage and 115 runs for the Tigers.

LIFETIME STATS: BA: .254, HR: 139, RBI: 683, H: 1,863, SB: 72

#282 Charles Herbert "Red" Ruffing

RHP, Red Sox, Yankees, White Sox, 1924–42, 1945–47. Hall of Fame, 1967

Ruffing's career was completely turned around by a trade from the Red Sox to the Yankees. After twice losing 20 or more games in Boston in 1928 and 1929, Ruffing logged 20 or more wins in four consecutive seasons with New York, from 1936 to 1939. He ranked 12 times among league leaders in wins, complete games and shutouts. He ranked among strikeout leaders in 13 seasons. In the postseason, Ruffing was even tougher, compiling a 7–2 record with a 2.63 ERA over seven World Series.

LIFETIME STATS: W: 273, L: 225, SV: 16, ERA: 3.80, SO: 1,987, CG: 335

#283 Raleigh "Biz" Mackey

C-SS-3B, San Antonio Giants, Darby Daisies, Indianapolis ABCs, Hilldale, Baltimore Elite Giants, Philadelphia Stars, Washington Elite Giants, Nashville Giants, Newark Eagles (Negro Leagues),1918–47. Hall of Fame, 2006

Mackey was considered, after Josh Gibson, to be the best all-around catcher in the Negro Leagues. Mackey was an excellent handler of pitchers and was on a par with Gibson as a defensive player. While not as thunderous a hitter as Gibson, the switch-hitting Mackey could hit for average. From 1923 to 1932, he hit .300 or better for various teams, and in 1924, he hit .423 for Hilldale.

LIFETIME STATS: BA: .332, H: 1,383

#284 Bernabe "Bernie" Williams
OF, Yankees, 1991–2007

Williams has been one of the most consistent players for the Yankees in their most recent dynasty. A four-time Gold Glove winner, Williams led the American League in 1998 with a .339 batting average. He was named the 1996 ALCS MVP, batting .474 with two home runs and six RBI, leading the Yankees to victory over the Orioles. Williams has batted .278 over 21 postseason series, with 19 home runs and 66 RBI. He hit .300 or better in eight consecutive seasons, 1995–2002.

LIFETIME STATS: BA: .305, HR: 241, RBI: 1,062, H: 1,950, SB: 143

#285 Dominic Paul "Dom" DiMaggio
OF, Red Sox, 1940–42, 1946–53

He may have played in the shadow of big brother Joe for many years, but "Dom" was a superb defensive center fielder and a better hitter than he has been given credit for. He led the American League in 1950 with 11 triples and 15 stolen bases. Topping the league in runs in 1950 and 1951, DiMaggio scored 100 or more runs in six seasons. He also batted .300 or better four times. A seven-time All Star, DiMaggio hit safely in 34 consecutive games in 1949, and had a 27-game hitting streak in 1951.

LIFETIME STATS: BA: .298, HR: 87, RBI: 618, H: 1,680, SB: 100

#286 Wallace Keith "Wally" Joyner
1B, Angels, Royals, Padres, Braves, 1986–2001

Joyner was named Angels' MVP in 1987, hitting 34 home runs, a team record for first basemen. He also scored a career-high 100 runs with 117 RBI that year. Joyner logged 100 or more RBI his first two years in the majors, becoming the ninth player in major league history to accomplish that feat. He batted .455 in the 1986 ALCS against Boston in a losing effort, with a home run and two doubles for the Angels.

LIFETIME STATS: BA: .289, HR: 204, RBI: 1,106, H: 2,060, SB: 60

#287 Forrest Harrill "Smoky" Burgess
C, Cubs, Phillies, Reds, Pirates, White Sox, 1949, 1951–67

Burgess set a since-surpassed record with 507 pinch at-bats and 145 pinch hits in his career. He hit the Reds' 221st home run in the 1956 season to match a National League team record. Burgess also caught Harvey Haddix's 12-inning perfect game for the Pirates in 1959 against the Braves. Burgess batted .333 in the Pirates' 1960 World Series win against the Yankees.

LIFETIME STATS: BA: .295, HR: 126, RBI: 673, H: 1,318, SB 13

#288 Hugh Ambrose "Hughie" Jennings

SS-1B, Louisville Colonels, Orioles, Brooklyn Superbas, Phillies, Tigers, 1891–1903, 1907, 1909, 1912, 1918. Hall of Fame, 1945

Jennings is best known as a third base coach for the Tigers who belted out his expressive "EEE-Yah!" yell to rally the team. But he was a formidable infielder in his playing days. He batted .328 or better in five consecutive seasons with Baltimore, 1894–98, while scoring 125 runs or more a season. Jennings logged more than 100 RBI in three consecutive seasons, 1894–96. He batted .401 in 1896, still a major league record for shortstops. A solid defensive player, Jennings topped league shortstops in putouts three times and fielding percentage four times.

LIFETIME STATS: BA: .311, HR: 18, RBI: 840, H: 1,527, SB: 359

#289 Jay Stuart Bell

SS-2B, Indians, Pirates, Royals, Diamondbacks, Mets, 1986–2003

Bell, an excellent defensive player, won a Gold Glove as the Pirates' shortstop in 1993. At the plate, Bell ranked among league runs-scored leaders four times, and topped the National League in sacrifice hits twice, 1990–91. Bell peaked offensively in 1999 with the Diamondbacks, hitting 38 home runs with 112 RBI and 132 runs scored. He batted .414 in the 1991 NLCS, with a home run and two doubles, though the Pirates lost to the Braves.

LIFETIME STATS: BA: .265, HR: 195, RBI: 860, H: 1,963, SB: 91

#290 Charley Gardner "Old Hoss" Radbourn

RHP-OF, Buffalo Bisons, Providence Grays, Boston Beaneaters, Boston Reds, Cincinnati Reds, 1880–91. Hall of Fame, 1939

Dubbed "Old Hoss" for his consistency and durability, Radbourn had a career year in 1884, leading National League pitchers with a 1.38 ERA, 59 wins and 441 strikeouts for the Grays. Radbourn, not much of a "hoss" at 5'9", 168 pounds, won more games that year than four National league teams. Despite a short career because of a burned-out arm, Radbourn collected the 18th-most wins of all time. He topped league pitchers in strikeouts twice and threw the eighth-most complete games in major league history. The Hoss won 20 or more games in nine seasons of his 11-year career.

LIFETIME STATS: W: 309, L: 195, SV: 2, ERA: 2.67, SO: 1,830, CG: 489

#291 Kenton Lloyd "Ken" Boyer

3B-OF, Cardinals, Mets, White Sox, Dodgers, 1955–69

A five-time winner of the Gold Glove award for National League third basemen, Boyer was the best all-around third baseman in the National League in the 1960s, leading his position five times in double plays. Named 1964 National League MVP, Boyer scored 100 runs, hit 24 home runs and had a league-leading 119 RBI for the Cardinals. He hit a grand slam in Game Four of the 1964 World Series to give the Cardinals a win over the Yankees, then homered again in Game Seven to clinch the Series.

LIFETIME STATS: BA: .287, HR: 282, RBI: 1,141, H: 2,143, SB: 105

#**292** Ralph McPherran Kiner

OF, Pirates, Cubs, Indians, 1946–55. Hall of Fame, 1975

Kiner was one of the great power hitters of his era. He led the National League in home runs over seven consecutive seasons with the Pirates, 1946–1952, including a career-high 54 home runs in 1949. Combined with his 51 homers in 1947, that made Kiner the first National Leaguer to hit 50 homers in two seasons. He topped the league three times in slugging percentage. Kiner also collected 100 or more runs and 100 or more RBI six times. He hit at least 20 home runs in nine of his 10 major league seasons.

LIFETIME STATS: BA: .279, HR: 369, RBI: 1,015, H: 1,451, SB: 22

#**293** Octavio Antonio "Tony" Fernandez

SS-3B-2B, Blue Jays, Padres, Mets, Reds, Yankees, Indians, Brewers, 1983–95, 1997–99, 2001

The acrobatic Fernandez won the Gold Glove award for American League shortstops four consecutive seasons, from 1986 to 1989. At the plate, he ranked seven times among triples leaders, topping the AL in 1990 with 17 for the Blue Jays. Fernandez is one of the best World Series hitters ever, batting .395 with 13 RBI in two Series. He hit a series-winning home run for the Indians in Game Five of the 1997 ALCS to defeat the Orioles.

LIFETIME STATS: BA: .288, HR: 94, RBI: 844, H: 2,276, SB: 246

#294 Robert Jose "Bob" Watson

OF-1B, Astros, Red Sox, Yankees, Braves, 1966–84

A hitting machine, Watson batted .300 or better in seven seasons. He played in 65 games with 149 at-bats in 1983, batting .309. If that level of participation counts as a "year," then he had seven seasons over .300. He collected 100 or more RBI in two consecutive seasons for the Astros, 1976–77. In 1979 with the Red Sox, Watson became the first player to hit for the cycle in both the American League and the National League. Watson homered in his first World Series at-bat in 1981, helping the Yankees defeat the Dodgers in Game One, although the Yankees eventually lost the Series.

LIFETIME STATS: BA: .295, HR: 184, RBI: 989, H: 1,826, SB: 27

#295 Rocco Domenico "Rocky" Colavito

OF, Indians, Tigers, Kansas City A's, White Sox, Dodgers, Yankees, 1955–68

"The Rock" hit 30 or more home runs seven times in his career, and collected 100 or more RBI in six seasons. He led the American League with 42 home runs for the Indians in 1959. That year, he became the first Indian to have two consecutive seasons with 40 or more home runs, as he socked 41 the season before. Colavito ranked among league home run leaders nine times. He topped AL batters with 108 RBI in 1965.

LIFETIME STATS: BA: .266, HR: 374, RBI: 1,159, H: 1,730, SB: 19

#296 Albert "Al" Oliver Jr.

OF-1B-DH, Pirates, Rangers, Expos, Giants, Phillies, Dodgers, Blue Jays, 1968–85

Another outfielder who was consistently productive, Oliver hit .300 or better 11 times in his career, including nine consecutive seasons, from 1976 to 1984. Oliver led the National League with a .331 batting average, 109 RBI, 204 hits and 43 doubles for the Expos in 1982. He ranked among league hits leaders nine times. In 1980, playing for Texas, Oliver had 209 hits and 117 RBI. Thus, in conjunction with his 1982 stats, Oliver became the first player to collect 200 hits and 100 RBI in a season for both leagues.

LIFETIME STATS: BA: .303, HR: 219, RBI: 1,326, H: 2,743, SB: 84

#297 Eric Keith Davis

OF, Reds, Dodgers, Tigers, Orioles, Cardinals, Giants, 1984–94, 1996–2001

Davis won three Gold Glove awards for National League outfielders, from 1987 to 1989. He also ranked among league home run leaders, 1986–89. Davis hit 25 or more home runs six times in his career. He was a combination of power and speed, as in 1986 with the Reds, Davis became the second player ever to hit 20 home runs and steal 80 bases in a single season. He stole 35 or more bases four times.

LIFETIME STATS: BA: .269, HR: 282, RBI: 934, H: 1,430, SB: 349

#298 Jose Cruz

OF, Cardinals, Astros, Yankees, 1970–88

Cruz was an unheralded star for the Astros in the 1970s and early 1980s. He led the National League in 1983 with 189 hits for the Astros, and was named Houston's MVP four times. He hit .300 or better in six seasons, and stole 30 or more bases five times. Cruz batted .400 with a triple and four RBI in the Astros' 1980 NLCS loss to the Phillies. He ranked among NL leaders in triples four times.

LIFETIME STATS: BA: .284, HR: 165, RBI: 1,077, H: 2,251, SB: 317

#299 Ernesto Natali "Ernie" Lombardi

C, Brooklyn Dodgers, Reds, Boston Braves, New York Giants, 1931–47. Hall of Fame, 1986

A fearsome hitter who, by the end of his career, may have been one of the slowest players in baseball, Lombardi was named National League MVP in 1938, posting 19 home runs, 167 hits and 95 RBI for the Reds, with a league-leading .342 batting average. That accomplishment meant Lombardi became only the second catcher ever to capture a batting title. Tough and durable, Lombardi hit .300 or better 10 times and ranked among league leaders in slugging percentage in eight seasons. He caught consecutive no-hitters for Johnny Van der Meer in 1938.

LIFETIME STATS: BA: .306, HR: 190, RBI: 990, H: 1,792, SB: 8

#**300** John Michael "Johnny" Pesky

SS-3B-2B, Red Sox, Tigers, Senators, 1942, 1946–54

Johnny Pesky is another player who has been overlooked by many experts. He batted .300 or better six times in his career and led the American League three times in hits. He ranked among league leaders in on-base percentage for six seasons. Pesky scored 100 or more runs in each of his first six seasons with the Red Sox and logged 200 or more hits in his first three seasons with Boston. He also set a Boston franchise rookie record with 205 hits in 1942. Pesky holds, with Marty Barrett, the Boston team record for catching players off base with the old "hidden ball trick," doing it three times. It should have been four, but teammate Bobby Doerr called time in a game against the Orioles in the 1940s. Pesky, with the ball hidden in his glove, glared at Doerr and threw the ball in.

LIFETIME STATS: BA: .307, HR: 17, RBI: 404, H: 1,455, SB: 53

#**301** Jack Glasscock

SS-2B, Cleveland Blues, Cincinnati Outlaw Reds, St. Louis Maroons, Indianapolis Hoosiers, Giants, Pirates, Louisville, Washington, 1879–95

One of the finest-fielding shortstops of his era, Glasscock played without a glove from 1879 to 1890, yet managed to lead league shortstops in fielding percentage and assists six times each during that period. Dubbed "Pebbly Jack" for his habit of clearing out pebbles, imaginary or otherwise, from the left side of the infield, Glasscock also impressed with his bat as he hit over .300 five times, winning the batting crown in 1890 with a .336 mark, going six-for-six in a September game that year. He was known as an innovator at his position as Glasscock was one of the first to signal his catcher on who would cover second on a steal attempt, and also was among the first shortstops to back up his second baseman.

LIFETIME STATS: BA: .290, HR: 27, RBI: 825, H: 2,040, SB: 372

#302 Bill Mazeroski

2B, Pirates, 1956–72. Hall of Fame, 2001

Everyone remembers the big home run Bill Mazeroski hit in Game Seven of the 1960 World Series to win the world championship for the upstart Pittsburgh Pirates over the heavily favored New York Yankees in a wild 10–9 win. But Mazeroski is not in the Hall of Fame just for that one glorious moment; he is considered by many to be the greatest fielding second baseman of all time. An eight-time Gold Glover, Mazeroski set major league records for participating in 1,706 double plays, including eight straight seasons leading the league in that department. Called "No Hands" for the way he seemed to merely redirect the ball as the middleman of a double play, the West Virginia native also led the league in chances a record eight seasons, and in assists a major-league-record nine consecutive seasons.

LIFETIME STATS: BA: .260, HR: 138, RBI: 853, H: 2,016, SB: 27

#303 Bert "Campy" Campaneris

SS-2B-3B, A's, Rangers, Angels, Yankees, 1964–83

Campaneris was a speedy shortstop who anchored the infield for the Championship A's teams of 1972–74. Early in his career, he became the first player to play all nine positions in one major league game. "Campy" broke into the majors with a bang as he homered on the first pitch he saw against Jim Kaat and the Minnesota Twins in 1964. Campaneris, also nicknamed "the Road Runner," led the league in triples in his second season, and led the league in stolen bases six times. He stole 50 or more bases seven times in his career, pilfering a high of 62 in both 1968 and 1969. In 1971, "Campy" was hit by a pitch, perhaps intentionally by Detroit's Lerrin

LaGrow in the American League Championship Series, and the A's short-stop responded by throwing his bat, narrowly missing the Tiger hurler. American League President Joe Cronin suspended Campaneris for the rest of the playoffs, but reinstated him for the World Series.

LIFETIME STATS: BA: .259. HR: 79, RBI: 646, H: 2,249, SB: 649

#**304** Joe "Iron Man" McGinnity

RHP, Baltimore (NL), Dodgers, Baltimore (AL), Giants, 1899–1908. Hall of Fame, 1946

Some say that "Iron Man" Joe McGinnity earned his nickname by often pitching both ends of a doubleheader (once winning three twin bills in a month), while others say he worked in the off-season in an iron factory in Oklahoma. The right-hander broke in with a splash, winning 28 games for John McGraw's 1899 Orioles. With Brooklyn the following year, McGinnity led the league in innings pitched (his first of four times), and won a league best 28 games, including five of the last six games as Brooklyn won the pennant. The "Iron Man" went 31–20 in 1903 and an eye-popping 35–8 in 1904, leading the league with an .814 winning percentage. He "slumped" to 21–15 and 27–12 for the following two seasons, all the while logging more than 300 innings each season.

LIFETIME STATS: W: 246, L: 142, SV: 24, ERA: 2.66, SO: 1,068, CG: 314

#305 Hugh Duffy

OF, Cubs, Chicago (PL), Boston (AA), Braves, Milwaukee (AL), Phillies, 1888–1901, 1904–06. Hall of Fame, 1945

The 5'7" Duffy was an excellent hitter, sporting a career batting average of .324, while hitting a still-record .440 in 1894, also leading the league in slugging (.694), hits (237), doubles (51), homers (18) and RBI (145), becoming the first ever Triple Crown winner. Overall, he hit over .300 10 times in a row from 1889 to 1898. He also won another home-run title in 1897, and had five hits in a game seven times in his career. The speedy Duffy stole 40 or more bases nine times in his career with a career high of 85 in 1891. He joined the Braves and future Hall of Fame outfielder Tommy McCarthy, forming one of the best outfield duos of the time period. They were dubbed "the Heavenly Twins," for their defensive prowess.

LIFETIME STATS: BA: .328, HR: 103, RBI: 1,299, H: 2,314, SB: 599

#306 Cecil Cooper

1B-DH, Red Sox, Brewers, 1971–87

Cecil Cooper started out in Boston, but didn't reach his potential until he was sent to Milwaukee in 1976. A first baseman with solid, if not spectacular, power, Cooper blended in well in Milwaukee. Cooper led the American League twice in doubles and RBI. His career high in batting average was an impressive .352 in 1980, second in the league. Cooper got the most important hit in the Brewers young history as he singled home two runs in the 1982 ALCS, beating the Angels, and propelling the "Brew Crew" to their second World Series appearance to date.

He hit .300 eight times in his career. Cooper hit three homers and knocked in six in the seven-game World Series loss to the Cardinals.

LIFETIME STATS: BA: .298, HR: 241, RBI: 1,125, H: 2,192, SB: 89

#**307** Alvin Dark

SS-3B, Braves, Giants, Cardinals, Cubs, Phillies, 1946, 1948–60

Dark came up with the Boston Braves, winning the National League Rookie of the Year award in 1948, hitting .322 and helping the Braves win the pennant. He only hit .167 in the ensuing World Series. Dubbed "Blackie" because of his jet-black hair, Dark, a former LSU football star, was traded to the New York Giants.
It was Dark's single that started the Giants' winning rally in the ninth inning in the famous Bobby Thomson homer game that won the pennant for the Giants. He hit over .300 four times, and hit over 20 home runs and scored over 100 runs twice each in his fine career. Dark was no slouch with the glove either, as he led NL shortstops three times each in double plays and putouts.

LIFETIME STATS: BA: .289, HR: 126, RBI: 757, H: 2,089, SB: 59

#**308** Rick Monday

OF-1B, A's, Cubs, Dodgers, 1966–84

The left-hand-hitting Rick Monday was the first player taken in the first-ever amateur draft in 1965 by the then Kansas City A's after leading Arizona State to the NCAA championship and being named the College Player of the Year. Monday made the All Star team in 1968 and tied Lou Gehrig's record of making RBI in 10 consecutive games. Traded to the Cubs, Monday found the cozier dimensions of Wrigley Field to his liking, hitting 20 or more homers three times, peaking at 32 in 1976. Monday was not a relief pitcher, but came up with one of the more famous "saves" in baseball. In a 1976 game against the Dodgers in Los Angeles, Monday spotted two young men about to light the American flag on fire. Before they could light Old Glory ablaze, Monday swooped over and grabbed the flag away from the miscreants, prompting the Dodger crowd to give Monday a standing ovation and to break into a spontaneous rendition of "God Bless America."

LIFETIME STATS: BA: .264, HR: 241, RBI: 775, H: 1,619, SB: 98

#**309** Wally Schang

C, OF, A's, Red Sox, Yankees, Browns, Tigers, 1913–31

Schang broke in with the Philadelphia A's in 1913, and promptly helped Connie Mack's team to the world championship, hitting .357 in his first Fall Classic. He was traded to the Red Sox in 1918, and helped them win their last championship, leading all hitters with an impressive .444 average in the Series win over the Cubs. Traded to the Yankees in 1921, Schang helped New York to their first-ever flag in 1921 and their first World Series win in 1923. Schang hit over .300 six times in his career, and had a reputation as an excellent handler of pitchers. Schang even stole 121 bases in his career, a rarity for a catcher.

LIFETIME STATS: BA: .284, HR: 59, RBI: 710, H: 1,506, SB: 121

#310 Robin Ventura

3B-1B, White Sox, Mets, Yankees, Dodgers, 1989–2004

The Chicago White Sox signed the highly heralded Robin Ventura off the campus of Oklahoma State University where he was honored as the College Player of the Decade by Baseball America. While a Cowboy, he fashioned a 58-game hitting streak and helped the USA win the gold medal in the 1988 Seoul Olympics, hitting .409. In 1995, Ventura became just the eighth player in major league history to hit two grand slams in one game, the first to accomplish that feat in 25 years. He signed a free-agent contract with the New York Mets in 1999, and became the first player in baseball history to hit a grand slam in both ends of a doubleheader. Ventura was a leader for the 1999 Mets, clouting 32 homers and knocking in a career-best 120 runs, while he continued to shine defensively at third base, winning his sixth Gold Glove. He went to the crosstown Yankees in 2002 and hit 27 homers and knocked in 93, while playing a fine third base. As of 2003, Ventura was the majors' active leader in career grand slams with 16.

LIFETIME STATS: BA: .267, HR: 294, RBI: 1,182, H: 1,885, SB: 24

#311 Lee May

1B-DH, Reds, Astros, Orioles, Royals, 1965–82

May was a right-handed power hitter who hit 20 or more home runs 11 straight years in his career, and went over the 30-homer mark three times, peaking with 39 in 1971, his last year as a Red. He appeared in his first and only World Series as a regular in 1970, hitting .389 with two homers and eight RBI. Traded to Houston in 1972, May's power numbers declined in the cavernous Astrodome, but he still averaged 27 homers in his three seasons there. As many power hitters are apt to do, the 6'3" May was prone to striking out, whiffing over 100 times on 10 occasions in his career.

LIFETIME STATS: BA: .267, HR: 354, RBI: 1,244, H: 2,031, SB: 39

#312 Fred "Dixie" Walker
OF, Yankees, White Sox, Tigers, Dodgers, Pirates
1931, 1933–49

Hailing from Georgia (hence the nickname), Walker languished in the Yankee farm system until 1933, but blossomed in 1937 after a trade to the White Sox, hitting 16 triples and a .302 batting average. Walker is the brother of Harry "the Hat" Walker and they both hold the distinction of being the only brothers to win batting titles, Dixie in 1944, and Harry in 1947. Traded to the Dodgers in 1939, Dixie Walker was loved in Brooklyn. Dubbed "the People's Choice," he hit .308 against the hated Giants in his first full season in Flatbush, and hit over .300 in all but one of his seasons there, including that league-leading year of 1944, when he hit a career-high .357. Walker, to his discredit, when hearing of Branch Rickey's plans to promote Jackie Robinson to the Dodgers, launched a petition stating that he and the players who signed it would refuse to play with Robinson. When this move failed, Walker asked to be traded, and he was granted his wish, but a year later. Walker and Robinson did coexist on the 1947 Dodger team without incident, however. Walker ended up in Pittsburgh.

LIFETIME STATS: BA: .306, HR: 105, RBI: 1,023, H: 2,064, SB: 59

#313 Chuck Knoblauch
2B-OF-DH, Twins, Yankees, Royals, 1991–2002

Knoblauch came to the Minnesota Twins in 1991 and hit .281 with 25 stolen bases, and was a key performer in the Twins run to become the first team to go from last place to a world title. For his efforts, the 5'9" Texan was named the AL Rookie of the Year. He continued his fine play in the Series against the Braves, hitting .308. A four-time All Star, Knoblauch hit .297 in 1992, and peaked in 1996, when he hit .341 with 197 hits and 140 runs. He led the league in doubles in 1994 with 45. Knoblauch stole 30 or more bases seven times in his career, peaking in 1997 with 62. He was traded to the Yankees in 1998, and struggled to a .265 average, and had some defensive difficulties. Still Knoblauch managed to hit when it counted as he hit .375 in the World Series win over San Diego that year, including a homer that tied the game in the first contest.

LIFETIME STATS: BA: .298, HR: 98, RBI: 615, H: 1,839, SB: 407

#314 Rafael Corrales "Raffy" Palmeiro
1B-OF-DH, Cubs, Rangers, Orioles, 1986–2005

Palmeiro was an underappreciated star in his first three years with the Cubs, even though he hit .307 in his first full year there and made the All Star team.

He was traded to Texas and moved from the outfield to first base. After struggling a bit, Palmeiro found his groove and hit .319 in 1990 and .322 in 1991. He was traded to the Orioles and really hit his stride there, hitting .300 or better twice. From 1995 to 1998, while playing for the Orioles, he averaged 40 home runs a year.

Palmeiro returned to Texas, and his home run production increased, hitting between 37 and 47 homers a year for the next six seasons. He became a consistent, feared slugger.

In 2004, Palmeiro's contract with the Rangers ran out, and he re-signed with the Orioles. He had always been popular in Baltimore, and in 2004, he continued to be. But rumors of steroid abuse began to dog him, and as Major League baseball started to crack down on performance-enhancing substances, Palmeiro's production dropped dramatically in 2005, his last year.

Palmeiro reached the 3,000-hit plateau, which usually is an automatic ticket to the Hall of Fame. Time will tell if his alleged steroid use prevents him from admission.

LIFETIME STATS: BA: .288, HR: 585, RBI: 1,835, H: 3,020, SB: 97

#**315** Luke Easter

1B, Cincinnati Crescents, Homestead Grays (Negro Leagues), Indians, 1949–54

Easter played in the Negro Leagues for three years, playing catcher and first base. The Indians bought the muscular, 6'4", 240-pound Easter for the 1949 season. In 1950 Easter really started making an impact, belting 28 homers and knocking in 107, one of two times he eclipsed the 100 mark in RBI. He was known for his tape-measure homers, as he belted a memorable 477-foot blast in the upper deck of Cleveland's Municipal Stadium in 1950. The left-hand-hitting Easter had his best power year with the Tribe in 1952 when he clouted 31 homers. Bad knees limited Easter's playing time and he retired from an already abbreviated playing career in 1954 only to continue to hit tape-measure homers in minor league venues (reportedly Easter hit a 550-foot home run that went clear out of Buffalo's Offerman Stadium).

LIFETIME STATS: BA: .274, HR: 93, RBI: 340, H: 472, SB: 1

#316 Ken Griffey Sr.

OF-1B-DH, Reds, Yankees, Braves, Mariners, 1973–91

After playing sparingly in his first two seasons with the Reds, Ken Griffey Sr. became an integral part of Cincinnati's "Big Red Machine" in 1975 as he hit .305, then came in second in the NL with a .336 mark in 1976. He was also in double figures in steals seven times with the Reds, peaking at 34 in 1976. Griffey hit a career .312 in three National League Championship Playoff series. In Game Seven of the 1975 World Series, Griffey scored the tying and the winning runs as the Reds won their first crown since 1940. In 1982, he moved to New York and hit over .300 twice more before going to the Braves in mid-1986. He was a lethal pinch hitter in 1987, going an amazing 11 for 18. He briefly returned to the Reds, and then signed with the Seattle Mariners to play with his son. Playing left and center in the Mariner outfield, they became the first father and son combination to play at the same time. Griffey once said that playing in the majors with his son was his greatest thrill in baseball.

LIFETIME STATS: BA: .296, HR: 152, RBI: 859, H: 2,143, SB: 193

#317 Lon "The Arkansas Hummingbird" Warnecke

RHP, Cubs, Cardinals, 1930–1943, 1945

Warnecke was so nicknamed because he was from Arkansas and could play the guitar. He came up to the Cubs in 1930, but really made an impact with them in 1932 when the right-hander led the league in wins (22), winning percentage (.786), ERA (2.37) and shutouts (4) in helping the Cubbies win the National League pennant. He declined to a more modest 18–13 the following year, but led the loop in complete games with 26. In 1934, the 6'2" righty started the season by hurling back-to-back one-hitters on the road. A three-time 20-game winner, Warnecke was sent to the Cardinals, where he pitched effectively for them from 1937 until 1942. In an August game in 1941, he no-hit the Reds 2–0.

LIFETIME STATS: W: 192, L: 121, SV: 1, ERA: 3.18, SO: 1,140, CG: 192

#**318** Brett Butler

OF, Braves, Indians, Giants, Mets, Dodgers, 1981–97

Butler displaced MVP Dale Murphy in the Braves' center field in 1982. (Murphy moved to right.) The speedy Butler stroked a league-leading 13 triples in 1983 and swiped 39. Butler was also perhaps the best drag bunter of his time. The 5'10", 160-pound speedster was traded to the Indians in 1984, and he promptly drove American League catchers crazy, stealing a career best 52 bases and scoring 108 runs that year. In 1985 he hit .311, and scored 108 runs. He would eclipse the century mark in runs scored four more times in his career. In 1986, Butler led the American League in triples with 14, becoming only the second man to lead both leagues in that department (Hall of Famer Sam Crawford was the other). Butler also shone defensively as he led the AL in fielding with a .998 fielding average in 1985.

LIFETIME STATS: BA: .290, HR: 54, RBI: 576, H: 2,375, SB: 558

#319 Willie Davis

OF, Dodgers, Expos, Rangers, Cardinals, Padres,
Angels, 1960–76, 1979

When Davis came up with the Dodgers in 1960, he was
regarded as one of the fastest players in the game, especially going from first to third. In 1962, he teamed with
Maury Wills to set a record for stolen bases by two teammates when Wills stole 104 and Davis pilfered 32. He
was a three-time Gold Glove award winner. But he could also struggle afield,
as Davis twice led the league in errors. Offensively, Davis went on a 31-game
hitting streak in 1969, the longest skein in the league since 1945, and then
went on another streak of 25 games. He hit an impressive .311 that year, and
hit .305 the following summer. In 1971, Davis became a member of a Buddhist sect, and openly practiced his religion in the clubhouse. Davis, thinking
he would fit right in in predominately Buddhist Japan, signed a contract
with a team in that country in 1977. He found out otherwise, as both Japanese teams he played for complained of his chanting before games.

LIFETIME STATS: BA: .279, HR: 182, RBI: 1,053, H: 2,561, SB: 398

#320 Joe Kelley

OF-1B, Braves, Pirates, Baltimore (NL), Dodgers,
Orioles, Reds, 1891–1908. Hall of Fame, 1971

Kelley came up with the Braves and then went to the
Pirates, but it was with the early Baltimore Orioles of the
National League that he made his mark. He hit over .300
for all of the six full seasons he played in Baltimore, finishing one season at .393 and another at .388. He led the Orioles to three
straight pennants. The fleet-footed Kelley stole 30 or more bases six times

in his career, including 87 in 1896, when he hit .364. Between 1894 and 1896, Kelley scored a whopping 461 runs. In 1894, Joe Kelley had a day to remember when he went a perfect nine-for-nine in a doubleheader as in the first game he rapped three singles and a triple, and in the second game he collected four doubles and a single. Groundskeeping in 1894 was not what it is today in baseball. Kelley was known to hide a reserve ball in the high grass of left field in case he had to use it. The trick backfired on Kelley one game when two balls were simultaneously thrown into the infield.

LIFETIME STATS: BA: .317, HR: 65, RBI: 1,194, H: 2,220, SB: 443

#**321** Pedro Guerrero

1B-OF-3B, Dodgers, Cardinals, 1978–92

Guerrero was signed by the Cleveland Indians in 1973 as a slender 16-year-old shortstop, but after a few years in the Indian farm system, he was sent to the Dodgers for Bruce Ellingsen, in perhaps the worst deal the Tribe ever made. Guerrero began to grow into his body, and after a stint on the disabled list, he began to hit his stride. In 1980 he hit .322 in part-time play. In 1981, the Puerto Rico native became the regular right fielder and hit 12 homers and had 48 RBI in the strike-shortened year. He helped the Dodgers win the World Series over the Yankees, hitting two homers and knocking in seven runs, earning him a share of the Series MVP award. Guerrero was one of the National League's best hitters in the 1980s, putting up fine offensive numbers like the 32-homer, 100-RBI season of 1982 and another 32-homer season with 103 RBI in 1983.

LIFETIME STATS: BA: .300, HR: 215, RBI: 898, H: 1,618, SB: 97

#**322** Larry Wayne "Chipper" Jones
3B-SS-OF-DH, Braves, 1993–present

Jones was nicknamed "Chipper" when he played high school ball in Florida for his dad, and thus, a "chip off the old block." He became a Brave starter in 1995 and put up decent numbers. But for the next eight years in a row, 1996–2003, Jones had 100 or more RBI. In 1999 he had his best year to date, earning him the MVP award. That year Jones hit .319 with 45 homers and 110 RBI and 41 doubles. He also excelled on the base paths with 25 steals that year, and showed a keen eye at the plate as he drew 126 walks. Seven times in his career, the consistent, durable Jones has hit 25 or more homers, and in 2001 he had a career-best .330 batting average.

LIFETIME STATS: BA: 304, HR: 454, RBI: 1,561, H: 2,615, SB: 149

#**323** Joe Carter
OF-1B-DH, Cubs, Indians, Padres, Blue Jays, Orioles, Giants, 1983–98

Only nine players have batted in 100 or more runs 10 times in their careers. Joe Carter is one of them, joining such illustrious names as Babe Ruth, Lou Gehrig, Willie Mays and Hank Aaron. In 1986, Carter had his first big year with the Indians by garnering 200 hits for the first and only time in his career, hitting .302 and smacking 29 homers with 121 RBI. In Game Six of the 1993 World Series against the Phillies at Toronto, Carter was at the plate to face Philadelphia closer Mitch "Wild Thing" Williams with the Jays trailing 6–5 in the bottom of the ninth. Carter then stroked a low fastball over the left field fence to clinch the World

Series for the Blue Jays, their second in a row. Carter thus joined Bill Maze-roski as the only players to hit walk-off homers to clinch a World Series title.

LIFETIME STATS: BA: .259, HR: 396, RBI: 1,445, H: 2,184, SB: 231

#**324** Bob Boone
C, Phillies, Angels, Royals, 1972–90

Boone is the son of Ray Boone and the father of present major leaguers Bret and Aaron Boone, and was regarded as his era's best defensive catcher. He won seven Gold Gloves. In 1987 he also broke Al Lopez's major league record for games caught, a record that had stood for 30 years. In 1978 he led NL catchers in fielding percentage. In 1980, in the World Series against the Royals, he hit an impressive .412 with four RBI as the Phillies won the World Series. He was traded to the Angels in 1982, and threw out 63 of 109 runners attempting to steal in his first year there. He again blossomed with the bat in the postseason as he hit .455 in a 1986 ALCS loss to the Red Sox.

LIFETIME STATS: BA: .254, HR: 105, RBI: 826, H: 1,838, SB: 38

#**325** Roy White
OF-DH, Yankees, 1965–79

In 1966, though not a regular, White led the Yankees in stolen bases with 14, and as many aging Yankee stars retired, the slender 5'10" White became their only name player and cleanup hitter. He became one of the few players in baseball history to hit triples from both sides of the plate in the same game, and also did the same in homers five times. Despite a weaker-than-average throwing arm, White was a superb left fielder for the Yanks, playing the entire season of 1971 without making an error, the first Yankee ever to do so. Except for his first and last years, White was in double figures in steals every year. In the 1978 World Series, White hit .333. He started the Yankee comeback in Game Three when he homered to send the Yankees on their way back from a two-game deficit to sweep the next four from the Dodgers.

LIFETIME STATS: BA: .271, HR: 160, RBI: 758, H: 1,803, SB: 233

#**326** Jim Bottomley

1B, Cardinals, Reds, Browns 1922–37. Hall of Fame, 1974

"Sunny Jim" Bottomley, so-called because of his affable nature, was a strong left-handed cleanup hitter. He slugged .500 for his career, and hit a career high .371 in his first full season with the Cardinals. Bottomley certainly "had a day" on September 16, 1924, when he drove in a record 12 runs in a twin bill against the Brooklyn Dodgers with two homers, including a grand slam, a double, and three singles. The left-handed first baseman had 110 or more RBI from 1924 to 1929, peaking at 137 in 1929 and leading the league twice in that category during that span. The Illinois native led the NL in the rare combination of triples (20) and homers (31) in 1928, the year he won the MVP award. He once stroked three triples in a game. In 1931, Bottomley finished third in the National League batting race by percentage points to Chick Hafey at .3489, and Bill Terry at .3486, to Bottomley's .3482 in the closest NL batting race ever.

LIFETIME STATS: BA: .310, HR: 219, RBI: 1,422, H: 2,313, SB: 58

#327 Darren Daulton

C-OF, Phillies, Marlins, 1983–97

Daulton had a tough time in his first three seasons with the Phillies, often landing on the disabled list. During those three seasons, he incurred two knee surgeries. In 1992, Daulton showed he could become a star in his league, hitting 27 homers, and a league-best 109 RBI. A true leader, he helped the Phillies to the National League pennant the following year with 24 homers and 105 RBI. Once again the injury bug hit and the unfortunate Daulton was out for much of 1994 and again in 1995. This forced him from behind the plate as by this time he had undergone eight left-knee operations. The resilient Daulton came back for the 1997 campaign, and played the outfield, but was then traded to the upstart Florida Marlins, who won the NL pennant. Daulton had a great World Series, hitting .389, including a homer and two doubles, and despite all the injuries and rehab, came away with a championship ring as the Marlins beat the Indians in the seven-game Series.

LIFETIME STATS: BA: .245, HR: 137, RBI: 588, H: 891, SB: 50

#328 Joe Adcock

1B-OF, Reds, Braves, Indians, Angels, 1950–66

Adcock was a hard-hitting first baseman who started out with the Reds and found his way blocked at first base by another powerful hitter, Ted Kluszewski. Adcock's wish to be traded was granted in 1953 when he was dealt to the Braves. Adcock had some fine seasons there. On July 31, 1954, he homered four times and struck a double in Ebbets Field against the Dodgers to set the major league record for total bases in a game (18). He also tied the record for most home runs in a game. Adcock could hit some tape-measure shots as he, along with Henry Aaron and Lou Brock, became the only players to homer into the cavernous Polo Grounds' bleachers. Adcock had 10 grand slams as a player, with 26 multiple-homer games.

LIFETIME STATS: BA: .277, HR: 336, RBI: 1,122, H: 1,832, SB: 20

#**329** Dave "Beauty" Bancroft
SS, Phillies, Giants, Braves, Dodgers, 1915–30. Hall of Fame, 1974

Bancroft broke in with the Philadelphia Phillies in 1915, and acquired his nickname there when he would say "Beauty" every time his pitcher would break off a great pitch. Bancroft had quick hands, great range, and was an intelligent player. Many consider him to be one of the best-fielding shortstops ever. He helped the Phillies win the pennant in 1915 and to a second-place finish the next season. The switch-hitter was sent to John McGraw's Giants in 1920, where he flourished, hitting over .300 the next three years there, and continuing his defensive wizardry at shortstop. Bancroft had a six-for-six day in 1920, and hit for the cycle in 1921, while leading NL shortstops in assists, putouts, and double plays.

LIFETIME STATS: BA: .279, HR: 32, RBI: 591, H: 2,004, SB: 145

#330 Bruce Sutter

RHP, Cubs, Cardinals, Braves, 1976–88. Hall of Fame, 2006

Bruce Sutter was a relief pitcher who had exceptionally long hands and a limber wrist. He used them to throw the devastating split-fingered fastball, which the batters found hard to pick up since it looks like a fastball coming into the plate, only to dip downward. For nine years Sutter used this pitch and became the most dominant closer in the National League. The 6'2" reliever had 27 saves in 1978 for the lowly Cubs, and had a great year in 1979 when he notched 37 saves with a 2.22 ERA and won the Cy Young award, only the second reliever to receive that award. Sutter also got the win in the All Star game for the second year in a row, a feat matched only by Don Drysdale. Sutter was dealt to the Cardinals, and was their closer for four years, leading the league in saves for three out of the four years he was in St. Louis. In 1982 Sutter had a win and two saves in the World Series, as the Cardinals annexed their first world championship in 15 years. In 1984 Sutter had his finest save year with 45, tying the then–major league record.

LIFETIME STATS: W: 68, L: 71, SV: 300, ERA: 2.83, SO: 861, CG: 0

#331 Kirk Gibson

OF-DH, Tigers, Dodgers, Royals, Pirates, 1979–95

Gibson was a Michigan native who was also a star football receiver at Michigan State, and chose to sign with his hometown Detroit Tigers. The youthful Gibson was a fine combination of hustle, speed and power. In 1984, Gibson hit 27 homers, knocked in 91 and was the MVP of the ALCS sweep of the Royals. He hit two homers in the Game Five clincher in the World Series win over the Padres. In 1988 he signed with the Dodgers and hit .290 in helping them to the NL pennant. Sustaining a pulled left hamstring and strained ligaments in his right knee, Gibson was listed as doubtful to play in the World Series. In the 9th inning of Game One, the AL champion A's were up 4–3, with ace closer Dennis Eckersley pitching. The Dodgers had a runner on first when Gibson got the call. He limped up to the plate and the A's closer quickly got two strikes on him. Then Gibson, with a one-legged swing, hit the next pitch miraculously over the right-field fence for a 5–4 Dodger win. Los Angeles went on to win the Series. Gibson's homer and joyous limp around the bases have been called the greatest moment in Los Angeles' sports history.

LIFETIME STATS: BA: .268, HR: 255, RBI: 870, H: 1,553, SB: 284

#**332** Chuck Klein

OF, Phillies, Cubs, Pirates, 1928–44. Hall of Fame, 1980

The left-handed Klein was perhaps the best hitter in the National League from 1929 to 1933. Ideally suited for cozy Baker Bowl in Philadelphia, where the distance down the right-field line was only 280 feet, Klein averaged 36 homers, 139 RBI and hit .359 in that span. In his first full season, he led the league in homers with 43 and hit .356. His best season was in 1930 when he hit .386, belted 59 doubles, scored 158 runs, knocked in 170 runs and slugged a gaudy .687. Defensively, he was adroit at solving the nuances of the corrugated tin wall at his home field as he rang up an unbelievable 44 assists that season as well as participating in 10 double plays. He was named MVP in 1932, and won the Triple Crown in 1933 with 28 homers, 120 RBI and a .368 batting average. Overall, Klein led the league in homers four times, in RBI twice, and was an All Star twice.

LIFETIME STATS: BA: .320, HR: 300, RBI: 1,201, H: 2,076, SB: 79

#333 Larry Gardner
3B-2B, Red Sox, A's, Indians, 1908–24

The left-hand-hitting Gardner played both second and third base for the outstanding Red Sox teams of the 1910s, playing on three world championship teams. A collegiate star second baseman at the University of Vermont, Gardner hit .315 in the 1912 championship season, second on the team to Hall of Famer Tris Speaker, and had 86 RBI. In the World Series that year, he had five RBI, leading the Sox. In 1916, with Speaker traded away, Gardner led the Red Sox in hitting with a .308 average, and led the squad in RBI with 62. In that year's World Series, the diminutive (5'8") Vermonter hit two homers as the Red Sox won it all again.

LIFETIME STATS: BA: .289, HR: 27, RBI: 934, H: 1,931, SB: 165

#334 Don Newcombe
RHP, Dodgers, Reds, Cleveland, 1949–51, 1954–60

Newcombe came up to the Dodgers in 1949 and was promptly shelled in his first start. Instead of farming him out as Newcombe expected, manager Burt Shotton gave him words of encouragement. Shotton's patience paid off as the big right-hander then shut out the Reds 3–0 in his next outing on the way to a 17–8 record and the Rookie of the Year award. He went 19–11 in 1950 and 20–9 in 1951. He also led the league in strikeouts in 1951 with 164. "Big Newk" missed the next two seasons due to military service, and was 9–8 in 1954. He rebounded in the Dodgers only championship season in Brooklyn (1953) by fashioning a 20–5 mark. In 1956 Newcombe had things working on all cylinders as he went an astounding 27–7, and became the first pitcher to win the Cy Young award and the MVP award the same season, thus also becoming the only player to win the Rookie of the Year, the Cy Young and the MVP awards in his career.

LIFETIME STATS: W: 149, L: 90, SV: 7, ERA: 3.56, SO: 1,129, CG: 136

#**335** George Gore

OF, Cubs, Giants, New York (PL), Cardinals, 1879–92

The fun-loving Gore was one of the stars of the early Cub dynasty in the 1880s. In 1880, he led the league in hitting with a .360 mark and slugging with a .463 average. He hit over .300 eight times in his career. He was on four pennant-winning teams in the 1880s. The fleet-footed Gore scored 100 or more runs seven times in his career, peaking in 1886 when he dented the plate 150 times. That year he also drew 102 walks, particularly noteworthy since nine balls were needed to draw a walk back then. The speedy center fielder was called "Piano Legs" because of his powerful upper thighs. Gore hit two doubles and three triples in a single game in 1885 to set a then-record of five extra bases in a game. He stole seven bases in an 1881 game. Gore was sent to New York, where he continued to shine, hitting over .300 two more times in his career. Gore is one of only three players with more than 4,000 at-bats that has scored more runs (1,327) than games played (1,310).

LIFETIME STATS: BA: .302, HR: 46, RBI: 618, H: 1,642, SB: 170

#336 John Montgomery "Monte" Ward

SS-2B-RHP-OF, Providence (NL), Giants, Brooklyn (PL), Dodgers, 1878–94. Hall of Fame, 1964

Ward was a Renaissance man in the early days of baseball. He was a very good position player as well as a pitcher. The right-handed pitcher had a fine rookie season for Providence, winning 22 and leading the league with a dazzling ERA of 1.51, winning two games in one day on one occasion. The following season Ward went 47–19, leading the league in winning percentage and strikeouts, while the Grays won the National League pennant. He followed that up with a 39–24 year logging 595 innings in the process. He threw a perfect game on June 17 against Buffalo. On days that he wasn't pitching, Ward would play the infield, eventually moving there full-time. He hit left-handed, and went to the Giants, where he hit .338 and led the league in steals with 111 in 1887. While with Brooklyn in 1890, he hit .335 with 188 hits and 63 steals. He led the loop in that department in 1892 when he pilfered 88.

LIFETIME STATS: BA: .275, HR: 26, RBI: 867, H: 2,104, SB: 540. W: 164, L: 102, SV: 3, ERA: 2.10, SO: 920, CG: 244

#337 Gil McDougald

2B-3B-SS, Yankees, 1951–60

The versatile McDougald could play any infield position except first base with skill and dexterity. Coming up as a second baseman, Yankee manager Casey Stengel wanted him to try third base, and eventually shortstop on occasion. In his rookie season he hit .306, played 55 games at second and 82 games at third and won the AL Rookie of the Year award. In a 1951 game, he collected six RBI in one inning, tying an AL record. In 1952 he led AL third basemen in double plays, and in 1957 he led league shortstops in the same category. McDougald also shined in the postseason when in 1951 he became the first rookie to hit a grand slam in the World Series.

LIFETIME STATS: BA: 276, HR: 112, RBI: 576, H: 1,291, SB: 45

#338 Greg "The Bull" Luzinski
OF-DH, Phillies, White Sox, 1970–84

Luzinski became a regular with the Phillies in 1972, hitting 18 homers as a rookie, then improving to 29 homers the following season. Dubbed "the Bull" because of his massive body and powerful right-handed-hitting swing, Luzinski joined with fellow slugger Mike Schmidt to form a formidable one-two punch in the heart of the Phillies batting order: The duo averaged nearly 66 homers a season from 1975 to 1980. In 1975 Luzinski clouted 34 homers, led the NL in RBI with 120 and hit .300. In 1977 he hit 39 homers, had 130 RBI and a .309 batting average. He was sent to the White Sox, where he became the team's full-time designated hitter. His best power year in Chicago was 1983 when he hit 32 homers with 95 RBI and helped the White Sox win the division. Three of his homers cleared the Comiskey Park roof.

LIFETIME STATS: BA: .276, HR: 307, RBI: 1,128, H: 1,795, SB: 37

#339 Cecil Travis
SS-3B-OF, Senators, 1933–41, 1945–47

Travis broke in with the Senators on May 16, 1933, and turned in a five-for-five game. The left-handed hitter loved slapping the ball to the opposite field early in his career, and played very well defensively at either third base or shortstop. A three-time All Star, the slender Georgian hit over .300 seven times as a starter, peaking at .359 in 1941 when Travis came in second to Ted Williams in the American League batting race. Travis did lead the league in hits that season with 218. He also collected 19 triples that year. Learning to use the whole field, Travis also hit a solid .344 in 1937. After 1941, like so many other major leaguers, Travis entered the military service, missing three seasons, and part of a fourth. When he returned, he just couldn't recapture the timing needed to hit consistently, and he retired in 1947.

LIFETIME STATS: BA: .314, HR: 27, RBI: 657, H: 1,544, SB: 23

#340 Frank White
2B-SS, Royals, 1973–90

White was a great-fielding second baseman who played his entire career in Kansas City. He won eight Gold Gloves, including six in a row, and led American League second sackers in fielding percentage three times. In 1977, he played in 62 straight games without committing an error. Offensively, White wasn't exactly an automatic out either, hitting .255 lifetime. He had decent power as he reached double figures in homers seven times and twice hit 20 or more homers in a season, stroking 22 in 1985 and 1986. He was also a threat on the base paths, stealing 20 or more bases three times in his career. In 1980 White hit a remarkable .545 in the ALCS sweep of the Yankees, earning him the MVP award for that series. He also hit a homer off Cardinal ace Joaquin Andujar that helped the Royals win Game Three of the World Series five years later.

LIFETIME STATS: BA: .255, HR: 160, RBI: 886, H: 2,006, SB: 178

#**341** Elwood "Bingo" DeMoss

2B-SS, Topeka Giants, Kansas City Giants, Chicago American Giants, Indianapolis ABC's, Detroit Stars, Cleveland Giants, Chicago Brown Bombers, Brooklyn Brown Bombers (Negro Leagues), 1905–43

"Bingo" DeMoss, so named because he consistently made contact with the ball, was considered to be the best second baseman in black baseball at the turn of the 20th century. His reflexes and throwing arm made it seem as though he didn't touch the ball on double-play relays, just redirected it to first. A right-handed hitter who could hit the ball where it was pitched, DeMoss was an important man in the lineup, though he rarely hit the .300 mark. He settled in as an ideal number-two hitter, moving the runner along with either a hit or run or a well-placed bunt. DeMoss often laid a bunt down and beat it out with his excellent speed. Some reports say that he had the ability to put a reverse spin on the ball when he bunted it to make it even more difficult for a charging infielder. DeMoss helped the Indianapolis ABC's to the Negro League championship in 1916, and captained three other championship squads.

LIFETIME STATS (incomplete): BA: .286, SB: 346

#**342** Eddie Cicotte

RHP , Tigers, Red Sox, White Sox, 1905, 1908–20

Cicotte had a poor three-game trial with the Tigers (1–1, 3.50 ERA) in 1908, and was farmed out, not to resurface until three years later with the Red Sox. In just over four seasons there, he was barely over a .500 pitcher at 51–46. In 1912 he was traded to the White Sox, where he won 18 games the next year. Cicotte eventually became a great shineball or spitball pitcher, as the pitch was still legal then. In 1916, he went 15–7, second in the league with a minuscule ERA of 1.78. Cicotte fashioned a 28–12 mark the following season with an ever-better 1.53 ERA, leading the league that year in wins, ERA and innings pitched. In 1919 he won a league high 29, lost only seven, and led the league in winning percentage (.806) and complete games (30). Cicotte had a clause in his contract that would give him a bonus if he won 30 games, and records show that he only pitched 18 more innings after September 5. Some speculate that tight-fisted owner Charlie Comiskey ordered manager Kid Gleason to hold Cicotte back. This could have been the reason why Cicotte joined seven others in accepting money to throw the 1919 World Series to the Reds.

LIFETIME STATS: W: 208, L: 149, SV: 25, ERA: 2.38, SO: 1,374, CG: 249

#**343** Harry Stovey

OF-1B, Worcester (NL), Philadelphia (AA), Boston (PL), Braves, Baltimore (NL), Dodgers, 1880–93

Stovey was one of baseball's stars of the 1880s. His real name was Harry Duffield Stowe, but he changed his name so his mother wouldn't know he was playing baseball. The right-hander could do it all as he led the league in homers five times, triples and runs scored four times, slugging percentage three times, stolen bases twice and RBI and doubles once. The Philadelphia native once hit two triples in the same inning and three for the game in an 1884 contest and hit for the cycle in 1888. The right-handed Stovey is only one of three players with over 4,000 at bats to score more runs (1,492) than games played (1,486). George Gore and Billy Hamilton are the others.

LIFETIME STATS: BA: .289, HR: 122, RBI: 908, H: 1,771, SB: 509

#344 George Edward "Rube" Waddell

LHP, Louisville (NL), Pirates, Cubs, A's, Browns, 1897, 1899–1910. Hall of Fame, 1946

Waddell was a eccentric fireballing southpaw whose fastball was compared to the great Walter Johnson's. Connie Mack called him one of the best left-handers he ever saw. Mack should know. From 1902 to 1905, Waddell won 21 or more games. He also led the league in strikeouts for six straight seasons. He set a major league record for strikeouts in a season with 349, a mark that stood for over 70 years until broken by Nolan Ryan. In 1905, he went 27–10 and led the AL in wins, games, ERA and strikeouts. An arm injury that year slowed Waddell down and he never again approached the numbers he put up earlier in his career. Waddell was a flake, but, probably not mentally ill, as some have portrayed him. At one time, he wrestled alligators in the off-season in Florida. He also held up a game once because he was playing marbles with children outside the park. In 1908, Mack traded him to the Browns. In July, Waddell got his revenge as he struck out 16 A's, tying the AL record for strikeouts in a game at the time.

LIFETIME STATS: W: 193, L: 143, SV: 5, ERA: 2.16, SO: 2,316, CG: 261

#345 Herman "Germany" Long

SS-2B, Kansas City (AA), Braves, Yankees, Tigers, Phillies, 1889–1904

Long, born of German immigrants, hit .275 as a rookie with Kansas City in 1889. From there he was sent to the Boston Beaneaters, and helped them win three straight pennants. Long made a large number of errors, but according to many experts of his day, he was considered one of the best shortstops in the game because of his tremendous range and athleticism. He is ranked second all-time in chances per game. One day, Long couldn't reach a ball with his glove, so he stuck out his foot, deflected the ball with his toe, caught it, and threw the runner out. Long was a good hitter, and had his greatest offensive season in 1896, when he hit .343 with 105 runs scored and 100 RBI. Over the years, he was a serious threat on the base paths as he stole 20 or more bases 14 straight years. He also led the league in homers in 1900 with 12, though his batting average started to decline.

LIFETIME STATS: BA: .277, HR: 91, RBI: 1,055, H: 2,127, SB: 534

#346 Tim McCarver

C-1B, Cardinals, Phillies, Expos, Red Sox, 1959–80

McCarver played in eight games with the Cardinals in 1959 and in six games for the 1980 Phillies, thus becoming a four-decade player. He also did some great things between those years. He was one of the top defensive catchers in the league in the '60s and '70s. He played well in the national spotlight, making a hit in every one of the seven games in the 1964 World Series win over the Yankees and hitting a team best .478. In Game Five, he hit a game-winning three-run homer in the top of the 10th, giving the Redbirds a 5–2 win. The Tennessee native could run for a catcher as he became the only catcher ever to lead the league in triples, collecting 13 in 1966. In 1967 McCarver had his best offensive season, hitting 14 homers, knocking home 69 and hitting .295, finishing second in the MVP race to teammate Orlando Cepeda. At the end of his career, McCarver was best known as Phillie ace Steve Carlton's personal catcher.

LIFETIME STATS: BA: .271, HR: 97, RBI: 645, H: 1,501, SB: 61

#347 Jim "Junior" Gilliam
2B-3B-OF, Dodgers, 1953–66

After being a member of the Negro National League All Stars for three years, Gilliam was signed by the Dodgers and arrived in 1953. Replacing the legendary Jackie Robinson at second base, Gilliam won the Rookie of the Year award, led the league in triples, and set a rookie record for walks with 100. Gilliam played either second or third in the Dodgers infield, and showed his versatility by playing the outfield and even first base on two occasions. In 1956, the 5'10" Gilliam hit .300 and was on the NL All Star team. He also scored at least 100 runs for the fourth successive year, had 43 RBI and stole 21 bases. Gilliam was also a good fielder as he tied a major league record for second basemen by accumulating 12 assists in a nine-inning game.

LIFETIME STATS: BA: .265, HR: 65, RBI: 558, H: 1,889, SB: 203

#348 Jim Sundberg

C, Rangers, Brewers, Royals, Cubs, 1974–89

Sundburg started out with the Texas Rangers and the durable backstop played 16 seasons, appearing in more games behind the dish than all but three other catchers: Carlton Fisk, Gary Carter and Bob Boone. His defensive skills were never questioned as he led the American League in total chances six times, in putouts and assists six times, in fielding percentage six times and in double plays four times. In his career, he collected six Gold Gloves, and his .995 fielding percentage in 1979 set a new record. Runners were loath to challenge that strong and accurate right arm, since he threw out more than half of the would-be stealers. Sundberg also was very durable at shaking off nagging injuries, appearing in 140 or more games behind the plate each year from 1975 to 1980.

LIFETIME STATS: BA: .248, HR: 95, RBI: 624, H: 1,493, SB: 20

#349 Edgar Martinez

DH-3B-1B, Mariners, 1987–2004

Martinez is one of the great right-hand hitters in this era. Not an especially good defensive player, partly because of his bad knees, Martinez has made up for that offensively as a designated hitter par excellence for the Seattle Mariners since 1987. He led the American League twice in batting, once in 1992 with a .343 average and again in 1995 when he hit .356, thus becoming the first right-handed hitter to win two batting crowns since the great Joe DiMaggio way back in 1940. He has hit over .300 ten times in his career and has batted in 100 or more runs six times. Martinez has very good power as he once hit 37 homers, but it is his doubles he is best known for. This "doubles machine" hit 35 or more two-baggers eight times in his career, peaking twice at 52 and leading the league twice in that department, becoming the first to do so in successive seasons since Joe Medwick in 1936 and 1937.

LIFETIME STATS: BA: .312, HR: 309, RBI: 1,261, H: 2,247, SB: 49

#350 Luis "El Tiante" Tiant
RHP, Indians, Twins, Red Sox, Yankees, Pirates, 1964–82

"El Tiante" came up with the Indians in mid-1964 and posted a 10–4 mark. In 1968, Tiant went 21–9, led the league with nine shutouts, and fashioned a minuscule 1.60 ERA, also leading the league in that category. After two subpar years, Tiant, seemingly washed up, signed with the Red Sox. He went 1–7 with a hefty 4.85 ERA in 1971. Red Sox management stuck with Tiant, though, and their patience paid off as Tiant, perfecting his trademark spinning delivery, rebounded the next year to a 15–6 record, led the league with a sterling 1.91 ERA, prompting the *Sporting News* to award him the Comeback Player of the Year award. The right-handed Cuban won 20 or more games three of the next four years in Beantown. In 1975, Tiant was the hero of the postseason. He shut down the three-time defending World Series champion A's in Game One of the ALCS, winning 7–1 on a three-hitter. The Red Sox swept Oakland. In Game One of the World Series, Tiant shut the mighty Reds down 6–0. In Game Four, a gritty Tiant survived the Reds and a pitch count of 158 to eke out a 5–4 win to square the Series at two games apiece. Tiant went 21–12 in 1976, his last big year with Boston, and then tailed off winning 12 and 13 games the next two seasons. He then signed a free-agent pact with the Yankees, and went 13–8 with them in 1979.

LIFETIME STATS: W: 229, L: 172, SV: 15, ERA: 3.30, SO: 2,416, CG: 187

The Women Players

Philip K. Wrigley, owner of baseball's Chicago Cubs, was forced to chew on this financial dilemma at the onset of World War II. With so many of America's young males fighting overseas, baseball was taking a beating at all levels here in the States. Not only was the talent at the top level being compromised but also owners of minor-league and semipro teams were taking a strong hit in the wallet.

Wrigley summoned his general manager, Ken Sells, and gave him a directive to come up with a plan that would breathe fresh air into the suffocating sport. Sells led a committee that ultimately suggested a girls' softball league. Thus, in the spring of 1943, the new league was formed.

Sells was named president of the league and before the initial season was too deep, the board renamed the league the All American Girls' Baseball League (AAGBBL).

It became a work in progress, and while the rules of the game mirrored greatly the rules of professional baseball, the women who played the game certainly provided fans with a very unique form of entertainment.

A smaller ball was used in the beginning that was thrown in underhand fashion. Ultimately, the women were allowed to pitch in a sidearm style that resembled more closely the major-league style of throwing.

The league, which ran from 1943 to 1954, gave some 600 women the chance to compete professionally. That stretch of years is recalled now as both a poignant and exciting time in the history of our national pastime.

The league even had its own "Victory Song."

"Batter up! Hear that call!
The time has come for one and all
To play ball. For we're the members of the All-American League.
We've come from cities near and far,

We've got Canadians, Irishmen and Swedes,
We're all for one and one for all,
We're All-American.

Each girl stands, her head so proudly high,
Her motto Do or Die.
She's not the one to use or need an alibi.
Our chaperones are not too soft
They're not too tough,
Our managers are on the ball.
We've got a president who really knows his stuff.
We're all for one and one for all,
We're All-American.

To further show the American spirit, the teams when introduced would form a "V" on the field.

The following is a list of eight players who anchored the league and who remain now somewhat cult figures of that time in the nation's history, when women stepped forward and helped fill a big gap in the nation's consciousness while the men were away fighting for the same freedom that allowed them to play.

1. Dorothy "Dottie" Schroeder

She was the only women to play all 12 seasons in the All-American League and was a standout performer at shortstop for the South Bend Blue Sox, Kenosha Comets, Fort Wayne Daisies and Kalamazoo Lassies.

A mainstay of the league, Schroeder was Player of the Year in both 1951 and 1953. She held league records in games played (1,249), at bats (4,129) and runs batted in (431).

Blessed with a positive and strong personality, Schroeder played at 5'8" and 150 pounds, wearing her hair in two long braids. She batted .211 lifetime, pretty good considering the league used a dead ball through the 1949 season.

2. Jean Faut

A native of East Greenville, Pennsylvania, Faut tried out for the league in 1946 and soon became perhaps the best overhand pitcher the league ever saw. Her blond hair and blue eyes made her a leading lady of the league.

Faut was responsible for the only two perfect games in league history while pitching for the South Bend Blue Sox. The first was a 2–0 win over the Rockford Peaches in 1951; the second came in 1953 against the Kalamazoo Lassies. Faut's lifetime record was 140–64 with an earned run average of 1.23.

She led the league with 12 shutouts in 1949. Her best season came in 1949, when Faut went 24–8 with a 1.10 earned run average. She pitched 261 innings and whiffed 120.

3. Edie (Perlick) Keating

Keating is considered by league historians to be one of the top 20 women to have played in the All-American League. A consistent hitter and outfielder for eight seasons with the Racine Bells, Keating was called the consummate team player while authoring a lifetime batting average of .240. She had 481 career stolen bases and was a league All Star three times. She set a Racine record for RBI with 63 in 1944.

4. Betsy Jochum

One of the league's strongest players, Jochum might have hit the leagues longest home run one evening while playing for the South Bend Blue Sox against the Minneapolis Millerette's and their ace Dottie Wiltse. In a game won by the Blue Sox, 8–7, Wiltse hit a home run out near the flagpole in deep center field. One South Bend rooter gave Jochum $25 for the blast. It was fairly common during the history of the league for fans to reward the players financially for good hits or overall good play.

Jochum had great speed and was able to track down balls in the outfield. She stole 358 bases in her career, including a career-high 127 in 1944. A career .246 hitter, she switched to pitching when the league allowed mound workers to throw overhand in 1948. She fashioned a 14-13 record with a 1.51 ERA in 215 innings.

5. Dottie (Wiltse) Collins

It was a day and night that Dotty Wiltse would never forget. The Rockford Peaches were in first place in the league and visiting the Fort Wayne Daisies for a doubleheader. Rockford was humbled that day by Wiltse, who pitched both games and won by scores of 5–1 and 1–0.

Later that evening, two young men made a beer delivery to Wiltse and five teammates. One of those young men was Harvey Collins, who had been discharged from the service. Collins, who met Wiltse that night, didn't know at the time he was meeting his future wife. Eight days later Wiltse repeated her two-for-one performance against the Grand Rapids Chicks. Wiltse won the nine-inning opener 14–0 and the seven-inning nightcap 3–1. Wiltse was one of the top underhanded pitchers of the league's early era. In 1945, she produced a 29–10 record and an amazing 0.83 ERA. Wiltse led the league in strikeouts that year with 293. Her lifetime record was 117–76.

6. Doris Sams

Sams was so potent as both a pitcher and an outfielder, she became the first player chosen to the All Star team at two positions.

That honor came in 1947 and didn't come as a shock to those in the know. Pitching for the Muskegon Lassies, Sams pitched a perfect game in August of 1947, a 2–0 win over the Fort Wayne Daisies. Her record that year was 11–4 with a fine ERA of 0.98. On the offensive side of the ledger, Sams batted .280 and drove in 41 runs. She was Player of the Year in both 1947 and 1949. Sams was a five-time All Star in her eight-year career. As a member of the Knoxville Lassies, she often took home runs away from other players by making plays at the outfield fence. Her .290 lifetime average is sixth on the league's all-time list.

7. Earlene "Beans" Risinger

Risinger might not have been Hall of Fame material, as the pretty 6-foot-1 redhead posted a 73–80 mound record over her seven years in the league. It should be noted, though, that Risinger was often able to come up on the winning side of meaningful games.

It's Risinger's story, however, that best represents the heart and soul of the league. Her story in some ways is reflective of many of the stories of how many of the players came one day to find themselves in a professional baseball league.

Born in an Oklahoma town of less than two dozen, Risinger worked through her high school years in the local cotton fields for little money. The family, it's said, didn't have enough cash to buy the local paper. But her father, "Soupy," played sandlot ball on the weekends and the young daughter became not just a fan of the game but a pretty good player under the coaching of her father.

Just out of high school, Risinger read about an exhibition game being played by the All-American League in nearby Oklahoma City. There was also a tryout session being held and young Risinger made the grade.

But she backed out of the offer to play in the league and went back to the cotton fields. A couple of years later she went back for another tryout, and this time a more mature Risinger accepted the offer and was able to fashion a pretty decent career.

8. Connie Wisniewski

Signed by the Milwaukee Chicks in 1943 following a tryout, Wisniewski, 23, posted a 23–10 pitching record and helped the team win a league championship. The team, however, had little support in Milwaukee and moved in 1945 to Grand Rapids, Michigan, and that's where the legend began.

She went 32–11 her first year in Grand Rapids and finished the year with an ERA of .81. She also earned the nickname "Iron Woman" for pitching and winning both ends of a doubleheader against the Racine Belles.

Wisniewski was Player of the Year in 1945 and led the league in winning percentage for three straight seasons.

In 1946, she pitched 40 complete games. In 1948, her offense began to rival her pitching exploits. She hit .289 and led the league with 409 total bases.

#351 John "Johnny" Roseboro
C, Dodgers, Twins, Senators, 1957–70

Roseboro became the Dodgers' regular catcher in 1958 and caught at least 100 games in 11 out of the next 12 years. He caught two of Sandy Koufax's four no-hitters. The best year at the plate for the left-hand-hitting back-stop was in 1961, when he hit 18 homers and had 59 RBI, both career highs. In a heated 1965 game against the hated Giants, Roseboro was behind the plate catching Sandy Koufax while Juan Marichal was at the plate. Roseboro caught the pitch and on the throw back, whizzed the ball past the ear of Marichal. The incensed Marichal then attacked Rose-boro with the bat and bloodied his face. Roseboro, who admitted to provoking the incident, never thought that Marichal would retaliate with his bat. NL President Warren Giles suspended Marichal for nine days and fined him $1,750, and barred Marichal from making the Giants' final trip to Los Ange-les. Roseboro was traded in 1968 to the Twins, and helped them win the American League West championship in 1969. The following season he was sent to the Senators, where he retired midseason after hitting .233.

LIFETIME STATS: BA: .249, HR: 104, RBI: 548, H: 1,206, SB: 67

#352 Jimmy Ryan
OF-SS, Cubs, Chicago (PL), Senators, 1885–1903

Ryan came up to Cap Anson's White Stockings (forerun-ner of the Cubs) in 1885, and became a starter in 1886. A rarity in that he threw left, but batted right, Ryan played a fine right field for Chicago, helping them to their second straight pennant. In 1887 the fleet-footed Ryan was moved to center field and hit over .300 for the next three seasons and stole 30 or more bases each year over that span. Overall, he would hit over .300 11 times in his career. The 1888 season was a tremendous year for Ryan, as he led the league in homers with 16, doubles with 33, hits with 182 and slugging percentage with a .515 mark. Ryan jumped to the Chicago entry of the Players League in 1890 and hit .340, but went back to Anson's team the next season after the Players League folded. The versatile Ryan played all three outfield positions and hit a career best .361 in 1894. He was a threat on the base paths as he stole 27 or more bases nine times in his career.

LIFETIME STATS: BA: .306, HR: 118, RBI: 1,093, H: 2,502, SB: 418

#**353** Jack Fournier

1B-OF, White Sox, Yankees, Cardinals, Dodgers, Braves, 1912–18, 1920–27

Fournier would have been an ideal designated hitter, had he been born 60 years later. He was tremendous offensively but defensively was often pretty uninterested. He rang up .351, .334, and .350 batting averages in the years between 1923 and 1925. In 1915, the left-handed-hitting Fournier led the league in slugging percentage along with 20 doubles and 18 triples. In 1924 Fournier led the American League in homers with 27. He hit over .300 seven times in his career. His best day came in a 1923 game when he went a perfect six-for-six with two doubles and a homer. But, during these same years of offensive achievements, he was frequently at the top of the league in errors.

LIFETIME STATS: BA: .313, HR: 136, RBI: 859, H: 1,631, SB: 145

#354 Ken Caminiti

3B, Astros, Padres, Rangers, Braves, 1987–2001

The switch-hitting Caminiti came up with the Houston Astros, and for the early part of his career was a good, not great, player. But he was traded to the San Diego Padres for the 1995 season, and had a resurgence hitting .302 with 26 homers and 94 RBI. His fielding also peaked, and Caminiti won the first of three straight Gold Gloves. Caminiti rally put it together in 1996 as he hit 40 homers, had 130 RBI, and hit .326, easily copping the National League's Most Valuable Player award. Caminiti had two more solid seasons, with 26 homers and 90 RBI in 1997 and 29 homers and 82 RBI in 1998. He also clouted two homers helping the Padres beat the Atlanta Braves in the NLCS in 1998, but injuries plagued him in the Series that year against the Yankees.

LIFETIME STATS: BA: .272, HR: 239, RBI: 983, H: 1,710, SB: 88

#355 Bobby Wallace

SS-3B, Cleveland (NL), Cardinals, Browns, 1894–1918. Hall of Fame, 1953

Wallace started out as a pitcher and won 10 games and hurled two shutouts in 1896. But then the right-hander turned his attention to third base in 1897, and then to shortstop for the next 17 years. Always considered a superior fielder, Wallace set a record of handling 17 chances in a single game in 1902. He hit better than .300 twice, and finished second in the National League in homers in 1899 with a career high 12. In 1897 and 1899, he drove in over 100 runs. In 1902, he signed with the Browns and his hitting declined, but he continued to be quick on the base paths, accumulating 143 career triples and stealing 201 bases.

LIFETIME STATS: BA: .268, HR: 34, RBI: 1,121, H: 2,309, SB: 201

#**356** Harold Baines

DH-OF, White Sox, Rangers, A's, Orioles, Indians, 1980–2001

The lefty-swinging Baines batted over .300 eight times in his 22-year career and came close to that hallowed mark a number of other times. He became the youngest player in White Sox history to have 100 homers. In 1984, Baines smacked a game-winning homer in the 25th inning against Milwaukee, ending baseball's longest game. The 6'2" Baines slugged 20 or more homers six years in a row with Chicago while he was playing the outfield. His knees started to bother him, so Baines became his team's DH for most of the rest of his career, and he continued to put up consistent numbers.

LIFETIME STATS: BA: .289, HR: 384, RBI: 1,628, H: 2,866, SB: 34

#**357** Jose Canseco

OF-DH, A's, Rangers, Red Sox, Blue Jays, Devil Rays, Yankees, White Sox, 1985–2001

Canseco came up with the Oakland A's in the '80s and along with Mark McGwire formed the "Bash Brothers," a lethal power combination in the A's batting order. Canseco hit 33 homers and had 117 RBI and won the Rookie of the Year award in 1986. In 1988 he combined both power and speed as he came the charter member of the "40-40 Club," when he hit 42 homers and had 40 steals while hitting a career-best .307 and winning the MVP award. He helped the A's win it all in 1989, then hit 81 homers and had 223 RBI the next two seasons. Canseco seemed to be destined for greatness, but injuries and dumb plays prevented that. He was traded to Texas, and endured the embarrassment of a fly ball bouncing off the top of his head, and over the wall for a homer for an opponent. On one occasion, he appeared as a relief pitcher for the Rangers, only to blow out his elbow and disable himself for the rest of the season in 1993.

LIFETIME STATS: BA: .266, HR: 462, RBI: 1,407, H: 1,877, SB: 200

#**358** James Bentley "Cy" Seymour
OF-LHP, Giants, Baltimore (AA), Reds, Braves, 1896–1910, 1913

Seymour started out as a hard-throwing left-handed pitcher in the early part of his career. "Cy" was short for Cyclone, and he lived up to his name as he led the National League in strikeouts in 1898, and went 18–14 in 1897 and 25–19 in 1898. Arm woes curtailed his hurling heroics, however, but the Albany, New York, native could also hit. He hit over .300 seven times in his career and really put it all together in 1905. In that glorious year, he led the league in hitting with a lusty .377, and slugging at a fine .559. He also led the league that year in doubles with 40, triples with 21 and RBI with 121. The fleet center fielder could also be a threat on the base paths as he stole 20 or more bases six times in his career.

LIFETIME STATS: BA: .303, HR: 52, RBI: 799, H: 1,723, SB: 222. W: 61, L: 56, SV: 1, ERA: 3.76, SO: 584, CG: 104

#359 Darryl Strawberry

OF-DH, Mets, Dodgers, Giants, Yankees, 1983–99

Strawberry seemed destined to break many of baseball's cherished records, but injuries and personal problems got in the way. He started out in May 1983, hitting 26 homers and winning the Rookie of the Year award. He hit 26 or more homers nine times in his career, eight with the Mets. The 6'6" 200-pound Strawberry twice hit 39 homers with the Mets in 1987 and 1988, while driving in more than 100 runs both years. An eight-time All Star, "Straw" went home to the Dodgers as a free agent in 1991 and had a good first season there with 28 homers and 99 RBI, but the following years were dismal due to back, and later, drug problems. Playing for New York in 1996, Strawberry hit 11 homers for the Bombers, including three in an August game, and won another game in the bottom of the ninth with his 300th career home run. Knee injuries prevented Strawberry from playing much of 1997, but he came back again with 24 homers in only 101 games in 1998 before being diagnosed with colon cancer just before the postseason. The Yankees dedicated the postseason to him, winning the World Series over San Diego.

LIFETIME STATS: BA: .259, HR: 335, RBI: 1,000, H: 1,401, SB: 221

#360 Don Baylor

DH-OF-1B, Orioles, Angels, Yankees, Red Sox, Twins, A's, 1970–88

Baylor helped the Orioles to American League East titles in 1973 and 1974, but didn't have a great season until 1975 with 25 homers and 32 steals. A renowned streak hitter, Baylor's nickname was "Groove." He once had four homers in successive at bats over two games. Over his career, Baylor led by example, showing a combination of speed, power, and hustle. He stole a career total of 285 bases, including 52 in 1976, and walloped 338 homers. Baylor crowded the plate and would not give in to pitchers, which lead to him being hit by pitches a then-record 267 times. After a year in Oakland, Baylor signed with the Angels, and in 1979 was the AL MVP, leading the majors with 120 runs and 139 RBI. In 1986 he helped the Red Sox win the pennant with 31 homers and 94 RBI.

LIFETIME STATS: BA: .260, HR: 338, RBI: 1,276, H: 2,135, SB: 285

#**361** Raymond "Ray" Brown

RHP, Indianapolis ABCs, Detroit Wolves, Homestead Grays, 1932–45. Hall of Fame, 2006

Brown, a muscular right-hander, is one of the more forgotten men of the old Negro Leagues. That's a darn shame, because he holds the league record, and probably the all-time professional record, for most games won in a row: 22. Brown was born in Ashland Grove, Ohio, and attended Wilberforce University, eventually graduating in 1935. But long before then, he was playing professionally in various midwest leagues. Brown had an explosive sinker ball and a great fastball, but his best pitch was a looping curve that broke over the plate like it was falling off a table. In 1938, he was 15–0 for the Grays, who easily won the Negro National League pennant. Brown had won his last five decisions of 1937, and was 2–0 in 1939 before losing. Brown also played in the Puerto Rican League in the winter of 1938, going 7–0. It was a good year to be Ray Brown.

LIFETIME STATS: (Negro Leagues) W: 146, L: 55

#362 Roy Thomas

OF, Phillies, Pirates, Braves, 1899–1911

Thomas was the ideal leadoff hitter of his era as the left-handed slap-hitter would foul off pitches incessantly until he got the pitch he wanted or the pitcher walked him. Many believe that Thomas's propensity for fouling off many pitches led to the rule change that foul balls would count as strikes. More often than not, the opposing pitcher walked him as Thomas led the National League in bases on balls seven of his first nine years in the league. He was only a .290 lifetime hitter, but his keen eye and quality at bats led him to a career on-base percentage of .413, an amazing 123 points above his career batting average. Seven times in his career, the pesky Thomas walked 100 or more times in a season. When he was on base, he was also a threat to steal, as he accumulated 244 career stolen bases, with 42 coming in his rookie season in 1899. Thomas also scored often, tallying 137 runs in his first season, and scored 1,011 in his 13-year career. The speedy Thomas also excelled defensively in center field where he led NL outfielders in putouts in 1903 and 1905, in assists in 1905, and in fielding percentage in 1906.

LIFETIME STATS: BA: .290, HR: 7, RBI: 299, H: 1,537, SB: 244

#363 Bob Johnson

OF, A's, Senators, Red Sox, 1933–45

Called "Indian Bob" because he was half Cherokee, Johnson established himself as a solid, consistent hitter in his 13-year career in the American League. A right-handed hitter, Johnson came up with the A's and in his rookie season, stroked 69 extra-base hits, including 44 doubles.

In a 1934 games he went a perfect six-for-six, with two homers and a double. Over his career the six-foot Johnson hit over 20 homers nine times. In 1934 he hit 34 homers and had 92 RBI while hitting .307 and stealing 12 bases. His highest batting average was .338 in 1939. Feeling he was underpaid in Philadelphia, he asked for a trade and Connie Mack obliged in 1943 when he was sent to Washington. Johnson lasted only one year there, as he was sent to Boston. He found Fenway Park to his liking. He hit only 17 homers there in 1944, but pounded 40 doubles, hit .324 and led the American League in on-base percentage that year.

LIFETIME STATS: BA: .296, HR: 288, RBI: 1,283, H: 2,051, SB: 96

#364 Kent Hrbek

1B-DH, Twins, 1981–94

Hrbek was a local boy who made good, coming out of a Bloomington, Minnesota, high school and signing and playing his entire career with the hometown Twins. In his first full year in the majors, the husky Hrbek hit .301 and slugged 23 homers, coming in second to Cal Ripkin in the Rookie of the Year balloting. Hrbek hit 41 doubles, along with a .297 average in 1983, and in 1984 had one of his finest seasons, hitting .311 and slugging 27 homers with 107 RBI. In 1987 Hrbek helped lead the Twins to their first-ever world championship hitting a career-high 34 homers in the process, and stroking a grand slam homer in the World Series in Game Six, which the Twins won, forcing the decisive Game Seven, which the Twins also won. The fine-fielding first baseman led the league in fielding at his position in 1988, hitting .312, and in 1988, despite injuries, hit 25 homers and had 84 RBI. Hrbek never won a Gold Glove, but he led the American League first basemen again in fielding in 1990.

LIFETIME STATS: BA: .282, HR: 293, RBI: 1,086, H: 1,749, SB 37

#365 Tim Wallach

3B-1B, Expos, Dodgers, Angels, 1980–96

The right-handed-hitting Wallach homered in his first major league at bat in 1980, and played 13 seasons with the Montreal Expos. A three-time Gold Glove winner, Wallach had his finest offensive year in 1987 when he hit 26 homers and knocked in a career-best 123, while hitting a league-leading 42 doubles and batting .298. Two years later the five-time All Star led the league again in doubles with 42. Wallach was the team captain of the Expos, but the Californian was traded closer to home after the 1992 season, when he was sent to the Dodgers. He hit 23 homers for the Dodgers in 1994.

LIFETIME STATS: BA: .257, HR: 260, RBI: 1,125, H: 2,085, SB: 51

#366 Ray Schalk

C, White Sox, Giants, 1912–29. Hall of Fame, 1955

Schalk was a baby-faced 20-year-old when he broke in with his hometown White Sox, and on one occasion, had to convince a security guard that he was a player. Schalk caught four no-hitters, including Charlie Robertson's 1922 perfect game. Schalk led American League catchers eight times in fielding and eight straight seasons in putouts. In addition, he led the junior circuit four times in double plays, and twice in assists. Schalk was also a very durable receiver, catching 100 or more games for 12 seasons, and his .989 fielding average in 1922 set a then–American League record. He was also a very intelligent player, being one of the first catchers to back up first and third base, and he was the first catcher to make a putout at all four bases

LIFETIME STATS: BA: .253, HR: 11, RBI: 594, H: 1,345, SB: 177

#367 Lonny Frey

2B-SS, Dodgers, Cubs, Reds, Yankees, Giants,
1933–43, 1946–48

Frey came up with the Dodgers in 1933. In 1937 the
5'10", 160-pound left-handed hitter, who also switch-hit
from 1933 to 1938, was sent to the Cubs, playing sparingly there. He resurrected his career in Cincinnati, where
he was sent in 1938. First of all, the Reds moved Frey
from shortstop to second base, and installed him into the regular lineup. Frey
responded, fielding well and hitting .291 in 1939 and leading the league in
stolen bases in 1940 with 22, as the Reds won back-to-back pennants, winning the World Series in 1940. A three-time All Star, Frey led National League
second basemen twice each in fielding percentage and double plays. After losing two years due to military service, Frey came back to the Reds in 1946,
and then was a bench player with the Yankees and the Giants, retiring in 1948.

LIFETIME STATS: BA: .269, HR: 61, RBI: 549, H: 1,482, SB: 105

#368 Walker Cooper

C, Cardinals, Giants, Reds, Braves, Pirates, Cubs,
1940–57

Cooper had the misfortune of being in an organization
that had a rich farm system, the major reason he didn't
come up to the Cardinals until he was 25. Cooper had
his breakout season in 1942, hitting .281 and being
named to the National League All Star Team. The right-
handed Cooper hit .318 and had 81 RBI in 1943, and
came in second in the balloting for MVP behind teammate Stan Musial. The
Cardinals, with Cooper hitting .317, won the pennant again in 1944 and

beat the Browns in the World Series. He missed most of 1945 because he was in the Navy. He returned with the Giants, and in 1947 hit a career-high and uncharacteristic 35 homers with 122 RBI.

LIFETIME STATS: BA: .285, HR: 173, RBI: 812, H: 1,341, SB: 18

#369 Carl Furillo
OF, Dodgers, 1946–60

"Skoonj," as Furillo was affectionately called by the Flatbush faithful, hit an impressive .322 and had 106 RBI in 1949. Hailing from Reading, Pennsylvania, and possessing a cannon of an arm, he was also called "the Reading Rifle." In 1950 and 1951 he led National League outfielders in assists. Furillo had a phenomenal 1953, hitting .344 and winning the NL batting title. He credited an off-season cataract operation for helping him see the ball much better. Furillo could also make the clutch play in World Series competition, robbing Johnny Mize of homer in Game Five of the 1952 World Series, and clouting a game-tying ninth-inning home run in the 1953 Fall Classic.

LIFETIME STATS: BA: .299, HR:192, RBI: 1,058, H: 1,910, SB: 48

#370 Wilbur Cooper
LHP, Pirates, Cubs, Tigers, 1912–26

Cooper came up to the Pirates late in the 1912 season, but became a full-fledged member of the Pirates' starting rotation with a 16–15 mark in 1914. The lefty from West Virginia really hit his stride in 1917, going on a tear, winning at least 17 games each of the next eight years. He was a 20-game winner four times in that streak. Cooper went 24–15 in 1920 and led the league in wins (22) in 1921, and complete games (27) in 1922, on the way to an impressive career total of 279. Cooper currently holds the all-time Pirate complete-game record with 263. Cooper specialized in picking runners off third base. He would whirl and throw the ball to third and Hall of Famer Pie Traynor would dive and tag the unsuspecting base runner. The pair picked off seven base runners in 1924 alone. Cooper wasn't a bad hitter either as he hit .239 lifetime.

LIFETIME STATS: W: 216, L: 178, SV: 14, ERA: 2.89, SO: 1,252, CG: 279

#371 Jud "Boojum" Wilson

3B-1B, Baltimore Black Sox, Homestead Grays, Pittsburgh Crawfords, Philadelphia Stars (Negro Leagues), 1922–45. Hall of Fame, 2006

Wilson was a tough competitor who used any means necessary, including intimidation, to win. He was built like a wrestler, and wouldn't hesitate to fight opponents, even umpires, who got in his way. His nickname comes from the sound his line drives made off distant fences. Wilson was also an excellent player, as he hit .407 in 1927. In 1930, he led the league in doubles and hit .372, all while playing for the Baltimore Black Sox. A three-time Negro League All Star, Wilson had some fine years with the Philadelphia Stars, leading the league in hitting in 1934 with a .412 average and helping the Stars to the pennant that year. He was appointed team captain to try to channel his aggressive energy, and to an extent it worked— until the playoffs, when he punched an umpire.

LIFETIME STATS: BA: .354, HR: 94, H: 1,481

#372 Ross Youngs

OF, Giants, 1917–26. Hall of Fame, 1972

Youngs came up to the New York Giants in 1917 and quickly became one of manager John McGraw's favorite players. He only played 10 seasons, all with the Giants, as his career was tragically cut short because of a fatal kidney disease. The speedy Youngs helped the Giants win four straight pennants from 1921 to 1924, and became the first player in World Series history to get two hits in the same inning in the 1921 Fall Classic. "Pep," as he was called, hit .300 or better in seven of eight full seasons in his abbreviated career, hitting a career-high .356 in 1924. The left-handed-hitting Youngs was among league leaders for stolen bases five times in his career and led the league in doubles and runs once each. The fleet Texan stole home 10 times, and once hit three triples in a game. John McGraw kept pictures of only two players on his desk: one was the great Christy Mathewson; the other was Ross Youngs.

LIFETIME STATS: BA: .322, HR: 42, RBI: 592, H: 1,491, SB: 153

#373 Clyde "Deerfoot" Milan

OF, Senators, 1907–22

Milan was nicknamed "Deerfoot" because of his blazing speed. He led the American League with a then-record 88 stolen bases in 1912, then stole another 75 the following year. A left-handed hitter with little power, Milan had a tough time in the majors at first, but then started to slap the ball to all fields and use his speed more effectively. In 1911 he hit .315 and stole 58 bases, and hit over .300 the next two years. Milan also used his speed in the outfield as he would play a shallow center field only to coast back and catch long fly balls. His last big year was in 1920 when he hit .322.

LIFETIME STATS: BA: .285, HR: 17, RBI: 617, H: 2,100, SB: 495

#374 Tom Haller
C, Giants, Dodgers, Tigers, 1961–72

Haller signed with the Giants in 1958 after a successful career as the University of Illinois's quarterback. As a left-handed hitter with some power, he hit 18 homers and 55 RBI in part-time action as he platooned with Ed Bailey for the 1962 season, and the Giants went to the World Series against the Yankees. Haller hit .286 in his only Series action and hit a homer and had three RBI as he caught four of the seven games. He became the Giants' starting catcher in 1965, hitting 16 homers. The following year he had his best power year, hitting a career-best 27 homers and knocking in 67. A three-time All Star, Haller was traded to the rival Dodgers in 1968. He only hit four homers, but batted a career-high .286, and caught 139 games while setting a National League record for double plays for a catcher with 23. He caught for three more years with Los Angeles before going to the American League and the Tigers.

LIFETIME STATS: BA: .257, HR: 134, RBI: 504, H: 1,011, SB: 14

#375 Hal Trosky Sr.
1B, Indians, White Sox, 1933–41, 1944, 1946

Born Harold Arthur Troyavesky, Hal Trosky was brought up by the Cleveland Indians in the last part of the 1933 season, becoming their starting first baseman in 1934. He made his presence felt right away, swatting 35 homers, with 142 RBI and an impressive .330 batting average. The left-handed-hitting Trosky also hit three homers in a May game that year. In 1936, he led the American League in RBI with a career high of 162, posting career bests in homers with 42 and batting average with a .343 mark. He continued to hit well, hitting .334 and .335 in 1938 and 1939 and .295 in 1940 with 25 homers. His play started to decline in 1941, and he decided to retire after the 1946 season because of recurring migraine headaches.

LIFETIME STATS: BA: .302, HR: 228, RBI: 1,012, H: 1,561, SB: 28

#376 Bobby Veach
OF, Tigers, Red Sox, Yankees, Senators, 1912–25

The left-handed-hitting Veach was a steady left fielder during the 1910s. Usually overshadowed by Hall of Famers Ty Cobb and Sam Crawford, Veach was a star in his own right. He hit over .305 eight times in his career, and drove in over 100 runs six times, tying Crawford for the American League lead in 1915 with 112 RBI. He also led the league in that department in 1917 with 103 RBI, and led the loop again with 78 RBI in the war-shortened 1918 season. The following year he led the league in hits, doubles, and triples, but finished second to Cobb in the batting race as Cobb hit .384 and Veach .355. He was sent to Boston in 1924, where he hit .295

LIFETIME STATS: BA: .310, HR: 64, RBI: 1,166, H: 2,064, SB: 195

#377 Jim O'Rourke
OF-C-3B-1B, Middletown Mansfields, Boston Red Stockings, Boston Red Caps, Providence Grays, Buffalo Bisons, New York Giants, Senators, 1872–93, 1904. Hall of Fame, 1945

The National League was formed in 1876, and O'Rourke had the distinction of being the first player in NL history to get a hit, going on to hit .327 that year. The following year Boston won the pennant, with the right-handed O'Rourke hitting a gaudy .362 and leading the league in runs and on-base percentage. In 1879 he jumped to Providence, prompting the Boston owner to propose the inclusion of a reserve clause in player contracts. O'Rourke's new club won the pennant as he hit .348. O'Rourke went back to Boston in 1880 and led the league for a third time in home runs, and became player-manager for Buffalo in 1881. In 1884 he led the league with 162 hits and came in second with a .347 batting average. His next stop was with the New York Giants in 1885, where he led the league in triples with 16, and was on the 1888 and 1889 championship teams.

LIFETIME STATS: BA: .311, HR: 62, RBI: 1,203, H: 2,643, SB: 224

#378 Tony Pena

C, Pirates, Cardinals, Red Sox, Indians, White Sox, Astros, 1980–97

Pena was one of the best defensive catchers in the majors in the '80s and early '90s. A four-time Gold Glove winner, he had a strong, accurate arm that stymied would-be base-stealers. He hit 10 or more homers six times in his career. The right-hand-hitting Dominican batted .286 or more four times in Pittsburgh. In 1987 he went to the Cardinals. In his first year there, his offensive production suffered due to injuries, but he had a terrific postseason, hitting .381 in the NLCS against the Giants, and then .409 in a losing effort against the Twins in the World Series.

LIFETIME STATS: BA: .260, HR: 107, RBI: 708, H: 1,187, SB: 80

#379 Brian Downing
DH-OF-C, White Sox, Angels, Rangers, 1973–92

In 1979 the right-hand-hitting Downing hit .326 with 12 homers and 75 RBI, all the while playing excellent defense behind the plate, as the Angels won the American League West title. Downing broke his ankle in 1980, which led him to play the outfield for the rest of his career, where he broke the record for an outfielder for most consecutive errorless chances with 330. As the Angels won the AL West in 1986, Downing hit .267 with 20 homers and a career-best 95 RBI. Because of his keen batting eye and not his speed, Downing often hit leadoff. He led the league in walks in 1987 while hitting a career-high 29 homers.

LIFETIME STATS: BA: .267, HR: 275, RBI: 1,073, H: 2,099, SB: 50

#380 Bill White
1B-OF, Giants, Cardinals, Phillies, 1956, 1958–69

White hit a home run in his first major league at bat in 1956, and led the league in both putouts and assists that year. He missed all of the 1957 season and part of the 1958 season serving in the Army. A five-time All Star, White was a solid hitter with occasional power, as he hit 20 or more homers and had over 100 RBI for three straight years. He won a Gold Glove award each year from 1960 to 1966. He hit a career-best 27 homers in 1963. In 1966 the lefty-hitting White was traded to the Phillies where he hit 22 homers and had 103 RBI in his last good season. After retiring, he became a broadcaster and later the president of the National League.

LIFETIME STATS: BA: .286, HR: 202, RBI: 870, H: 1,706, SB: 103

#381 Joe Judge

1B, Senators, Dodgers, Red Sox, 1915–34

Judge was a smooth-fielding, contact-hitting first baseman who played most of his career with the Washington Senators. He and Hall of Famer Sam Rice, who played with Washington from 1915 to 1933, hold the all-time record for most career hits by two teammates. Standing a shade over 5'6", Judge was not your prototypical first baseman, but he was smooth around the bag and led the American League in fielding five times, and had an impressive career fielding average of .993. In 1922 he participated in a record 131 double plays. Not a power hitter, Judge hit the ball to all fields, hitting over .300 nine times in his career. He once hit three triples in one game.

LIFETIME STATS: BA: .298, HR: 71, RBI: 1,037, H: 2,352, SB: 213

#382 George Kell

3B-1B, Tigers, Red Sox, White Sox, Orioles, 1943–59. Hall of Fame, 1983

Kell hit .320 in 1947 and .304 in 1948, but in 1949 he won his only batting title in a close race with Ted Williams. Kell nosed out the Splendid Splinter, .342911 to .342756, which denied Williams his third Triple Crown. Kell struck out only 13 times all season that year. Kell was also the first third baseman since 1912 in either league to win a batting championship. The next year the Arkansas native kept right on hitting, posting a .340 mark and leading the league with 56 doubles and 218 hits. In 1957 he finished up playing third base in Baltimore and tutoring a young Oriole rookie named Brooks Robinson, who entered the Hall of Fame on the same day as George Kell in 1983.

LIFETIME STATS: BA: .306, HR: 78, RBI: 870, H: 2,054, SB: 51

#383 Virgil Trucks

RHP, Tigers, Browns, White Sox, Tigers, A's, Yankees, 1941–43, 1945–58

Virgil "Fire" Trucks, so called because of his blazing fast-ball, started out with the Tigers, having successful 14–8 and 16–10 seasons in 1941 and 1942. He missed two years due to the war. The 1952 season was an ambiguous one for the burly right-hander. The bad news was he was a dismal 5–19. The good news was that two of his wins (40 percent of them) were no-hitters. At the time of this feat Johnny Vander Meer and Allie Reynolds were the only hurlers who had pitched two no-hitters (since joined by Sandy Koufax and Nolan Ryan). Both were 1–0 masterpieces, one against the lowly Senators, the other against the mighty Yankees.

LIFETIME STATS: W: 177, L: 135, SV: 30, ERA: 3.39, SO: 1,534, CG: 124

#384 Andy Van Slyke

OF-1B-3B, Cardinals, Pirates, Orioles, Phillies, 1983–95

Van Slyke came up to the Cardinals in 1983, and became their regular right fielder in 1985, hitting .259 and stealing 34 bases, while stroking 13 homers, second on the team. He also displayed his strong arm, collecting 13 assists. Traded to the Pirates, he blossomed in the Steel City, moving to center field where he would win five straight Gold Gloves. Van Slyke had a banner year in 1992 when he came in second in the batting race with a .324 season and led the loop with 45 doubles and 199 hits. Van Slyke had an amazing 80.6-percent success rate in stealing bases, stealing 245 times out of 304 attempts.

LIFETIME STATS: BA: .274, HR: 164, RBI: 792, H: 1,562, SB: 245

#385 Walter James Vincent "Rabbit" Maranville

SS-2B, Braves, Pirates, Cubs, Dodgers, Cardinals, 1912–33, 1935. Hall of Fame, 1954

Maranville was only a .258 lifetime hitter, but he was one of the best-fielding shortstops of his time. The diminutive Maranville was also known to be a prankster who kept his teammates loose during the long seasons. In 1914, teamed with former Cub Johnny Evers, Maranville helped the 1914 "Miracle Braves" win the pennant and then shock the heavily favored A's in a stunning four-game sweep in the World Series. Maranville hit .308 in that Series. He led the league in putouts six times, in assists four times, and chances per game three times.

LIFETIME STATS: BA: .258, HR: 28, RBI: 884, H: 2,605, SB: 291

#386 Albert Spalding

RHP-OF-1B, Boston (NA), Cubs, 1871–78. Hall of Fame, 1939

In 1871 Albert Spalding joined the Boston team in the National Association, baseball's first league. In their first season they only played 33 games, and Spalding pitched in 31 of them, going 19–10 as the Red Stockings came in second. For the next four years, they won championships every year, with right-handed hurler Spalding ringing up an incredible record of 186–43, including a 54–5 record in 1875. Spalding then was lured by a big money offer from Chicago owner William Hulbert, and signed with the White Stockings as the National League started play in 1876. Chicago won the very first pennant behind the solid pitching of Spalding, who compiled an amazing 47–12 record with a microscopic 1.75 ERA while acting as player-manager.

LIFETIME STATS: W: 253, L: 65, SV: 11, ERA: 2.14, SO: 142, CG: 281, BA: .313, HR: 2, RBI: 327, H: 613, SB: 10

#387 Eddie "The Brat" Stanky

2B-SS, Cubs, Dodgers, Braves, Giants, Cardinals, 1943–53

Branch Rickey once said of the pesky Stanky: "He can't hit, he can't run, he can't field, and he can't throw. He can't do a thing but beat you." In three full seasons with Brooklyn, from 1945 to 1947, Stanky led the National League in walks twice and in on-base percentage and runs once. Three times in his career he had equal to or more walks than hits, the only major leaguer to accomplish that. Stanky helped the Boston Braves to the 1948 pennant, hitting a career-best .320 during the season, and then had an impressive .524 on-base percentage in the World Series loss to the Indians.

LIFETIME STATS: BA: .268, HR: 29, RBI: 364, H: 1,154, SB: 48

#**388** Harlond Clift

3B, Browns, Senators, 1934–45

One of the best players ever for the St. Louis Browns, a second-division club, Clift was one of the top power-hitting third basemen of his era. He led AL third basemen in homers four straight years, and set a record for third basemen when he hit 29 in 1937. He then bettered the record, hitting 34 the next season, good for third overall in the league that year. The right-handed-hitting Georgian hit over .300 twice and slugged over .500 three times. Clift was also good with the glove as he set records for participating in 50 double plays and having 405 assists (since broken). He twice had 118 RBI, scored 100 or more runs seven times, and drew over 100 walks in a season on six occasions.

LIFETIME STATS: BA: .272, HR: 178, RBI: 829, H: 1,558, SB: 69

#**389** Mickey Tettleton

C-DH-OF-1B, A's, Orioles, Tigers, Rangers, 1984–97

The switch-hitting Tettleton slugged 26 homers and had 65 RBI for the Orioles in 1989. His power numbers declined in 1990 to 15 homers and 51 RBI, but he drew over 100 walks, the first of five times Tettleton would accomplish that feat in his career. He was traded to Detroit and in his first three seasons there he hit 30 or more home runs and in 1993 had a career-best 110 RBI, the first and only time he went over the century mark in that department. The negative side to Tettleton's game was his propensity for striking out (career 1307). "Fruit Loops," as he was called because he said he liked the cereal, hit 17 homers in the strike-shortened 1994 season.

LIFETIME STATS: BA: .241, HR: 245, RBI: 732, H: 1,132, SB: 23

#**390** Dave Cash

2B, Pirates, Phillies Expos, Padres, 1969–80

Cash came up as a second baseman with the Pirates and filled in for the aging veteran Bill Mazeroski, hitting .314 in part-time duty in 1970. Traded to the Phillies in 1974, Cash made the most of the opportunity, hitting over .300 his first two seasons there. The speedy Cash also led the National League in triples with 12 in 1976 and stole 10 or more bases six times in his career. Cash set a record for durability for a second baseman appearing in 443 consecutive games. He signed with Montreal as a free agent, and in 1977 continued to play well, hitting .289, stealing a career-high 21 bases and stroking 42 doubles, second in the league.

LIFETIME STATS: BA: .283, HR: 21, RBI: 426, H: 1,571, SB: 120

#**391** Sam Thompson

OF, Detroit (NL), Phillies, Tigers, 1885–98, 1906. Hall of Fame, 1974

"Big Sam" Thompson stood only 6'2" and weighed 207 pounds, but he was big for his day, and was one of baseball's first big sluggers in the "dead ball" era. He hit over .300 eight times in his career, and was regarded as the best right fielder of his era. In 1887 Thompson led the National League with 203 hits, 23 triples, a .372 batting average, a .571 slugging percentage and the most RBI in one season in the 19th century, 166. In 1894 Thompson became part of the only .400-or-better outfield as he and Ed Delahanty hit .407 and Billy Hamilton hit .404.

LIFETIME STATS: BA: .331, HR: 127, RBI: 1,299, H: 1,979, SB: 229

#392 Stan Coveleski

RHP, A's, Indians, Senators, Yankees, 1912, 1916–28.
Hall of Fame, 1969

Coveleski, born Stanislaus Kowalewski, came to baseball out of a Pennsylvania coal mine. He was a consistent winner for Cleveland from 1916 to 1924, winning 20 or more games four times in that span. In 1920, Coveleski went 24–14 with a 2.49 ERA, and led the league in strikeouts with 133. The Indians won the world championship in 1920 and Coveleski was a main reason why, as he threw five-hitters in Games One, Four and Seven, shutting out Brooklyn in Game Seven, 5–0 and compiling a 0.67 ERA. The following year, despite the personal tragedy of losing his wife unexpectedly and the death of teammate Ray Chapman, the Pennsylvania left-hander went 23–13, the last time he would win 20 for the Tribe.

LIFETIME STATS: W: 215, L: 142, SV: 21, ERA: 2.89, SO: 981, CG: 224

#393 Sherm Lollar

C, Indians, Yankees, Browns, White Sox, 1946–63

Lollar caught 100 or more games for Chicago eight years. A superb handler of pitchers, he led American League catchers four times in fielding. In 1962, he tied an American League record by catching six popups in one game. At the plate he was a lifetime .264 hitter with occasional power as he hit 20 or more homers twice in his career. His best offensive year was in 1959, the Year of the "Go-Go" White Sox team that won its first AL pennant in 40 years, when he hit 22 homers with a career-tying 84 RBI.

LIFETIME STATS: BA: .264, HR: 155, RBI: 808, H: 1,415, SB: 20

#394 Curt Flood

OF, Reds, Cardinals, Senators, 1956–69, 1971

Flood played very briefly with the Reds, but made his mark on the field with the St. Louis Cardinals where he played a great center field for 12 seasons. In 1961, the right-handed Flood became a starter and hit .322. He would hit over .300 five more times in his career. Starting in 1963, Flood won seven straight Gold Glove awards. He also played 226 errorless games, a National League record, and handled 568 straight chances flawlessly, a major league mark. In 1967, the fleet-footed Flood completed an unassisted double play, the first by an outfielder since 1945. In 1964, the 5'9", 165-pound Houston native led the National League with 211 hits and in 1967 hit a career-best .335.

LIFETIME STATS: BA: .293, HR: 85, RBI: 636, H: 1,861, SB: 88

#395 Bobby Bonilla

3B-OF-1B-DH, White Sox, Pirates, Mets, Orioles, Marlins, Dodgers, Braves, Cardinals, 1986–2001

Bonilla hit .300 in 1987 for the Pirates, and blossomed in 1990 as he and the young Barry Bonds were a potent combination in the Pittsburgh batting order. Bonilla smashed 32 homers and knocked in 120 runs, finishing second to Bonds in the MVP balloting. In 1991 he hit .302 and led the league with 44 doubles. The Bronx native then opted to go to the Mets via free agency and struggled in his first season at Shea. He rebounded in 1993 with 34 homers and 87 RBI and was named to the NL All Star team for a fifth year, an honor he would receive once more in his career. He moved on to Baltimore in mid-1995 and finished the year with 99 RBI, playing half of the year in the outfield.

LIFETIME STATS: BA: .279, HR: 287, RBI: 1,173, H: 2,010, SB: 45

#396 James Augustus "Catfish" Hunter

RHP, A's, Yankees, 1965–79. Hall of Fame, 1987

"Catfish" Hunter was so nicknamed by A's owner Charlie Finley, basically, as a publicity stunt. Never playing a day in the minors, the crafty right-hander threw the majors' first regular-season perfect game in 46 years when he beat the Twins in 1968. Hunter won 20 or more games five years in a row. The ace of the A's' three-time world champion staff, Hunter won a league-leading 25 games in 1974 and lost only 12. He led the league with a 2.49 ERA and won the Cy Young award. After the 1974 season, Hunter had a contract dispute with Oakland. He was then signed by New York, where he fashioned a 23–14 mark in 1975 and helped the Yankees win the pennant in 1976 and world championships in 1977 and 1978. Hunter was diagnosed in 1998 with amyotrophic lateral sclerosis, or Lou Gehrig's disease, and died in 1999.

LIFETIME STATS: W: 224, L: 166, SV: 1, ERA: 3.26, SO: 2,012, CG: 181

#397 Pete Runnels

1B-2B-SS, Senators, Red Sox, Astros, 1951–64

Runnels came up with the Washington Senators in the early '50s and was used all over the infield, except for third base. Shipped to Boston, the slap-hitting contact-hitting Runnels loved batting there, peppering the left field and hitting over .300 all five years he played in Beantown. His hitting was good enough to win two American League batting crowns, once in 1960 when he hit .320 and once in 1962, when he hit .326 at the age of 35. A three-time All Star, Runnels was traded in 1963 to the Houston Colt 45's for power-hitting Roman Mejias, but only hit .253 there and then retired in 1964.

LIFETIME STATS: BA: .291, HR: 49, RBI: 630, H: 1,854, SB: 37

#398 Carney Lansford

3B-1B, Angels, Red Sox, A's, 1978–92

The right-handed-hitting Lansford came up with the Angels in 1978 and hit .294 in his rookie season. He was traded to Boston in 1981, and led the league in batting with a .336 average. He was sent to the A's, where he hit over .300 his first two seasons. In 1986 and 1987 he hit 19 home runs each year. In 1989 his homer production dwindled to two, but Lansford found his batting stroke erupting for a .336 season, good for second in the league. Lansford was in double figures nine times in stolen bases, including a career-high 37 in 1989 and 29 the year before on the way to lifetime total of 224. Hobbled by injuries for most of 1991, the San Jose native returned for one more season in 1992, hitting .262.

LIFETIME STATS: BA: .290, HR: 151, RBI: 874, H: 2,074, SB: 224

#399 Dick Bartell

SS-3B-2B, Pirates, Phillies, Giants, Cubs, Tigers, 1927–43, 1946

Bartell, dubbed "Rowdy Richard" for his brash, aggressive personality, was a well-traveled player who wore out his welcome often. A two-time All Star, the fiery 5'9", 160-pound Bartell was a good fielding shortstop who hit .300 or better six times in his career. He came up with the Pirates and hit .302 and .320 in his first two full seasons there. He was traded to the Phillies, where he hit over .300 two of his four years there and was named to the NL All Star squad. His next stop was New York, where he helped the Giants win two straight flags in 1936 and 1937. He hit a robust .381 in the World Series of 1936, and was an All Star again in 1937.

LIFETIME STATS: BA: .284, HR: 79, RBI: 710, H: 2,165, SB: 109

#**400** John Mayberry

1B-DH, Astros, Royals, Blue Jays, Yankees, 1968–82

Mayberry languished on the Astros' bench for four seasons until he was traded to the Kansas City Royals in 1972. The 6'3", 220-pound Mayberry made the most of the opportunity as he was consistently the top power threat in the Royals' lineup the next six seasons. The lefty-swinging and -throwing Mayberry had his best season in 1975 when he socked 34 homers, had 106 RBI, hit .291, slugged .547, had 38 doubles and scored 95 runs. All but the batting average were career highs for the big first baseman. The Detroit native was excellent with the glove at first base, leading the junior circuit three times in putouts, and twice in fielding and double plays.

LIFETIME STATS: BA: .253, HR: 255, RBI: 879, H: 1,379, SB: 20

#**401** Willie Dean McGee

OF, Cardinals, A's, Giants, Red Sox, 1982–99

A three-time National League Gold Glove winner, McGee was voted NL MVP in 1985, hitting a league-leading .353 for the Cardinals. He also topped the NL with 216 hits and 18 triples in 1985, stealing a career-high 56 bases. McGee stole 30 or more bases five seasons in his career. He hit .370 in the Cardinals' 1987 seven-game World Series loss to the Twins, and was voted to the All Star team four times.

LIFETIME STATS: BA: .295, HR: 79, RBI: 856, H: 2,254, SB: 352

#402 Thomas Michael Glavine

LHP, Braves, Mets, 1987–2008

Glavine was a two-time Cy Young award winner with the Braves, in 1991 and 1998. He ranked among the top three Cy Young candidates six times in his career. Voted World Series MVP in 1995, Glavine led the Braves to victory over the Indians while allowing only four hits in 14 innings' work. He logged a 2.47 ERA over eight World Series games. Glavine led the NL in wins five times, and was named to the All Star team eight times.

LIFETIME STATS: W: 305, L: 203, SV: 0, ERA: 3.54, SO: 2,607, CG: 56

LUNDY
BASE BALL

#403 Dick Lundy

SS-2B-3B, Bacharach Giants, New York Lincoln Giants, Hilldale, Baltimore Black Sox, Philadelphia Stars, Newark Dodgers, New York Cubans, Newark Eagles, Jacksonville Eagles (Negro Leagues), 1916–1939

Lundy hit .484 in 1921 to top the Bacharach Giants. He also led the Giants to pennants in 1926 and 1927 as a player-manager. He hit .325 in the 1926 Black World Series in a losing effort against the Chicago American Giants. Lundy was considered one of the best shortstops in the Negro Leagues in the 1920s. He earned the nickname "King Richard" for his superb defensive play on that side of the infield.

LIFETIME STATS (incomplete): BA: .307

#404 Delmar Wesley "Del" Crandall

C, Boston Braves, Milwaukee Braves, Giants, Pirates, Indians, 1949–50, 1953–66

Crandall won the National League Gold Glove for catchers four times as a Milwaukee Brave, 1958–60 and 1962, while leading league catchers in fielding percentage each of those years. He was voted to the All Star team eight times. Crandall hit a home run in both the Braves' 1957 World Series win over the Yankees and their World Series loss the next year, also to the Yankees.

LIFETIME STATS: BA: .254, HR: 179, RBI: 657, H: 1,276, SB: 26

#405 Donald Alvin "Don" Buford

OF-2B-3B, White Sox, Orioles, 1963–72

Buford scored 99 runs in three consecutive seasons with the Orioles, 1969–71, leading the AL in 1971. He stole 51 bases in 1966 for the White Sox, and ranked among the top 10 in the AL for drawing walks from 1969 to 1972. Buford hit four home runs over three World Series with the Orioles, 1969–71, including a leadoff home run off the Mets' Tom Seaver to open the 1969 World Series.

LIFETIME STATS: BA: .264, HR: 93, RBI: 418, H: 1,203, SB: 200

#406 Andres Jose "The Big Cat" Gallaraga

1B, Expos, Cardinals, Rockies, Braves, Rangers, Giants, Angels, 1985–2004

Galarraga hit .300 or better nine times in 18 seasons, including an NL-best .370 with Colorado in 1993. He won two Gold Gloves with the Expos, 1989–90, and ranked among the top-10 league MVP vote-winners six times in his career. In 1988 Galarraga led the NL with 184 hits. He also led the NL in 1996 with 47 home runs and 150 RBI. Galarraga ranks second all-time in career strike-outs for batters with 2,000, behind Reggie Jackson.

LIFETIME STATS: BA: .288, HR: 399, RBI: 1,425, H: 2,333, SB: 128

#407 Mariano Rivera

RHP, Yankees, 1995–present

The all-time saves leader with more than 600. It's difficult to figure out where to rank Rivera, who is clearly the ultimate specialist in baseball. But his postseason stats are, in a word, astounding! He has allowed eight earned runs in 96 innings, and sports a 7–1 record with 30 saves. His postseason ERA is 0.75. In 14 of the 21 playoff series in which he has been involved, Rivera has an ERA of 0.00. There has been no more automatic result in baseball history. The all-time saves leader with more than 600.

LIFETIME STATS: W: 75, L: 57, SV: 603, ERA: 2.21, SO: 1,111, CG: 0

#**408** Colbert Dale "Toby" Harrah

3B-SS-2B, Senators, Rangers, Indians, Yankees,
1969–1986

Harrah led American League third basemen in fielding
percentage in 1983. He hit a career-high .304 in 1982
with the Indians, logging 25 home runs and an AL second-best .398 on-base percentage. He perennially ranked
among league leaders in walks, and scored 100 runs a
season twice with the Indians, his career best. Harrah was voted to the All
Star team four times.

LIFETIME STATS: BA: .264, HR: 195, RBI: 918, H: 1,954, SB: 238

#**409** August John "Augie" Galan

OF-1B-3B-2B, Cubs, Brooklyn Dodgers, Reds, New
York Giants, Philadelphia A's, 1934–49

As a Cub in 1937, Galan became the first major leaguer
to hit home runs from both sides of the plate in the same
game. He led the National League that year with 23 stolen
bases. In 1935, Galan led the NL with 133 runs and 22
stolen bases. He did not hit into one double play in 646
at-bats that season. Galan topped the NL in walks in 1943 and 1944.

LIFETIME STATS: BA: .287, HR: 100, RBI: 830, H: 1,706, SB: 123

#**410** John Andrew Smoltz

RHP, Braves, Red Sox, Cardinals, 1988–2009

The steady Smoltz has been one of the most consistent performers on the Braves' pitching staff over the past decade. He came into his own in 1996, winning the Cy Young award and posting a 24–8 record with a 2.94 ERA and 276 strikeouts, the latter leading the league and a career high. Smoltz also led the NL in strikeouts in 1992 with 215. He was also named MVP of the NCLS that year, notching wins in Games One and Four as the Braves defeated the Pirates. He switched to the bullpen and led the NL in saves in 2002 with 55. He has also set the record for most postseason pitching wins, with 12.

LIFETIME STATS: W: 213, L: 155, SV: 154, ERA: 3.33, SO: 3,084, CG: 53

#**411** Abram Harding "Hardy" Richardson

2B-OF-3B, Buffalo Bisons, Detroit Wolverines, Boston Reds, Senators, New York Giants, 1879–92

Richardson led the National League in 1886 with 189 hits and 11 home runs for Detroit, while hitting a career-high .351. He hit .300 or better in seven of his 14 professional seasons, and led the Players League in 1890 with 146 RBI for Boston. Richardson consistently ranked among league leaders in runs and extra-base hits for most of his career.

LIFETIME STATS: BA: .299, HR: 70, RBI: 822, H: 1,688, SB: 205

#412 Matt Williams

3B-SS, Giants, Indians, Diamondbacks, 1987–2003.

Had it not been for the baseball strike which shortened the 1994 season, baseball fans would likely have been talking about Matt Williams, not Mark McGwire, breaking Roger Maris's 1961 home-run record. When the season was shut down, Williams already had 43 homers in only 112 games, well ahead of the pace set by Maris in 1961. The 6'2" Williams had more homers by the age of 29 than any other third baseman in baseball history (229). Overall, Williams has hit 30 or more homers six times in his career. Defensively, he has won four Gold Gloves. A five-time All Star, Williams was traded to the Indians in 1997, where he helped the Tribe win the AL pennant. He went to Arizona in 1998, and in 1999 he exploded for 35 homers and a career high 142 RBI in leading the Diamondbacks to a division title.

LIFETIME STATS: BA: .268, HR: 378, RBI: 1,218, H: 1,878, SB: 53.

#413 Delmer "Del" Ennis

OF, Phillies, Cardinals, Reds, White Sox, 1946–59

The consistent Ennis logged 90 or more RBI in nine of his 14 seasons in the majors. He led the NL in 1950 with 126 RBI, while also hitting a career-best 31 home runs. Ennis ranked among league leaders in RBI for most of his career, and ranks 90th all-time in that category. He was voted to the All Star team three times.

LIFETIME STATS: BA: .284, HR: 288, RBI: 1,284, H: 2,063, SB: 45

#**414** Lonas Edgar "Ed" Bailey Jr.

C, Reds, Giants, Milwaukee Braves, Cubs, California Angels, 1953–66

A five-time All Star, Bailey hit eight pinch-hit home runs over the course of his career. Hitting 28 home runs in 1956, he helped the Reds tie a National League record with 221 team home runs. He briefly formed a battery with his brother, Jim, who joined the Reds as a pitcher in 1959. Bailey ruined a Yankee shutout with a ninth-inning home run in Game Three of the 1962 World Series, though the Giants ultimately lost the game and the Series.

LIFETIME STATS: BA: .256, HR: 155, RBI: 540, H: 915, SB: 17

#**415** John "Johnny" Logan Jr.

SS, Boston Braves, Milwaukee Braves, Pirates, 1951–63

A four-time All Star, Logan led the National League with 31 sacrifice hits in 1956. He led the NL in games in 1954 and 1955, playing 154 games each season, and topping the league with 37 doubles in 1955. Logan appeared in two World Series with the Braves, homering in the team's winning 1957 effort against the Yankees.

LIFETIME STATS: BA: .268, HR: 93, RBI: 547, H: 1,407, SB: 19

#416 Charles Sylvester "Chick" Stahl

OF, Boston Beaneaters, Boston Pilgrims, 1897–1906

Stahl hit over .300 in five of his 10 professional seasons, including a career-high .354 as a rookie. He collected six hits in one game in 1899 for the Beaneaters. In the first World Series in 1903, Stahl hit three triples for the Pilgrims, leading them to victory over the Pirates. He topped the AL with 19 triples in 1904. Stahl committed suicide in 1907, blaming the pressures of managing the Boston Red Sox.

LIFETIME STATS: BA: .305, HR: 36, RBI: 622, H: 1,546, SB: 189

#417 Arthur "Art" Fletcher

SS-3B-2B, New York Giants, Phillies, 1909–20, 1922

Fletcher was hit by a pitch 141 times in his career, ranking him 20th on the all-time list. He placed among the top 10 league RBI leaders four consecutive years, from 1913 to 1916. Fletcher played in four World Series with the Giants, all losing efforts. A superb defensive shortstop, he led National League shortstops for two seasons in fielding percentage and assists, 1917–18.

LIFETIME STATS: BA: .277, HR: 32, RBI: 675, H: 1,534, SB: 159

#**418** Waite Charles Hoyt

RHP, New York Giants, Red Sox, Yankees, Tigers, Philadelphia A's, Brooklyn Dodgers, Pirates, 1918–38. Hall of Fame, 1969

As a member of the 1927 Yankees, Hoyt led the American League with 22 wins and notched a second-place 2.63 ERA. He logged a 1.83 ERA over seven World Series, including six with the Yankees in the 1920s and one with the A's in 1931. In the 1921 World Series, he pitched three complete games with a 0.00 ERA. Hoyt led the AL with eight saves in 1928. Hoyt was a vaudeville star as well as a ballplayer, and often sang in speakeasies in cities around the league while he played ball.

LIFETIME STATS: W: 237, L: 182, SV: 52, ERA: 3.59, SO: 1,206, CG: 226

#**419** Curtis Montague Schilling

RHP, Orioles, Astros, Phillies, Diamondbacks, Red Sox, 1988–2007

Even without the bloody sock, Curt Schilling would have worked his way into the pantheon of great pitchers. He is a three-time runner-up for the Cy Young Award, a three-time 20-game winner and one of the best postseason hurlers in this or any other era.

The Anchorage, Alaska, native (that information will win you a bet, for sure) was drafted by the Orioles, but he was a very late bloomer. He didn't really hit his stride until he was 30, going 17–11 for the Phillies in 1997. He was traded to the Diamondbacks in 2001, and was half of a killer one-two pitching punch, with Randy Johnson. Arizona beat the Yankees in the World Series that year, and Schilling and Johnson were co-MVPs.

Schilling went to Boston in 2004, and when he incurred a foot injury in the American League Divisional Series against the Angels, things looked bleak. But a novel medical procedure (we don't have the space to walk you though it—just take it from me, it was novel) on his left foot enabled him to pitch Game Six against the Yankees in the American League Championship Series and Game Two against St. Louis in the World Series. He won both games, and his sock, covered in blood from busted sutures, is now in the Hall of Fame.

LIFETIME STATS: W: 213, L: 142, SV: 22, ERA: 3.46, SO: 3,086, CG: 83

#**420** John Wesley "Johnny" Callison

OF, White Sox, Phillies, Cubs, Yankees, 1958–73

Callison led the National League in doubles in 1966 and triples in 1962 and 1965. He earned the second-most NL MVP votes in 1964, hitting 31 home runs with 104 RBI. Callison was named MVP of the 1964 All Star game after hitting a two-out, ninth-inning home run off Dick Radatz to seal the NL win.

LIFETIME STATS: BA: .264, HR: 226, RBI: 840, H: 1,757, SB: 74

#**421** Leonard Kyle "Lenny," "Nails" Dykstra

OF, Mets, Phillies, 1985–96

The feisty Dykstra, nicknamed "Nails" for his toughness, led the National League in hits in 1990 and 1993 with 192 and 194, respectively, and runs scored in 1993, with 143. He stole 30 or more bases a year six times in his 12-

year career. His two-run, ninth-inning home run in the 1986 NLCS clinched the Mets' win over the Astros. Dykstra hit .348 in the Phillies' 1993 World Series against Toronto, hitting four home runs.

LIFETIME STATS: BA: .285, HR: 81, RBI: 404, H: 1,298, SB: 285

#422 Derrill Burnham "Del" Pratt

2B-1B, St. Louis Browns, Yankees, Red Sox, Tigers, 1912–24

Pratt led the American League in 1916 with 103 RBI for the Browns. He ranked among league leaders in doubles, from 1912 to 1916, and again from 1920 to 1922, while topping the AL in games, 1913–16. Pratt hit .300 or better six times over a 13-year career, including each of his last five seasons. He ranked among the top seven AL leaders in total bases, 1912–16.

LIFETIME STATS: BA: .292, HR: 43, RBI: 968, H: 1,996, SB: 247

#423 Fielder Allison Jones

OF, Brooklyn Bridegrooms, White Sox, St. Louis Terriers, 1896–1908, 1914–15

Jones (Fielder was his real name) hit .300 or better in six seasons, and ranked among the top nine league leaders in bases on balls from 1900 to 1908. He averaged 33 stolen bases a year. Jones led the American League with 36 sacrifice hits in 1904, and ranks 37th all-time in sacrifice hits with 254. He became the first AL outfielder to carry out an unassisted double play.

LIFETIME STATS: BA: .285, HR: 21, RBI: 631, H: 1,920, SB: 359

#424 Kenneth "Kenny" Lofton

OF-DH, Astros, Indians, Braves, White Sox, Giants, Pirates, Cubs, Yankees, Phillies, Dodger, Rangers, 1991–2007

Lofton stole 30 or more bases in eight of his 13 professional seasons, including a career-high 70 steals in 1993 for the Indians. He set an AL rookie record with 66 steals in 1992, and went on to lead the league in stolen bases for five seasons, 1992–96. Lofton led the AL with 160 hits in 1994 and 13 triples the following season. A six-time All Star, he hit .300 or better in six seasons and won Gold Gloves in four consecutive seasons, 1993–96.

LIFETIME STATS: BA: .300, HR: 129, RBI: 763, H: 2,369, SB: 619

#425 Robert Abial "Red" Rolfe

3B-SS, Yankees, 1931–42

Rolfe, nicknamed "Red" because of his shock of red hair, led the American League with 139 runs, 213 hits and 46 doubles in 1939, while hitting a career-best .329. He hit .300 or better four times in his career and played on six World Series teams, including five world champions, 1936–39, and 1941. Rolfe scored at least 100 runs each year he played more than 100 games, and twice led AL third basemen in fielding percentage.

LIFETIME STATS: BA: .289, HR: 69, RBI: 497, H: 1,394, SB: 44

#**426** Garry Lewis Templeton

SS, Cardinals, Padres, Mets, 1976–91

In 1977 Templeton became the youngest shortstop since 1900 to reach 200 hits in a season. He led the National League with 211 hits in 1979. That year, he became the first switch-hitter to collect 100 hits from each side of the plate in one season. He topped the NL in triples, 1977–79, and ranked third in NL batting average in 1977 and 1980.

LIFETIME STATS: BA: .271, HR: 70, RBI: 728, H: 2,096, SB: 242

#**427** Jackson Riggs Stephenson

OF-2B, Indians, Cubs, 1921–34

Stephenson hit .300 or better in 12 of his 14 professional seasons, and ranks 23rd among all-time batting-average leaders. He led the National League with 46 doubles in 1927. Stephenson had one of his best offensive years in 1929 with the Cubs, hitting .362 with 17 home runs and 110 RBI. He won the fifth-most votes in 1932 NL MVP balloting, batting .324 with 189 hits and 85 RBI.

LIFETIME STATS: BA: .336, HR: 63, RBI: 773, H: 1,515, SB: 53

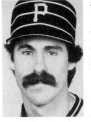

#**428** Philip Mason "Phil" Garner

2B-3B, A's, Pirates, Astros, Dodgers, Giants, 1973–88

Garner ranked among the top five league leaders in triples five times in his career. As a Pirate, he batted .500 in the 1979 World Series against Baltimore, hitting safely in all seven games. He hit .417 with a home run in the Pirates' three-game sweep of the Reds in the NLCS that year. A three-time All Star, Garner averaged .309 over five career postseason series.

LIFETIME STATS: BA: .260, HR: 109, RBI: 738, H: 1,594, SB: 225

#**429** Roger Thorpe Peckinpaugh

SS, Indians, Yankees, Senators, White Sox, 1910–27

Peckinpaugh was voted the 1925 American League MVP as a Senator. Two years earlier, he led the AL with 40 sacrifice hits. He collected 314 career sacrifice hits, placing him eighth among all-time leaders in that category. Peckinpaugh had a 29-game hitting streak in 1919, and knocked in the winning run in Game Two of the Senators' 1924 World Series against the New York Giants.

LIFETIME STATS: BA: .259, HR: 48, RBI: 739, H: 1,876, SB: 205

#430 William Ellsworth "Dummy" Hoy

OF, Washington Nationals, Buffalo Bisons, St. Louis Browns, Reds, Louisville Colonels, White Sox, 1888–1902

Hoy stole 82 bases in 1888 with the Nationals, leading the National League. He stole 30 or more bases in 11 seasons, and ranks 17th among all-time stolen base leaders with 594. He led the league with 296 times on base in 1891 for the Browns. A deaf-mute, Hoy is believed to be the reason umpires developed hand signals to accompany their play calls.

LIFETIME STATS: BA: .287, HR: 40, RBI: 726, H: 2,044, SB: 594

#431 Terry Lee Steinbach

C-DH-1B, A's, Twins, 1986–99

Steinbach knocked in seven runs including a home run to help the A's defeat the Giants in the 1989 World Series. He broke out offensively in the 1996 season, his last year with the A's, collecting a career-high 140 hits, with 35 home runs and 100 RBI. A three-time All Star, Steinbach was named MVP of the 1988 All Star game.

LIFETIME STATS: BA: .271, HR: 162, RBI: 745, H: 1,453, SB: 23

#432 Kenneth Frederick "Ken" Keltner

3B, Indians, Red Sox, 1937–44, 1946–50

Keltner ranked five times among the top nine American League leaders in doubles and triples. He was partly responsible for ending Joe DiMaggio's 56-game hitting streak on July 17, 1941, catching two of his line drives. The seven-time All Star peaked offensively in 1948, hitting 31 home runs and driving in 119 runs.

LIFETIME STATS: BA: .276, HR: 163, RBI: 852, H: 1,570, SB: 39

#433 Louis Rogers "Pete," "The Gladiator" Browning

OF-3B, Louisville Colonels, Cleveland Infants, Pirates, Reds, St. Louis Browns, Brooklyn Grooms, 1882–94

Browning, called "the Gladiator" for his battles with fly balls, hit .300 or better in 10 full professional seasons and posted his league's best batting average three times. He ranks 13th all-time for career batting average leaders. Browning led the league in 1885 with 174 hits for the Colonels, and topped the league again in 1890 with 40 doubles for the Infants. The Louisville Slugger line of baseball bats is named after Browning, who was born in Louisville.

LIFETIME STATS: BA: .341, HR: 46, RBI: 659, H: 1,646, SB: 258

#**434** Willard "Home Run" Brown

OF, Kansas City Monarchs (Negro Leagues), St. Louis Browns, 1936–1950. Hall of Fame, 2006

The power-hitting Brown was a fleet outfielder for most of his career with the Kansas City Monarchs. Many fans at that time believed Brown was a better home run hitter than the legendary Josh Gibson. In fact, Gibson himself conferred Brown's nickname.

Brown began his career as a shortstop with the Monarchs and hit .361 his first year. He stayed at that position for a few more years, moving into the outfield in 1938.

Brown won six Negro American League home run titles and hit .300 or better 16 consecutive years. He played one year in the majors with the St. Louis Browns, but, greatly bothered by racism in the Major Leagues at the time, he returned to the Monarchs in 1948.

LIFETIME STATS: BA: 366, HR: 188

#**435** Julio Cesar Franco

SS-2B-DH-1B, Phillies, Indians, Rangers, White Sox, Brewers, Devil Rays, Braves, 1982–2003

Franco led the AL with a .341 batting average in 1991 for the Rangers, notching one of his best offensive seasons that year with 201 hits, 108 runs and 36 stolen bases. He ranks eighth among active players in career hits, and ninth among active players in at bats, with 7,869. Franco hit .300 or better in seven full seasons.

LIFETIME STATS: BA: .300, HR: 173, RBI: 1,194, H: 2,586, SB: 281

#436 Manuel De Jesus "Manny" Sanguillen

C-OF-DH-1B, Pirates, A's, 1967, 1969–80

Sanguillen ranked among the top 10 NL MVP candidates in 1971. Three times in his career, he ranked among the top 10 league leaders in batting average and triples. The three-time All Star clinched a Game Two win for the Pirates over Baltimore in the 1979 World Series with a two-out, ninth-inning single. Sanguillen was one of the best bad-ball hitters in the league during his career.

LIFETIME STATS: BA: .296, HR: 65, RBI: 585, H: 1,500, SB: 35

#437 Gary Nathaniel Matthews Sr.

OF, Giants, Braves, Phillies, Cubs, Mariners, 1972–87

Named 1973 National League Rookie of the Year with the Giants, Matthews batted .300 with 162 hits. He led the NL in on-base percentage in 1984, his first year with the Cubs. Matthews recorded his best offensive season with the Braves in 1979, hitting .304 with 27 home runs, 90 RBI and 97 runs. Named the 1983 NLCS MVP, Matthews hit .429 for Philadelphia with three home runs and eight RBI against the Dodgers.

LIFETIME STATS: BA: .281, HR: 234, RBI: 978, H: 2,011, SB: 183

#438 Floyd Caves "Babe" Herman

OF-1B, Brooklyn Robins, Reds, Cubs, Pirates, Tigers, Brooklyn Dodgers, 1926–37, 1945

Herman ranked among the top 10 league leaders in home runs eight times in his career. He led the National League in 1932 with 19 triples for the Reds, and topped the NL in 1931 with 77 extra-base hits. Herman ranks 43rd among all-time leaders with a .532 slugging percentage. He batted .300 or better in eight seasons. Playing for Brooklyn in 1930, Herman hit .393 with 130 RBI, 35 home runs and 241 hits. He and Bob Meusel are the only players to hit for the cycle three times.

LIFETIME STATS: BA: .324, HR: 181, RBI: 997, H: 1,818, SB: 94

#439 Clarence Howeth "Ginger" Beaumont

OF, Pirates, Boston Doves, Cubs, 1899–1910

Beaumont led the National League in 1902 as a Pirate with a .357 batting average. As a rookie, he batted .352. Beaumont ranked among league batting average leaders seven times and led the league in hits for four seasons. He hit .300 or better in seven seasons and led the NL in 1903 with 137 runs.

LIFETIME STATS: BA: .311, HR: 39, RBI: 617, H: 1,759, SB: 254

#**440** Raymond Johnson "Ray" Chapman

SS, Indians, 1912–20

Chapman ranked among the top two American League hitters in sacrifice hits five times in his career. His 334 career sacrifice hits place him sixth among all-time leaders. He led the AL with 84 runs and 84 walks in 1918. Chapman died after being hit in the head by a pitch from Yankee Carl Mays on August 16, 1920. He was batting .303 with 132 hits at the time.

LIFETIME STATS: BA: .278, HR: 17, RBI: 364, H: 1,053, SB: 233

#**441** John W. "Jimmie" Crutchfield

OF, Birmingham Black Barons, Indianapolis ABC's, Pittsburgh Crawfords, Newark Eagles, Toledo Crawfords, Indianapolis Crawfords, Chicago American Giants (Negro Leagues), 1930–45

The hustling Crutchfield hit .286 in his rookie year with the Black Barons, and batted a career-high .330 with the ABC's. He was named to the East-West All Star team four times. The diminutive (5'7", 150 pounds) Crutchfield, who was often called the "Black Lloyd Waner," after the Pittsburgh Pirates star, was an excellent bunter and dependable hit-and-run man.

LIFETIME STATS: BA: .327

#442 George Edward Martin Van Haltren

OF-LHP-SS, Cubs, Brooklyn Ward's Wonders, Orioles, Pirates, New York Giants, 1887–1903

Van Haltren hit .300 or better 12 times in his career, ranking among league leaders in hits nine times, and in runs eight times. He led the National League with 21 triples in 1896. As a Giant, Van Haltren led the NL in stolen bases in 1900 with 45. He stole 30 or more bases 10 times in his career. His pitching career in the majors was brief: After he walked 16 batters in a game (still a major league record) in 1887, Chicago manager Cap Anson decided Van Haltern was better off in the outfield.

LIFETIME STATS: BA: .316, HR: 69, RBI: 1,014, H: 2,532, SB: 583

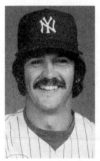

#443 Ronald Ames "Ron," "Gator" Guidry

LHP, Yankees, 1975–88

Guidry had one of the greatest seasons for a pitcher in major league history in 1978, winning the American League Cy Young award, posting a 1.74 ERA with 248 strikeouts and a 25–3 record, and also leading the league with nine shutouts that year. He won 20 or more games in a season three times in his career. Guidry's 2.78 ERA led the AL in 1979. A five-time Gold Glove winner, from 1982 to 1986, he was also a four-time All Star.

LIFETIME STATS: W: 170, L: 91, SV: 4, ERA: 3.29, SO: 1,778, CG: 95

#444 Lawrence Robert "Larry" Bowa

SS, Phillies, Cubs, Mets, 1970–85

The fiery Bowa led National League shortstops in fielding percentage six times, winning Gold Glove awards in 1972 and 1978. He topped the NL in 1972 with 13 triples and 18 sacrifice hits. Bowa placed third in 1978 NL MVP voting. A five-time All Star, he stole 20 or more bases nine times in his career.

LIFETIME STATS: BA: .260, HR: 15, RBI: 525, H: 2,191, SB: 318

#445 Ichiro Suzuki

OF, Mariners, 2001–present

Ichiro is a man who has succeeded on both sides of the Pacific Rim, first as a star in Japan's Pacific League, and now in the American League. Ichiro led the Pacific League in batting seven times, was a three-time MVP and a seven-time Gold Glove winner. Coming to the United States in 2000, he was an immediate star with Seattle. In 2004, Ichiro broke a 74-year-old record, making 262 hits, to pass George Sisler's old mark of 257. He has had 200 or more hits 10 times.

LIFETIME STATS (ML ONLY): BA: .326, HR: 95, RBI: 605, H: 2,428, SB: 423

#446 Thomas Mitchell "Tommy" Herr

2B, Cardinals, Twins, Phillies, Mets, Giants, 1979–91

A devastating double-play combination with shortstop Ozzie Smith, Herr led the National League three times in double plays for the Cardinals. He finished fifth in NL MVP voting in 1985, batting .302 with 180 hits, 110 RBI, 97 runs and 31 steals. Herr batted .333 with four doubles and a home run in the 1985 NLCS to help the Cardinals defeat the Dodgers.

LIFETIME STATS: BA: .271, HR: 28, RBI: 574, H: 1,450, SB: 188

#447 Lafayette Napoleon "Lave" Cross

3B-C-SS-OF-2B Louisville Colonels, Philadelphia A's, Phillies, Cardinals, Cleveland Spiders, Brooklyn Superbas, Senators, 1887–1907

Cross ranked among league leaders six times in hits and RBI. As a Phillie in 1894, he hit .386 with 125 RBI, 123 runs, 204 hits and seven home runs, his best offensive season. Cross played several positions over his career, and in 1897 set a major league record as a second baseman with 15 assists in a 12-inning game. He batted .290 or better in seven consecutive seasons, 1898–1904.

LIFETIME STATS: BA: .292, HR: 47, RBI: 1,371, H: 2,645, SB: 301

#448 Lloyd James "Little Poison" Waner

OF, Pirates, Boston Braves, Reds, Brooklyn Dodgers, 1927–42, 1944–45. Hall of Fame, 1967

Waner hit .300 or better 10 times in his career. He set a major league rookie record with 223 hits in 1927 with the Pirates and went on to collect 986 hits in his first five seasons with the Pirates. Waner led the National League in putouts four times. He topped the league in 1927 with 133 runs, in 1929 with 20 triples and in 1931 with 214 hits.

LIFETIME STATS: BA: .316, HR: 27, RBI: 598, H: 2,459, SB: 67

#449 Herbert Jefferis "Herb," "The Knight of Kennet Square" Pennock

LHP, Philadelphia A's, Red Sox, Yankees, 1912–17, 1919–34. Hall of Fame, 1948

Pennock led the American League in 1928 with five shutouts. He went 5–0 over five World Series with a 1.95 ERA, including four complete games. Pitching for the Yankees in the 1927 World Series, Pennock threw a three-hitter against the Pirates, retiring the first 22 batters. He ranked among the top nine league leaders in winning percentage nine times. His nickname came from his birthplace, Kennet Square, Pennsylvania.

LIFETIME STATS: W: 240, L: 162, SV: 33, ERA: 3.60, SO: 1,227, CG: 247

#450 Gary Joseph Gaetti

3B-1B, Twins, Angels, Royals, Cardinals, Cubs, Red Sox, 1981–2000

A four-time Gold Glove winner, Gaetti was named the 1987 ALCS MVP, hitting two home runs in his first two series at bats, leading the Twins to victory over Detroit. He started two triple plays in the same game for the Twins against the Red Sox in 1990. Gaetti set a record for Twins' third basemen with a .973 fielding percentage in 1987.

LIFETIME STATS: BA: .255, HR: 360, RBI: 1,341, H: 2,280, SB: 96

#451 William George "Billy" Rogell

SS-3B, Red Sox, Tigers, Cubs, 1925, 1927–28, 1930–40

Rogell led American League shortstops in fielding percentage over three straight seasons, 1935–37, and in assists, 1934–35. He peaked offensively as a Tiger in 1934, batting .296 with 100 RBI and 175 hits. Rogell tallied four RBI in Game Four of the 1934 World Series, though the Tigers would ultimately lose to the Cardinals.

LIFETIME STATS: BA: .267, HR: 42, RBI: 609, H: 1,375, SB: 82

#452 Walter Kevin McReynolds

OF, Padres, Mets, Royals, 1983–94

McReynolds led National League outfielders in putouts in 1984 and 1985 with the Padres, and in assists in 1988, the year he gathered the third-most NL MVP votes. He ranked among league home run and RBI leaders three times. His three-run home run in Game Three of the 1984 NLCS helped lead the Padres to victory over the Cubs.

LIFETIME STATS: BA: .265, HR: 211, RBI: 807, H: 1,439, SB: 93

#453 Burleigh Arland Grimes

RHP, Pirates, Brooklyn Robins, New York Giants, Boston Braves, Cardinals, Cubs, Yankees, 1916–34. Hall of Fame, 1964

The last man who could legally throw a spitball in the majors, Grimes led the National League in wins in 1921 and 1928, and ranks 31st all-time in career wins. He placed among the top eight league leaders in ERA six times, and among the top five strikeout leaders eight times. He notched five 20-win seasons and led the league four times in complete games. With Brooklyn in 1921, Grimes led the NL with 136 strikeouts.

LIFETIME STATS: W: 270, L: 212, SV: 18, ERA: 3.53, SO: 1,512, CG: 314

#454 John Scott "Jack" Morris

RHP, Tigers, Twins, Blue Jays, Indians, 1977–94

Morris won 17 or more games eight times in his career, leading the American League in wins in 1981 and 1992. He topped the league in strikeouts in 1983 with 232. Morris ranked among the top nine Cy Young vote-winners seven times, and led the AL in 1990 with 11 complete games. Named the 1991 World Series MVP, Morris won the first game against the Braves and clinched the Series for the Twins by pitching 10 innings without giving up a run in Game Seven.

LIFETIME STATS: W: 254, L: 186, SV: 0, ERA: 3.90, SO: 2,478, CG: 175

#455 James Thomas "Deacon" McGuire

C-1B, Toledo Blue Stockings, Detroit Wolverines, Phillies, Cleveland Blues, Rochester Broncos, Senators, Brooklyn Superbas, Tigers, Yankees, Red Sox, Cleveland Naps, 1884–88, 1890–1908, 1910, 1912

McGuire hit .300 or better with the Senators from 1894 to 1897. He was the oldest player in the major leagues for six seasons, reaching 48 in his last season. McGuire caught games in 26 seasons, more than any other catcher. He peaked offensively in 1895 with the Senators, batting .336 with 97 RBI, 179 hits, 30 doubles, 10 home runs and 16 stolen bases.

LIFETIME STATS: BA: .278, HR: 45, RBI: 840, H: 1,748, SB: 117

#456 James Edward "Tip" O'Neill

OF, New York Giants, St. Louis Browns, Chicago Pirates, Reds, 1883–92

O'Neill hit .300 or better in six full seasons. In 1887 he hit a league-leading .435 for the St. Louis Browns, also leading the league that year with 167 runs, 225 hits, 14 home runs, 52 doubles and 19 triples. O'Neill led the league the following year with a .335 batting average. He was known as "Tip" for his penchant for fouling off balls at the plate. O'Neill batted .400 for St. Louis in the 1886 World Series exhibition against the Chicago White Sox, hitting two home runs.

LIFETIME STATS: BA: .326, HR: 52, RBI: 757, H: 1,386, SB: 161

#457 Max Frederick "Camera Eye" Bishop

2B, Philadelphia A's, Red Sox, 1924–35

Bishop ranked among American League leaders in on-base percentage eight times in his career. He ranks 19th all-time with a .423 on-base percentage. Bishop led the AL with 128 walks in 1929, and ranked among the top eight league leaders in bases on balls nine other times. He was nicknamed "Camera Eye" for his excellent eye for balls and strikes at the plate.

LIFETIME STATS: BA: .271, HR: 41, RBI: 379, H: 1,216, SB: 43

#458 Juan Alberto Gonzalez

OF-DH, Rangers, Tigers, Indians, 1989–2005

Gonzalez was named the American League MVP in 1996 and 1998. He led the AL in 1998 with 50 doubles and 157 RBI. Gonzalez batted .438 with five home runs as a Ranger in a losing 1996 AL Division Series against the Yankees. He tallied 100 or more RBI in eight seasons, hit 30 or more home runs in seven years and led the AL in home runs, 1992–93.

LIFETIME STATS: BA: .296, HR: 429, RBI: 1,387, H: 1,901, SB: 26

#459 Michael Stephen "Mickey" Lolich

LHP, Tigers, Mets, Padres, 1963–79

The portly Lolich collected 200 or more strikeouts a season seven times in his career. He led the American League in 1971 with 308 strikeouts, 25 wins and 29 complete games, and ranked among the top three Cy Young vote-winners, 1971–72. Lolich was named the 1968 World Series MVP, throwing three complete-game wins with a 1.67 ERA, leading the Tigers to victory over the Cardinals. He ranks 14th among all-time strikeout leaders.

LIFETIME STATS: W: 217, L: 191, SV: 11, ERA: 3.44, SO: 2,832, CG: 195

#**460** Chester Earl "Chet" Lemon

OF, White Sox, Tigers, 1975–90

Lemon broke two American League records in 1977, notching 524 chances as an outfielder and 512 putouts. He led the AL in 1979 with 44 doubles. He ranked among the top eight league leaders in the hit-by-pitch category for 13 consecutive seasons. The three-time All Star ranks 17th all-time in that category, having been hit by 151 pitches in his career.

LIFETIME STATS: BA: .273, HR: 215, RBI: 884, H: 1,875, SB: 58

#**461** Alfonso Ramon "Al" Lopez

C, Brooklyn Dodgers, Boston Braves, Pirates, Indians, 1928, 1930–47. Hall of Fame, 1977

Lopez led National League catchers in fielding percentage and assists three times. He tied an NL record in 1941, catching 114 games without a passed ball. His 1,918 games caught was a major league record for several years. After his playing career ended, Lopez managed the Indians and White Sox. His .581 managerial winning percentage ranks ninth among all-time leaders.

LIFETIME STATS: BA: .261, HR: 51, RBI: 652, H: 1,547, SB: 46

#462 Edwin David "Eddie" Joost

SS-2B-3B, Reds, Boston Braves, Philadelphia A's, Red Sox, 1936–37, 1939–55.

Joost ranked among league leaders four times in runs scored and on-base percentage. He led the National League in 1947 with 24 sacrifice hits. Joost drew 100 or more walks a season six years in a row, from 1947 to 1952, with more walks than hits in 1947 and 1949. He led AL shortstops in putouts, 1947–49 and 1951.

LIFETIME STATS: BA: .239, HR: 134, RBI: 601, H: 1,339, SB: 61

#463 Roy Edward "Squirrel" Sievers

OF-1B, St. Louis Browns, Senators, White Sox, Phillies, 1949–65

Sievers was named 1949 American League Rookie of the Year, batting .306 with 16 home runs and 91 RBI for the Browns. He led the AL in 1957 as a Senator with 114 RBI, 42 home runs and 70 extra-base hits. A four-time All Star, Sievers drove in 90 or more runs eight times in his career. He acquired his nickname as a basketball player: Sievers was always hanging around the "cage."

LIFETIME STATS: BA: .267, HR: 318, RBI: 1,147, H: 1,703, SB: 14

#464 Albert Fred "Red" Schoendienst

2B-OF, Cardinals, Giants, Milwaukee Braves, 1945–63. Hall of Fame, 1989

Schoendienst led National League second basemen in fielding percentage seven times, and also hit .300 or better seven times. He led the NL in 1957 with 200 hits. He was one of the best switch-hitters of his era, and his 14th-inning home run in the 1950 All Star game clinched the NL victory. A 10-time All Star, Schoendienst led the league with 26 stolen bases in his rookie year. In 1989, he was elected to the Hall of Fame as a manager.

LIFETIME STATS: BA: .289, HR: 84, RBI: 773, H: 2,449, SB: 89

#465 Harold Abraham "Hal" McRae

OF-DH, Reds, Royals, 1968, 1970–87

McRae hit .300 or better in six seasons. In the postseason he ratcheted up his hitting, batting .400 over four World Series. He topped the American League in 1976 with a .407 on-base percentage. McRae led the AL in 1977 with 54 doubles and 86 extra-base hits, and again topped the league in 1982 with 46 doubles and 133 RBI. He peaked in power in 1982 with 27 home runs and 133 RBI.

LIFETIME STATS: BA: .290, HR: 191, RBI: 1,097, H: 2,091, SB: 109

#466 Harold Patrick "Pete" Reiser

OF-3B, Brooklyn Dodgers, Boston Braves, Pirates, Indians, 1940–42, 1946–52

Reiser led the National League in 1941, batting .343 with 117 runs, 39 doubles and 17 triples, becoming the youngest major league batting champion at 22. He led the league in 1942 with 20 stolen bases and again in 1946 with 34 stolen bases. Reiser set a major league record in 1946 by stealing home seven times.

LIFETIME STATS: BA: .295, HR: 58, RBI: 368, H: 786, SB: 87

#467 Ricardo Adolfo Jacobo "Rico" Carty

OF-DH-1B, Milwaukee Braves, Atlanta Braves, Rangers, Cubs, A's, Indians, Blue Jays, 1963–67, 1969–70, 1972–79

Carty led the National League in 1970 with Atlanta, batting .366 with a .454 on-base percentage. He hit .300 or better six times in his career, peaking offensively in 1970, with 175 hits, 84 runs and 101 RBI. His .330 batting average in his rookie year was eclipsed in the NL only by Roberto Clemente.

LIFETIME STATS: BA: .299, HR: 204, RBI: 890, H: 1,677, SB: 21

#**468** Paul Andrew O'Neill

OF, Reds, Yankees, 1985–2001

O'Neill, the spiritual leader of the Yankees in the late 1990s, hit .300 or better in six consecutive seasons, 1993–98. He led the American League in 1994 with a .359 batting average, and gathered the fifth-most MVP votes. O'Neill played in six World Series from 1990 to 2001. A five-time All Star, he hit .474 for the Yankees in a victorious 2000 World Series against the Mets, with two doubles and two triples.

LIFETIME STATS: BA: .288, HR: 281, RBI: 1,269, H: 2,105, SB: 141

#**469** John Rikard "Rick" Dempsey

C, Twins, Yankees, Orioles, Indians, Dodgers, Brewers, 1969–92

Dempsey led American League catchers in assists in 1979 and in fielding percentage in 1981 and 1983. He was named MVP of the 1983 World Series, batting .385 overall. Dempsey knocked in the game-winning RBI in Game Two for the Orioles and clinched the Series over the Phillies in the fifth and final game with a double and a home run.

LIFETIME STATS: BA: .233, HR: 96, RBI: 471, H: 1,093, SB: 20

#470 Ronald Ray "Ron" Fairly

1B-OF-DH, Dodgers, Expos, Cardinals, A's, Blue Jays, Angels, 1958–78

Fairly led National League first basemen in fielding percentage as a Dodger in 1963. Slow afoot, but with an excellent eye at the plate, Fairly ranked among league leaders five times in bases on balls. Fairly's .422 on-base percentage was second-best in the NL in 1973. He batted .379 with two home runs in the Dodgers' 1965 World Series win over the Twins.

LIFETIME STATS: BA: .266, HR: 215, RBI: 1,044, H: 1,913, SB: 35

#471 Travis Calvin Jackson

SS-3B, New York Giants, 1922–36. Hall of Fame, 1982

Jackson ranked among the top ten National League MVP vote-winners four times, and placed among league home run leaders four times. Jackson had a strong arm and better-than-average range, and led league shortstops in assists four times. Twice Jackson led league shortstops in double plays and fielding percentage. He hit .300 or better six times in his career.

LIFETIME STATS: BA: .291, HR: 135, RBI: 929, H: 1,768, SB: 71

#472 Herold Dominic "Muddy" Ruel

C, St. Louis Browns, Yankees, Red Sox, Senators, Tigers, White Sox, 1915, 1917–34

Ruel led American League catchers three times each in fielding percentage, putouts, double plays and assists. His 12th-inning double drove in the winning run in the 1924 World Series, leading the Senators to victory over the New York Giants. Ruel peaked offensively in 1923 with Washington, batting .316 with 24 doubles, 142 hits and 63 runs scored. He got his nickname from his childhood, where he would play games of catch using a ball of mud.

LIFETIME STATS: BA: .275, HR: 4, RBI: 534, H: 1,242, SB: 61

#473 Kenneth Ray "Ken" Williams

OF, Reds, St. Louis Browns, Red Sox, 1915–16, 1918–29

Williams hit .300 or better eight times in his career, including six consecutive seasons with the Browns, from 1920 to 1925. He led the American League in 1922 as a Brown with 39 home runs, 155 RBI and 84 extra-base hits. That same season, he also stole 37 bases while batting .332, making him the first player to hit 30 or more home runs with 30 or more stolen bases and a batting average of at least .300.

LIFETIME STATS: BA: .319, HR: 196, RBI: 913, H: 1,552, SB: 154

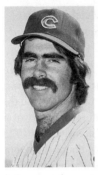

#**474** William Joseph "Bill" Buckner

1B-OF-DH, Dodgers, Cubs, Red Sox, Angels, Royals, 1969–90

Throw away his error in Game Six of the 1986 World Series, and one is left with a Bill Buckner who was a solid hitter. He led the National League as a Cub in 1980 with a .324 batting average. He topped the NL in doubles twice, in 1981 and 1983, and ranked among league leaders in hits seven times. Buckner set a major league record in 1985 with 184 assists at first base for the Red Sox. He led active players in 1990 with 2,707 career hits.

LIFETIME STATS: BA: .289, HR: 174, RBI: 1,208, H: 2,715, SB: 183

#**475** John Jordan "Buck" O'Neil

1B, Miami Giants, Shreveport Acme Giants, Memphis Red Sox, Kansas City Monarchs (Negro Leagues), 1938–55

O'Neil led the Negro National League with a .353 batting average in 1946. An excellent clutch hitter, O'Neil hit .333 with two home runs in the Black World Series that year. A smooth-fielding first baseman through his career, O'Neil also became the first black coach to be officially hired by the major leagues, signing with the Cubs in 1962.

LIFETIME STATS (incomplete): BA: .333

#476 Eugene Richard "Gene" Woodling

OF, Indians, Pirates, Yankees, Orioles, Senators, Mets, 1943, 1946–47, 1949–62

Woodling batted .300 or better five times in his career. He batted .318 over five consecutive victorious World Series with the Yankees, from 1949 to 1953. Woodling peaked offensively in 1957 with the Indians, batting .321 with 78 RBI and 19 home runs. He ranked among the top eight AL leaders in on-base percentage with the Indians and Orioles, 1957–60.

LIFETIME STATS: BA: .284, HR: 147, RBI: 830, H: 1,585, SB: 29

#477 John Landis "Johnny" Bassler

C, Indians, Tigers, 1913–14, 1921–27

For three consecutive seasons, Bassler ranked among the top seven American League players in MVP voting, 1922–24. He also ranked among the top eight AL players in on-base percentage, 1922–24. Bassler hit .300 or better in three full seasons with the Tigers, recording peak offensive numbers in 1924, when he batted .346 with 20 doubles, 131 hits and 68 RBI.

LIFETIME STATS: BA: .304, HR: 1, RBI: 318, H: 704, SB: 13

#478 Elburt Preston "Elbie" Fletcher

1B, Boston Braves, Pirates, 1934–35, 1937–43, 1946–47, 1949

Fletcher led the National League in on-base percentage for three consecutive seasons, 1940–42, and led the league in walks, 1940–41. He ranked among league base-on-balls leaders for most of his career. Fletcher placed among the top four league leaders in times on base, 1940–43. He recorded his best power numbers in 1940 as a Pirate, hitting 16 home runs with 104 RBI.

LIFETIME STATS: BA: .271, HR: 79, RBI: 616, H: 1,323, SB: 32

#479 Elwood George "Woody" English

SS–3B, Cubs, Brooklyn Dodgers, 1927–38

English led National League shortstops in putouts in 1931, the year he gathered the fourth-most NL MVP votes. He topped NL third basemen in fielding percentage in 1933. English posted career-best numbers in 1930 with the Cubs, batting .335 with 14 home runs, 59 RBI, 17 triples, 214 hits and 152 runs scored.

LIFETIME STATS: BA: .286, HR: 32, RBI: 422, H: 1,356, SB: 57

#480 Thomas Edward "Tommy" John Jr.

LHP, Indians, White Sox, Dodgers, Yankees, Angels, A's, 1963–74, 1976–89

John ranked among the top eight Cy Young award vote-winners four times, 1977–80. He placed six times among league ERA leaders, and led the league in shutouts three times. John ranks sixth among all-time leaders with 700 games started. He underwent mid-career arm surgery in a procedure now synonymous with his name. John posted three seasons with 20 or more wins following the surgery. He was 46 years old in his final season.

LIFETIME STATS: W: 288, L: 231, SV: 4, ERA: 3.34, SO: 2,245, CG: 162

#481 Michael Joseph "Mike" Griffin

OF, Orioles, Philadelphia A's Brooklyn Bridegrooms, 1887–98

Griffin hit .300 or better six times, including his last five consecutive seasons with Brooklyn, 1894–98. He led the league in runs scored with 152 in 1889, and later led the National League with 36 doubles in 1891. Griffin stole 30 or more bases eight times in his career. His 94 stolen bases in 1887 with the Orioles set a major league record for rookies that held until 1985.

LIFETIME STATS: BA: .296, HR: 42, RBI: 719, H: 1,753, SB: 473

#**482** Sidney "Sid" Gordon

OF-3B, New York Giants, Boston Braves, Milwaukee Braves, Pirates, 1941–43, 1946–55

Gordon ranked among the top nine National League home run leaders five years in a row, from 1948 to 1952. He placed five times among league leaders in on-base percentage and bases on balls. Gordon collected the fourth-most NL MVP votes in 1948, batting .299 with 30 home runs, 107 RBI and 100 runs. Born and raised in Brooklyn, he was a popular star when he played for the Giants.

LIFETIME STATS: BA: .283, HR: 202, RBI: 805, H: 1,415, SB: 19

#**483** Charles Andrew "Duke" Farrell

C-3B-OF-1B, Cubs, Red Sox, Chicago Pirates, Pittsburgh Pirates, Senators, New York Giants, Brooklyn Superbas, 1888–1905

Farrell led the National League in pinch hits three times. He notched a pinch hit for Boston during the first World Series in 1903. Farrell led the league with 110 RBI and 12 home runs for Boston in 1891. Farrell hit 12 or more triples a season, 1890–94, and ranks 93rd among all-time triples leaders with 123.

LIFETIME STATS: BA: .275, HR: 51, RBI: 912, H: 1,564, SB: 150

#484 Dudley Michael "Mike" Hargrove

1B-OF-DH, Rangers, Padres, Indians, 1974–85

Hargrove was named 1974 American League Rookie of the Year, batting .323 with 134 hits and 66 RBI for the Rangers. He hit .300 or better five times, and ranked among league leaders in on-base percentage for most of his career, topping the AL in 1981 with a .424 percentage for the Indians. Hargrove led the AL in walks in 1976 and 1978, and topped AL first basemen in assists twice.

LIFETIME STATS: BA: .290, HR: 80, RBI: 686, H: 1,614, SB: 24

#485 Felipe Rojas Alou

OF-1B, Giants, Milwaukee Braves, Atlanta Braves, A's, Yankees, Expos, Brewers, 1958–74

Alou led the National League in 1966 with 218 hits and 122 runs for the Braves. That year he also hit a personal-best .327 with 31 home runs. Alou led the NL in 1968 with 210 hits. He scored the winning run for the Giants in the 1962 playoffs against the Dodgers. Alou ranked among the top 10 NL MVP vote-winners in 1966 and 1968.

LIFETIME STATS: BA: .286, HR: 206, RBI: 852, H: 2,101, SB: 107

#486 James Lee "Jim" Kaat

LHP, Senators, Twins, White Sox, Phillies, Yankees, Cardinals, 1959–83

Kaat was agile and quick, despite being 6'4". He won the Gold Glove for pitchers 16 consecutive times, 1962–77. He led the AL with five shutouts in 1962 and 25 wins in 1966. Kaat ranks 13th among all-time leaders for games started with 625. Winning 20 or more games three times in his career, he set a Twins franchise record with 189 wins. He holds a major league record with 25 years as a pitcher.

LIFETIME STATS: W: 283, L: 237, SV: 18, ERA: 3.45, SO: 2,461, CG: 180

#487 Henry John "Hank" Sauer

OF, Reds, Cubs, Cardinals, New York Giants, San Francisco Giants, 1941–42, 1945, 1948–59

Sauer was named the National League MVP as a Cub in 1952. That year, he led the NL with 37 home runs, 121 RBI and 71 extra-base hits. Sauer ranked among the top 10 NL home run leaders seven times in his career, and hit 30 or more home runs in a season six times. Sauer was the first major leaguer to hit three home runs in one game twice in his career off the same pitcher (Curt Simmons of Philadelphia).

LIFETIME STATS: BA: .266, HR: 288, RBI: 876, H: 1,278, SB: 11

#488 Charles Wesley "Charlie" Bennett

C-OF, Milwaukee Grays, Worcester Ruby Legs, Detroit Wolverines, Boston Beaneaters, 1878, 1880–93

Bennett ranked among league home run leaders five times in his career, and six times among leaders in bases on balls. He started a three-year streak hitting .300 or better for the Wolverines in 1881. Bennett hit seven home runs with 64 RBI that year, both second-best in the National League. He lost both of his legs in a train accident in 1894. Bennett was popular in Detroit, and when the Tigers began operations in the American League in 1901, their first home field was named Bennett Field.

LIFETIME STATS: BA: .256, HR: 55, RBI: 533, H: 978, SB: 42

#489 Cecil Grant Fielder

1B-DH, Blue Jays, Tigers, Yankees, Angels, Indians, 1985–98

Fielder led the American League as a Tiger with 51 home runs and 132 RBI in 1990, and again with 44 home runs and 133 RBI in 1991. Still with the Tigers, he again led the AL in 1992 with 124 RBI. Fielder ranked among the top 10 AL MVP candidates three times. In 1990, he became the first AL player to reach 50 home runs since 1961.

LIFETIME STATS: BA: .255, HR: 319, RBI: 1,008, H: 1,313, SB: 2

#490 Frederick Charles "Freddie" Lindstrom

3B-OF, New York Giants, Pirates, Cubs, Brooklyn Dodgers, 1924–36. Hall of Fame, 1976

Lindstrom batted .300 or better seven times in his 13-year career, and led the National League in 1928 with 231 hits. That year, he earned the second-most votes for NL MVP. Lindstrom collected 231 hits again in 1930 while batting .379, with a personal-best 22 home runs and 127 runs. He ranked among league leaders in doubles four times.

LIFETIME STATS: BA: .311, HR: 103, RBI: 779, H: 1,747, SB: 84

#491 Robert Brown "Bobby" Thomson

OF-3B, New York Giants, Milwaukee Braves, Cubs, Red Sox, Orioles, 1946–60

Thomson ranked five times among league home run and RBI leaders. He hit 20 or more home runs eight times in his career. Thomson placed among the top eight NL MVP candidates in 1951, hitting 32 home runs with 101 RBI. He is best known for his three-run, ninth-inning home run off Brooklyn's Ralph Branca to clinch the pennant for the Giants in 1951.

LIFETIME STATS: BA: .270, HR: 264, RBI: 1,026, H: 1,705, SB: 38

#492 Terry Lee Pendleton

3B, Cardinals, Braves, Marlins, Reds, Royals, 1984–98

Pendleton won the National League Gold Glove for third basemen three times. He was named the NL MVP in 1991, leading the league with a .319 batting average, 187 hits and 303 total bases for the Braves. Pendleton hit .311 in 1992, with a career-high 105 RBI, 199 hits, 98 runs and 39 doubles. Over five World Series, he batted .298.

LIFETIME STATS: BA: .270, HR: 140, RBI: 946, H: 1,897, SB: 127

#493 Jesus Manuel Marcano "Manny" Trillo

2B-3B-1B, A's, Cubs, Phillies, Indians, Expos, Giants, Reds, 1973–89

A three-time Gold Glove winner for National League second basemen, Trillo played 89 consecutive games without an error in 1982, posting a then-record .9937 fielding average at second base. The four-time All Star was named MVP of the 1980 NLCS, batting .381 with four RBI in the Phillies' victory over Houston.

LIFETIME STATS: BA: .263, HR: 61, RBI: 571, H: 1,562, SB: 56

#494 John Garrett Olerud

1B-DH, Blue Jays, Mets, Mariners, Yankees, Red Sox, 1989–2005

Olerud has won three American League Gold Gloves at first base since 2000. As a Blue Jay in 1993, he led the AL with a .363 batting average, .473 on-base percentage and 54 doubles, placing third in AL MVP voting that year. He ranked among league leaders in bases on balls nine times. With 1,198 career walks, Olerud ranks eighth among active players in bases on balls.

LIFETIME STATS: BA: .295, HR: 255, RBI: 1,230, H: 2,239, SB: 94

#495 Francis Joseph "Lefty" O'Doul

OF, Yankees, Red Sox, New York Giants, Phillies, Brooklyn Dodgers, 1919–23, 1928–34

O'Doul led the National League in 1929 with a .398 batting average and 254 hits for the Phillies. He topped the league again as a Dodger in 1932, batting .368, and holds the fourth-highest career batting average of all time. He ranked among league home run leaders four times. O'Doul peaked offensively in 1929, with 32 home runs, 152 runs, 254 hits and 122 RBI.

LIFETIME STATS: BA: .349, HR: 113, RBI: 542, H: 1,140, SB: 36

#**496** William Henry "Bucky" Walters

RHP, Boston Braves, Red Sox, Phillies, Reds, 1931–48, 1950

Walters began his career as an infielder, but converted to a pitcher in 1934 at the suggestion of his manager in Philadelphia, Jimmie Wilson. It was a fortuitous decision. Walters was named the National League MVP in 1939, leading the league with a 2.29 ERA, 27 wins and 137 strikeouts, while batting .325 for the Reds. He led the league in 1940 with a 2.48 ERA and 22 wins, and again topped the league in 1944 with 23 wins. A six-time All Star, Walters led the league in complete games over three consecutive seasons, 1939–41.

LIFETIME STATS: W: 198, L: 160, SV: 4, ERA: 3.30, SO: 1,107, CG: 242

#**497** Robert Arthur "Bob" O'Farrell

C, Cubs, Cardinals, New York Giants, Reds, 1915–35

O'Farrell was named the National League MVP in 1926, batting .293 with 144 hits for the Cardinals. He clinched the 1926 World Series for the Cardinals by throwing out Babe Ruth at second in an unsuccessful steal attempt. O'Farrell batted .304 in that Series. He caught a 1929 Carl Hubbell no-hitter as a Giant, and formed a battery with Dizzy Dean and Grover Alexander.

LIFETIME STATS: BA: .273, HR: 51, RBI: 549, H: 1,120, SB: 35

#498 Gerald Wayne "Jerry" Grote

C, Astros, Mets, Dodgers, Royals, 1963–64, 1966–78, 1981

A poor hitter early in his career with Houston, Grote's contract was purchased by the Mets in 1966. Grote seemed to grow up in New York, and became a superb defensive catcher with occasional pop in his bat. Grote caught every inning of the 1969 National League Championship Series and World Series, as the Mets won their first world title.

LIFETIME STATS: BA: .252, HR: 39, RBI: 404, H: 1,092, SB: 15

#499 Roy David McMillan

SS, Reds, Milwaukee Braves, Mets, 1951–66

McMillan won the National League Gold Glove award for shortstops for three consecutive seasons, 1957–59, the first three years the award was granted. He led the NL with 31 sacrifice hits in 1954 and turned 129 double plays that year, an NL record for shortstops at the time. McMillan played a record 584 consecutive games at shortstop, 1951–55.

LIFETIME STATS: BA: .243, HR: 68, RBI: 594, H: 1,639, SB: 41

#**500** Lee Arthur Smith

RHP, Cubs, Red Sox, Cardinals, Yankees, Orioles,
Angels, Reds, Expos, 1980–97

A three-time Rolaids Relief award winner, Smith led the
league four times in saves, and ranked 14 times among
the top nine league leaders in saves. Smith, a hulking
6'6" and 225 pounds, posted three seasons with 40 or
more saves, 1991–93, with the Cardinals and Yankees.
He stands as the all-time leader in saves, also ranking first
with 802 games finished.

LIFETIME STATS: W: 71, L: 92, SV: 478, ERA: 3.03, SO: 1,251, CG: 0

#**501** Miller James Huggins

2B, Reds, Cardinals, 1904–1916. Hall of Fame, 1964

Huggins led the National League with a .432 on-base
percentage for the Cardinals in 1913, and topped the
league four times in walks. Frequently ranked among
league-leading second basemen in putouts, double plays,
assists and fielding percentage, Huggins grew to fame
after his playing career ended, managing the Yankees to their first six pennants and three World Series wins. He was eventually inducted into the Hall
of Fame for his managerial success.

LIFETIME STATS: BA: .265, HR: 9, RBI: 318, H: 1,474, SB: 324

#502 Michael Joseph Tiernan

OF, New York Giants, 1887–99

Tiernan hit .300 or better seven times in his career, and ranked among league batting-average leaders five times. He led the National League in 1889 with 147 runs and 96 walks. Tiernan topped the league the following year with 13 home runs and then again in 1891 with 16 home runs. He stole 30 or more bases seven times in his career.

LIFETIME STATS: BA: .311, HR: 106, RBI: 851, H: 1,834, SB: 428

#503 Ferris Roy Fain

1B, Philadelphia A's, White Sox, Tigers, Indians, 1947–55

Fain led the American League in batting in 1951, hitting .344 for the A's. He topped the league again in 1952, batting .327 with 43 doubles, also leading the AL that year with a .438 on-base percentage. His .424 career on-base percentage ranks 15th among all-time leaders. He posted the most assists and double plays among AL first basemen four times in his career.

LIFETIME STATS: BA: .290, HR: 48, RBI: 570, H: 1,139, SB: 46

#**504** John J. "Jack" Clements

C, Philadelphia Quakers, Phillies, Cardinals, Cleveland Spiders, Boston Beaneaters, 1884–1900

Clements ranked among league leaders in home runs and slugging percentage five times in his career. In 1898 with Philadelphia, he became the first left-hander to catch 1,000 games. Clements peaked offensively in 1893 with the Phillies, hitting a career-high 17 home runs, with 80 RBI and 64 runs.

LIFETIME STATS: BA: .286, HR: 77, RBI: 687, H: 1,226, SB: 55

#**505** John B. "Dusty" Baker Jr.

OF-1B, Braves, Dodgers, Giants, A's, 1968–86

Baker won a National League Gold Glove for outfielders in 1981, and ranked among the top eight league leaders in batting average three times in his career. He hit 20 or more home runs six times, with a career-high 30 in 1977 for the Dodgers. Named the 1977 NLCS MVP, Baker drove in eight runs over four games, including a two-run home run to win the series.

LIFETIME STATS: BA: .278, HR: 242, RBI: 1,013, H: 1,981, SB: 137

#506 Michael Joseph "Turkey Mike," "Mike" Donlin

OF-1B, St. Louis Perfectos, Orioles, Reds, New York Giants, Boston Braves, Pirates, 1899–1906, 1908, 1911–12, 1914

Donlin hit .300 or better in five full seasons, and ranked among the top three batting-average leaders five times. He led the National League in 1905 with 124 runs, hitting a personal-best .356 with 216 hits for the Giants. Donlin placed five times among the league's home run and on-base percentage leaders, and stole 20 or more bases six times.

LIFETIME STATS: BA: .333, HR: 51, RBI: 543, H: 1,282, SB: 213

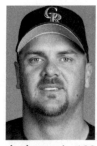

#507 Larry Kenneth Robert Walker

OF-1B-2B-3B-DH, Expos, Rockies, Cardinals, 1989–2005

A seven-time Gold Glove winner, Walker was named the 1997 National League MVP, batting .366 with a league-leading 49 home runs and a career-high 130 RBI, 46 doubles, 208 hits, 143 runs and 33 stolen bases. He led the NL in batting average three times, and topped the league in 1994 with 44 doubles. Walker hit 20 or more home runs eight times.

LIFETIME STATS: BA: .313, HR: 383, RBI: 1,311, H: 2,160, SB: 230

#508 Tommy Harper

OF-3B-DH-2B, Reds, Indians, Seattle Pilots, Brewers, Red Sox, Angels, A's, Orioles, 1962–76

Harper led the National League in 1965 with 126 runs for the Reds, then stole 73 bases in 1969 for the Pilots to top the AL. With the Brewers the following year, he led the league with 70 extra-base hits and became the fifth player ever to hit 30 home runs and steal 30 bases in a single season. Harper stole 54 bases for the Red Sox in 1973 and was named the team's MVP that year.

LIFETIME STATS: BA: .257, HR: 146, RBI: 567, H: 1,609, SB: 408

#509 Harold Delano "Butch" Wynegar

C, Twins, Yankees, Angels, 1976–88

Wynegar was named to the American League All Star team his first two years in the majors. He recorded his best power numbers in those two years and notched a career-high 139 hits each season. Wynegar caught Dave Righetti's 1983 no-hitter as a Yankee, and led AL catchers in double plays in 1980 with the Twins.

LIFETIME STATS: BA: .255, HR: 65, RBI: 506, H: 1,102, SB: 10

#510 Kevin Donnell Mitchell

OF-3B-DH, Mets, Padres, Giants, Mariners, Reds, Red Sox, Indians, A's, 1984, 1986–98

Mitchell was named the 1989 National League MVP, leading the league with 47 home runs, 87 extra-base hits, 125 RBI and a .635 slugging percentage. He batted .353 in the 1989 NLCS, helping the Giants defeat the Cubs with two home runs and seven RBI. Mitchell gathered the ninth-most NL MVP votes in 1994, batting .326 with 30 home runs for the Reds.

LIFETIME STATS: BA: .284, HR: 234, RBI: 760, H: 1,173, SB: 30

#511 Andrew "Andy" Pafko

OF-3B, Cubs, Brooklyn Dodgers, Milwaukee Braves, 1943–59

A five-time All Star, Pafko posted his best offensive numbers in 1948 with the Cubs, including a career-high .312 batting average, 26 home runs, 171 hits and 101 RBI. He hit .304 with the 1950 Cubs, logging 36 home runs and 92 RBI. Pafko won the fourth-most NL MVP votes in 1945, batting .298 with 110 RBI for Chicago.

LIFETIME STATS: BA: .285, HR: 213, RBI: 976, H: 1,796, SB: 38

#512 Martin Whiteford "Marty" Marion

SS, Cardinals, St. Louis Browns, 1940–50, 1952–53

Named the 1944 National League MVP, Marion helped the Cardinals defeat the Browns in the World Series that year with three doubles and two RBI. He led NL shortstops in double plays, assists and putouts in 1946, then topped league shortstops in fielding percentage, double plays and putouts the following year. Marion was named to the All Star team eight times.

LIFETIME STATS: BA: .263, HR: 36, RBI: 624, H: 1,448, SB: 35

#513 Roland Glen "Rollie" Fingers

RHP, A's, Padres, Brewers, 1968–82, 1984–85. Hall of Fame, 1992

Fingers won the Cy Young and American League MVP awards in 1981 with the Brewers, leading the league with 28 saves and posting a 1.04 ERA. Named 1974 World Series MVP, he helped the A's defeat the Dodgers by winning the first game and notching two saves later in the Series. Fingers led the league three times in saves and collected the seventh-most career saves of all time.

LIFETIME STATS: W: 114, L: 118, SV: 341, ERA: 2.90, SO: 1,299, CG: 4

#514 Joseph Oden "Joe" Rudi

OF-1B-DH, Kansas City A's, Oakland A's, Angels, Red Sox, 1967–82

Rudi won three American League Gold Gloves for outfielders. He batted .300 over three victorious World Series with Oakland, including two home runs and nine RBI. His seventh-inning home run in the A's 1974 World Series against the Dodgers provided the winning run. Rudi topped the AL in 1972 with 181 hits, and in 1974 with 39 doubles.

LIFETIME STATS: BA: .264, HR: 179, RBI: 810, H: 1,468, SB: 25

#515 Charles Wesley "Charley" Jones

OF, Keokuk Westerns, Hartford Dark Blues, Reds, Cubs, Boston Beaneaters, New York Metropolitans, Kansas City Cowboys, 1875–80, 1883–88

Jones ranked among league home run leaders for most of his career. He led the National League in 1879 with nine home runs, 85 runs and 62 RBI for Boston, then became the first player to hit two home runs in one inning the following year. Jones led the league with 80 RBI in 1883 and in 1884 with a .376 on-base percentage for the Reds.

LIFETIME STATS: BA: .298, HR: 56, RBI: 552, H: 1,114, SB: 20

#516 John Tortes "Chief" Meyers

C, New York Giants, Brooklyn Dodgers, Boston Braves, 1909–17

Meyers ranked three times among the top 10 National League MVP vote-winners, 1911–13, batting at least .312 in those three seasons. He led the NL with a .441 on-base percentage in 1912. Meyers batted .357 in the 1912 World Series with a triple and three RBI, although the Giants ultimately lost to Boston.

LIFETIME STATS: BA: .291, HR: 14, RBI: 363, H: 826, SB: 44

#517 Edward Joseph "Ed" Konetchy

1B, Cardinals, Pirates, Pittsburgh Rebels, Boston Braves, Brooklyn Dodgers, Phillies, 1907–21

Konetchy ranked among league batting average and home run leaders six times in his career. He led the Federal League in 1915 with 59 extra-base hits, and holds the 15th-most career triples of all time with 182. He collected 100 or more hits in 14 consecutive seasons and hit .300 or better four times. Konetchy led the NL in 1911 with 38 doubles.

LIFETIME STATS: BA: .281, HR: 74, RBI: 992, H: 2,150, SB: 255

#518 Terrance Edward "Terry" Kennedy

C, Cardinals, Padres, Orioles, Giants, 1978–91

A four-time All Star, Kennedy became the second catcher to start All Star games for both leagues. He was named the Padres' MVP in 1982, batting .295 with 97 RBI and a career-best 21 home runs, 42 doubles, 166 hits and 75 runs. Kennedy caught 934 games from 1981 to 1987 with the Padres and Orioles, the second most in the majors.

LIFETIME STATS: BA: .264, HR: 113, RBI: 628, H: 1,313, SB: 6

#519 David Andrew "Dave" Stieb

RHP, Blue Jays, White Sox, 1979–93, 1998

Stieb ranked among the top seven American League Cy Young candidates four times. He topped the AL in 1982 with 19 complete games and five shutouts and led the league with a 2.48 ERA in 1985. Stieb threw three one-hitters in the 1988 season. A seven-time All Star, he placed seven times among the top 10 league leaders in wins, 1981–84, and 1988–90.

LIFETIME STATS: W: 176, L:137, SV: 3, ERA: 3.44, SO: 1,669, CG: 103

#**520** Jack Eugene "Jackie" Jensen

OF, Yankees, Senators, Red Sox, 1950–59, 1961

Named the 1958 American League MVP, Jensen batted a career-best 35 home runs with 122 RBI for Boston. He won an AL Gold Glove in 1959. Jensen logged 100 or more RBI in five seasons with the Red Sox and led the AL in RBI three times. He topped the league in 1954 with 22 stolen bases and in 1956 with 11 triples. Jensen also hit 20 or more home runs six times in his career.

LIFETIME STATS: BA: .279, HR: 199, RBI: 929, H: 1,463, SB: 143

#**521** David Allen "Davey" Johnson

2B-1B, Orioles, Braves, Phillies, Cubs, 1965–75, 1977–78

A three-time Gold Glove winner as a second baseman for the Orioles, Johnson led AL second basemen in putouts, double plays and fielding percentage at various times. He hit two home runs in the 1970 ALCS to help the Orioles defeat the Twins. Johnson peaked offensively with the Braves in 1973, hitting 43 home runs with 99 RBI.

LIFETIME STATS: BA: .261, HR: 136, RBI: 609, H: 1,252, SB: 33

#**522** James "Jimmie" Wilson

C, Phillies, Cardinals, Reds, 1923–40

As a Cardinal, Wilson led National League catchers in putouts and double plays three times and assists twice. At 40 years old, he caught six of seven games in the 1940 World Series for the Reds, batting .353 against the Tigers and logging the only stolen base in the Series. Wilson batted .300 or better in four seasons.

LIFETIME STATS: BA: .284, HR: 32, RBI: 621, H: 1,358, SB: 86

#**523** Vernon Louis "Lefty" Gomez

LHP, Yankees, Senators, 1930–43. Hall of Fame, 1972

Gomez led American League pitchers in 1934 with 26 wins, 158 strikeouts and a 2.33 ERA, and again in 1937 with 21 wins, 194 strikeouts and a 2.33 ERA. He also topped the league in shutouts three times. Gomez went 6–0 over five winning World Series with the Yankees. He won 20 or more games a season four times.

LIFETIME STATS: W: 189, L: 102, SV: 9, ERA: 3.34, SO: 1,468, CG: 173

#524 George Robert Stone
OF, Red Sox, St. Louis Browns, 1903, 1905–10

Stone ranked four times among league leaders in batting average, hits, home runs and runs. He topped the American League in 1905 with 187 hits, then led the league in 1906 with a .358 batting average, a .501 slugging percentage and a .417 on-base percentage. Stone peaked offensively in 1906 with 208 hits, 25 doubles and 20 triples.

LIFETIME STATS: BA: .301, HR: 23, RBI: 268, H: 984, SB: 132

#525 Roy Smalley III
SS-DH-OF, Rangers, Twins, Yankees, White Sox, 1975–87

Smalley was the number-one draft pick of the Texas Rangers in 1974 but was traded to the Twins in 1976. Smalley was a switch-hitter with very good power for a shortstop. In 1978 and again in 1979, he led the majors in home runs by a shortstop with 19 and 24, respectively. Back problems in 1981 limited his effectiveness, and he was sent to the Yankees in 1982, where he played well in a relief role.

LIFETIME STATS: BA: .257, HR: 163, RBI: 694, H: 1,454, SB: 27

#526 Maurice Samuel "Mo" Vaughn

1B-DH, Red Sox, Angels, Mets, 1991–2000, 2002–03

Named the 1995 American League MVP, Vaughn batted .300 with 39 home runs, a career-best 11 stolen bases and a league-leading 126 RBI for the Red Sox. He posted his best offensive numbers the next season, batting .326 with a career-high 44 home runs, 143 RBI and 207 hits. Vaughn hit .300 or better five times for Boston, 1994–98.

LIFETIME STATS: BA: .293, HR: 32,8 RBI: 1,064, H: 1,620, SB: 30

#527 John Alban "Johnny" Edwards

C, Reds, Cardinals, Astros, 1961–74

Edwards won two National League Gold Glove awards for catchers, 1963–64. He set a major league season record with 1,221 total chances as a catcher in 1969 with the Astros. Edwards briefly held the National League record for total career chances with 9,745. He batted .364 for the Reds in the 1961 World Series against the Yankees.

LIFETIME STATS: BA: .242, HR: 81, RBI: 524, H: 1,106, SB: 15

#528 Bill Madlock Jr.

3B–2B–DH-1B, Rangers, Cubs, Giants, Pirates, Dodgers, Tigers, 1973–87

Madlock led his league three times in batting average. He hit .300 or better in seven full seasons, including a career-best .354 in 1975 with the Cubs. Madlock was named co-MVP of the All Star game that year, along with John Matlack of the Mets. He batted .375 in the 1979 World Series, helping the Pirates defeat the Orioles.

LIFETIME STATS: BA: .305, HR: 163, RBI: 860, H: 2,008, SB: 174

#529 Charles Louis "Chief" Zimmer

C, Detroit Wolverines, New York Metropolitans, Cleveland Blues, Cleveland Spiders, Louisville Colonels, Pirates, Phillies, 1884, 1886–1903

Zimmer regularly led NL catchers in putouts, double plays and assists with the Spiders, 1889–99. Considered the first catcher to position himself directly behind the batter for every pitch, Zimmer posted his best batting average, .340, in 1895, logging 107 hits and 14 stolen bases. He was the oldest player in the majors for the last four years of his career.

LIFETIME STATS: BA: .269, HR: 26, RBI: 625, H: 1,224, SB: 151

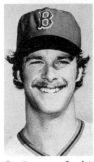

#530 Richard Paul "Rick," "The Rooster" Burleson

SS-2B, Red Sox, Angels, Orioles, 1974–84, 1986–87

Burleson won an American League Gold Glove in 1979 with the Red Sox, and ranked three times among league hit leaders. He set a major league record with 147 double plays for the 1980 Red Sox. A four-time All Star, Burleson set another record in 1982, recording 15 assists in a 20-inning game against the Mariners. Nicknamed the Rooster for his fiery play, Burleson was one of the team leaders during his tenure in Boston.

LIFETIME STATS: BA: .273, HR: 50, RBI: 449, H: 1,401, SB: 72

#531 William Joseph "Bill" Bradley

3B, Cubs, Cleveland Blues, Brooklyn Tip-Tops, Kansas City Packers, 1899–1910, 1914–15

Bradley led American League third basemen four times in fielding percentage, three times in double plays and twice in putouts. He ranked among league leaders in doubles six times. Bradley led the AL in sacrifice hits, 1907–08, and hit .300 or better with Cleveland, 1902–04. He posted his best numbers in 1902, batting .340 with 11 home runs, 187 hits and 104 runs.

LIFETIME STATS: BA: .271, HR: 33, RBI: 552, H: 1,471, SB: 181

#**532** William Donald "Bill" Doran

2B, Astros, Reds, Brewers, 1982–93

Doran led National League second basemen with 461 assists as a rookie with the Astros in 1983, then topped NL second basemen in fielding percentage, 1988–89. He stole 20 or more bases a season six times in his career, including a personal-best 42 stolen bases for the 1986 Astros. Doran ranked among league leaders in bases on balls four times.

LIFETIME STATS: BA: .266, HR: 84, RBI: 497, H: 1,366, SB: 209

#**533** George Charles "Boomer" Scott Jr.

1B-3B, Red Sox, Brewers, Royals, Yankees, 1966–79

Scott won the American League Gold Glove for first basemen eight times, 1967–68 and 1971–76. He became the second rookie first baseman ever to start in the All Star game. Scott logged some of his best numbers in 1975 with the Brewers, leading the league with 109 RBI and tying Oakland's Reggie Jackson for the league lead with 36 home runs.

LIFETIME STATS: BA: .268, HR: 271, RBI: 1,051, H: 1,992, SB: 69

#**534** Jeffrey Franklin "Jeff" Kent

2B-3B-1B-SS-DH, Blue Jays, Mets, Indians, Giants, Astros, Dodgers, 1992–2008

Named National League MVP in 2000 with the Giants, Kent hit .334 that year, with 33 home runs, 125 RBI, 41 doubles, 196 hits and 114 runs. He tallied 100 or more RBI in each of his six seasons with the Giants, 1997–2002. Kent hit 20 or more home runs nine times in his career, and led the NL in 2002 with 81 extra-base hits.

LIFETIME STATS: BA: .297, HR: 377, RBI: 1,518, H: 2,841, SB: 94

#535 Willie James Wilson
OF, Royals, A's, Cubs, 1976–94

Wilson ranked among the American League's top five base stealers, 1978–88, and led the league in 1979 with 83 stolen bases. He ranked among the AL top five in triples, 1979–88. Leading the league in 1980 with 230 hits and 133 runs, Wilson won a Gold Glove that year as well. He topped the AL in 1982 with a .332 batting average.

LIFETIME STATS: BA: .285, HR: 41, RBI: 585, H: 2,207, SB: 668

#536 Stephen Francis "Steve" O'Neill
C, Indians, Red Sox, Yankees, St. Louis Browns, 1911–25, 1927–28

O'Neill set a record for catchers in 1916 with 36 double plays for the Indians. He led American League catchers in double plays four times, and topped league catchers in fielding percentage and assists in 1918. O'Neill ranked among league leaders in on-base percentage, 1920–22, also hitting at least .311 those three seasons for the Indians.

LIFETIME STATS: BA: .263, HR: 13, RBI: 537, H: 1,259, SB: 30

#537 Urban Charles "Red" Faber

RHP, Chicago White Sox, 1914–33. Hall of Fame, 1964

Faber topped the American League with the lowest ERA and most complete games, 1921–22. He won 20 or more games in a season four times and ranked among the league's top-10-wins leaders seven times. Faber posted 10 consecutive winning seasons, 1914–23. He earned three wins in Chicago's 1917 World Series victory over the New York Giants.

LIFETIME STATS: W: 254, L: 213, SV: 28, ERA: 3.15, SO: 1,471, CG: 273

#538 Frank "Wildfire" Schulte

OF, Cubs, Pirates, Phillies, Senators, 1904–18

Named the National League MVP in 1911 as a Cub, Schulte led the league that year with 21 home runs, 107 RBI and 72 extra-base hits. Along with Willie Mays, he was one of only two players to post more than 20 stolen bases, home runs, doubles and triples in one season. Schulte batted .321 over four World Series. He was known as "Wildfire," not for his temper, but because he owned a horse named "Wildfire."

LIFETIME STATS: BA: .270, HR: 92, RBI: 792, H: 1,766, SB: 233

#539 Daniel Raymond "Quiz" Quisenberry

RHP, Royals, Cardinals, Giants, 1979–90

Quisenberry won the Rolaids Relief award five times and ranked among the top five Cy Young candidates five times as well, 1980 and 1982–85. He led the American League in saves five times. Quisenberry set a major league record, since broken, with 45 saves in 1983, and led the league four times in games finished. He posted a 2.08 ERA in the Royals' 1985 World Series win over the Cardinals.

LIFETIME STATS: W: 56, L: 46, SV: 244, ERA: 2.76, SO: 379, CG: 0

#540 Garry Lee Maddox

OF, Giants, Phillies, 1972–86

Maddox won eight National League Gold Glove awards. He led the league three times in doubles, triples and stolen bases. Maddox stole 20 or more bases eight times in his career, and led the NL in outfield putouts twice. He clinched the NLCS for the Phillies in 1980 with a 10th-inning double in Game Five.

LIFETIME STATS: BA: .285, HR: 117, RBI: 754, H: 1,802, SB: 248

#541 Leonardo Lazaro "Leo" Cardenas

SS-3B, Reds, Twins, Angels, Indians, Rangers, 1960–75

Cardenas won the National League Gold Glove for shortstops in 1965 with the Reds. He led NL shortstops twice in fielding percentage and putouts and once in double plays. A five-time All Star, Cardenas led American League shortstops in assists and double plays in 1969 with the Twins, also tying a league record with 570 putouts that year.

LIFETIME STATS: BA: .257, HR: 118, RBI: 689, H: 1,725, SB: 39

#542 John Kelly "Buddy" Lewis

3B-OF, Senators, 1935–41, 1945–47, 1949

Lewis hit .300 or better four times in his career. He led the American League in 1939 with 16 triples, and ranked seven times among league triples leaders. Lewis placed five times among the top-10-hits leaders in the AL and collected 170 or more hits in a season seven times. He also scored 100 or more runs four times.

LIFETIME STATS: BA: .297, HR: 71, RBI: 607, H: 1,563, SB: 83

#543 Philip Joseph "Phil" Cavarretta

1B-OF, Cubs, White Sox, 1934–55

Cavarretta was named the National League MVP in 1945, batting a league-leading .355 with 97 RBI and 34 doubles for the Cubs. He also topped the NL with a .449 on-base percentage that year. Cavarretta tied Stan Musial for the league lead with 197 hits in 1944. He hit .317 over three World Series, including a .462 average in the 1938 Series against the Yankees.

LIFETIME STATS: BA: .293, HR: 95, RBI: 920, H: 1,977, SB: 65

#544 Earl Jesse Battey Jr.

C, White Sox, Senators, Twins, 1955–67

Battey won three American League Gold Glove awards, from 1960 to 1962, and placed three times among the top 10 AL MVP vote-winners. A four-time All Star, Battey peaked offensively in 1963 with 26 home runs and 84 RBI for the Twins. He hit .280 in 1962, leading all major league catchers. The durable Battey caught 805 of the Twins' first 970 games despite a host of knee, finger and other injuries.

LIFETIME STATS: BA: .270, HR: 104, RBI: 449, H: 969, SB: 13

#545 Antonio Nemesio "Tony" Taylor

2B-3B-1B, Cubs, Phillies, Tigers, 1958–76

Taylor ranked nine times among National League stolen-base leaders, stole 20 or more bases in a season six times, and stole home six times for the Phillies. He set a Phillies franchise record playing 1,003 games at second base. Taylor ranked among league triples leaders four times. He posted career-high numbers in 1963 with 102 runs, 180 hits and 10 triples.

LIFETIME STATS: BA: .261, HR: 75, RBI: 598, H: 2,007, SB: 234

#546 Frank Elton Snyder

C-1B, Cardinals, Giants, 1912–27

Snyder led National League catchers three times in fielding percentage. He played in four World Series with the Giants, batting .364 with one home run and three RBI in the 1921 Series and .333 in the next year's Series, both against the Yankees. Snyder ranked twice among the NL batting-average leaders, 1915 and 1922.

LIFETIME STATS: BA: .265, HR: 47, RBI: 525, H: 1,122, SB: 37

#547 Clark Calvin Griffith

RHP, St. Louis Browns, Boston Reds, Cubs, White Sox, Yankees, Reds, Senators, 1891, 1893–1907, 1909–10, 1912–14. Hall of Fame, 1946

Griffith won 20 or more games in a season seven times in his career, including six consecutive seasons with the Cubs, 1894–99. He threw a National League–leading 38 complete games in 1897 and led the NL the following year with a 1.88 ERA. Griffith topped the NL with four shutouts in 1900 and the AL with five shutouts in 1901 for the White Sox.

LIFETIME STATS: W: 237, L: 146, SV: 6, ERA: 3.31, SO: 955, CG: 337

#548 David Russell "Gus" Bell Jr.

OF, Pirates, Reds, Mets, Milwaukee Braves, 1950–1964

A four-time All Star, Bell ranked three times among National League leaders in home runs and RBI. He placed among league leaders in hits and doubles with the Reds, 1953–56. Bell collected 100 or more RBI four times with Cincinnati. He led the league in 1951 with 12 triples, and hit a career-best 30 home runs in 1953.

LIFETIME STATS: BA: .281, HR: 206, RBI: 942, H: 1,823, SB: 30

#**549** Dwight Eugene "Doc" Gooden

RHP, Mets, Yankees, Indians, Astros, Devil Rays,
1984–94, 1996–2000

Gooden won the National League Cy Young award in
1985, leading the league with a 1.53 ERA, 24 wins, 268
strikeouts and 16 complete games. Named 1984 Rookie
of the Year, he recorded a career-high 276 strikeouts while
giving up a career-low seven home runs. Gooden's 276
strikeouts came over only 218 innings, setting a major
league rookie record. However, injuries and drug and personal problems beset
Gooden throughout the 1990s.

LIFETIME STATS: W: 194, L: 112, SV: 3, ERA: 3.51, SO: 2,293, CG: 68

#**550** James Kevin Brown

RHP, Rangers, Orioles, Marlins, Dodgers, Padres,
Yankees, 1988–2005

Brown recorded 200 or more strikeouts in four consecutive seasons, 1997–2000, and led the American League
with 21 wins for Texas in 1992. He topped the NL with
a 1.89 ERA and three shutouts for the Marlins in 1996,
winning the second-most Cy Young award votes. Brown
threw a no-hitter for the Dodgers against the Giants in 1997, and led the
NL with a 2.58 ERA in 2000.

LIFETIME STATS: W: 211, L: 144, SV: 0, ERA: 3.28, SO: 2,397, CG: 72

#551 Robert Randall "Robby" Thompson
2B, Giants, 1986–96

Thompson won the National League Gold Glove award for second basemen in 1993. He led the NL in 1986 with 18 sacrifice hits and finished second in Rookie of the Year voting. Thompson topped the league with 11 triples in 1989. His two-run home run in the 1987 NLCS gave the Giants a Game Three win over the Cardinals.

LIFETIME STATS: BA: .257, HR: 119, RBI: 458, H: 1,187, SB: 103

#552 David Christopher Justice
OF-DH, Braves, Indians, Yankees, A's, 1989–2002

Justice was amazingly consistent: He hit exactly 21 home runs in a season four times, and hit 20 or more homers nine times in his career. His best season was 1993, when he hit 40 home runs, had 120 RBI and scored 90 runs for the Braves. Justice hit .300 or better three times.

LIFETIME STATS: BA: .279, HR: 305, RBI: 1,017, H: 1,571, SB: 53

#553 Owen Joseph "Donie" Bush
SS, Tigers, Senators, 1908–23

Bush stole 34 or more bases eight times for the Tigers. He topped the league in 1917 with 112 runs and ranked among league leaders in runs 10 times, scoring 100 or more four times. Bush led the league twice in sacrifice hits; his 337 career sacrifice hits are fifth-most of all time. He led the American League five times in bases on balls.

LIFETIME STATS: BA: .250, HR: 9, RBI: 436, H: 1,804, SB: 404

#**554** Donald Wayne "Don" Money
3B-2B-DH-SS-1B-OF, Phillies, Brewers, 1968–83

Money led National League third basemen with a .978 fielding percentage, 139 putouts and 31 double plays in 1972 for the Phillies. He led American League third basemen in fielding percentage with the Brewers, 1973–74. A four-time All Star, he posted his best offensive numbers in 1977 with 25 home runs, 83 RBI and 86 runs.

LIFETIME STATS: BA: .261, HR: 176, RBI: 729, H: 1,623, SB: 80

#**555** Frank Andrew McCormick
1B, Reds, Phillies, Boston Braves, 1934, 1937–48

McCormick was named the 1940 National League MVP, batting .309 with a league-leading 191 hits and 44 doubles. He hit 100 or more RBI four times in his career and batted .300 or better six times. A nine-time All Star, McCormick led the league with 128 RBI in 1939 with the Reds, and topped the league in hits from 1938 to 1940.

LIFETIME STATS: BA: .299, HR: 128, RBI: 951, H: 1,711, SB: 27

#**556** Frank James Malzone

3B, Red Sox, Angels, 1955–66

A three-time Gold Glove winner, 1957–59, Malzone ranked among American League leaders in hits and doubles, 1957–60. He produced 87 RBI or more five times with the Red Sox and drove in a career-high 103 runs as a rookie. Malzone led AL third basemen in fielding percentage, putouts, assists and double plays in 1957.

LIFETIME STATS: BA: .274, HR: 133, RBI: 728, H: 1,486, SB: 14

#**557** Jacob Peter "Jake" Beckley

1B, Pittsburgh Alleghenys, Pittsburgh Burghers, New York Giants, Reds, Cardinals, 1888–1907. Hall of Fame, 1971

Beckley hit .300 or better in 12 full seasons, including six consecutive seasons, 1899–1904, with the Reds and Cardinals. He led the league with 69 extra-base hits in 1890. His 243 career triples ranks fourth all-time. Beckley holds the all-time record for first basemen with 23,709 career putouts. He regularly ranked among league leaders in doubles, triples, extra-base hits and RBI.

LIFETIME STATS: BA: .308, HR: 86, RBI: 1,575, H: 2,930, SB: 315

#558 Louis "Big Bertha" Santop

C-OF, Fort Worth Wonders, Oklahoma Monarchs,
Philadelphia Giants, New York Lincoln Giants,
Chicago American Giants, Lincoln Stars, Brooklyn
Royal Giants, Hilldale (Negro Leagues), 1909–26

The imposing (6'4") Santop was one of the early draws
in the Negro Leagues. He used a heavy bat, and belted
tape-measure home runs even in an era where home runs were in short sup-
ply. He was nicknamed "Big Bertha" after the World War I German howitzer,
also known for long blasts. He hit over .400 at least twice in his career, and
long before 1932, when Babe Ruth reportedly "called his shot" in the World
Series, teammates say Santop often announced to fans in the stands that he
would hit a home run—and would then do so.

LIFETIME STATS: BA: .318

#559 Paul A. Hines

OF-1B-2B, Washington Nationals, Washington Blue
Legs, Chicago White Stockings, Providence Grays,
Indianapolis Hoosiers, Pittsburgh Alleghenys, Boston
Beaneaters, Washington Statesmen, 1872–91

Hines earned baseball's first Triple Crown, leading the
National League with a .358 batting average, four home
runs and 50 RBI for the Grays in 1878. He batted .300
or better 11 times in his career. Hines led the NL in 1879 with 146 hits and
a .357 batting average. He ranked among doubles leaders 12 times, topping
the league three times.

LIFETIME STATS: BA: .302, HR: 57, RBI: 855, H: 2,134, SB: 163

#**560** Thomas Jefferson Davis "Tommy" Bridges

RHP, Tigers, 1930–46

Bridges won 20 or more games in three consecutive years, 1934–36, and led the American League in 1936 with 23 wins and 175 strikeouts. He topped the league in 1935 with 163 strikeouts. Bridges earned a 4–1 record over four World Series. He ranked among league leaders in ERA, strikeouts and shutouts for most of his career.

LIFETIME STATS: W: 194, L: 138, SV: 10, ERA: 3.57, SO: 1,674, CG: 200

#**561** Donald Martin "Don" Slaught

C, Royals, Rangers, Yankees, Pirates, Angels, White Sox, Padres, 1982–97

Slaught posted some of his strongest offensive numbers in 1993 with the Pirates, batting .300 with a career-high 113 hits and 55 RBI. He tallied a personal-best 48 runs and 27 doubles in 1984, his first full season with the Royals. Slaught hit .300 or better six times, though many of his seasons as a platoon catcher were not complete years.

LIFETIME STATS: BA: .283, HR: 77, RBI: 476, H: 1,151, SB: 18

#562 William Dale "Billy" Goodman

2B-1B-3B-OF, Red Sox, Orioles, White Sox, Astros, 1947–62

Goodman led the American League batting .354 for the Red Sox in 1950, collecting the second-most AL MVP votes that year and recording a career-high 68 RBI. He hit .293 or better in 11 consecutive seasons, 1948–58. Goodman led AL first basemen in fielding percentage in 1948 and ranked among league leaders in doubles and batting average, 1952–55.

LIFETIME STATS: BA: .300, HR: 19, RBI: 591, H: 1,691, SB: 37

#563 Charles James "Chick" Hafey

OF, Cardinals, Reds, 1924–35, 1937. Hall of Fame, 1971

Hafey led the National League with a .349 batting average for the Cardinals in 1931. He hit .300 or better eight times, including seven consecutive seasons, 1927–33. Hafey played in the first All Star game in 1933, notching the game's first hit in the second inning. He ranked among NL home run leaders, 1927–31, and led the league with a .590 slugging percentage in 1927.

LIFETIME STATS: BA: .317, HR: 164, RBI: 833, H: 1,466, SB: 70

#564 Preston Rudolph "Rudy" York

1B-C, Tigers, Red Sox, White Sox, Philadelphia A's, 1934, 1937–48

York led the American League in 1943 with a .527 slugging percentage, 118 RBI, 34 home runs and 67 extra-base hits. He ranked among AL home run leaders, 1937–47, and RBI leaders, 1940–47. A seven-time All Star, York batted .307 in his rookie year with 35 home runs and 103 RBI for the Tigers. That year, he put together a stupendous August, hitting 18 home runs and breaking Babe Ruth's record for most homers in a month.

LIFETIME STATS: BA: .275, HR: 277, RBI: 1,152, H: 1,621, SB: 38

#565 Frank Peter Joseph "Frankie" Crosetti

SS-3B, Yankees, 1932–48

Crosetti led American League shortstops in putouts and double plays in both 1938 and 1939. He topped the AL with 27 stolen bases in 1938. A tough player who tried to get on base any way he could, Crosetti led the league eight times in being hit by opposing pitchers. He played for six world championship Yankees teams and led the AL with 656 at bats in 1939.

LIFETIME STATS: BA: .245, HR: 98, RBI: 649, H: 1,541, SB: 113

#566 Jacob Ellsworth "Jake" Daubert

1B, Brooklyn Robins, Reds, 1910–24

Daubert was named the 1913 National League MVP, leading the league with a .350 batting average. He topped the league again the following year, batting .329. Daubert hit .300 or better 10 times in his career, including six consecutive seasons with Brooklyn, 1911–16. He twice topped the league in triples. Daubert's 392 career sacrifice hits rank him second among all-time leaders.

LIFETIME STATS: BA: .303, HR: 56, RBI: 722, H: 2,326, SB: 251

#567 Urban James Shocker

RHP, Yankees, St. Louis Browns, 1916–28

Shocker led the American League with 27 wins in 1921. He topped the league again in 1922 with 149 strikeouts. Shocker won 20 or more games in four consecutive seasons with the Browns, 1920–23, and completed 17 or more games a season, 1920–24. He pitched for 13 years in the majors without posting a losing season. Yankee teammate Babe Ruth said Shocker's knowledge of opposing hitters was the most complete of any pitcher he played with.

LIFETIME STATS: W: 187, L: 117, SV: 25, ERA: 3.17, SO: 983, CG: 200

#**568** Willie Watterson Horton

OF-DH, Tigers, Rangers, Indians, A's, Blue Jays, Mariners, 1963–80

Horton hit a career-high 36 home runs in 1968 for the Tigers, then logged a personal-best 180 hits and 106 RBI 11 years later for the Mariners. He threw out Lou Brock at home for the Tigers in Game Five of the 1968 World Series against the Cardinals. Horton, a four-time All Star, hit .304 in the Series with a double, a triple, a home run and three RBI.

LIFETIME STATS: BA: .273, HR: 325, RBI: 1,163, H: 1,993, SB: 20

#**569** William Benjamin "Ben" Chapman

OF-3B-2B, Yankees, Senators, Red Sox, Indians, White Sox, Brooklyn Dodgers, Phillies, 1930–41, 1944–46

The speedy Chapman led the American League four times in stolen bases, including three consecutive seasons, 1931–33, with the Yankees. He stole a career-high 61 bases in 1931, and ranked among the league's top eight base stealers, 1931–40. He logged 100 or more runs a season six times. Chapman hit .294 with six RBI in the Yankees' 1932 World Series win against the Cubs.

LIFETIME STATS: BA: .302, HR: 90, RBI: 977, H: 1,958, SB: 287

#570 Glenn Alfred Beckert

2B, Cubs, Padres, 1965–75

Beckert won a National League Gold Glove in 1968. He made 189 hits that year, third-most in the NL, while topping the league with 98 runs. He recorded the fewest strikeouts in the NL five times in his career. Beckert hit a personal-best .342 in 1971 for the Cubs. A four-time All Star, he led NL second basemen in assists in 1965.

LIFETIME STATS: BA: .283, HR: 22, RBI: 360, H: 1,473, SB: 49

#571 William Beck "Bill" Nicholson

OF, Philadelphia A's, Cubs, Phillies, 1936, 1939–53

Nicholson led the National League in 1943 with 29 home runs and 128 RBI for the Cubs. He topped the league again in 1944 with 33 home runs and 122 RBI, as well as 116 runs and 317 total bases. Nicholson, a five-time All Star, hit four consecutive home runs with the Cubs during a 1944 doubleheader against the New York Giants.

LIFETIME STATS: BA: .268, HR: 235, RBI: 948, H: 1,484, SB: 27

#572 Thomas Michael "Tom" Tresh

OF-SS-3B, Yankees, Tigers, 1961–69

Tresh was named the 1962 American League Rookie of the Year, hitting 20 home runs that season, along with a career-high .286 batting average, 93 RBI, 178 hits and 94 runs. He won an AL Gold Glove for outfielding in

1965. Tresh hit home runs both right- and left-handed in a single game three times in his career.

LIFETIME STATS: BA: .245, HR: 153, RBI: 530, H: 1,041, SB: 45

#**573** Paul L. D. Blair
OF, Orioles, Yankees, Reds, 1964–80

An eight-time Gold Glove winner for outfielding, Blair led the American League in 1967 with 12 triples. He topped the league in 1969 with 13 sacrifice hits. Blair homered in the 1966 World Series to give the Orioles a Game Three win over the Dodgers. He also hit .474 in the Orioles' 1970 World Series against the Reds.

LIFETIME STATS: BA: .250, HR: 134, RBI: 620, H: 1,513, SB: 171

#**574** Gus Triandos
C-1B, Yankees, Orioles, Tigers, Phillies, Astros, 1953–65

Triandos caught a perfect game for Jim Bunning with the Phillies in 1964. He tied an American League record for catchers with 30 home runs in 1958 for the Orioles, and ranked among American League home run leaders 1958–59, hitting 55 home runs over two seasons for the Orioles. He was named to the AL All Star team in three consecutive years, 1957–59.

LIFETIME STATS: BA: .244, HR: 167, RBI: 608, H: 954, SB: 1

#575 Edward Nagle "Ned" Williamson

3B-SS, Indianapolis Blues, Chicago White Stockings, Chicago Pirates, 1878–90

Williamson led the National League in 1884 with 27 home runs, setting a major league record that wouldn't be broken until 1919 when Babe Ruth hit 29 home runs. This was in part because in 1884, the ground rules at his home park were changed, and what had been ground rule doubles in 1883, became home runs in 1884. Williamson, by the way, led the NL with 49 doubles in 1883, also setting a major league record. Williamson topped league third basemen and shortstops multiple times in fielding percentage, double plays and assists.

LIFETIME STATS: BA: .255, HR: 64, RBI: 667, H: 1,159, SB: 88

#576 Roberto Francisco "Bobby" Avila

2B-3B, Indians, Orioles, Red Sox, Milwaukee Braves, 1949–59

Avila won the American League batting championship in 1954, hitting .341 for the Indians. He also led the league that year with 19 sacrifice hits, and placed eight times among sacrifice hits leaders, 1951–58. Avila ranked among AL hits leaders four times with the Indians, 1951–54, and topped the league with 11 triples in 1952.

LIFETIME STATS: BA: .281, HR: 80, RBI: 467, H: 1,296, SB: 78

#**577** Thomas Peter "Tom" Daly

2B-C-3B, Chicago White Stockings, Washington Nationals, Brooklyn Superbas, White Sox, Reds, 1887–96, 1898–03

Daly hit .300 or better five times in his career. He led the National League in 1901 with 38 doubles for Brooklyn. Daly recorded some of his best offensive numbers in 1894 for Brooklyn, batting a career-high .341 with 135 runs, 168 hits, eight home runs and 51 stolen bases. He stole 30 or more bases five times in his career.

LIFETIME STATS: BA: .278, HR: 49, RBI: 811, H: 1,582, SB: 385

#**578** Dennis Patrick Aloysius "Denny" Lyons

3B, Providence Grays, Philadelphia A's, St. Louis Browns, New York Giants, Pirates, 1885–97

Lyons ranked among league leaders in batting average, from 1887 to 1891. He led the American Association in 1890 with a .461 on-base percentage and a .531 slugging percentage, while also topping league third basemen in fielding average. Lyons placed among the top eight league leaders in home runs, 1887–1892. In 1887 he set a major league record for a third baseman with 255 putouts.

LIFETIME STATS: BA: .310, HR: 62, RBI: 755, H: 1,333, SB: 224

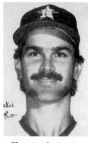

#579 Richard William "Dickie" Thon

SS-2B-3B, Angels, Astros, Padres, Phillies, Rangers, Brewers, 1979–93

Thon led National League shortstops in 1983 with 533 assists and 20 home runs for the Astros. He topped the NL in 1982 with 10 triples. During those two seasons, he stole 71 bases. Thon homered in Houston's losing effort in the 1986 NLCS against the Mets. He peaked offensively in 1983 with 177 hits and 79 RBI.

LIFETIME STATS: BA: .264, HR: 71, RBI: 435, H: 1,176, SB: 167

#580 Richard William "Rube" Marquard

LHP, New York Giants, Brooklyn Dodgers, Reds, Boston Braves, 1908–25. Hall of Fame, 1971

Marquard won 20 or more games in three consecutive seasons with the Giants, 1911–13. He led the National League in 1911 with 237 strikeouts, then topped the league in 1912 with 26 wins. Marquard posted a 1.58 ERA in 1916 for the Dodgers, second best in the NL, while collecting a career-high five saves. He went 2–0 in the 1912 World Series, though the Giants lost to the Red Sox. He got his nickname because of his resemblance to another "Rube," "Rube" Waddell.

LIFETIME STATS: W: 201, L: 177, SV: 19, ERA: 3.08, SO: 1,593, CG: 197

#581 Herman Thomas "Tommy" Davis Jr.

OF-DH-3B-1B, Dodgers, Mets, White Sox, Seattle Pilots, Astros, A's, Cubs, Orioles, Angels, Royals, 1959–76

Davis earned National League Batting Champion honors in two consecutive seasons for the Dodgers, 1962–63. He led the NL in 1962 with a career-high .346 batting average, 230 hits and 153 RBI. Davis hit .300 or better in five full seasons. He also hit .400 with two triples in the 1963 World Series, leading the Dodgers to victory over the Yankees.

LIFETIME STATS: BA: .294, HR: 153, RBI: 1,052, H: 2,121, SB: 136

#582 Samuel Blake "Sam" Chapman

OF, Philadelphia A's, Indians, 1938–41, 1945–51

Chapman hit 20 or more home runs a season five times in his career. He logged his best offensive year for the A's in 1941, with a career-high .322 batting average, 25 home runs, 29 doubles, nine triples and 178 hits. In 1949 Chapman hit 24 home runs, third-most in the American League. He topped AL outfielders four times in putouts.

LIFETIME STATS: BA: .266, HR: 180, RBI: 773, H: 1,329, SB: 41

#583 George Antonio Bell

OF-DH, Blue Jays, Cubs, White Sox, 1981, 1983–93

Bell was named American League MVP in 1987, leading the league with 134 RBI and 83 extra-base hits, while collecting 47 home runs, 188 hits and 111 runs for the Blue Jays. He drove in 100 or more runs four times, and hit 25 or more home runs six times. Bell hit three home runs in the Blue Jays' 1988 opening day game.

LIFETIME STATS: BA: .278, HR: 265, RBI: 1,002, H: 1,702, SB: 67

#584 Ralston Burdett "Rollie" Hemsley

C, Pirates, Cubs, Reds, St. Louis Browns, Indians, Yankees, Phillies, 1928–44, 1946–47

Hemsley led American League catchers in double plays three times with the Browns, and topped league catchers with 105 assists in 1935. He batted a career-high .309 for the 1934 Browns. A five-time All Star, Hemsley led AL catchers in fielding percentage for the 1940 Indians.

LIFETIME STATS: BA: .262, HR: 31, RBI: 555, H: 1,321, SB: 29

#**585** George Lange Kelly

1B-2B-OF, New York Giants, Pirates, Reds, Cubs, Brooklyn Dodgers, 1915–17, 1919–30, 1932. Hall of Fame, 1973

Kelly batted .300 or better seven times in his career, including six consecutive seasons for the Giants, 1921–26. He hit 100 or more RBI in four consecutive seasons, 1921–24. Kelly led the National League in 1920 with 94 RBI and again in 1924 with 136 RBI. He topped the league with 23 home runs in 1921 and ranked among the league's top six home runs hitters, 1920–26.

LIFETIME STATS: BA: .297, HR: 148, RBI: 1,020, H: 1,778, SB: 65

#**586** George Andrew Hendrick Jr.

OF-1B, A's, Indians, Padres, Cardinals, Pirates, Angels, 1971–88

Hendrick hit .300 or better four times for the Padres and Cardinals, and also ranked among National League RBI leaders four times. He posted his best offensive numbers in 1980 with the Cardinals, batting .302 with a career-high 173 hits, 109 RBI, 33 doubles and 25 home runs. Hendrick batted .321 in the 1982 World Series with five RBI, leading the Cardinals to victory over the Brewers.

LIFETIME STATS: BA: .278, HR: 267, RBI: 1,111, H: 1,980, SB: 59

#587 Anthony Francis "Tony" Cuccinello

2B-3B, Reds, Brooklyn Dodgers, Boston Braves, New York Giants, White Sox, 1930–40, 1942–45

Cuccinello hit .300 or better five times in his career, including his first two years in the majors, batting .312 in 1930 and .315 in 1931 for the Reds. He batted .308 for the White Sox in 1945, logging the second-best average in the American League. Cuccinello led National League second basemen in double plays and assists three times.

LIFETIME STATS: BA: .280, HR: 94, RBI: 884, H: 1,729, SB: 42

#588 Quincy Trouppe

C-OF, St. Louis Stars, Detroit Wolves, Homestead Grays, Kansas City Monarchs, Chicago American Giants, Indianapolis ABC'S, Cleveland Buckeyes, New York Cubans (Negro Leagues), 1930–49, Cleveland Indians, 1952

Trouppe was a terrific catcher in the Negro Leagues, who also played 14 winters in Latin America. He hit over .300 lifetime, and hit as high as .352 for the Chicago American Giants in 1948. He was selected for five Negro League All Star games, four as a catcher in the mid- to late 40s. He was a player-manager in the league and led the Cleveland Buckeyes to championships in 1945 and 1947. In 1952, he was signed by the Cleveland Indians, but unfortunately batted only 10 times, getting one hit, but stealing three bases in that limited action. His autobiography, which is aptly named Twenty Years Too Soon, was published in 1977.

LIFETIME STATS: BA: .311, HR: 97

#589 Edwin John "Ed" McKean

SS-OF, Cleveland Blues, Cleveland Spiders, St. Louis Perfectos, 1887–99

McKean hit .300 or better five times in his career, including four consecutive seasons with the Spiders, 1893–96, while also driving in 112 or more runs in each of those four seasons. He stole 76 bases in his rookie year with the Blues, then went on to hit a career-best .357 in 1894 with 198 hits. McKean led the National League twice in games and at bats.

LIFETIME STATS: BA: .302, HR: 66, RBI: 1,124, H: 2,083, SB: 323

#590 Carroll Christopher "Chris" Chambliss

1B, Indians, Yankees, Braves, 1971–86, 1988

Named 1971 American League Rookie of the Year, Chambliss batted .275 with 114 hits and 48 RBI for the Indians. He ranked six times among league leaders in doubles. A Gold Glove winner, Chambliss hit a series-clinching, ninth-inning home run in Game Five of the 1976 ALCS, leading the Yankees to victory over the Royals.

LIFETIME STATS: BA: .279, HR: 185, RBI: 972, H: 2,109, SB: 40

#**591** Eppa Rixey

LHP, Phillies, Reds, 1912–17, 1919–33. Hall of Fame, 1963

Rixey won 20 or more games a season four times in his career, leading the National League in 1922 with 25 wins for the Reds. He posted a career-best 1.85 ERA in 1916 with the Phillies, notching 22 wins, 20 complete games and 134 strikeouts. His 1,195 career assists on the mound ranks 10th all-time among pitchers. Rixey also topped the league with four shutouts in 1924.

LIFETIME STATS: W: 266, L: 251, SV: 14, ERA: 3.15, SO: 1,350, CG: 290

#**592** George Farley Grantham

2B-1B, Cubs, Pirates, Reds, New York Giants, 1922–34

Grantham hit .300 or better in eight of his 13 major league seasons, and ranked among National League leaders in on-base percentage for six consecutive seasons, 1924–29. He ranked among league leaders in walks eight times. Grantham hit a career-high 36 doubles in 1923, second-best in the NL. He stole 43 bases that year, his first full season with the Cubs.

LIFETIME STATS: BA: .302, HR: 105, RBI: 712, H: 1,508, SB: 132

#**593** Lonnie Smith

OF-DH, Phillies, Cardinals, Royals, Braves, Pirates, Orioles, 1978–94

Smith led the National League with 120 runs in 1982 for the Cardinals. He stole 68 bases that season, second-best in the NL, and led his team with a .307 batting average, 182 hits, 35 doubles and 69 RBI. He led the NL in 1989 with a .415 on-base percentage for the Braves. Smith stole 30 or more bases five times in his career, and also hit .300 or better five times.

LIFETIME STATS: BA: .288, HR: 98, RBI: 533, H: 1,488, SB: 370

#**594** George Robert "Birdie" Tebbetts

C, Tigers, Red Sox, Indians, 1936–42, 1946–52

Tebbetts led American League catchers in 1940 with 10 double plays and 89 assists for the Tigers, while also logging a career-best 572 putouts. He topped league catchers in 1941 with 83 assists. A four-time All Star, Tebbetts posted a .296 batting average for the Tigers in 1940 with 112 hits and 24 doubles.

LIFETIME STATS: BA: .270, HR: 38, RBI: 469, H: 1,000, SB: 29

#**595** Charles Jacob "Charlie" Hollocher

SS, Cubs, 1918–24

Hollocher led National League shortstops with a .963 fielding percentage in 1921 and a .965 percentage in 1922. He topped the league in 1918, his rookie year, with 161 hits, 202 total bases and 509 at bats. His .379 on-base percentage in 1918 was second-best in the NL. Hollocher hit .300 or better in four of his seven professional seasons.

LIFETIME STATS: BA: .304, HR: 14, RBI: 241, H: 894, SB: 99

#**596** Chris Edward Speier

SS-3B-2B, Giants, Expos, Cardinals, Twins, Cubs, 1971–89

Speier led National League shortstops in 1975 with a .982 fielding percentage for the Giants. He hit .357 with a home run in the 1971 NLCS, although the Giants lost to the Pirates. A three-time All Star, Speier drove in three runs and batted .400 in the 1981 NLCS, helping the Expos beat the Phillies.

LIFETIME STATS: BA: .246, HR: 112, RBI: 720, H: 1,759, SB: 42

#597 Michael Francis "Mickey" Welch

RHP, Troy Trojans, New York Giants, 1880–92. Hall of Fame, 1973

Welch won 20 or more games in seven consecutive seasons with the Giants, 1883–89. He recorded 345 strikeouts in 1884, then went 44–11 in 1885 with a 1.66 ERA. Welch ranked nine times among league leaders in ERA and wins, and also logged the sixth-most complete games in baseball history. He posted a 2.65 ERA over two complete games to help the Giants beat the St. Louis Browns in the 1888 World Series.

LIFETIME STATS: W: 307, L: 210, SV: 4, ERA: 2.71, SO: 1,850, CG: 525

#598 Robert William "Bob" Meusel

OF-3B, Yankees, Reds, 1920–30

Meusel hit .300 or better in seven of his 11 major league seasons, and drove in 100 or more runs five times. He led the American League in 1925 with a career-best 33 home runs, 79 extra-base hits and 138 RBI. Meusel ranked among the league's slugging percentage leaders for six consecutive seasons, 1920–25, and also topped the Yankees five times in stolen bases. A solid defensive player, he had the best outfield arm in the majors in the mid- to late 1920s.

LIFETIME STATS: BA: .309, HR: 156, RBI: 1,067, H: 1,693, SB: 142

#**599** John Dwight "Jack" Chesbro

RHP, Pirates, Yankees, Red Sox, 1899–1909. Hall of Fame, 1946

Chesbro led the National League in 1902 with 28 wins and eight shutouts for the Pirates. He topped the league again in 1904 with 41 wins and 48 complete games. He also notched a career-high 239 strikeouts and a career-low 1.82 ERA that year. The 41 wins are a modern major league record. Chesbro won 20 or more games a season five times, and ranked among league strikeout leaders in five consecutive seasons, 1902–06.

LIFETIME STATS: W: 198, L: 132, SV: 5, ERA: 2.68, SO: 1,265, CG: 260

#**600** Mark Henry Belanger

SS, Orioles, Dodgers, 1965–82

An eight-time Gold Glove winner, Belanger led American League shortstops in assists, double plays and fielding percentage at various times in his career. He led the AL with 15 sacrifice hits in 1973 and 23 sacrifice hits in 1975. Belanger hit a home run in baseball's first ALCS in 1969, helping the Orioles defeat the Twins.

LIFETIME STATS: BA: .228, HR: 20, RBI: 389, H: 1,316, SB: 167

#601 Albert Walter "Sparky" Lyle

LHP, Red Sox, Yankees, Rangers, Phillies, White Sox, 1967–82

Lyle twice led the American League in saves, in 1972 (35) and 1976 (23). In 1977 he was 13–5 with 26 saves as the Yankees won their first World Series since 1962. That performance earned him the Cy Young award. Twice in his career, Lyle posted an ERA under 2.00.

LIFETIME STATS: W: 99, L: 76, SV: 238, ERA: 2.88, SO: 873, CG: 0

#602 Augustus "Gus" Weyhing

RHP, Philadelphia A's, Brooklyn Ward's Wonders, Phillies, Pirates, Louisville, Senators, Cardinals, Brooklyn Superbas, Cleveland Blues, Reds, 1887–1901

Weyhing won 30 or more games in four consecutive seasons, 1889–1892, and 20 or more in three others. He had three seasons with an ERA under 3.00, 1888, 1889 and 1892. His best statistics were logged before 1893, when the mound was only 50 feet from home plate. He led the league in hit batsmen in 1887 with 37.

LIFETIME STATS: W: 264, L: 232, SV: 4, ERA: 3.89, SO: 1,665, CG: 448

#603 Richard Walter "Richie" Zisk

OF-DH, Pirates, White Sox, Rangers, Mariners, 1971–83

Zisk replaced Roberto Clemente in 1973 as the Pirate's right fielder, notching a career-high .324 batting average. He hit .311 in 1981 as a DH and set a Mariner record that year with home runs in five consecutive games. Zisk played in two league championship series, averaging .400 over six games. He was a two-time All Star, 1977–78.

LIFETIME STATS: BA: .287, HR: 207, RBI: 792, H: 1477, SB: 8

#604 Daniel Francis "Danny" Murphy

2B-OF, Giants, A's, Brooklyn Tip-Tops, 1900–15

Murphy had seven seasons hitting .300 or better. He played in three World Series with the A's, stroking a .400 batting average in the 1910 Series against the Cubs. In his 1902 debut for the A's, he hit six-for-six, including a grand slam off Boston's Cy Young.

LIFETIME STATS: BA: .289, HR: 44, RBI: 702, H: 1,563, SB: 193

#605 Norman Leroy "Norm" Sieburn

1B-OF, Yankees, A's, Orioles, Angels, Giants, Red Sox, 1956–68

Sieburn won a Gold Glove as the Yankees' left fielder in 1958, then was traded to Kansas City in 1959 in a seven-player deal that brought Roger Maris to New York. He tallied a career-high 185 hits, 25 home runs, 117 RBI and a .308 batting average in 1962 with the A's. He was named to the All Star team three times, 1962–64.

LIFETIME STATS: BA: .272, HR: 132, RBI: 636, H: 1,217, SB: 18

#606 Virgil Lawrence "Spud" Davis

C, Cardinals, Phillies, Reds, Pirates, 1928–41, 1944–45

Davis batted .300 or better in 10 of his 16 professional seasons, including a seven-year streak from 1929–35. His career-high mark of .349 for the 1933 Phillies was second-best in the NL, as was his .395 on-base percentage. He led NL catchers in double plays in 1932.

LIFETIME STATS: BA: .308, HR: 77, RBI: 647, H: 1,312, SB: 6

#607 Gregory "Greg" Vaughn

OF-DH, Brewers, Padres, Reds, Devil Rays, Rockies, 1989–2003

Vaughn hit 40 or more home runs in three seasons, including a career-high 50 for the 1998 Padres. That year, Vaughn was third in the NL in home runs, behind Sammy Sosa of the Cubs and the Cardinals' Mark McGwire, both of whom shattered Roger Maris' long-standing record. He was named to the All Star team four times.

LIFETIME STATS: BA: .242, HR: 355, RBI: 1,072, H: 1,475, SB: 121

#608 Omar Enrique "Little O" Vizquel

SS, Mariners, Indians, Giants, Rangers, White Sox, 1989–2011

Vizquel won nine consecutive Gold Glove awards, 1993–2001. He boasts a career .983 fielding percentage, the all-time best for a shortstop playing in more than 1,000 games. He twice stole more than 40 bases in a season for the Indians, in 1997 and 1999, and played in 11 postseason series. He was voted an All Star three times.

LIFETIME STATS: BA: .272, HR: 80, RBI: 944, H: 2,841, SB: 401

#**609** Harry "Jasper" Davis

1B-OF, Giants, Pirates, Louisville Colonels, Senators, A's, Indians, 1895–1917

Davis led the AL in home runs from 1904 to 1907. He also led the league in RBI in 1905 and 1906 with 83 and 96 respectively. He played in three World Series, hitting .353 in the A's 1910 World Series defeat of the Cubs. Davis also drove in five runs in the 1911 World Series, leading the A's to victory over the New York Giants.

LIFETIME STATS: BA: .277, HR: 75, RBI 952, H: 1,841, SB: 285

#**610** Walter Arlington "Arlie," "The Freshest Man on Earth" Latham

3B, Buffalo Bisons, St. Louis Browns, Chicago Pirates, Reds, Senators, Giants, 1880–1909

Latham scored 100 or more runs nine times, including 152 in 1886 to lead the AA. He stole 739 career bases, leading the AA in 1888 when he stole 109 bases for the Browns. As a player-coach for the Giants in 1909, Latham successfully stole second against the Phillies at the age of 50, making him the oldest player to steal a base. The most colorful man in baseball in the 1890s, he got his nickname from his incessant chatter in the field, constantly encouraging his pitcher and disparaging the batter.

LIFETIME STATS: BA: .269, HR: 27, RBI: 563, H: 1,833, SB: 739

#611 Fredrick Alfred "Freddy" Parent

SS-OF, St. Louis Perfectos, Red Sox, White Sox, 1899–1911

Parent contributed to the Red Sox' (Pilgrims, as they were known) victory over the Pirates in the first World Series in 1903, averaging .290 over eight games. That same year, he knocked in a career-high 80 RBI and hit 17 triples. Parent was on the field for four no-hitters, including a perfect game by Boston's Cy Young.

LIFETIME STATS: BA: .262, HR: 20, RBI: 471, H: 1,306, SB: 184

#612 William Edward "Willie" Kamm

3B, White Sox, Indians, 1923–35

The White Sox bought his minor league contract from the San Francisco Seals in 1922 for a then-record sum of $100,000. Considered the best defensive player of his era, Kamm was among AL leaders in fielding statistics for most of his 13-year career, logging a lifetime fielding percentage of .967. His fielding prowess made him fifth in the 1928 AL MVP voting, despite hitting just over .300 with only one home run.

LIFETIME STATS: BA: .281, HR: 29, RBI: 826, H:1,643, SB: 126

#613 Orel Leonard Quinton Hershiser IV

RHP, Dodgers, Indians, Giants, Mets, 1983–2000

Hershiser's big year was 1988, when he won the NL Cy Young award, along with a Gold Glove and MVP awards in both the National League Championship Series and World Series. Hershiser became the first NL player to win MVP awards for both postseason series. He pitched two complete-game wins in the 1988 World Series, helping the Dodgers defeat the A's. He pitched 59 consecutive scoreless innings that year, breaking a 20-year record held by former Dodger Don Drysdale.

LIFETIME STATS: W: 204, L: 150, SV: 5, ERA: 3.48, SO: 2,014, CG: 68

#614 Rickey Eugene "Rick" Reuschel

RHP, Cubs, Yankees, Pirates, Giants, 1972–91

Reuschel is among the Cubs' all-time leaders in strikeouts, wins and games. He won a Gold Glove in 1985 and again in 1987. He won 10 or more games in his first nine seasons with the Cubs, 1972–80, including a 20-10 season in 1977 that made him third in NL Cy Young award voting. He was a three-time All Star, 1977, 1987 and 1989.

LIFETIME STATS: W: 214, L:191, SV: 5, ERA: 3.37, SO: 2,015, CG: 102

#**615** Patrick Henry "Patsy" Dougherty

OF, Red Sox, Yankees, White Sox, 1902–11

Dougherty led the AL in 1903 with 107 runs, 195 hits and 590 at bats, and topped the league in 1908 with 47 stolen bases. He was a pitcher's nightmare, breaking up four no-hitters in a 10-year career. "Patsy" hit two home runs and two triples to help the Red Sox defeat the Pirates in the first World Series.

LIFETIME STATS: BA: .284, HR: 17, RBI: 413, H: 1,294, SB: 261

#**616** Thomas Francis "Kelly," "Tommy" Holmes

OF, Braves, Dodgers, 1942–52

Holmes had a career year in 1945, leading the NL with 28 home runs, 224 hits and 47 doubles. He had a .352 batting average that season, second-best in the league. Holmes set an NL record by hitting safely in 37 consecutive games, broken by Pete Rose in 1978. Also in 1945, he became the only player ever to lead his league in home runs and fewest strikeouts, nine.

LIFETIME STATS: BA: .302, HR: 88, RBI: 581, H: 1,507, SB: 40

#617 Benjamin Ambrosio "Ben" Oglivie

OF-DH, Red Sox, Tigers, Brewers, 1971–86

Oglivie led the AL with 41 home runs in 1980 for the Brewers. He also tallied 118 RBI that year, second best in the league. He hit three home runs in a game three times for the Brewers that year. His 34 home runs in 1982 helped deliver the Brewers to the World Series against, which they would lose to the Cardinals. Oglivie was a three-time All Star, in 1980, 1982 and 1983.

LIFETIME STATS: BA: .273, HR: 235, RBI: 901, H: 1,615, SB: 87

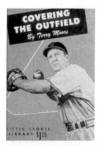

#618 Terry Bluford Moore

OF, Cardinals, 1935–42, 1946–48

The well-respected Moore served as the captain of two Cardinals World Series teams, both winners, against the Yankees in 1942 and the Red Sox in 1946. Among the NL top 10 in stolen bases from 1935 to 1938, and in 1940 and 1942, Moore entered the military in the fall of 1942, returning to professional baseball four years later. He was a four-time All Star.

LIFETIME STATS: BA: .280, HR: 80, RBI: 513, H: 1,318, SB: 82

#**619** Alan Dean Ashby

C, Indians, Blue Jays, Astros, 1973–89

During his career, Ashby tied the NL record for catching the most no-hitters with three, pitched by Ken Forsch in 1979, Nolan Ryan in 1981 and Mike Scott in 1986. He caught more games than anyone in Astros franchise history with 911 and became the first Astro to hit home runs both left- and right-handed in one game in 1982. An excellent defensive receiver, he led the league's catchers in fielding percentage in 1987.

LIFETIME STATS: BA: .245, HR: 90, RBI: 513, H: 1,010, SB: 7

#**620** Spotswood Poles

OF, Philadelphia Giants, New York Lincoln Giants, Brooklyn Royal Giants, Lincoln Stars, Hilldale (Negro Leagues), 1909–23

Known as "the black Ty Cobb," Poles stole 41 bases over 60 games in 1911 in the Negro Leagues. Poles hit .487 in 1914, and scored 11 runs for the New York Lincoln Giants in the 1915 Black World Series. He joined the army in 1917 and earned a Purple Heart in WWI. Poles is credited with a .440 average in nine "All Star" games against white big leaguers.

LIFETIME STATS: BA: .335

#621 Harvey Edward Kuenn

OF-SS-3B, Tigers, Indians, Giants, Cubs, Phillies, 1952–66

In 1953 Kuenn was the AL Rookie of the Year playing for the Tigers, notching a league-leading 209 hits. He topped the AL in hits four times while with the Tigers. He hit .353 to win the American League batting championship in 1959. Kuenn hit over .300 in eight full seasons and was an eight-time All Star, from 1953 to 1960.

LIFETIME STATS: BA: .303, HR: 87, RBI: 671, H: 2,092, SB: 68

#622 James Thomas "Jimmy" Williams

2B-3B, Pirates, Orioles, New York 1899–1909

Williams was among the league leaders in home runs for six of his 11 seasons in the majors. He led his league three times in triples, with a career high 27 in 1899 for the Pirates. That year, Williams hit nine home runs and 116 RBI, both third best in the league. He led the league's second basemen twice in fielding percentage, in 1903 and 1905.

LIFETIME STATS: BA: .275, HR: 49, RBI: 796, H: 1,507, SB: 151

#**623** Andrew Wasil "Andy" Seminick

C, Phillies, Reds, 1943–57

Seminick was a solid defensive catcher who had some power: He hit 10 or more homers nine times in his career, including eight years in a row, 1946 to 1953. He hit two home runs in a five-home-run eighth inning in for the Phillies in a 1949 game against the Reds. Then he hit a third home run in the same game. Seminick was voted to the All Star team that year. He hit a career-high .288 with 24 home runs and 113 hits in 1950.

LIFETIME STATS: BA: .243, HR: 164, RBI: 556, H: 953, SB: 23

#**624** Howard Michael "Hojo" Johnson

3B-SS-OF, Tigers, Mets, Rockies, Cubs, 1982–95

As a Met, Johnson had three years with 30 or more home runs and stolen bases: 1987, 1989 and 1991. He set the NL record for home runs by a switch-hitter in 1987 with 36. He broke his own record in 1991, when he led the league with 38 home runs and 117 RBI.

LIFETIME STATS: BA: .249, HR: 228, RBI: 760, H: 1,229, SB: 231

#625 John Milton "Mickey" Rivers

OF-DH, Angels, Yankees, Rangers, 1970–84

In New York, Rivers was known as "Mick the Quick." He stole 70 bases as an Angel in 1975 to lead the AL. Rivers logged 190 stolen bases from 1974 to 1978. His forte was the postseason. Rivers had a .308 batting average over six postseason series, including three World Series as a Yankee, 1976–78. Rivers led the AL in triples in 1974 and 1975 with the Angels.

LIFETIME STATS: BA: .295, HR: 61, RBI: 499, H: 1,660, SB: 267

#626 George John "Whitey" Kurowski

3B, Cardinals, 1941–49

Kurowski hit .300 or better four times in his nine-season career. He also led the NL in putouts three times and in fielding percentage twice. He ranked among NL leaders in home runs from 1943 to 1947. Kurowksi hit a ninth-inning home run in the fifth game of the 1942 World Series against the Yankees to break a 2–2 tie and take the Series.

LIFETIME STATS: BA: .286, HR: 106, RBI: 529, H: 925, SB: 19

#627 Oscar Emil "Happy" Felsch
White Sox, 1915–20

Part of the 1919 Black Sox scandal team, Felsch was banned from baseball in 1920 after six seasons in the majors. He was in his prime, hitting .300 or better in three seasons. Felsch knocked in 100 or more runs in two seasons, 1917 and 1920. He was one of the best all-around players of his era. Felsch shares record for double plays in a season by an outfielder, with 15.

LIFETIME STATS: BA: .293, HR: 38, RBI: 446, H: 825, SB: 88

#628 Walter William "Billy" Pierce
LHP, Tigers, White Sox, Giants, 1945–64

Billy Pierce won 15 or more games eight times in his career, including back-to-back 20-win seasons for the White Sox in 1956 and 1957. He was an "inning-eater," leading the American League in complete games four times in his career and pitching more than 200 innings nine times in that span.

LIFETIME STATS: W: 211, L: 169, SV: 32, ERA: 3.27, SO: 1,999, CG: 193

#**629** James Joseph "Jimmy" Dykes

3B-2B-1B-SS, A's, White Sox, 1918–39

One of the most versatile players of the 1920s and 1930s, Dykes began his career as a second baseman for the A's and ended it as a third baseman for the White Sox. In between, he played wherever he was needed, and usually played very well. He was also an excellent pinch hitter, with a .321 career average. He hit .421 to lead Philadelphia in the 1929 World Series.

LIFETIME STATS: BA: .280, HR: 108, RBI: 1,071, H: 2,256, SB: 70

#**630** Zoilo Casanova "Zorro" Versalles

SS-3B-2B, Senators, Twins, Dodgers, Indians, Braves, 1959–71

Versalles was one of the best defensive shortstops of his era, winning Gold Gloves twice as the Twins' shortstop, in 1963 and 1965. Named 1965 AL MVP, he led the league with 126 runs, 45 doubles and 12 triples and also stole a career-high 27 bases that year. He helped lead the Twins to the 1965 World Series, which they ultimately lost to the Dodgers.

LIFETIME STATS: BA: .242, HR: 95, RBI: 471, H: 1,246, SB: 97

#631 Claude Cassius "Little All Right" Ritchey

2B-SS, Reds, Louisville Colonels, Pirates, Boston Doves, 1897–1909

The diminutive (5'6", 167 pounds) Ritchey was a five-time NL fielding percentage leader at second base for Pittsburgh. He also led the NL three times in double plays, working mostly along with Honus Wagner at shortstop for the Pirates. He notched 31 sacrifice hits in 1898 for the Colonels to lead the National League.

LIFETIME STATS: BA: .273, HR: 18, RBI: 673, H: 1,618, SB: 155

#632 Henry Leval "Hank" Severeid

C, Reds, Browns, Senators, Yankees, 1911–13, 1915–26

Severeid was one of the most durable catchers of his era. He caught 1,225 games over 15 seasons, appearing in more than 100 games each year from 1916–24, with the exception of his year in the military in 1918. One of his claims to fame was being knocked unconscious in a 1916 game by the Red Sox' Babe Ruth, who barreled into him while he was defending the plate. He hit .300 or better five seasons in a row, 1921–1925.

LIFETIME STATS: BA: .289, HR: 17, RBI: 539, H: 1,245, SB: 35

#**633** Victor Woodrow Wertz

OF-1B, Tigers, St. Louis Browns, Orioles, Indians, Red Sox, Twins, 1947–63

Wertz, as Willie Mays will tell you, could hit the baseball. He made more than 100 RBI a season five times. He ranked among the top 10 AL MVP candidates in 1949, 1950, 1956 and 1957. Wertz logged a career-high 133 RBI in 1949 with the Tigers. His claim to fame, though, was making one of the most famous outs in World Series history: He hit the ball in the 1954 World Series that Mays tracked down with a legendary over-the-shoulder catch. Wertz still batted .500 for the Indians in that Series, though the New York Giants swept the Indians in four games.

LIFETIME STATS: BA: .277, HR: 266, RBI: 1,178, H: 1,692, SB: 9

#**634** Jesse Joseph "Pop" Haines

RHP, Reds, Cardinals, 1918, 1920–37. Hall of Fame, 1970

Haines was a very consistent pitcher for a very long time, which was the principal factor in his election to the Hall of Fame. He won more games for the Cardinals than anyone but Bob Gibson, yet he won 20 or more games in a season only three times. Seven times he won between 11 and 13 games. Haines pitched in four World Series and won two games with a 1.08 ERA in the Cardinals' 1926 World Series victory over the Yankees.

LIFETIME STATS: W: 210, L: 158, SV: 10, ERA: 3.64, SO: 981, CG: 208

#635 Joseph Anthony "Joe" Kuhel
1B, Senators, White Sox, 1930–47

Kuhel was a tremendous defensive first baseman, probably the best of his era. In a 1941 doubleheader against the A's, Kuhel recorded 17 putouts in the first game and 23 in the second, breaking a record set by Hal Chase in 1906. Kuhel hit a career-best .322 with 107 RBI in 1933, helping take the Senators to the World Series. He led AL first basemen that year in putouts with 1,498. In 1940, Kuhel hit a personal-best 27 home runs for the White Sox.

LIFETIME STATS: BA: .277, HR: 131, RBI: 1,049, H: 2,212, SB: 178

#636 Leo Ernest "Ernie" Whitt
C, Red Sox, Blue Jays, Braves, Orioles, 1976–78, 1980–91

One of the most popular members of the expansion Blue Jays, Whitt was also a very good defensive catcher and handler of pitchers. As a Blue Jay, he hit three of a major league single-game-record-setting 10 team home runs against the Orioles in 1987. Voted to the All Star team in 1985, Whitt led American League catchers in putouts with 803 in 1987.

LIFETIME STATS: BA: .249, HR: 134, RBI: 534, H: 938, SB: 22

#637 William Mitchell "Billy" Nash

3B, Richmond Virginians, Boston Beaneaters, Boston Doves, Phillies, 1884–98

Nash was a great two-way star for Boston in the late 1880s and early 1890s, with a stint in the Players League mixed in there in 1890. He had 90 or more RBI in six of his 15 seasons and averaged 28 stolen bases a year. Nash also led third baseman in fielding percentage four times while with the Beaneaters. In 1893 he logged a career year with the Beaneaters, hitting .291 with 10 home runs, 123 RBI and 30 stolen bases.

LIFETIME STATS: BA: .275, HR: 60, RBI: 977, H: 1,606, SB: 265

#638 John Phelan "Stuffy" McInnis

1B-SS, Philadelphia A's, Red Sox, Indians, Boston Braves, Pirates, Phillies, 1909–27

McInnis was a good-hitting first baseman with limited range. Still, he committed only one error at first base in 152 games for the 1921 Red Sox to log a .999 fielding average. He would lead the league in fielding six times in his career. McInnis hit over .300 in 12 of his 19 seasons and appeared in five World Series, winning four times.

LIFETIME STATS: BA: .307, HR: 20, RBI 1,062, H: 2,405, SB: 172

#**639** Henry "Heinie" Zimmerman
3B-2B-SS-1B, Cubs, New York Giants, 1907–19

A versatile player early in his career, Zimmerman played all four infield and all three outfield positions for the Cubs. In 1912, his second year as a regular for Chicago at third, he led the NL with a .372 batting average, 14 home runs, 41 doubles, 207 hits and a .571 slugging percentage. Zimmerman led the league in RBI twice. He was suspended from the Giants toward the end of the 1919 season and next year banned from baseball for conspiring to fix games.

LIFETIME STATS: BA: .295, HR: 58, RBI 796, H: 1,566, SB: 175

#**640** William Ellis "Bill" Russell
SS-2B-OF, Dodgers, 1969–86

Russell was one of the more underrated postseason players. He participated in 10 postseason series, averaging .294. Russell played in four World Series, including the Dodgers' 1981 win over the Yankees. He led the NL in games played in 1973 with 162. He was among league leaders in at bats that year and from 1977 to 1979. Russell played more games for the Dodgers than anyone in franchise history except Hall of Famer Zach Wheat.

LIFETIME STATS: BA: 263, HR: 46, RBI: 627, H: 1,926, SB: 167

#**641** Alfred Karl "Kip" Selbach

OF-SS-2B, Senators, Reds, New York Giants, Orioles, Boston Pilgrims, 1894–1906

Selbach batted over .300 in seven of his 13 professional seasons and logged 100 RBI in 1896 with the Senators. The fireplug-like (5'7", 190 pounds) Selbach was among NL leaders in 1900 with a .337 batting average, his career best. He led the NL in triples in 1895 with 22. In 1904, Selbach caught the final out in left field to clinch the pennant for the Boston Red Sox.

LIFETIME STATS: BA: .293, HR: 44, RBI: 779, H: 1,803, SB: 334

#**642** James Luther "Luke" Sewell

C, Indians, Senators, White Sox, St. Louis Browns, 1921–39, 1942

Tough and durable, Sewell set an AL record for playing 20 seasons as an active catcher. He was named to the All Star team during his 1937 season with the White Sox. Sewell was among the top 10 AL MVP candidates in 1927, the year he set career-high marks with a .294 batting average and 138 hits. He repeated among the top 10 MVP candidates in 1937.

LIFETIME STATS: BA: .259, HR: 20, RBI: 696, H: 1,393, SB: 65

#643 William Robert "Bob" Allison
OF-1B, Senators, Twins, 1958–70

Allison was named the 1959 AL Rookie of the Year, hitting 30 home runs and 85 RBI for the Senators. He hit 29 home runs or more five times in his career. In 1963, he led the American League in runs with 99 for the Twins. Allison and Twins teammate Harmon Killebrew became the first two major leaguers to each hit a grand slam in the same inning in 1962.

LIFETIME STATS: BA: .255, HR: 256, RBI: 796, H: 1,281, SB: 84

#644 Marquis Dean Grissom
OF, Expos, Braves, Indians, Brewers, Dodgers, Giants, 1989–2005

One of the best defensive outfielders of the 1990s, Grissom was a four-time Gold Glove outfielder, 1993–96. He committed only one error over 158 games in center field for the 1996 Braves. Voted ALCS MVP in 1997 for his efforts to lift the Indians over the Orioles. Grissom ranks 19th among active players in career hits and seventh among active players for stolen bases with 425.

LIFETIME STATS: BA: .272, HR: 227, RBI: 967, H: 2,251, SB: 429

#645 Denis John Menke

SS-3B-2B-1B, Milwaukee Braves, Atlanta Braves, Astros, Reds, 1962–74

The versatile Menke was twice voted an All Star, in 1969 and in1970. He peaked in 1970 with the Astros, batting .304 with 92 RBI and 171 hits, all career-high numbers. He homered off Catfish Hunter in Cincinnati's 1972 World Series against the A's, though the Reds ultimately lost in seven games.

LIFETIME STATS: BA: .250, HR: 101, RBI: 606, H: 1,270, SB: 34

#646 George Henry "Dode" Paskert

OF, Reds, Phillies, Cubs, 1907–21

Paskert led National League outfielders in fielding percentage in 1917 while with the Phillies. Admired for his smooth fielding style and exceptional range, Paskert had his best offensive season in 1912, batting .315 with 170 hits for the Phillies. He stole a career-high 51 bases for the 1910 Reds, on his way to 293 lifetime stolen bases. He was among league leaders in bases on balls six times.

LIFETIME STATS: BA: .268, HR: 42, RBI: 577, H: 1,613, SB: 293

#647 Richard Joseph "Richie" Hebner

3B-1B, Pirates, Phillies, Mets, Tigers, Cubs, 1968–85

Hebner led National League rookies with a .301 batting average for the Pirates in 1969. He would go on to play in nine postseason series, setting an NL record for most LCS appearances, with eight. He led the 1979 Mets with 79 RBI. Hebner hit a career-high 82 RBI in 104 games with the 1980 Tigers. He also hit 25 home runs with the Pirates in 1973.

LIFETIME STATS: BA: .276, HR: 203, RBI: 890, H: 1,694, SB: 38

#648 Stephen Wayne "Steve" Yeager

C, Dodgers, Mariners, 1972–86

Yeager played in 11 postseason series with the Dodgers and four World Series. He was named co-MVP in the 1981 World Series against the Yankees, along with Ron Cey and Pedro Guerrero. Yeager hit two home runs in that Series, including a shot off Ron Guidry to win Game Five. He tied the NL record for catchers in 1972 with 22 putouts in a game.

LIFETIME STATS: BA: .228, HR: 102, RBI: 410, H: 816, SB: 14

#649 Henry E. "Ted" Larkin

1B-OF, Philadelphia A's, Indians, Senators, 1884–93

Larkin was one of the early stars of big league baseball, hitting .300 or better six times in his 10-season career. Ranking among league leaders in extra-base hits and home runs for much of his career, Larkin topped the American Association in doubles in 1885 and 1886. He hit a career-high .330 with 112 RBI for the Indians in 1890, and stole 37 bases for the A's in 1887.

LIFETIME STATS: BA: .303, HR: 53, RBI: 836, H: 1,429, SB: 129

#650 William Michael "Bill" Joyce

3B-1B, Brooklyn Ward's Wonders, Boston Reds, Brooklyn Grooms, Senators, New York Giants, 1890–92, 1894–98

Joyce still ranks sixth in all-time career on-base percentage, with .435. He hit .300 or better four consecutive years, 1894–97. In 1896, Joyce led the NL in home runs with 13. He hit 17 home runs in both 1894 and 1895 for the Senators. He notched a career-best .355 batting average in 1894. An excellent base runner, Joyce stole 20 or more bases in each of his eight major league seasons, totaling 264 in all.

LIFETIME STATS: BA: .294, HR: 70, RBI: 607, H: 970, SB: 264

#651 Larry Alton Parrish

3B-OF-DH, Expos, Rangers, Red Sox, 1974–88

Parrish became the 13th player to record seasons of 30 or more home runs in both the AL and NL. He was named Expos Player of the Year in 1979 with a .307 batting average, 82 RBI and 30 home runs, and was voted to the All Star team for that year. He was vote an All Star for the second time in 1987, hitting 100 RBI and 32 home runs by the end of the season.

LIFETIME STATS: BA: .263, HR: 256, RBI: 992, H: 1,789, SB: 30

#652 Jeff Blauser

SS-2B-3B, Braves, Cubs, 1987–99

The defensive mainstay of the Braves for most of the 1990s, Blauser blew hot and cold offensively throughout most of his career. A two-time All Star, he twice topped .300, in 1993 and 1997. But the free-swinging Blauser also struck out 100 or more times in four seasons in his career.

LIFETIME STATS: BA: .262, HR: 122, RBI: 513, H: 1,187, SB: 65

#653 Cletis Leroy "Clete" Boyer

3B-SS-2B, Kansas City A's, Yankees, Braves, 1955–57, 1959–71

The very versatile Boyer led NL third basemen in fielding percentage in 1967 and 1969. He also won a Gold Glove for third base work with the Braves in 1969. He was one of three brothers to play in the majors. Clete and his brother Ken became the first siblings to each hit home runs in the same World Series game when the Yankees played the Cardinals in 1964.

LIFETIME STATS: BA: .242, HR: 162, RBI: 654, H: 1,396, SB: 41

#654 Bret William Saberhagen

RHP, Royals, Mets, Rockies, Red Sox, 1984–95, 1997–2001

In 1985 at the age of 21, Saberhagen became the youngest pitcher to win a Cy Young award. He led the 1985 Royals to a World Series victory over the Cardinals, pitching two complete games with an 0.50 ERA and winning the World Series MVP award. In 1989, he won the AL Cy Young award again, leading the league in complete games with 12, and posting 23 wins.

LIFETIME STATS: W: 167, L: 117, SV: 1, ERA: 3.34, SO: 1,715, CG: 76

#655 J. Preston "Pete" Hill

OF-2B, Philadelphia Giants, Leland Giants, Chicago American Giants, Detroit Stars, Philadelphia Madison Stars, Milwaukee Bears, Baltimore Black Sox (Negro Leagues),1904–25. Hall of Fame, 2006

The swift Hill was a tremendous line-drive hitter who once hit safely in 115 of 116 games as an American Giant in 1911. That season, the team finished the year 106–7, and was considered one of the greatest Negro League teams ever. A very consistent hitter, Hill led the Detroit Stars with a .388 batting average in 1921 at the age of 41.

LIFETIME STATS (Negro Leagues games only): BA: .306, H: 477

#656 Victor Gazaway "Vic" Willis

RHP, Boston Beaneaters, Pirates, Cardinals, 1898–1910. Hall of Fame, 1995

Willis started his major league career with a bang, winning 25 games in his first season with Boston. He would go on to win 20 or more games a season eight times over his 13-season career. In 1902 Willis set a National League record with 45 complete games. He completed 388 of the 471 games he started in his career. He ranks 19th lifetime in complete games and shutouts (50).

LIFETIME STATS: W: 249 L: 205, SV: 11, ERA: 2.63, SO: 1,651, CG: 388

#657 Ronald Edwin Gant

OF-2B-3B, Braves, Reds, Cardinals, Phillies, Angels, Rockies, A's, Padres, 1987–93, 1995–2003

The swift Gant became the third player ever to have back-to-back seasons with 30 or more stolen bases and home runs in 1991 with the Braves. He also displayed some power, hitting 25 or more home runs in seven seasons. Gant logged a career-best 36 home runs and 117 RBI in 1993, his last year with Atlanta. He currently ranks 20th among active players, with 321 career home runs.

LIFETIME STATS (THROUGH 2003): BA: .256, HR: 321, RBI: 1,008, H: 1,651, SB: 243

#**658** Brady Kevin Anderson

OF-DH, Red Sox, Orioles, Indians, 1988–2002

As an Oriole in 1992, Anderson became the first AL player ever to reach the milestones of 20 home runs, 50 steals and 75 RBI in one season. In 1994, Anderson stole 31 bases in 32 attempts. Between his 1994 and 1995 seasons, Anderson stole 36 consecutive bases without getting caught. He led the American league with 92 extra-base hits in 1996, the same year he hit a career-best 50 home runs.

LIFETIME STATS: BA: .256, HR: 210, RBI: 761, H: 1,661, SB: 315

#**659** Jesse Lee Barfield

OF, Blue Jays, Yankees, 1981–92

Barfield was a superb defensive outfielder, winning a Gold Glove with the Blue Jays in 1986 and in 1987. Known for his strong arm, Barfield led American League outfielders in assists three years in a row, from 1985 to 1987. He also hit 20 or more home runs six times in his career. His personal best numbers came in 1986 with 40 home runs and 108 RBI.

LIFETIME STATS: BA: .256, HR: 241, RBI: 716, H: 1,219, SB: 66

#**660** Oswald Lewis "Ossie" Bluege

3B-SS-2B, Senators, 1922–39

Bluege was a fixture at third base for the Senators from 1923 to 1933. Among top 10 AL MVP candidates in 1925, Bluege turned in a .287 batting average and 150 hits. At 5'11" and 165 pounds, Bluege was not a sturdy-looking guy, but he ranked among top-10 batters hit by pitches for nine of his 18 seasons. He hit a career-best 98 RBI with eight home runs in 1931.

LIFETIME STATS: BA: .272, HR: 43, RBI: 848, H: 1,751, SB: 140

#**661** Clifford Earl Torgeson

1B, Boston Braves, Phillies, Tigers, White Sox, Yankees, 1947–61

As a Brave in 1950, Torgeson led the National League in runs scored with 120. The following year, he reached career highs with 24 home runs and 92 RBI. Torgeson boasted the best batting average in the 1948 World Series, hitting .389 over five games, though the Braves ultimately lost to the Indians.

LIFETIME STATS: BA: .265, HR: 149, RBI: 740, H: 1,318, SB: 133

#662 George Frederick "Doggie" Miller

C-OF-3B-SS-2B, Pirates, St. Louis Browns, Louisville Colonels, 1884–96

The versatile Miller had a career-best year in 1894 with the Browns, hitting eight home runs with 86 RBI, and leading his team with a .339 batting average and 163 hits. He collected the 10th-most hits in the National League as a Pirate in 1891 with 156. That was the year he played 41 games at catcher, 37 games at shortstop and 34 games at third base.

LIFETIME STATS: BA: .267, HR: 33, RBI: 567, H: 1,380, SB: 260

#663 Ivey Brown Wingo

C, Cardinals, Reds, 1911–29

One of the more durable catchers of his generation, Wingo briefly held the record for most career games caught upon his retirement in 1929, with 1,233. Wingo played for Cincinnati in the infamous 1919 World Series with the Chicago Black Sox, and hit .571 in the Series. He ranks seventh among catchers in career assists with 1,487, and also holds the 20th-century record for catchers' career errors, with 234.

LIFETIME STATS: BA: .260, HR: 25, RBI: 455, H: 1,039, SB: 87

#664 Donald Eulen "Don" Kessinger
SS-2B, Cubs, Cardinals, White Sox, 1964–79

"Kess," as he was known to his Cub teammates, was a two-time Gold Glove winner, 1969–70, as well as a six-time All Star, from 1968 to 1972 and in 1974. In the middle of his career, Kessinger led NL shortstops multiple times in various categories, including putouts, double plays, assists and fielding percentage. He batted six-for-six during an extra-inning game in 1970 with the Cubs. In 1969, he went 54 games without an error, a shortstop record at the time.

LIFETIME STATS: BA: .252, HR 14, RBI: 527, H: 1,931, SB: 100

#665 Nathaniel Frederick "Fred" Pfeffer
2B-SS, Troy Trojans, Chicago White Stockings, Chicago Pirates, Louisville Colonels, New York Giants, 1882–97

Pfeffer's unofficial nickname was "the Dandelion," because he could really "pick" ground balls. He was among the league leaders in home runs five times, from 1884 to 1887, and again in 1891. He posted a career-high 25 home runs and 101 RBI in 1884 with the White Stockings. In a playoff series against the St. Louis Browns of the American Association in 1885, Pfeffer hit .407 over a seven-game series. He was known as the first infielder to cut off a catcher's throw to second, then throw out a runner at the plate, foiling a double steal.

LIFETIME STATS: BA: .255, HR: 94, RBI: 1,019, H: 1,671, SB: 382

#666 John Anthony "Johnny" Romano

C, White Sox, Indians, Cardinals, 1958–67

A two-time All Star in 1961 and 1962, Romano registered peak career numbers in those years with the Indians, hitting 21 home runs and 80 RBI in 1961, and 25 home runs and 81 RBI in 1962. He led the Indians in RBI and home runs in 1962. Romano hit 10 homers or more for seven consecutive years. The husky (some say overweight) Romano was slowed by a hand injury after the 1963 season.

LIFETIME STATS: BA: .255, HR: 129, RBI: 417, H: 706, SB: 7

#667 Harry M. Steinfeldt

3B-2B, Reds, Cubs, Boston Braves, 1898–1911

Third baseman Steinfeldt was the fourth infielder in the Cubs' legendary Tinker-to-Evers-to-Chance infield. He was a solid hitter, leading the National League with 176 hits and 83 RBI in 1906, his first year with the Cubs, when he also posted his best batting average, .327. He also led the NL in doubles in 1903 with 32. Steinfeldt played in four World Series, winning two with the Cubs over the Tigers, in 1907 and 1908.

LIFETIME STATS: BA: .267, HR: 27, RBI: 762, H: 1,576, SB: 194

#668 Charles Theodore "Chili" Davis

OF-DH, Giants, Angels, Twins, Royals, Yankees, 1981–99

Davis was a durable outfielder, ranking third in all-time career home runs by switch-hitters with 350. He also ranks in the top 100 all-time in most hits, home runs, RBI and extra-base hits. A three-time All Star in 1984, 1986 and 1994, Davis homered twice in the Twins' 1991 World Series victory over the Braves. Davis averaged 23 home runs and 91 RBI over a 19-season career.

LIFETIME STATS: BA: .274, HR: 350, RBI: 1,372, H: 2,380, SB: 142

#669 William J. "Kid" Gleason

2B-RHP, Phillies, St. Louis Browns, Orioles, New York Giants, Tigers, White Sox, 1888–1908, 1912

As a pitcher, Gleason garnered four seasons with 20 or more wins, including a 38–17 year with the Phillies in 1890. He moved to second base with the Giants, and hit .319 with 106 RBI and 43 stolen bases in 1897. Gleason twice led NL in sacrifice hits, 1904–05, with 35 and 43 respectively. Perhaps he is best known as the unsuspecting manager of the 1919 "Black" Sox, several of whose players threw the World Series.

LIFETIME STATS: W: 138, L: 131, SV: 6, ERA: 3.79, SO: 744, CG: 240. BA: .261, HR: 15, RBI: 823, H: 1,944, SB: 328

#670 Ron Hansen

SS-3B, Orioles, White Sox, Senators, Yankees, Royals, 1958–72

Hansen was named AL Rookie of the Year in 1960 as an Oriole, hitting 22 home runs with 86 RBI. The next year, he led American League shortstops in double plays with 110. He went on to lead his teams in that category three times in his career, and topped AL shortstops four times in assists over 15 seasons. As a Senator, Hansen completed an unassisted triple play in a 1968 game against the Indians.

LIFETIME STATS: BA: .234, HR: 106, RBI: 501, H: 1,007, SB: 9

#671 Keith Anthony "Tony" Phillips

OF-2B-3B-SS-DH, A's, Tigers, Angels, White Sox, Blue Jays, Mets, 1982–99

Philips's 114 runs with Detroit led the American League in 1992. Patient at the plate, Phillips topped the AL twice in bases on balls and ranks 30th in career walks. Phillips tied a major league record in 1986 with 12 assists at second base in a game for Oakland. He played in two World Series, hitting a home run in Oakland's four-game sweep of the Giants in 1989.

LIFETIME STATS: BA: .266, HR: 160, RBI: 819, H: 2,023, SB: 177

#672 Adrian "Addie" Joss

RHP, Indians, 1902–10. Hall of Fame, 1978

Joss packed a solid career into only eight full seasons. He ranks second in all-time lowest ERA, with a 1.89 career average, and led the American League in ERA in 1904 and 1908. Joss led the AL in wins in 1907 with 27. He won 20 or more games in a season four consecutive years, 1905–08. He threw a perfect game against the White Sox in 1908. In all, Joss completed 234 of his 260 career starts. He died in 1911 of meningitis.

LIFETIME STATS: W: 160, L: 97, SV: 5, ERA: 1.89, SO: 920, CG: 234

#673 Samuel Blair "Sam" Mertes

OF-2B, Phillies, Cubs, White Sox, Giants, Cardinals, 1896, 1898–1906

The swift Mertes ranked among league leaders for stolen bases from 1899 to 1905. Over that span, he averaged 45 stolen bases a year. Mertes led American League outfielders in assists with the 1902 White Sox, and the following year topped National League outfielders in fielding percentage as a Giant. Mertes was also an offensive threat, leading the NL in RBI (104) and doubles (32) in 1903.

LIFETIME STATS: BA: .279, HR: 40, RBI: 721, H: 1,227, SB: 396

#674 Michael Lewis "Mike" Greenwell

OF-DH, Red Sox, 1985–96

"Greenie" hit .300 or better in seven of his 12 major league seasons. He ranked second in AL MVP voting in 1988, hitting .325 with 22 home runs and 119 RBI. The successor in left field to Jim Rice, Greenwell averaged 93 RBI a season for Boston. He burst out of the gate his rookie year, homering for his first three hits with Boston in 1985. He hit a career-best 22 home runs with 119 RBI in 1988 and was a two-time All Star, in 1988 and 1989.

LIFETIME STATS: BA: .303, HR: 130, RBI: 726, H: 1,400, SB: 80

#675 Forest Glenn Wright

SS, Pirates, Brooklyn Robins, White Sox, 1924–33, 1935

Wright had unusual power for a shortstop, and was among league leaders in home runs and RBI in 1925 and 1930. He averaged 105 RBI over 11 seasons. In 1930, his second season in Brooklyn, Wright hit .321 with 126 RBI and 22 home runs. Wright was an agile fielder, leading the National League in double plays and assists his first two seasons in Pittsburgh. He also made an unassisted double play for the Pirates in a 1925 game against the Cardinals.

LIFETIME STATS: BA: .294, HR: 94, RBI: 723, H: 1,219, SB: 38

#676 Frederick Joseph "Freddy" Patek

SS, Pirates, Royals, Angels, 1968–81

The diminutive (5'5") Patek was nonetheless a terror on the base paths, and was one of the top six stolen base leaders 1971–78 in the American League. Patek led the AL in steals in 1977 with 53 and averaged 38 stolen bases a year, collecting 385 over a 14-season career. He led the league in triples with 11 in 1971. Patek was not a great hitter during the regular season, managing a career best of only .267 in 1971. But he hit .389 in both the 1976 and 1977 ALC against the Yankees.

LIFETIME STATS: BA: .242, HR: 41, RBI: 490, H: 1,340, SB: 385

#677 Mateo Rojas "Matty" Alou

OF-1B, Giants, Pirates, Cardinals, A's, Yankees, Padres, 1960–74

The best hitting of the three Alou brothers, Matty hit .300 or better in seven seasons. He led the National League in 1966 with a .342 average for the Pirates. Three years later, Matty topped the NL with 231 hits and 41 doubles. Brothers Jesus and Felipe played with him briefly on the Giants in 1963. Alou came over to the American League in 1972, and hit .381 in the A's ALCS against Detroit at age 34 to help deliver Oakland to the World Series.

LIFETIME STATS: BA: .307, HR: 31, RBI: 427, H: 1,777, SB: 156

#678 Joseph Vance "Joe" Ferguson

C-OF, Dodgers, Cardinals, Astros, Angels, 1970–83

Ferguson set a major league record for catchers in 1973 with only three errors in 700 or more chances. In addition to leading the league in fielding percentage, he also led NL catchers that year in double plays with 17. Not blessed with a lot of power, Ferguson did hit a career-best 25 home runs with 88 RBI in 1973. He hit a two-run home run off Vida Blue to lead the Dodgers to their only win over the A's in the 1974 World Series.

LIFETIME STATS: BA: .240, HR: 122, RBI: 445, H: 719, SB: 22

#679 Wilbert Robinson

C, Philadelphia A's, Orioles, Cardinals, 1886– 1902. Hall of Fame, 1945

Robinson, called "Uncle Robbie" for his happy personality, hit a career-best .353 with 98 RBI for Baltimore in 1894. He once logged seven hits in one game for the Orioles. Although a relatively rotund player, he was known for his endurance, once catching a tripleheader and then a double-header the following day as an Oriole. He went on to manage the Brooklyn Dodgers, leading them to the NL pennant in 1916 and 1920, and was elected to the Hall of Fame as a manager.

LIFETIME STATS: BA: .273, HR: 18, RBI: 722, H: 1,388, SB: 196

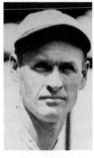

#680 Fred "Cy" Williams
OF, Cubs, Phillies, 1912–30

Williams was a slugging outfielder who led the National League in home runs four times. He shared the major league home run lead in 1923 with New York's Babe Ruth, when both hit 41 homers. Over the course of his 19-season career, Williams ranked among the top three in the NL for home runs 11 times. He could also hit for average, and batted .300 or better in six seasons. Williams belted seven career grand slams and also scored on 12 inside-the-park home runs.

LIFETIME STATS: BA: .292, HR: 251, RBI: 1,005, H: 1,981, SB: 115

#681 Ronald LeFlore
OF, Tigers, Expos, White Sox, 1974–82

LeFlore's story is an inspirational one, as he was signed by the Tigers while still in prison, serving a five-to-15 year sentence for armed robbery. He was a terror on the base paths, swiping 30 or more bases in six consecutive seasons, 1976–81. No jokes, please. Leflore stole 97 bases in 1980 with the Expos and ranks 46th in all-time stolen bases with 455. LeFlore led the AL in runs with 126 and stolen bases with 68 in 1978 as a Tiger. He hit safely in 27 straight games that year and strung together a 30-game hitting streak in 1976.

LIFETIME STATS: BA: .288, HR: 59, RBI: 353, H: 1,283, SB: 455

#682 Edwin Americus "Eddie" Rommel

RHP, Philadelphia A's, 1920–32

Rommel spent his entire career with the Athletics, and was usually the team's number two man, behind Lefty Grove. He led the American League in wins in 1922 with 27 and again in 1925 with 21. Also in 1922, Rommel finished second in AL MVP voting. He is known for one of the longest relief stints ever, 17 innings in an 18-inning 1932 game against the Indians. The A's ultimately lost, 18–17. A knuckleballer, Rommel was among the AL top eight in innings pitched from 1921 to 1925. He topped the league in games in 1923 with 56.

LIFETIME STATS: W: 171, L: 119, SV: 29, ERA: 3.54, SO: 599, CG: 147

#683 Douglas Lee "The Red Rooster" Rader

3B-1B, Astros, Padres, Blue Jays, 1967–77

Rader's nickname derived from his shock of flaming red hair. The agile Rader was a five-time NL Gold Glove winner, from 1970 to 1974. In addition, Rader led NL third basemen in assists three times, in 1970 and again in 1972 and 1973. His best year at the plate was 1972, when he had 90 RBI and socked 22 home runs for the Astros. Playing against the Cardinals in 1971, Rader tied an Astros franchise record of six RBI over the course of one game.

LIFETIME STATS: BA: .251, HR: 155, RBI: 722, H: 1,302, SB: 37

#684 Michael Lorri "Mike" Scioscia

C, Dodgers, 1980–92

Scioscia recorded the second-highest on-base percentage in the National League in 1985 with .407, while also hitting a career-best .296 with 26 doubles and 127 hits. Scioscia hit .364 in the Dodgers' 1988 NLCS win over the Mets, with a game-tying ninth-inning home run off Dwight Gooden in Game Four. After his playing career ended, Scioscia managed the Anaheim Angels to victory in the 2002 World Series.

LIFETIME STATS: BA: .259, HR: 68, RBI: 446, H: 1,131, SB: 29

#685 Wallace Wade "Wally" Moon

OF-1B, Cardinals, Dodgers, 1954–65

Moon was named NL Rookie of the Year in 1954, posting a .304 batting average, 76 RBI, 12 home runs, 193 hits and a career-best 18 stolen bases, beating out Hank Aaron. Moon was an offensive machine, leading the National League in triples in 1959 with 11. In 1959, he was traded to the Dodgers, and his home run shots over the right field wall of the Los Angeles Coliseum were called "Moon Shots." He won a Gold Glove with the Dodgers in 1960. Moon topped the NL in 1961 in on-base percentage, with .434.

LIFETIME STATS: BA: .289, HR: 142, RBI: 661, H: 1,399, SB: 89

#686 Roy Joseph Cullenbine

OF-1B, Tigers, Brooklyn Dodgers, St. Louis Browns, Senators, Yankees, Indians, 1938–47

Cullenbine was a reluctant batsman throughout his career. He was among the league leaders in walks from 1941 to 1947, topping the AL in 1945 by drawing 113 walks with the Tigers and Indians. Perhaps consequently, Cullenbine ranked among the top three in league on-base percentage four times. He still ranks 42nd in all-time on-base percentage with .408. But Cullenbine could hit, as his personal-best .335 batting average in 1946 and his .317 with 98 RBI for the Browns in 1941 attest. He ended up with 853 career bases on balls.

LIFETIME STATS: BA: .276, HR: 110, RBI: 599, H: 1,072, SB: 26

#687 Jeffrey Alan "Jeff" Burroughs

OF-DH, Senators, Rangers, Braves, Mariners, A's, Blue Jays, 1970–85

The muscular Burroughs spent four so-so years with the Senators and Rangers before busting out in 1974, when he was named AL MVP. Burroughs posted a .301 batting average with 25 home runs, while leading the league with 118 RBI for the Rangers. From 1973 to 1975, Burroughs ranked among the top five league leaders in home runs. Traded to Atlanta in 1977, Burroughs, hit a career-high 41 home runs for the Braves that year. Burroughs was an All Star as a Ranger in 1974 and as a Brave in 1978.

LIFETIME STATS: BA: .261, HR: 240, RBI: 882, H: 1,443, SB: 16

#**688** Arthur McArthur "Art" Devlin

3B-1B, New York Giants, Boston Braves, 1904–13

Devlin was not considered overly fast, but he was an excellent base runner, leading the NL In stolen bases in 1905 with 59 and averaging 35 stolen bases a year over a 10-season career. Devlin led NL third basemen in putouts and fielding percentage in 1908, and had the most assists among NL third basemen for three years from 1907 to 1909. He hit .250 with a double and three stolen bases during the 1905 World Series, helping the Giants to victory over the Philadelphia A's.

LIFETIME STATS: BA: .269, HR 10, RBI: 505, H: 1,185, SB: 285

#**689** Frederick "Fred" Tenney

1B-OF-C, Boston Braves, New York Giants, 1894–1909, 1911

Tenney was one of the most consistent hitters in the National League in the 1890s and 1900s. He hit .300 or better seven times from 1894 to 1903. He lead the NL in runs scored in 1908 with 101, and led the league in 1902 with 29 sacrifice hits. Tenney still ranks 20th on the all-time sacrifice hits leaders list with 275. In 1899, a career year with Boston, he batted .347 with 209 hits with 67 RBI and 28 stolen bases.

LIFETIME STATS: BA: .294, HR: 22, RBI: 688, H: 2,231, SB: 285

#690 Manuel Julian Javier

2B, Cardinals, Reds, 1960–72

Javier did not have a high career average—except when it came to the postseason. He batted .333 in four World Series. His biggest hit in that forum was a three-run home run in Game Seven of the 1967 World Series against the Red Sox to help lead the Cardinals to victory. Javier led the NL in sacrifice hits in 1960 with 15. He was voted twice to the All Star team, in 1963 and 1968. Javier was ranked among top 10 NL base stealers, from 1960 to 1963.

LIFETIME STATS: BA: .257, HR: 78, RBI: 506, H: 1,469, SB: 135

#691 William Edward "Bill" Melton

3B-DH-OF, White Sox, Angels, Indians, 1968–77

The slugging Melton led the American League in home runs in 1971 with 33. It was his second consecutive 33-home-run season. That home run crown was the first time in White Sox history that a player lead the league in home runs. He ultimately hit 154 home runs for the White Sox, which at the time led the White Sox franchise for career home runs. Melton was named to the All Star team in 1971, when he finished the season batting .269 with 86 RBI and 146 hits.

LIFETIME STATS: BA: .253, HR: 160, RBI: 591, H: 1,004, SB: 23

#692 August Rodney "Gus" Mancuso

C, Cardinals, Giants, Cubs, Brooklyn Dodgers, Phillies, 1928, 1930–45

Mancuso isn't remembered much these days, but he was ranked among the top 10 National League MVP vote-earners in 1933 and 1936. He was named to the All Star team in 1935 and 1937. Giant manager Bill Terry credited Mancuso's play as they key for the Giants' pennants in 1933, 1936 and 1937. In 1936, his best offensive year, Mancuso batted .301 with 63 RBI, nine home runs and 156 hits. He played in five World Series with the Cardinals and Giants.

LIFETIME STATS: BA: .265, HR: 53, RBI: 543, H: 1,194, SB: 8

#693 John Leonard "Pepper," "The Wild Horse of the Osage" Martin

OF-3B, Cardinals, 1928, 1930–40, 1944

The feisty Martin led the National League in stolen bases in 1933, 1934 and 1936. In addition, Martin led the league in runs scored in 1933, with 122. As good as Martin was during the regular season, it was his postseason play that made him a star. He batted .418 over three World Series, including .500 in the 1931 World Series, with five RBI and one home run to help the Cardinals stun the Philadelphia A's. That career average is the highest in World Series history by players with more than 50 at bats.

LIFETIME STATS: BA: .298, HR: 59, RBI: 501, H: 1,227, SB: 146

WILLIAM LANGE, Captain.
CHICAGO, 1896.

#694 William Alexander "Bill" Lange

OF-2B, Cubs, 1893–99

Lange had an abbreviated career because he retired to marry his girlfriend, a belle of San Francisco society. At the time, baseball players were thought to be ruffians, so Lange left the game to become a businessman. But as a player, he was great, hitting .300 or better in six of his seven seasons. He set the Cubs all-time season batting average record with .389 in 1895. He also ranked among league leaders in stolen bases from 1893 to 1897, including a league-topping 73 stolen bases in 1897. Lange was considered the best all-around outfielder of the 1890s. Oh yes, he divorced his wife after four years.

LIFETIME STATS: BA: .330, HR: 39, RBI: 578, H: 1,055, SB: 399

#695 Newton Henry "Newt" Allen

2B-SS-OF, Kansas City Tigers, All-Nations, Kansas City Monarchs, St. Louis Stars, Detroit Stars, Homestead Grays, Cincinnati Clowns (Negro Leagues), 1920–48

Allen was considered the best-fielding second baseman of the 1920s and 1930s. He spent most of his career with the Kansas City Monarchs, although there were brief stints with other teams. Allen had quick hands and a powerful throwing arm. The agile Allen was excellent at turning the double play. Available evidence indicates he began his career as a switch-hitter, but abandoned it as he got older. Allen played in three Black World Series with the Kansas City Monarchs, 1924, 1925 and 1942, as his team won all three. He hit seven doubles for the Monarchs in the first series against Hilldale.

LIFETIME STATS: BA: .288

#696 Ruben Angel Sierra

OF-DH, Rangers, A's, Yankees, Reds, Tigers, Reds, Blue Jays, White Sox, Mariners, Twins, 1986–2006

The much-traveled Sierra was the Rangers' MVP in both 1987 and 1988. In 1989, he led the American League with 119 RBI and 78 extra-base hits, as well as a .543 slugging percentage as a Ranger. He hit .307 with 25 home runs in 1991, and ranks 15th among active players in career at bats, with 7,539. Sierra has more sacrifice flies, 111, than any other active player. He was named to the All Star team four times.

LIFETIME STATS: BA: .268, HR: 306, RBI 1,322, H: 2,247, SB: 142

#697 Cleon Joseph Jones

OF, Mets, White Sox, 1963, 1965–76

Jones had a memorable 1969 season, helping the Mets reach the World Series, and posting career-best offensive numbers, including a .340 batting average, 92 runs scored, 75 RBI and 164 hits. He hit .429 with four RBI and one home run during the Mets three-game sweep of the Braves in the 1969 NLCS. He was voted to the All Star team in 1969. That was a career year, but Jones hit .297 with 29 doubles in 1968 and .319 with 24 doubles and 69 RBI in 1971. In 1974, his last year as a regular, Jones hit .282 with 23 doubles and 13 home runs.

LIFETIME STATS: BA: .281, HR: 93, RBI: 524, H: 1,196, SB: 91

#698 Adolfo "Dolf" Luque

RHP, Boston Braves, Reds, Brooklyn Dodgers, New York Giants, 1914–15, 1918–35

The Cuban-born Luque was also known as "the Pride of Havana" and led the NL in ERA in 1923, with a career-best 1.93, and again in 1925 with a 2.63 mark. The durable righty also led the league in 1923 with 27 wins and six shutouts. Overall Luque topped National League pitchers in shutouts three times, in 1921, 1923 and 1925. As a Giant, Luque earned a win in the fifth and final game of the 1933 World Series against the Senators.

LIFETIME STATS: W: 194, L: 179, SV: 28, ERA: 3.24, SO: 1,130, CG: 206

#699 Delino Lamont DeShields

2B-OF, Expos, Dodgers, Cardinals, Orioles, Cubs, 1990–2002

DeShields was a free-swinging, base-stealing second baseman who swiped 40 or more bases six times in his career, although he never led the league. His 463 thefts are 44th on the all-time list. DeShields' best season was in 1997, with the Cardinals, when he led the league in triples with 14, hit .295, stole 55 bases and popped a career-high 11 home runs. In all, DeShields hit .290 or better five times in his career

LIFETIME STATS: BA: .268, HR: 8,0 RBI: 561, H: 1,548, SB: 463

#700 Ralph Allen "Road Runner" Garr

OF, Braves, White Sox, Angels, 1968–80

The speedy Garr hit .300 or better during five seasons with the Braves and White Sox, and ranked among the league leaders in batting average five times. In 1974 Garr led the National League with a .353 batting average and 214 hits. He also led the NL in triples, in 1974 and again in 1975. Garr tallied more than 200 hits in a season three times with the Braves.

LIFETIME STATS: BA: .306, HR: 75, RBI: 408, H: 1,562, SB: 172

#701 Edward Robert "Eddie," "Eppie" Miller

SS-2B, Reds, Braves, Phillies, Cardinals, 1936–37, 1939–50

Miller led league shortstops in fielding from 1940 to 1943, and in 1945. Back with the Reds, the team he came up with, he topped the senior circuit with 38 doubles in 1947, and had a career high of 19 home runs and 87 RBI. He made the NL All Star squad seven times.

LIFETIME STATS: BA: .238, HR: 97, RBI: 640, H: 1,270, SB: 64

#702 John Joseph "Jack," "Rowdy Jack," "Peach Pie" O'Connor

C-OF-1B, Cincinnati (AA), Columbus (AA), Cleveland (NL), Cardinals, Phillies, Yankees, Browns, 1887–1904, 1906–07, 1910

"Rowdy Jack" spent 21 years in the majors, most notably from 1892 to 1898 with the Cleveland Spiders. He twice led the American Association catchers in fielding average, and in 1890 hit .324, his highest career average. He managed the pitiful 27–107 1910 Browns. His last day as a manager he had his third baseman play back so Cleveland's Nap Lajoie could drop down bunts so he could win the batting title over the despised Ty Cobb.

LIFETIME STATS: BA: .263, HR: 19, RBI: 738, H: 1,417, SB: 219

#703 Leon Lamar "Daddy Wags" Wagner

OF, Giants, Cardinals, Angels, Indians, White Sox, 1958–69

Named to the Sporting News Rookie Team of 1958, "Daddy Wags" resurrected his career thanks to the 1961 American League expansion club the Los Angeles Angels. The DH rule would have been ideal for Wagner, since he frequently swung for the fences with little regard for the defensive part of the game. He hit .280 with 28 home runs and 79 RBI as the fledgling Angels won an impressive 70 games. From 1961 to 1965 Wagner averaged 30 homers and 91 RBI.

LIFETIME STATS: BA: .272, HR: 211, RBI: 669, H: 1,202, SB: 54

#**704** William Haron "Bill" Bruton
OF, Braves, Tigers, 1953–1964

This slick-fielding center fielder led the NL in stolen bases his first three years and twice led the league in three-baggers. He also led the senior circuit in runs (112) and triples (13) in 1960. Though his knee forced him to miss the 1957 World Series, he bounced back the following year, hitting a robust .412 in the Fall Classic. He got traded to the Tigers, where he swatted a career high 17 home runs and garnered 74 RBI in 1962.

LIFETIME STATS: BA: .273, HR: 94, RBI: 545, H: 1,651, SB: 207

#**705** Samuel Filmore "Sammy" West
OF, Senators, Browns, White Sox, 1927–42

Taught outfield play by Hall of Famer Tris Speaker, West paid defensive dividends for the Senators, setting an AL record for defense with a .996 fielding average and leading the loop twice in fielding, putouts, and double plays as well as once in assists. He also hit better than .300 eight times in his career. In 1933, West got eight straight hits over two games, including a six-for-six game.

LIFETIME STATS: BA: .299, HR: 75, RBI: 838, H: 1,838, SB: 53

#706 Anthony John "Tony," "The Count," "The Apollo of the Box" Mullane

RHP, Detroit (NL), Lousville (AA), St Louis (AA), Toledo (AA), Cincinnati (AA), Cincinnati (NL), Baltimore (NL), Cleveland (NL), 1881–84, 1886–94

Mullane could throw with either hand as he would doff his glove and wait for a switch-hitter to dig in and then use the appropriate hand to throw his pitches. He won 30 or more games in his first five seasons, leading the American Association in shutouts twice. Mullane pitched 400 innings or more six times, and has 287 lifetime wins to his credit, but is not in the Hall of Fame. He also showed versatility by playing all other positions save for catching, as he switch-hit his way to a .243 career batting average

LIFETIME STATS: W: 284, L: 220, SV: 15, ERA: 3.05, SO: 1,803, CG: 468

#707 Bruce Petway

C-1B-OF, Leland Giants, Chicago American Giants, Detroit Stars (Negro Leagues), 1906–25

Petway gained notoriety in 1910, when, playing in a series of exhibition games against the Tigers, he reportedly threw out Ty Cobb three times in three attempts. Petway was a superior defensive catcher with a rocket arm, but he wasn't a great hitter. His best season in the Negro Leagues was hitting .331 in 1913 with the Chicago American Giants.

LIFETIME STATS: BA: .267

#**708** George Edward "Duffy" Lewis

OF, Red Sox, Yankees, Senators, 1910–17, 1919–21

Duffy Lewis was the left fielder for arguably the best defensive outfield in their era, with Tris Speaker in center and Harry Hooper manning right from 1910 to 1915. Fenway Park's left field had an incline affectionately known as "Duffy's Cliff," for the expert way Lewis played it. He was also adept at hitting two baggers, averaging 31 per season for nine years, and driving in 109 runs in 1912. Lewis also had the distinction of being the first to pinch-hit for Babe Ruth, then a rookie Red Sox pitcher, in 1914. He also hit .299 on three champion Red Sox clubs, including an impressive .444 in 1915.

LIFETIME STATS: BA: .284, HR: 38, RBI: 793, H: 1,518, SB: 113

#**709** John Martin Kruk

41B-OF, Padres, Phillies, White Sox, 1986–95

Kruk hit over .300 his first two years with the Padres, but slumped and then got dealt to the Phillies. Though his autobiography is entitled, "I Ain't An Athlete, Lady," the extraverted Kruk was embraced in Philly, and the burly Phil helped his team to the NL pennant in 1993 and hit .348 in the World Series. He was elected to the NL All Star team three times, and in his All Star Game appearance in 1993, he bowed to big southpaw Randy Johnson after the Big Unit threw a 100-mile-per-hour heater behind the left-handed-hitting Kruk.

LIFETIME STATS: BA: .300, HR: 100, RBI: 592, H: 1,170, SB: 58

#710 Clay Palmer "Hawk" Carroll

RHP, Braves, Reds, White Sox, Cardinals, Pirates, 1964–78

Sparky Anderson was called Captain Hook, but he had good reasons to go to his bullpen. One of them was the mainstay of the Big Red Machine's Pen—Clay "Hawk" Carroll, who recorded 88 relief wins and 143 saves, including 37 in 1972, then a major league record for a season, easily winning the Fireman of the Year Award. The Reds lost in five games to the Orioles in 1970 as Carroll got the only Red win, and Clay also won Game Seven in the classic 1975 Series against the Red Sox.

LIFETIME STATS: W: 96, L: 73, SV: 143, ERA: 2.94, SO: 681, CG: 1

#711 Michael Franklin "Mike," "Pinky" Higgins

3B, A's, Red Sox, Tigers, 1930, 1933–44, 1946

In 1938, Higgins set a major league record by hitting safely in 12 consecutive at bats and also drove in 106 runs twice in his career. He hit .333 in the 1940 World Series with Detroit, and was an AL All Star in 1934, 1936, and 1944. Higgins later managed the Bosox, earning the Sporting News Manager of the Year in his maiden season in Beantown (1957).

LIFETIME STATS: BA: .292, HR: 140, RBI: 1,075, H: 1,941, SB: 61

#712 William Joseph "Bill," "Moose" Skowron

1B, Yankees, Dodgers, Senators, White Sox, Angels, 1954–67

Dubbed "Mussolini" as an infant by his grandfather, "Moose" took advantage of the short porch in Yankee Stadium's right field with the perfect inside-out right-handed swing. He hit over .300 five times, including .340 his rookie season. An All Star six times, he also played in eight Series in nine years. Moose proved his mettle in the clutch as he led the Yanks to the 1958 World Championship over the Braves with the game winning RBI in Game Six, and then capped off his fine performance with a big three-run homer in Game Seven.

LIFETIME STATS: BA: .282, HR: 211, RBI: 888, H: 1,566, SB: 16

#713 Harold Craig Reynolds

2B, Mariners, Orioles, Angels, 1983-94

An All Star in 1987 and 1988, this smooth-fielding infielder also won the Gold Glove at second in 1988, 1989, and 1090. In 1987, Reynolds led the AL in total chances, putouts, assists and double plays. He also showed great speed on the base paths, swiping a Mariner-record 60 bases and leading the league in 1987, while batting ninth in the order! Reynolds is now a baseball analyst on ESPN.

LIFETIME STATS: BA: .258, HR: 21, RBI: 353, H: 1,233, SB: 150

#714 Dwayne Keith Murphy

OF, A's, Tigers, Phillies, 1978–89

Murphy's tremendous range in center field helped him win six straight Gold Gloves (1980–85) and led AL flychasers in putouts in 1980, 1982, and 1984. He also hit a gaudy .545 in the 1981 Division Series against the Royals and led the league in game winning RBI with 15 that year.

LIFETIME STATS: BA: .246, HR: 166, RBI: 609, H: 1,069, SB: 100

#715 Alvin Glenn Davis

1B-DH, Mariners, Angels, 1984–92

Davis was the Rookie of the Year in 1984 with 27 homers and 116 RBI. His stats declined in 1990 with his move to the DH role, but Davis was the early leader in most Mariner offensive categories (since surpassed). He was one of the Mariners' first stars.

LIFETIME STATS: BA: .280, HR: 160, RBI: 683, H: 1,189, SB: 7

#716 Robert Clinton "Bobby" Richardson

2B, Yankees, 1955–66

Playing on seven Yankee pennant winners, Richardson became the first and only player on a losing team to win the World Series MVP Award with his 12 RBI, including a grand slam against the Pirates, in 1960. He also snared the screaming liner off the bat of the Giants' Willie McCovey that saved Game Seven for the Yankees in 1962. He led the AL in double plays four times and won five straight Gold Gloves. Now a minister in his native South Carolina, Richardson garnered a league-best 209 hits in 1962 and came in second in the MVP balloting to his teammate Mickey Mantle.

LIFETIME STATS: BA: .266, HR: 34, RBI: 390, H: 1,432, SB: 73

#717 Joseph Gregg "JoJo," "The Gause Ghost," "The Thin Man" Moore
OF, Giants, 1930–41

This lefty-hitting slaphitter hit over .300 five times in his first seven seasons and set the table for renowned Giants' sluggers Bill Terry and Mel Ott. He helped the Giants win the 1933 World Series, including two hits in the same inning, and hit .391 in a Series loss to the Yanks in 1937, including a then-record nine hits in the five game Series.

LIFETIME STATS: BA: .298, HR: 79, RBI 513, H: 1,615, SB: 46

#718 Tommie Lee Agee
OF, Indians, White Sox, Mets, Astros, Cardinals, 1962–73

Agee was the AL Rookie of the Year in 1966. Agee was one of the best defensive infielders of the 1960s, appearing in two All Star Games and winning a pair of Gold Gloves. He is best known for the two sensational catches he made in Game Three for the Miracle Mets in their upset of the Baltimore Orioles. He even added a homer in the game.

LIFETIME STATS: BA: .255, HR: 130, RBI: 433, H: 999, SB: 167

#**719** Joseph Franklin "Joe" Vosmik

OF, Indians, Browns, Red Sox, Dodgers, Senators, 1930–41, 1944

Vosmik's best years ended after the age of 29, but the left fielder hit more than .300 in six of his first eight years, averaging 81 RBI and hit higher than .340 twice. Vosmik had a career year in 1935, leading the AL in hits with 216, doubles with 47, triples with 20 with 110 RBI and a .348 batting average. He also led the league in hits (201) with the 1938 Red Sox and hit .324.

LIFETIME STATS: BA: .307, HR: 65, RBI: 874, H: 1,682, SB: 23

#**720** Andres Antonio "Tony" Gonzalez

OF, Reds, Phillies, Padres, Braves, Angels, 1960–71

Gonzalez spent his first eight years with the Phils, when he led NL outfielders in fielding thrice, including in 1962, where he played errorless ball in 276 chances, becoming the first center fielder ever to field a perfect 1.000. He hit a high of .339 in 1967, good for second in the NL (and in the majors). He also hit .357 in the 1969 League Championship Series for the Braves in a losing effort against the Mets.

LIFETIME STATS: BA: .286, HR: 103, RBI: 615, H: 1,485, SB: 79

#**721** Danilo "Danny" Tartabull

OF-DH Mariners, Royals, Yankees, A's, White Sox,
Phillies, 1984–97

Son of major leaguer Jose Tartabull, a singles contact hitter, Danny was quite a different story; Danny had five
100 RBI seasons and three 30-home-runs years. The
younger Tartabull was an All Star in 1991 as he hit a
career best .316 with a .593 slugging percentage. The
Yankees signed him as a free agent in 1992, and the next year he hit 31 home
runs with 102 RBI, but also struck out a whopping 156 times.

LIFETIME STATS: BA: .273, HR: 262, RBI: 925, H: 1,366, SB: 37

#**722** Paul Howard "Dizzy" Trout

RHP, Tigers, Red Sox, Orioles, 1939–52, 1957

Forming a superb lefty-righty combo with lefty Hal Newhouser for the Tigers between 1944 and 1946, in 1944
Paul Howard "Dizzy" Trout went 27–14, compiling a
league-leading 2.12 ERA, with 33 complete games and
seven shutouts in 352 innings of work. He also hit .271
with five homers and 24 RBI. In 1945, he "slumped" to
18 wins, but showed his durability by pitching in six games in nine days in
the heat of that year's pennant race, leading the Tigers to the World Series.
Trout capped it off with a five-hitter in the Fall Classic against the Cubs for
the World Champion Tigers.

**LIFETIME STATS: W: 170, L: 161, SV: 35, ERA: 3.23, SO: 1,256,
CG: 158**

#723 Tito Francona

OF-1B Orioles, White Sox, Tigers, Indians, Cardinals, Phillies, Braves, A's, Brewers, 1956–70

Francona, father of big-league manager Terry Francona, was a contact hitter who proved to be a valuable bench player, especially toward the end of his career. In 1959, he hit .363, but didn't have enough at bats to qualify for the AL batting title, with only 999 at bats. He also slugged .566 for the Tribe that year. In 1961, Francona was an All Star, hitting .301 that season.

LIFETIME STATS: BA: .272, HR: 125, RBI: 656, H: 1,395, SB: 46

#724 Raymond Lewis "Ray" Lankford

OF, Cardinals, Padres, 1990–2002

Lankford combined power and speed for the Cardinals in the '90s, stealing 44 and 42 bases in 1991 and 1992. He also enabled the Cardinals to bat him either leadoff or cleanup, although he did strike out often. His best offensive years were in 1997 and 1998 as he hit 31 homers both years, with 98 and 105 RBI while hitting .295 and .293. Lankford was capable of going on torrid streaks, but he would also be mired in terrible slumps. The outspoken left fielder was traded to the Padres in 2001 after slumping to .253 in 2000.

LIFETIME STATS: BA: .272, HR: 232, RBI: 852, H: 1,510, SB: 256

#**725** James Christopher "Jim" Delahanty

2B-3B-OF, Cubs, Giants, Braves, Reds, Browns, Senators, Tigers, Brooklyn (FL), 1901–02, 1904–12, 1914–15

Brother of four other major leaguers, including Hall of Famer Ed, Jim Delahanty could play every position but catcher. In 1909, Joe helped the Tigers win their third consecutive pennant and was the leading hitter in the 1909 World Series, hitting at a .346 clip in a losing effort against the Pirates. His best campaign was 1911, as Delahanty hit .339 with 83 runs scored and 94 RBI.

LIFETIME STATS: BA: .283, HR: 19, RBI: 489, H: 1,159, SB: 151

#**726** Lawrence Curtis "Larry" Jackson

RHP, Cardinals, Cubs, Phillies, 1955–68

Jackson was named to the NL All Star team four times and he led the senior circuit with 24 wins in 1964 while hurling for the eighth place Cubs. He was regarded as a fine fielding pitcher, handling 109 chances flawlessly during that career year. After his playing career, Jackson served four terms in his native Idaho's state legislature.

LIFETIME STATS: W: 194, L: 183, SV: 20, ERA: 3.40, SO: 1,709, CG: 149

#727 Ellis Rena Burks

OF, Red Sox, White Sox, Rockies, Giants, Indians, 1987–2004

Burks, a very good clutch hitter in his career, hit .378 with men in scoring position for the Giants in 1999, third best in the league. He's also hit 10 grand slams in his first 13 years in the bigs and drove in seven runs in one game against his former team, the Rockies. Speaking of the Rockies, Burks came into his own in Colorado in 1996, where he hit .344, belted 40 homers, drove in 128 with 211 hits and had 32 stolen bases, finishing third in the NL MVP race. Burks and Hank Aaron are the only players in major league history with at least 40 HR, 200 hits, and 30 steals in the same season.

LIFETIME STATS: BA: .291, HR: 352, RBI: 1,206, H: 2,107, SB: 181

#728 Frank Witman "Frankie," "Blimp" Hayes

C, A's, Browns, Indians, White Sox, Red Sox, 1933–34, 1936–47

An All Star five times, Hayes was an excellent defensive catcher, leading AL catchers in total chances per game three times, and twice in fielding, putouts, and double plays. He also proved to be a durable backstop as he set an AL record of 155 games in 1944. Offensively, his high water mark was in 1939, when he hit .283 with 20 home runs and 83 RBI.

LIFETIME STATS: BA: .259, HR: 119, RBI: 628, H: 1,164, SB: 30

#729 James Carlisle "Red" Smith

3B-OF, Dodgers, Braves, 1911–19

Red Smith joined the miracle Boston Braves in August of 1914 just in time for the pennant drive. Helped by his sterling play at third base, the Braves won it all that year. Smith led all NL third sackers in putouts, assists, double plays, and total chances per game while also hitting .314. Unfortunately he missed the World Series due to injury. He also led the NL with 40 doubles with Brooklyn in 1913.

LIFETIME STATS: BA: .278, HR: 27, RBI: 514, H: 1,087, SB: 117

#730 Tully Frederick "Topsy" Hartsel

OF, Louisville, Reds, A's, 1898–1911

Hartsel was known to be a very patient contact hitter as he took advantage of his diminutive 5'5" frame and his keen eye at the plate to lead the league in bases on balls five times and on-base percentage twice. He was also a speedy base runner, as he led the loop in stolen bases once and pilfered 246 in his career.

LIFETIME STATS: BA: .276, HR: 31, RBI: 341, H: 1,336. SB: 247

#731 Oswaldo Jose "Ozzie" Guillen

SS, White Sox, Orioles, Braves, Devil Rays,
1985–2000

A three-time All Star, Guillen was the AL Rookie of the
Year in 1985 and a Gold Glove winner in 1990. He
swiped 36 bases in 1989 and was a steady contact hitter
and a threat on the bases throughout his career. Guillen
had great range as twice in his career he surpassed 800
total chances. He started out in the Padres chain, and he became the second
slick-fielding shortstop named Ozzie to be dealt by San Diego. (Ozzie Smith,
of course, is the other one). He proved to be clutch in the LCS in 1998 and
1999 for Atlanta, hitting .417 in 1998 and plating the tying run in the 1999
LCS against the Mets.

LIFETIME STATS: BA: .264, HR: 28, RBI: 619, H: 1,764, SB: 169

#732 James Erigena "Jimmy" Barrett

OF, Reds, Tigers, Red Sox, 1899–1908

Barrett had a great arm as he led outfielders in assists for
three of the first four years the American League existed.
He also had a keen eye at the plate, leading the league in
walks twice and hitting the .300 mark four times. Because
of his discipline at the plate and his ability to put the ball
in play, he also led the league in on-base percentage in 1903.

LIFETIME STATS: BA: .291, HR: 16, RBI: 255, H: 962, SB: 143

#**733** Vida Rochelle Blue

LHP, A's, Giants, Royals, 1969–83, 1985–86

After being farmed out in 1970, Blue came on like gang-busters, throwing an auspicious no-hitter against the Twins in September. Then came 1971. Not only did Blue post a 24–8 record, he threw eight shutouts, struck out 301, and had an unbelievable 1.82 ERA as he dominated AL batters. He was awarded both the Cy Young and the MVP Awards that year. He never approached that year again, but he did go 20–9 as the A's won their third straight championship in 1973. He won 22 in 1975 and then with the Giants went 18–10 in 1978 and became the first player to start for both teams in the All Star Game. Blue sat out the 1984 season because of a drug charge, and then resurfaced with the Giants for two mediocre seasons.

LIFETIME STATS: W: 209, L: 161, SV: 2, ERA: 3.26, SO: 2,175, CG: 143

#**734** Anthony Christopher "Tony" Kubek

SS-OF, Yankees, 1957–65

Kubek, known as a shortstop, could play any infield or outfield position. He was named Rookie of the Year in 1957 as he hit .297 and starred in the World Series against his hometown Milwaukee Braves team, clubbing two homers in a 12–3 Yank victory. The World Series gods didn't smile on Kubek in 1960 when he took a would-be double-play grounder in the throat, rendering him unable to speak as the Bucs rallied to go ahead and eventually win Game Seven 10–9 in 1960. A bad back forced Kubek to retire and he landed in the broadcast booth for NBC Sports, providing color commentary on baseball telecasts.

LIFETIME STATS: BA: .266, HR: 57, RBI: 373, H: 1,109, SB: 29

#**735** Charles Lincoln "Buck" Herzog
2B-3B-SS, Giants, Braves, Reds, Cubs, 1908–20

Buck Herzog had 312 career stolen bases—and 10 of them were of home. Once he stole second, third, and home in the same game and had 23 hits in 25 World Series games with the Giants, and in 1912, he hit .400 in the Fall Classic. Later on in his career, he was a player-manager and was part of a trade for three future Hall of Famers (Christy Mathewson, Edd Roush and Bill McKechnie) in 1916.

LIFETIME STATS: BA: .259, HR: 20, RBI: 445, H: 1,370, SB: 312

#**736** William Chester "Jake," "Baby Doll" Jacobson
OF, Tigers, Browns, Red Sox, Indians, A's, 1915, 1917, 1919–27

On Opening Day in Mobile, Alabama, in 1912, while the band was playing the then hit "Oh, You Beautiful Doll," Jake Jacobson smacked a home run, and a nickname was born. "Baby Doll" Jacobson was an excellent all-around player, surpassing .300 for seven straight years for a slugging Browns club. Though he was big for his day (6'3", 215 pounds), he was an outstanding outfielder, at one time holding 15 fielding records including 488 putouts on 1924.

LIFETIME STATS: BA: .311, HR: 83, RBI: 819, H: 1,714, SB: 86

#737 James Francis "Pud," "Gentle Jeems," "The Little Steam Engine" Galvin

RHP, Reds, Buffalo, Pittsburgh, Cardinals, 1879–92.
Hall of Fame, 1965

James Francis Galvin, called "Pud" (short for "Pudding," because of his 300 pounds and his girth) was a solid pitcher who usually lost as many games as he won. Galvin had a great pickoff move, once nailing three runners in one inning. Galvin had two seasons with 46 wins, another with 37, and seven others with between 20 and 29 victories. He also lost 20 or more games nine times and 30 or more once. Galvin is second only to Cy Young, with 5,941 innings pitched and 630 complete games.

LIFETIME STATS: W: 364, L: 310, SV: 2, ERA: 2.86, SO: 1,806, CG: 646

#738 Elmer Ellsworth Smith

LHP-OF, Cincinnati (AA), Pirates, Reds, Giants, Braves, 1886–89, 1892–1901

Babe Ruth wasn't the first to change positions from a pitcher to an outfielder. Elmer Smith, sometimes called Mike Smith in the record books, won 34 games in 1887 with a league-best 2.94 ERA, and then won 22 more the following season before being plagued by arm woes. Tearing up the minors with his bat, Smith returned as an outfielder with the Bucs, consistently hitting over .300, including a remarkable .356 in 1894 and .362 in 1896. Smith swung a 54-ounce bat and had great range and a strong arm in the outfield, despite his early pitching injuries.

LIFETIME STATS: W: 75, L: 57, ERA: 3.35, SO: 525, CG: 122, BA: .310, HR: 37, RBI: 663, H: 1,454, SB: 232

#**739** Henry Morgan "Hank" Gowdy

C, Giants, Braves, 1910–17, 1919–25, 1929–30

Gowdy was a great defensive catcher for the Braves, but also hit well in the clutch as he hit a lusty .545 in the shocking sweep of the mighty Philadelphia A's in the 1914 World Series. Gowdy missed all of 1918 as he was the first major league player to serve in World War I. Gowdy caught two no-hitters, George Davis on September 9, 1914 and, Tom Hughes on June 16, 1916.

LIFETIME STATS: BA: .270, HR: 21, RBI: 322, H: 738, SB: 59

#**740** Donald Albert "Don," "Tiger" Hoak

3B, Dodgers, Cubs, Reds, Pirates, Phillies, 1954–64

Nicknamed "Tiger" because of his former boxing career and his pugnacious attitude, Hoak was the tenacious leader of the 1960 World Champion Pirates team, hitting .282 with 16 homers and 79 RBI and topping the NL in runs with 97. Hoak was named to the NL All Star team in 1957, with the Reds, as he hit .293 with 19 home runs and 89 RBI while leading the league in doubles with 39. Don Hoak is the trivia answer in the movie "City Slickers" when the woman cattledriver asks: "Why are men so concerned with who played third base for the 1960 Pittsburgh Pirates?" as Billy Crystal, Daniel Stern, and Bruno Kirby all shout in unison, "DON HOAK!"

LIFETIME STATS: BA: .265, HR: 89, RBI: 498, H: 1,144, SB: 64

#**741** Wallace "Wally," "Peepsight" Moses

OF, A's, White Sox, Red Sox, 1935–51

Moses hit over .300 each of his seven seasons with the A's. In 1937, he clouted 25 homers and slugged .550. He also had a spectacular year on the base paths in 1943 as he stole 56 bases despite never stealing more than 21 in any other year. He hit .417 in his only World Series, with the 1946 Red Sox, getting four hits in one game. After his playing days were over, Moses became a highly regarded hitting coach.

LIFETIME STATS: BA: .291, HR: 89, RBI: 679, H: 2,138, SB: 174

#**742** Walter Clement "Wally" Pipp

1B, Tigers, Yankees, Reds, 1913, 1915–26

Because of a headache caused by a beaning, Pipp asked out of the Yankee lineup in 1925, and never got his job back because his replacement was none other than the "Iron Horse" himself, Lou Gehrig. Pipp was no slouch either, as he led the AL in HR in 1916 and 1917, hit .329 in 1922 and was the first sacker on the Bombers first three pennant winners. In 1924, Pipp hit .295, drove in 114 and led the league with a now unheard of total of 19 triples.

LIFETIME STATS: BA: .281, HR: 90, RBI: 997, H: 1,941, SB: 125

#743 Thomas P. "Tom," "Oyster" Burns

OF-SS, Wilmington (U), Baltimore (AA), Brooklyn (AA), Giants, 1884–85, 1887–95

Tom Burns, called Oyster supposedly because of his love for the food, was the captain of the 1887 Baltimore Orioles, slugging .519 and hitting 33 doubles, a league-leading 19 triples and a batting average of .341. He led the NL in 1890 during the "dead ball" Era with 13 homers and 128 RBI. After he hung up his spikes, he briefly became an umpire.

LIFETIME STATS: BA: .300, HR: 65, RBI: 832, H: 1,389, SB: 263

#744 Eugene Franklin "Bubbles" Hargrave

C, Cubs, Reds, Yankees, 1913–15, 1921–28, 1930

Bubbles Hargrave was the first catcher to win a batting title with a .353 average in 1926. Bubbles, who got his nickname because of his difficulty pronouncing the "B" sound, broke a string of six consecutive batting crowns by the Rajah, Hall of Famer Rogers Hornsby. Hargrave hit over .300 from 1922–27 with the Reds, and his best overall season was in 1923 when he hit .333 with 10 home runs and 78 RBI. He also led NL catchers in fielding in 1927.

LIFETIME STATS: BA: .310, HR: 29, RBI: 376, H: 786, SB: 29

#**745** August Richard "Gus" Suhr

1B, Pirates, Phillies, 1930–40

Suhr was best known for holding the National League record for consecutive games played, with 822, when he snapped the streak to attend his mother's funeral. Known as a great fielder, Suhr led NL first basemen in putouts and double plays in 1938. In 1930 he was walked six times in one game and that year he also drove in 107 runs.

LIFETIME STATS: BA: .279, HR: 84, RBI: 818, H: 1,446, SB: 53

#**746** Steven F. "Steve" Kemp

OF-DH, Tigers, White Sox, Yankees, Pirates, Rangers, 1977–86, 1988

Kemp enjoyed an All Star year in 1979, stroking 26 homers and knocking in 105 while slugging .543. He then knocked in 101 more in 1980 with Detroit. After a brief stint with the Chicago White Sox, Kemp signed with the Yankees, but the injury-plagued Kemp only hit 19 home runs in two seasons with the Bombers.

LIFETIME STATS: BA: .278, HR: 130, RBI: 634, H: 1,128, SB: 39

#747 Lawrence J. "Larry" Corcoran

RHP, Cubs, Giants, Washington (NL), Indianapolis (NL), 1880–87

Corcoran was superb in his first four years, including three no-hitters, a 43–14 record as a rookie, and a league-best 268 strikeouts and a microscopic 1.95 ERA. He also pitched 536 1/3 innings, running off 13 straight wins at one point. And he only weighed 120 pounds! He went 31–14 in 1881, and 27–12 in 1882, topping the league with a 1.95 ERA. In 1883, he was 34–20. Corcoran and his batterymate Silver Flint may have been the first pitcher-catcher tandem to use pitching signs. Arm trouble curtailed Corcoran's career.

LIFETIME STATS: W: 177, L: 89, SV: 2, ERA: 2.36, SO: 1,103, CG: 256

#748 Harold Homer "Hal," "Prince Hal" Chase

1B, Yankees, White Sox, Buffalo, Reds, Giants, 1905–19

Chase was regarded as a slick-fielding first baseman. Later in his career, however, he also reportedly threw games when he bet on his opponents. A rarity in that he threw left, but batted right, Chase led the NL in home runs in 1915, won the hitting title in 1916 and hit over .300 five times. The fleet-footed Chase stole 363 bases in his career. After many suspensions, Chase was finally banned from baseball in 1919.

LIFETIME STATS: BA: .291, HR: 57, RBI: 941, H: 2,158, SB: 363

#**749** Von Francis Hayes

OF-1B, Indians, Phillies, Angels, 1981–92

Hayes was traded to Philadelphia in December 1982 for five players, and helped the Phils reach the World Series in 1983. He led the NL in runs and doubles in 1986 and hit .305. Hayes was an All Star in 1989 when he hit 26 homers, three coming in a single game. He retired in 1992 because of injuries.

LIFETIME STATS: BA: .267, HR: 143, RBI: 696, H: 1,402, SB: 253

#**750** Jose Rosario Domec Cardenal

OF-1B, Giants, Angels, Indians, Cardinals, Brewers, Cubs, Phillies, Mets, Royals, 1963–80

Speedy, but considered moody, Cardenal played for nine clubs in 18 seasons. While with the Indians, he made two unassisted double plays from his outfield position. He blossomed in the friendly confines of Wrigley Field in 1972 and 1973 where he hit .300 for the first time as he paced the Cubbies in batting, steals, and doubles. In 1976, Cardenal went six-for-seven in an extra inning contest. He also helped the Royals in the stretch run of 1980, hitting an impressive .340, and finally won a World Series ring with Kansas City.

LIFETIME STATS: BA: .275, HR: 138, RBI: 775, H: 1,913, SB: 329

#**751** Lloyd Anthony Moseby

OF, Blue Jays, Tigers, 1980–91

Moseby didn't quite live up to very high expectations in Toronto, but he did have flashes of brilliance. In 1983, he became the first Jay to score 100 runs, had a 21-game hitting streak, hit .315, and stole 27 bases. In 1984, Moseby led the AL with 15 triples, stole 39 bases and had 92 RBI. He finished his major league career in Detroit, then played a year in Japan, and later on became a Blue Jay coach.

LIFETIME STATS: BA: .257, HR: 169, RBI: 737, H: 1,494, SB: 280

#**752** "Uncle Bill" Monroe

2B-1B-3B-SS, Chicago Union Giants, Chicago Unions, Philadelphia Giants, New York Quaker Giants, Brooklyn Royal Giants, Chicago American Giants (Negro Leagues), 1896–1914

Uncle Bill Monroe was an exciting infielder, mostly at second base, for some of the best black teams in the country during the early 1900s. He was on Rube Foster's Chicago American Giants when they won the 1913 and 1914 black Western Championships. Monroe got four hits in the 1914 Black World Series in Game Three as Monroe's Giants swept his former team, the Brooklyn Royal Giants. He once hit .333 in the Cuban Winter League and John McGraw thought he was capable of All Star play in the white major leagues.

LIFETIME STATS: BA: .305

#**753** John Bernard "Hans," "Honus" Lobert

3B-SS, Pirates, Cubs, Reds, Phillies, Giants, 1903, 1905–17

Hans Lobert was a four-time 300 hitter called Honus because he resembled the great Honus Wagner. The fleet-footed, though bow-legged Lobert stole 30 or more bases seven times, including six of home plate. He was once clocked running the bases in 13.8 seconds and was known to race anyone or anything including horses, cars, motorcycles and professional runners.

LIFETIME STATS: BA: .274, HR: 32, RBI: 482, H: 1,252, SB: 316

#**754** Willie Edward "Puddinhead" Jones

3B, Phillies, Indians, Reds 1947–61

Jones was the third baseman on the 1950 Phillies "Whiz Kids" pennant winner as he hit 25 homers, drove in 88, and scored an even 100 runs. He was named to the NL All Star squad that year as well as in 1951. "Puddinhead" led all Senior Circuit third-sackers in fielding five of six years, including four straight years (1953–56). He also tied a major league record in his rookie season by stroking four doubles in a row in one game.

LIFETIME STATS: BA: .258, HR: 190, RBI: 812, H: 1,502, SB: 40

#**755** James Ray "Jim" Hart
3B-OF, Giants, Yankees, 1963–74

Hart would have been the ideal DH, but he was born 10 years too early. He broke in in 1964 and hit 31 homers, a Giants rookie record and third in the league. He only hit 23 the following year, but hit a career best .299 and drove in 96 runs. He was a poor fielder as he led NL third basemen in errors in 1965, and even admitted to reporters that he hated playing defense. But with a bat in his hand, he was lethal, as he averaged 29 homers and 92 RBI and hit .291. Then his career went downhill due to alcohol and injuries. The last highlight of his career was in 1970 when he hit for the cycle and drove in six runs.

LIFETIME STATS: BA: .278, HR: 170, RBI: 578, H: 1,052, SB: 17

#**756** Octavio Victor "Cookie" Rojas
2B-OF, Reds, Phillies, Cardinals, Royals, 1962–77

Cuban-born Cookie Rojas was chosen as the Phillies' best second baseman ever in 1969. He was very versatile—he played all 10 positions in his career (including DH). He was very capable with the glove as he led NL second sackers with a .987 fielding average and in 1968 helped the Royals set a team record of 192 double plays and led the AL in fielding twice. He was an All Star from 1971 to 1974 with Kansas City and hit .308 in two League Championship Series with the Royals.

LIFETIME STATS: BA: .263, HR: 54, RBI: 593, H: 1,660, SB: 74

LU BLUE
FIRST BASE, DETROIT AMERICANS

#**757** Luzerne Atwell "Lu" Blue,

1B, Tigers, Browns, White Sox, Dodgers, 1921–33

Blue, though not your typical powerful first baseman, got on base often. Four times in his career, this switch-hitter drew more than 100 free passes, and had two seasons with 126 and 127 bases on balls. He also hit .300 or better in four of his first five seasons. Blue is one of the few major leaguers buried in Arlington National Cemetery, as he was a veteran of World War I.

LIFETIME STATS: BA: .287, HR: 44, RBI: 695, H: 1,696, SB: 151

#**758** Timothy James "Tim" Salmon

OF-DH, Angels, 1992–2005

In 1990, while in the minors, Tim Salmon was hit by a pitch in the jaw, but bounced back three months later and just three years later was honored as the AL's Rookie of the Year, with the Angels, a team he has spent his entire career with. He hit .283, with 31 homers and 95 RBI in that rookie year of 1993 (he was called up late in 1992 but was still considered a rookie in 1993). In 1995 Salmon continued to put up fine numbers with 34 home runs, 105 RBI and a .330 batting average. Two years later, he knocked in 129 more runs. He helped the surprising Angels capture the 2002 World Series over the Giants as he went four-for-four in Game Two, smacking two two-run homers, the last one the winning margin in an 11–10 Anaheim win. Salmon was also named the AL Comeback Player of the Year in 2002.

LIFETIME STATS: BA: .282, HR: 299, RBI: 1,016, H: 1,674, SB: 48

#759 Charles Taylor "Charlie," "Piano Legs" Hickman

1B-2B-OF-3B, Braves, Giants, Red Sox, Indians, Tigers, Senators, White Sox, 1897–1908

Because of his immense limbs that supported his 5'9" body, Hickman was dubbed "Piano Legs," and he was one of the first sluggers in the game, just missing a Triple Crown in 1902 with a .361 average, 11 homers and 110 RBI, second in all three categories. He committed a record 86 errors at third base in 1900. Managers would often move him elsewhere to keep his potent bat in the lineup, but hoping the ball wouldn't be hit to him. Hickman even tried pitching briefly, compiling a 10–8 record, including three shutouts and four saves.

LIFETIME STATS: BA: .295, HR: 59, RBI: 614, H: 1,176, SB: 72

#760 Joseph Anthony "Joe," "Jumpin' Joe" Dugan

3B-SS-2B, Athletics, Red Sox, Yankees, Braves, Tigers, 1917–29, 1931

"Jumping Joe" Dugan got his nickname from leaving, or "jumping," teams without authorization early in his playing days. He was obtained by the Yankees from Boston in the middle of the 1922 season, and the deal sparked so much controversy that the June 15 trading deadline was established. The tall, athletic Dugan became a fine third baseman; he started out slowly, only hitting .194 and .195 in his first two years, but rebounded to a career high of .322 in 1920. Dugan was a key to the early Yankee success as he was an integral part of five pennant winners with the Bronx Bombers, including the "Murderers' Row" team of 1927.

LIFETIME STATS: BA: .280, HR: 42, RBI: 571, H: 1,515, SB: 37

#761 William Barney McCosky

OF, Tigers, A's, Reds, Indians, 1939–42, 1946–48, 1950–53

McCoskey had a terrific first two seasons as the Tigers' leadoff hitter, batting .311 with 190 hits and 120 runs in 1939, and .340 with 200 hits (a league best) and 123 runs in 1940. He didn't have much power, but he made up for it by getting on base and getting his share of doubles and triples, leading the league in three-base hits with 19 in 1940. The Tigers' acquisition of slugger Rudy York to play first base forced the lumbering Hank Greenberg to play left, so center fielder McCoskey had even more real estate to cover. An injury to his neck forced the early retirement of this American League star.

LIFETIME STATS: BA: .312, HR: 24, RBI: 397, H: 1,301, SB: 58

#762 Robert Lee "Bob," "Parisian Bob" Caruthers

RHP-OF, St. Louis (AA), Brooklyn (AA), Dodgers, Browns, 1884–93

Though he also played the outfield and hit .282 lifetime, "Parisian Bob" was more known as a hurler, leading two different teams to five pennants in the mid- to late-1880s. He got his unique nickname by negotiating, along with his catcher, with his owner directly from Paris while vacationing there. From 1885 to 1889, he never won fewer than 29 games and even won a league-leading 40 in 1885 and 1889. He stood only 5'7" and weighed 138 pounds, but his deceptive delivery and his guile were a prescription for success. In 1886, Caruthers became the first pitcher to stroke four extra-base hits in one game when he swatted two homers, a double and a triple. The following year Caruthers started 39 games and played 61 in the field, hitting .357 with eight home runs and 49 stolen bases.

LIFETIME STATS: W: 218, L: 99, SV: 3, ERA: 2.83, SO: 900, CG: 298. BA: .282, HR: 29, RBI: 359, H: 695, SB: 152

#**763** Spurgeon Ferdinand "Spud" Chandler

RHP, Yankees, 1937–47

A four-time All Star, Spud Chandler, who made the majors when he was 29, set the record for career winning percentage for pitchers with over 100 or more games (.717). The right-handed control hurler was fabulous for the Yanks in 1943 when he went 20–4, leading the AL in victories, complete games (20), shutouts (5). and ERA (1.64), the lowest ERA in the league in over two decades. For his exploits, he was named AL MVP for that year. In 1940, Chandler even hit two home runs in a game, one of them a grand slam.

LIFETIME STATS: W: 109, L: 43, SV: 6, ERA: 2.84, SO: 614, CG: 109

#**764** Stanley Raymond "Bucky" Harris

2B, Senators, Tigers, 1919–29, 1931. Hall of Fame, 1975

Harris was known for his glove even though he did hit .300 for the only time in his career in 1920. He led AL second basemen in fielding percentage once, putouts four times, and double plays five consecutive times and his 483 putouts in 1922 set a league record that stood for over five decades. After the 1924 season, as the Senators foundered again, owner Clark Griffith surprised everyone including Harris by offering the 27-year-old Harris the managerial reins. Known as "The Boy Wonder" or "The Boy Manager," Harris led the Senators and Walter Johnson to the pennant. The Senators then upset the Giants to win the Series in Harris' first year as manager. The Senators repeated as AL champs, but lost to the Pirates in the Series.

LIFETIME STATS: BA: .274, HR: 9, RBI: 506, H: 1,297, SB: 167

#765 Cesar Leonardo "Pepito" Perez Tovar

OF-3B-2B-DH, Twins, Phillies, Rangers, A's, Yankees, 1965–76

A very versatile player, Tovar proved it one day in 1968 when he played all nine positions for the Twins against the A's. Tovar is also known as the no-hitter "breaker-upper" as he spoiled five no-hit bids in his career, getting the lone hit off the likes of Dave McNally, Mike Cuellar, Catfish Hunter, Barry Moore and Dick Bosman. In '71, Tovar hit .311, leading the league with 204 hits, and hit for the cycle in 1972 when he led the junior circuit in hit by pitches.

LIFETIME STATS: BA: .278, HR: 46, RBI: 435, H: 1,546, SB: 226

#766 Jerry Dean Lumpe
2B-3B-SS, Yankees, A's, Tigers, 1956–67

Lumpe was a contact hitter who had a tough time defensively at third and shortstop for the Yankees. Because of his fielding woes and better players playing in front of him, the Yanks dealt Lumpe in 1959 to their "trading buddies," the Kansas City A's, where Lumpe blossomed as a second baseman. His finest season was 1962 as he hit 10 homers, drove in 83, hit .301 and had a 20-game hitting streak. He was an All Star in 1964.

LIFETIME STATS: BA: .268, HR: 47, RBI: 454, H: 1,314, SB: 20

#767 Edmund John "Bing" Miller
OF, Senators, A's, Browns, Red Sox, 1921–36

Unsung but not unappreciated, Bing Miller was one of the many stars of Connie Mack's Athletics teams of 1929 to 1931, with the likes of Al Simmons, Jimmy Foxx, Mickey Cochrane and Lefty Grove, Hall of Famers all. His first tour of duty with Philadelphia started in 1922 where he hit .335 with 90 RBI and hit a robust .342 in 1924. He was traded away to the Browns, but Mack reacquired Miller in 1928, and Bing responded with a .329 average and 85 RBI. Miller hit .368 in the 1929 World Series and got the Series clinching hit in Game Five over the Cubs.

LIFETIME STATS: BA: .311, HR: 116, RBI: 990, H: 1,936, SB: 127

#768 James Gorman "Stormin' Gorman" Thomas

OF-DH, Brewers, Indians, Mariners, 1973–76, 1978–86

A fan favorite in Milwaukee, Thomas loved to swing for the fences even though he would frequently lead the league in strikeouts. In 1979, he led the league in homers with 45, while also leading the loop with 175 strikeouts, five coming in a nine-inning game that tied a major league record. Thomas was a very good center fielder with a strong arm, and the fans loved the Fu-Manchued, long-haired Thomas because he played the game so enthusiastically.

LIFETIME STATS: BA: .225, HR: 268, RBI: 782, H: 1,051, SB: 50.

#769 Davis Travis Fryman

3B-SS, Tigers, Indians, 1990–2002

Travis Fryman was originally a shortstop in the Tiger chain, but he soon realized he wasn't going to play short with Alan Trammel there, so Fryman learned to play third base. He had a tough go of it at first defensively, but his bat kept him in the lineup. He made the All Star team four times, but was then traded to the Diamondbacks, who traded him that winter to Cleveland. Fryman hit a career-best 28 homers in 1998 and had 22 more circuit clouts as well as 106 RBI and a .321 batting average in 2000.

LIFETIME STATS: BA: .274, HR: 223, RBI: 1,022, H: 1,776, SB: 72.

#770 Emil John "Dutch" Leonard

RHP, Dodgers, Senators, Phillies, Cubs, 1933–36, 1938–53

Despite rarely playing for a contender, Dutch Leonard posted some fine numbers in his lengthy career. Displaying a dancing knuckleball, Leonard had his best year in 1939, hurling 21 complete games while posting a 20–8 mark. Working for the second-division Senators, Leonard was selected to four All Star games while consistently putting up win totals in the teens. In 1947 Dutch was traded to the Phils where he won 17, and then it was on to Chicago, where he made his fifth All Star team, this time as a reliever.

LIFETIME STATS: W: 191, L: 181, SV: 44, ERA: 3.25, SO: 1,170, CG: 192

#771 Charles Ray Knight

3B, Reds, Astros, Mets, Orioles, Tigers, 1974, 1977–88

Ray Knight began his career with the Reds as the third base successor to Pete Rose and he hit .318. His production tailed off, and he was dealt to Houston where he hit .294 and .304. Traded to the Mets, he slumped in 1985 and was almost cut by New York in spring training of 1986, but it was a good thing he wasn't: Knight became one of the Mets' World Series heroes by scoring the tying run in Game Six and smashing a homer in Game Seven to put the Mets in front to stay. Knight hit .391 and won the Series MVP Award.

LIFETIME STATS: BA: .271, HR: 84, RBI 595, H: 1,311, SB: 14

#772 Theodore Crawford "Ted" Sizemore

2B-SS, Dodgers, Cardinals, Phillies, Cubs, Red Sox, 1969–80

Originally a catcher dubbed "Runt" by pitching ace Don Drysdale, Sizemore volunteered to learn a new position when Manager Walter Alston needed a second baseman in 1969. Evidently, Sizemore learned well, as he won the NL Rookie of the Year Award. In 1971, the Dodgers traded him to the Cardinals and Sizemore was a success there. Lou Brock credited Sizemore, a patient hitter, with giving him the opportunity to break the career stolen-base record as Brock led off and Sizemore batted second for the five years they played together on the Cards.

LIFETIME STATS: BA: .262, HR: 23, RBI: 430, H: 1,311, SB: 59

#773 Michael Andrew "Mike" Mcfarlane

C, Royals, Red Sox, A's, 1987–99

Mcarlane was a steady catcher for the Kansas City Royals teams of 1987 to 1998. He would show occasional power as he did in his best year, 1993, when he clubbed 20 homers, knocked in 67 and hit .273. He also had 221 career doubles and led the league twice in getting hit by pitches, in 1992 and 1994 when he was plunked a total of 33 times.

LIFETIME STATS: BA: .252, HR 129, RBI: 514, H: 906, SB: 12

#774 Victor Felipe "Vic" Power (Pellot)

1B-2B-3B-OF, A's, Indians, Twins, Dodgers, Phillies, Angels, 1954–65

One of the better fielding first baseman of all time, Power caught the ball one handed and won seven Gold Gloves. Coming up in the Yankee chain, his flamboyant, colorful style clashed with the then-conservative Yankees. Thus, the slick-fielding Power was traded to Kansas City, where he led AL first baseman in assists six times. He also hit well, as in his first year with the A's as he hit .319 with 34 doubles, 19 homers and 91 runs. He also hit over .300 in three out of four years in KC. Traded to Cleveland in '58, Power hit .312 with 37 doubles and led the AL with 10 triples for the entire season. He also stole home twice in the same game that season.

LIFETIME STATS: BA: .284, HR: 126, RBI: 658, H: 1,716, SB: 45

#775 Jay Campbell "Bone" Buhner

OF, Yankees, Mariners 1987–2000

Buhner came up with the Yankees, and in one of the most lopsided deals in Yankee history they traded him to Seattle for DH Ken Phelps. Phelps was a major disappointment for the Yanks, but Buhner developed into a powerful slugger with the Mariners. His first seven full seasons with Seattle, Buhner smashed 224 homers as he topped the 40 home run and 100 RBI mark three times. Taking on the Yankees in the five-game Divisional Series in 1995, Buhner ripped Yankee pitching at a .458 clip as the Mariners rebounded from a 2–0 deficit and swept three straight to win the series.

LIFETIME STATS: BA: .254, HR: 310, RBI: 965, H: 1,273, SB: 6

#776 Richard Larry "Dick," "Bass Jaws" Green

2B, A's, 1963–74

Green was a sure-handed second baseman for Charley Finley's three-time champion A's. He did display occasional power as he hit 10 or more home runs four times, and his best overall season offensively was in 1969 when he hit .275 with 64 RBI. But when it came time to shore up the defense in tight World Series tilts, Green was the A's man at second base, particularly in the 1974 Series win over the Dodgers. Green set a World Series record by participating in six double plays, three alone in Game Three with the series tied at one apiece.

LIFETIME STATS: BA: .240, HR: 80, RBI: 422, H: 960, SB: 26

#777 Scott Brian Fletcher

SS-2B-3B, Cubs, White Sox, Rangers, White Sox, Brewers, Red Sox, Tigers, 1981–95

Fletcher came up with the Cubs, but was soon traded to the south side of Chicago to the White Sox. He earned the starting shortstop job in 1983, helping the Chisox reach the postseason for the first time in 24 years. His next stop was Texas, and he responded to the tune of a career high of .300 in 1986. Fletcher seemed to develop an inconsistent pattern of hitting over the years, which may have contributed to his journeyman status. Fletcher returned to the White Sox, then signed a free-agent contract with Boston in 1993 and had a good year, hitting .285 with 16 steals, but the next year he slumped to only .227.

LIFETIME STATS: BA: .262, HR: 34, RBI: 510, H: 1,376, SB: 99

#778 Bibb August "Jockey" Falk

OF, White Sox, Indians, 1920–31

Falk came out of the University of Texas and had the distinction of replacing "Shoeless" Joe Jackson in left field for the 1920 White Sox. The lefty was a mainstay there for eight solid seasons, surpassing the .300 mark five times in that span. "Jockey," as he was called because of his merciless riding of opponents from the bench, had three more plus-.300 seasons with the Indians, where he was used mostly off the bench his last two seasons.

LIFETIME STATS: BA: .314, HR: 69, RBI: 784, H: 1,463, SB: 47

#779 Steven Allen "Steve" Finley

OF, Orioles, Astros, Padres, Diamondbacks, Dodgers, Angels, Giants, Rockies, 1989–2007

Finley, a four-time Golden Glove winner, also combines durability, power and speed in his game. He has had over 24 homers in a season three times, has been among the leaders in games played, and has a career total of 296 stolen bases, 44 of which came in 1992, when he also led the NL with 13 triples. Speaking of three-baggers, Finley leads all active major leaguers in that department with 108. He was dealt to the Padres and he helped them win the NL West in '96, hitting .298 and clubbing 30 homers. Finley was also an integral part of Arizona's championship drive of 2001, hitting .421 in the NLDS and .368 in the D'Backs Series win over the Yankees.

LIFETIME STATS: BA: .271, HR: 304, RBI: 1,167, H: 2,548, SB: 320

#**780** John Franklin "Silent John" Titus

OF, Phillies, Braves, 1903–13

Titus didn't make it to the majors until the age of 27, but once he was there, proved to be a consistent outfielder and hitter. He also was a durable player as he played in 143 games or more for seven straight years. His career high batting average was in 1912 when he hit .309. Two of his eccentricities were chewing on toothpicks while batting and sporting a handlebar mustache when few, if any, of his contemporaries did the same.

LIFETIME STATS: BA: .282, HR: 38, RBI 561, H: 1,401, SB: 140

#**781** Glenn Dee Hubbard

2B, Braves, A's, 1978–89

A tough, fiery competitor, Hubbard was a fine fielding second baseman for the Braves for most of his career as his lifetime fielding average was an impressive .983. He led his league in double plays three times and in assists twice. His best season at the plate was in 1983, when he hit .263 with a career-high 12 homers and 70 RBI as he was chosen on the NL All Star team. In '85, Hubbard had 12 assists in a nine-inning game, which tied a major league record. Born at a United States Air Force Base in Germany, he led the NL in sacrifices in 1982.

LIFETIME STATS: BA: .244, HR: 70, RBI: 448, H: 1,084, SB: 35

#782 Norman Arthur "Kid," "The Tabasco Kid" Elberfeld

SS-3B, Phillies, Reds, Tigers, Highlanders, Senators, Dodgers, 1898–99, 1901–11, 1914

Because of his tenacious nature, Kid Elberfeld was also called "The Tabasco Kid." He stood only 5' 7" and weighed 158 pounds, but the Kid played the game hard and expected the opposition to play the same way. He was spiked numerous times, and the tough Elberfeld would rub his wounds with whiskey and continue playing. After brief stints with the Phillies and Reds, Elberfeld became Detroit's starting shortstop in the maiden season of the AL in 1901, hitting .308 and leading AL shortstops in double plays and putouts. He was the regular shortstop for the Highlanders from 1903 to 1907.

LIFETIME STATS: BA: .271, HR: 10, RBI: 535, H: 1,235, SB: 213

#783 Arnold Malcolm "Mickey" Owen

C, Cardinals, Dodgers, Cubs, Red Sox 1937–45, 1949–51, 1954

Mickey Owen was named to the NL All Star squad all four years he played for Brooklyn. He served in the United States Navy in World War II, and then played in Mexico, but then discovered he missed playing in the big leagues. No team would sign the catcher, until Baseball Commissioner Happy Chandler reinstated him in 1949. Owen then joined the Cubs, went into coaching in the minors, then resurfaced for one last season with the Red Sox in 1954.

LIFETIME STATS: BA: .255, HR: 14, RBI: 378, H: 929, SB: 36

#**784** William Murray "Billy" Werber
3B, Yankees, Red Sox, A's, Reds, Giants, 1930, 1933–42

Werber was a very good third baseman and a very effective leadoff hitter with a great eye at the plate and occasional power. When he got on base, he was a threat on the base paths as he led the American League in steals on three occasions. He once caught an opposing catcher unawares and took second base on a walk. Werber became the first player to hit four doubles in a row in an AL game in 1935 and then did it again in the NL in 1940, becoming the first person to perform this hitting feat in both leagues. The Maryland native was very outspoken in his opposition to blacks playing in the major leagues after he retired from the game, saying that "the movement to admit black players was partly Communist-inspired."

LIFETIME STATS: BA: .271, HR: 78, RBI: 539, H: 1,363, SB: 215

#**785** Devon Markes "Devo" White
OF, Angels, Blue Jays, Marlins, Diamondbacks, Dodgers, Brewers, 1985–2001

A fabulous defensive outfielder with seven Gold Gloves to his credit, White had one of his finest seasons in 1987 when he became a regular with the Angels, as he combined speed and power to the tune of 24 homers, 32 steals, and 103 runs scored. Though he was an All Star in 1989, he and manager Doug Rader didn't get along and he was demoted to the minors for a short time. He rebounded with the Blue Jays as he hit .282 and stole 37 bases in 41 tries. He responded in the big games, establishing an American League record for lifetime batting average in the ALCS with a .392 BA in 74 at bats.

LIFETIME STATS: BA: .263, HR: 208, RBI: 846, H: 1,934, SB: 346

#786 Jody Rich Davis

C, Cubs, Braves, 1981–90

One of the more popular players on the Cubs teams of the 80s, the tall red-headed Davis was a dependable defensive catcher who also had some pop as he clouted 24 homers and hit .271 in 1983, his second full season in Chicago. Davis earned an All Star invitation in 1984, and helped the Cubbies win the NL East title. He did all he could to bring the World Championship to Wrigley Field by hitting two homers and seven hits against the Padres, but it was not to be as the Padres took the Series. He caught almost every game for the Cubs between 1984 and 1986, again making the All Star team in 1986. This grueling regimen finally caught up with the affable Davis, and after a brief stint with the Braves, he retired in 1990.

LIFETIME STATS: BA: .245, HR: 127, RBI: 490, H: 877, SB: 7

#787 Charles Henry "Charlie," "Chinski" Root

RHP, Browns, Cubs, 1926–41

Root was an excellent pitcher for the Cubs for many years, but he's constantly remembered for the homer he gave up to Babe Ruth in the 1932 World Series. Did the Bambino point to center field and "call his shot"? We do know that the Babe did hit a Ruthian clout to the farthest reaches of center field, but Root vehemently denied that the Sultan of Swat called his homer by saying if he thought he was, Root would have knocked him down with the next pitch. Root won 26 games for the Cubbies in 1927 and won at least 13 games 10 times in his illustrious career. He had a sterling 19–6 season in 1929, leading the NL in winning percentage (.760), and in 1930 he led the league in shutouts. His Achilles' heel was the postseason as Root was 0–4 with a whopping (especially for him) 6.75 ERA.

LIFETIME STATS: W: 201, L: 160, SV: 40, ERA: 3.59, SO: 1,459, CG: 177

#**788** Curtis Benton "Curt" Welch
OF, Toledo (AA), St Louis (AA), Philadelphia (AA), Baltimore (AA), Baltimore (NL), Cincinnati, Louisville, 1884–93

In the only winner-take-all (the money) championship series in professional-baseball history, Welch made an impressive slide to score the winning run to secure the championship and $15,000 for the St. Louis Browns club over the Chicago White Stockings in 1886. Welch was a terror on the base paths as he pilfered 453 bases, an unbelievable 95 in 1888 alone. At times during his career, the colorful Welch would trade used baseballs and other baseball-related items for free drinks in local taverns.

LIFETIME STATS: BA: .263, HR: 16, RBI: 503, H: 1,152, SB: 453

#**789** Lynford Hobart "Lyn," "Broadway" Lary
SS, Yankees, Red Sox, Senators, Browns, Indians, Dodgers, Cardinals, 1929–40

Lary played for the Yankees for five seasons, but never played in the World Series, being supplanted by Frankie Crosetti in the 1932 Series. He had a spectacular 1931, however, as he drove in 107 runs, setting the record for RBI for Yankee short-stops, scored 100 runs, had 54 extra-base hits, and drew 88 walks. Lary was one of four Bombers with over 100 RBI that year. He was dealt to Boston where he led AL shortstops in fielding in 1934. He was with the Browns in 1936, when he scored 112 runs, drew 117 walks and hit .289 along with leading the league in steals with 37. Then it was on to Cleveland, where Lary had the last good season of his career, hitting .290 and slamming 46 doubles.

LIFETIME STATS: BA: .269, HR: 38, RBI: 526, H: 1,239, SB: 162

#**790** John Thomas "Johnny" Allen

RHP, Yankees, Indians, Browns, Dodgers, Giants, 1932–44

Allen had both an explosive temper and an explosive fast-ball in his 13 years in the bigs. He also may have been the first man to throw a slider. Allen had a fine rookie mark, posting a 17–4 record in 1932, following it up with a 15-win campaign. Thinking his arm was sore and tiring of his temper tantrums, the Bombers traded Allen to Cleveland, where he won 20 games in 1936. The next year, Allen went 15–1. His .938 winning percentage was a major league record until it was broken by Roy Face's 18–1 slate in 1959. Allen went 14–8 in 1938, but then injuries curtailed his effectiveness and he retired in 1944, taking with him an impressive winning percentage of .654.

LIFETIME STATS: W: 142, L: 75, SV: 18, ERA: 3.75, SO: 1,070, CG: 109

#791 Harry Arthur "Cookie" Lavagetto

3B-2B, Pirates, Dodgers, 1934–41, 1946–47

Cookie Lavagetto was one-for-16 in World Series batting, as he strode to the plate with two outs in the ninth inning for the Dodgers in Game Four of the 1947 World Series against the Yankees. Not only was the game on the line, but Yankee hurler Bill Bevens had a no-hitter going and a 2–1 lead, but Lavagetto doubled in the tying and winning runs and became an instant hero in Flatbush. He was the regular second baseman for Brooklyn in 1937, but the following year, he moved to third base, and became an All Star for the next four seasons. His career year occurred in 1939, when he hit .300 on the nose with 10 homers and 87 RBI as well as scoring 93 runs. That year he also had six hits in one game.

LIFETIME STATS: BA: .269, HR: 40, RBI: 486, H: 945, SB: 63

#792 James Laurie "Deacon" White

C-3B-OF-1B-2B, Cleveland Forest Citys (NA), Boston Braves (NA), White Stockings, Braves, Reds, Buffalo Bisons (NL), Detroit Wolverines, Pirates, Buffalo Bisons (PL), 1871–90

White is considered the best bare-handed catcher of his time, a tough, smart player who never smoke, drank or cursed (hence the nickname). In fact, White was one of the few ballplayers who regularly went to church. The versatile White could play several positions, and won a batting title in 1875 as a catcher with Boston in the National Association, and then won another title as a first baseman with Boston in 1877, this time when the franchise was in the National League. White hit .300 or better 12 of his 20 years in the pros.

LIFETIME STATS: BA: .323, HR: 23, RBI: 977, H: 2,066, SB: 57

#793 Bandillo Jose "Bo" Diaz
C, Red Sox, Indians, Phillies, Reds, 1977–89

Diaz's first good year was the strike-shortened 1981, as he hit .313 for the Indians and was selected for the AL All Star team. He was traded in the off-season to Philadelphia, where he had his best year, with 18 homers and 85 RBI while batting .288. He again was traded, this time to the Reds and he contributed well to the tune of 15 homers, 82 RBI and another All Star invitation. Tragedy struck Diaz as he was struck and killed by lightning in his native Venezuela in 1990, just a year after he retired from baseball.

LIFETIME STATS: BA: .255, HR: 87, RBI: 452, H: 834, SB: 9

#794 Henry Albert "Hank" Bauer
OF, Yankees, A's, 1948–61

This hard-nosed crewcutted ex-Marine was a clutch performer, playing on nine pennant winners in a 10 year span, including seven world titles. He was a leader on the team, exhorting his teammates not to "mess with my money," meaning his anticipated World Series check. A three-time American League All Star, he was platooned regularly by Stengel in favor of either Gene Woodling or Enos Slaughter. He hit 26 home runs in 1956 and 18 leadoff homers in his career. He made a game-saving catch in the World Series clincher against the Giants in 1951, and from 1956 to 1958 he set a Series record with a 17-game hitting streak. Bauer was traded to Kansas City in a deal that brought Roger Maris to the Yankees.

LIFETIME STATS: BA: .277, HR: 164, RBI: 703, H: 1,424, SB: 50

#**795** Walter "Dobie" Moore

SS-OF, Kansas City Monarchs (Negro League), 1920–26

Dobie Moore was an outstanding shortstop for the Monarchs, displaying a cannon of an arm and excellent range. Casey Stengel ranked him as "one of the best shortstops who will ever live." Moore was also a tremendous hitter, ranking fourth all time in Negro League history with a .359 batting average, helping Kansas City to three pennants from 1923 to 1925. He also hit in the clutch, with batting averages of .300 and .364 in the 1924 and 1925 Black World Series. His career was cut short in 1926 as Moore was wounded in an accidental shooting.

LIFETIME STATS: BA: .325, HR: 50, H: 625

#**796** David Lee "Dave" Henderson

OF-DH, Mariners, Red Sox, Giants, A's, Royals, 1981–94

Known for his infectious smile and the sheer joy of playing the game, Dave Henderson was the very first pick by the Mariners in the 1977 draft. He was dealt to Boston in 1986, and became an important part of Red Sox lore when he hit a two-run home run in the 1986 ALCS against the Angels in a game the Sox eventually won. The Red Sox won the series three days later. His home run in Game Six of that year's Series gave the Red Sox a 10th-inning lead against the Mets, but the Mets came back to win that game and the following contest. He played briefly with the Giants before crossing the Bay with the A's, where he enjoyed playing on three straight pennant winners and being selected to participate in the 1991 All Star Game.

LIFETIME STATS: BA: .258, HR: 197, RBI: 708, H: 1,324, SB: 50

#**797** Daniel "Dan" Driessen

1B-3B-OF, Reds, Expos, Giants, Astros, Cardinals, 1973–87

Driessen came up to the Reds as a third baseman, but struggled at the hot corner, and eventually moved to first base for the departed Tony Perez. Driessen hit .301 in his rookie season. He had adequate power, was a very good base runner and was very patient at the plate, leading the league in walks with 93 in 1980. He also led the NL in fielding three times.

In the World Series sweep of the Yankees in 1976, Driessen became the National League's first designated hitter where he hit an outstanding .357.

LIFETIME STATS: BA: .267, HR: 153, RBI: 763, H: 1,464, SB: 154

#**798** Raymond Otis "Ray" Boone

3B-SS-1B, Indians, Tigers, White Sox, A's, Braves, Red Sox, 1948–60

The patriarch of three generations of major leaguers, Ray played so well at shortstop when he first came up that the injured Lou Boudreau, when he recovered, moved to third. Boone was traded to the Tigers in 1953 and blossomed in Motown as he hit 26 home runs his first season, 14 more than his previous high; his 114 RBI that year almost doubled his previous high. He was selected to the All Star team twice and in 1955 tied for the American League lead in RBI with 116. He is the father of Bob Boone, a fine catcher primarily with the Phillies and Angels and later a manager, and grandfather to Bob's sons, Bret and Aaron, who continue to play in the majors, with the Mariners and Yankees, respectively.

LIFETIME STATS: BA: .275, HR: 151, RBI: 737, H: 1,260, SB: 21

#**799** William Alex "Billy" North

OF, Cubs, A's, Dodgers, Giants, 1971–81

The speedy, fiery Billy North started out with the Cubs, but really started to make his mark in baseball with the Oakland A's in 1973, where he hit a career-best .285. The next year, as the A's were winning their second straight World Series crown, North led the AL in steals with 54, and peformed an unassisted double play from his centerfield position. He also got into a celebrated locker-room fight with Reggie Jackson, but the "Swingin' A's" kept winning anyway. In 1976, North again led the loop in steals with 75. North moved across the bay with the Giants as he stole another 58 bases, good for second in the senior circuit in 1979.

LIFETIME STATS: BA: .261, HR: 20, RBI: 230, H: 1,016, SB: 395

#800 Fernando Valenzuela

LHP, Dodgers, Angels, Orioles, Phillies, Padres, Cardinals, 1980–97

"Fernandomania" hit Los Angeles and the nation in 1981 when a portly lefty named Fernando Valenzuela took the mound for the Dodgers. He won his first eight outings, completing seven and hurling five shutouts, including 36 scoreless innings. He had eight shutouts all told that glorious year, tying a rookie record and leading the league in complete games and innings while compiling a 13–7 mark to easily win both the Rookie of the Year Award and the Cy Young Award. He won a game in the World Series as the Dodgers beat the Yankees. The lumpy Valenzuela looked like he was out of shape, but he was very durable; as the workhorse of the staff, he did not miss a start from 1981 to 1988 and even won a Gold Glove Award. In 1985 he posted a 17–10 mark and the following year led the NL in wins with 21, along with an NL-leading 20 complete games. In 1990, the screw-balling southpaw threw a no-hitter against the Cardinals.

LIFETIME STATS: W: 173, L: 153, SV: 2, ERA: 3.54, SO: 2,074, CG: 113

Japanese Baseball

If you know the name Horace Wilson, then you know Japanese baseball. The great American game was first seen in Japan in the early 1870s, when an American teacher named Horace Wilson introduced the game to students at Kaisei Gakko, now known as Tokyo University. Around 1880 the first organized Japanese team was formed at the Shimbashi Athletic Club. At the same time, many college teams were forming in the Tokyo area.

By the dawn of the 20th century, a high school team from the Tokyo area played and often defeated a team made up of American residents in Yokohama. The excitement that these games brought helped spark an interest in baseball and helped turn the game into a Japanese pastime. In a rivalry that reminds one of Harvard and Yale, Waseda University and Keio University began a heated campaign against one another in 1903. Mejii, Hosei, Rikkyo and Tokyo universities soon joined Waseda and Keio and formed what became known as the Big Six—the first collegiate league in Japan.

The first visit by major leaguers from America came in 1913, when Charles Comiskey and John McGraw headed a visit to Japan as part of a world tour. Through the first half of the 20th century, it was common to see university teams from both the U.S. and Japan cross the ocean for baseball visits.

In the early 1930s, an American major league, All Star team came over to play in Japan. Lou Gehrig was the big star on the team. Even though the Americans defeated the Japanese in all 17 games played, the series continued to fuel excitement for the game and for a professional league that the Japanese could call their own.

Soon after, the Nihon Baseball Club was formed and seven other professional clubs followed. Amateur ball continued to hold the greater interest of the Japanese public during the 1930s, but in postwar Japan, professional ball took roots and became the fan favorite.

Activity increased after World War II, with Japanese teams often heading to the U.S. for spring training. Some 400 major league players have since played in Japanese professional leagues.

Japan celebrates the game with its own Baseball Hall of Fame located in Tokyo. Some 200 players have been inducted since the facility was dedicated in 1959, which was 20 years after America's Hall in Cooperstown opened to the public.

Tokyo also showcases the great Tokyo Dome, which is home to two great franchises with rich history—the Yomiuri Giants and Nippon Ham Fighters.

The following are brief biographies of 15 of the greatest Japanese players.

1. Sadaharu Oh

The best player in the history of the league, Oh leads in just about all offensive categories. He smacked 868 home runs and drove in 2,170 runs. He finished with 2,786 hits and a .301 lifetime average. The son of a Chinese father and Japanese mother, Oh had trouble gaining acceptance among the fans. He signed as a pitcher and received a $60,000 bonus. But he soon went to first base where he struggled because he couldn't hit the curve. Oh took up practicing samurai swordsmanship and adopted the Mel Ott style of raising the lead foot in his swing. He did this without knowing who the great New York Giants' slugger was. In 1965, Oh hit 55 home runs in 140 games. He broke Hank Aaron's major league mark for home runs in 1978.

2. Katsuya Nomura

Talk about a career. Including his time as player-manager for the Nankai Hawks, Nomura was in the lineup for 28 years. That's a record for Japanese baseball and it might be a record for any league in the universe. Nomura was a catcher. He led the league in home runs for 10 consecutive years from 1962–71.

3. Isao Harimoto

Here's an interesting character. Harimoto was Korean-born and an awesome hitter. He had 3,085 hits in his career as an outfielder and was tempted to jump to the Los Angeles Dodgers or San Francisco Giants in the mid-1960s. The American teams felt that his Korean ancestry wouldn't make him feel so bonded to the Japanese League. Instead, Harimoto used the American offers to earn a spectacular contract with the Toei Flyers. The contract, some alcohol issues and an occasional lack of hustle made him a popular target for taunting by the fans.

4. Shiego Nagashima

He hit the most dramatic home run in Japanese baseball history. This third-sacker's blast in 1959 at Korakuen Stadium in Tokyo was a walk-off home run in a game played with Emperor Hirohito in the stands. He batted fourth behind Oh for many years as the duo helped the Tokyo Giants win nine pennants.

5. Hiromitsu Ochiai

This Japanese great retired after the 1998 season. He had more games at first base than any other player, but also managed to play all four infield positions. Hiromitsu had a career .311 average while swatting 510 home runs. He was disciplined at the plate and was issued a free pass 1,475 times. He is among the all-time leaders in many offensive categories. He played with four teams in his career starting with the Lotte Orions in 1979 and finishing with the Ham Fighters.

6. Masaichi Kaneda
The Cy Young of Japanese baseball. Kaneda holds a league record in wins (400), strikeouts (4,490), complete games (365) and innings pitched (5,526). He also piled up 82 shutouts and a lifetime ERA of 2.34. Kaneda, who played with the Kokutetsu Swallows for much of his career (1950–69) also recorded a league record 298 pitching defeats. The southpaw led the league in strikeouts 10 times, including 350 in 1955.

7. Kazuhisa Inao
Another great pitcher and a Kaneda contemporary, who spent his entire career (1956–69) with the Nishitetsu Lions. Arm trouble hampered Inao after the 1963 season. But for the first eight years of his career, he was 236–94. He was 35–6 in 1957 and 42–14 in 1962. Inao is the best right-handed hurler in Japanese history.

8. Koji Yamamoto
An outfielder with both power and speed, he was a key member of Hiroshima's pennant winners in 1979 and 1981. He went deep 42 times and drove in 113 in 1979 and had 43 homers and 103 RBI in 1981. A Gold Glove winner many times, he retired with 469 more stolen bases than anyone in league history.

9. Yutaka Fukumoto
The Rickey Henderson of Japanese baseball. In a style that emphasized power over speed, Fukumoto swiped 106 bases in 1972. His 95 thefts the following year have been the only threat to the 1972 mark. In 1979, at the age of 33, he led Japanese baseball with 60 steals.

10. Keishi Suzuki

This crafty lefty finished his career in 1985 in the top five career list in innings pitched, wins and strikeouts. He won 317 games all for the Kintetsu Buffaloes. He was a 20-game winner eight times.

11. Tetsuharu Kawakami

You could call this first baseman Japan's first superstar. He hit .338 for the Yomiuri Giants in 1939 when he was only 18 to become the youngest batting champion in league history. He would win five more batting titles and hit over .300 13 times.

12. Victor Starffin

This old-timer broke in with the Tokyo Kyojin in 1936 and won 303 games by the time he finished his career with the Tombo Unions in 1955. In the years 1939–40, Starffin went 80–27 and whiffed 527 batters.

13. Hisashi Yamada

Pitched his entire career (1969–1988) for the Hankyu Braves, finishing with a 284–166 mark. This right-hander was remarkably consistent and was a four-time 20-game winner.

14. Akira Bessho

A top-10 placement in all pitching categories, Bessho won two MVPs with the Tokyo Giants. A big man by Japanese baseball standards, Bessho stood over 6-feet tall and was a solid enough presence on the mound that his style was sometimes compared to Roger Clemens.

15. Kazuhiro Yamauchi

Always a Triple Crown threat during his long career, this outfielder posted 396 home runs and 2,271 hits in a career that began in 1952 with the Mainichi Orions and finished in 1970 with the Hiroshima Tokyo Carp.

#801 Alphonse Eugene "Al," "Fuzzy" Smith

OF-3B, Indians, White Sox, Orioles, Red Sox, 1953–64

A multi-talented athlete, Al Smith once scored an amazing 10 touchdowns in a high school game for his St. Louis high school and was also a Golden Gloves boxing champ. In the World Series of 1954, he hit the first pitch from Giants ace Johnny Antonelli in Game Two for a home run in a losing effort as the Indians were swept by the Giants. In 1955, Smith led the AL with 123 runs scored and hit an impressive .306. Smith was an All Star in 1955, when he hit .306, and in 1960, when he hit .315.

LIFETIME STATS: BA: .272, HR: 164, RBI: 676, H: 1,458, SB: 67

#802 Sixto Joaquin Lezcano

OF, Brewers, Cardinals, Padres, Phillies, Pirates, 1974–85

Debuting at the tender age of 20 with the Brewers, the versatile Lezcano started slowly his first few seasons, blossoming in 1977, as he hit 21 doubles and 21 homers and led all American League outfielders in assists the following year. His best year was in 1979, when he hit .321 with 28 homers and 101 RBI, slugged a robust .573 and also won a Gold Glove.

LIFETIME STATS: BA: .271, HR: 148, RBI: 591, H: 1,122, SB: 37

#803 Charles Albert "Chief" Bender

RHP, A's, Baltimore (FL), Phillies, White Sox, 1903–17, 1925. Hall of Fame, 1953

Charles Albert Bender was called "Chief," as he was one quarter Chippewa. He endured the racism with aplomb, but he signed his autograph "Charles Bender" and manager Connie Mack always called him "Albert." Bender joined the A's in 1903 and had a 17-14 record. Bender is credited by some as the inventor of the slider. In 1910, he won 23 games and had an impressive 1.58 ERA while leading the league in winning percentage (.821). Mack, who had such illustrious hurlers as Eddie Plank, Lefty Grove and Rube Waddell, once said that if he had one game he had to win, he would give the ball to Albert Bender.

LIFETIME STATS: W: 212, L: 127, SV: 34, ERA: 2.46, SO: 1,711, CG: 255

#804 Kevin Lee Seitzer

3B-1B-DH, Royals, Brewers, A's, Brewers, Indians, 1986–97

A consistent hitter, Seitzer had six over-.300 seasons, despite many injuries throughout his 12-year career. He broke in as a late season callup with the Royals in 1986 and replaced Kansas City legend George Brett at third. (Brett was shifted to first). The following year, Seitzer, still technically a rookie, hit .323 and led the league in hits with 207, being named to the AL All Star team in the process. He would have also been named the AL Rookie of the Year had it not been for Mark McGwire, who slugged 49 homers that year for the A's. Seitzer also had a memorable August game against Boston as he went six-for-six with two homers and seven RBI.

LIFETIME STATS: BA: .295, HR: 74, RBI: 613, H: 1,557, SB: 80

#805 Roger Maxwell "Doc," "Flit" Cramer

OF, Athletics, Red Sox, Senators, Tigers, 1929–48

Cramer depended on speed and his ability to hit the ball to all fields. At 6'2" and 185 pounds, considered big for his time, Cramer was not a power hitter, but was an excellent contact hitter. He batted leadoff, leading the league seven times in at bats, and once in hits with 200 in 1940. He also set an AL record and tied a major league mark by going six-for-six twice in his career, once in 1932, the other in 1935. In 1936 he was traded to the Red Sox, where he had his best years as he was named to the AL All Star team for four straight years (1937–40).

LIFETIME STATS: BA: .296, HR: 37, RBI: 842, H: 2,705, SB: 62

#806 Andrew "Rube" Foster

RHP-1B-OF, Chicago Union Giants, Cuban X-Giants, Philadelphia Giants, Leland Giants, Chicago American Giants, 1902–26. Hall of Fame, 1981

Foster was the first great pitching star of the Negro Leagues and later, its greatest manager. In 1902, the 6'4", 200-pound Foster was playing for a semi-pro team in Texas. He was credited with 51 wins that year, including a victory over the great Rube Waddell, from whom Foster got his nickname. In 1905, he won 51 of 55 games for the legendary Philadelphia Giants, and was the dominating black pitcher of that era. Foster had a blazing fastball, an accurate curve ball and changed speeds better than most pitchers. Foster led the Philadelphia Giants to a pair of Negro League championships in 1905–06. In 1911, Foster became the manager of the Chicago American Giants. Foster was a terrific manager, who preached the hit-and-run, the double steal and bunting for base hits. The Chicago Americans won several Negro National League championships, including five in a row from 1918–22. In one game in 1919, the Chicago Americans were down, 18–0 after six innings. The team rallied to tie the game 18–18 with nine runs in the ninth, and the game was called because of darkness. In 1981, Foster was elected to the Hall of Fame on the basis of his contributions to baseball.

LIFETIME STATS: not available

#807 George Daniel "Buck" Weaver
SS-3B, White Sox, 1912–20

Weaver was one of seven Chicago White Sox to be banned from baseball for life following the 1919 World Series. Weaver's crime was that he knew about the infamous plan to fix the Series, but chose not to tell anyone in authority about it. Ironically, he had a fantastic Series, hitting .324 with four doubles and a triple and fielded 27 chances flawlessly. Weaver was regarded as a fine fielding third baseman, who would play so shallow he would negate the bunting game, a tactic often used in the "dead bal"l era. Despite a petition signed by 14,000 Chicagoans and numerous personal appeals to the Commissioner, Weaver was never allowed back in the majors.

LIFETIME STATS: BA: .272, HR: 21, RBI: 420, H: 1,308, SB: 172

#808 Delbert W. "Del" Rice

C, Cardinals, Braves, Cubs, Orioles, Angels, 1945–61

Rice, a smart defensive catcher in his early days with the Cardinals, hit .500 in the Cardinals' 1946 World Series win over the Red Sox. He played most of his career with St. Louis, never hitting much for average, but had the occasional pop as he hit 12 homers in 1947 and 11 in 1952. He was also named to the NL All Star squad in 1953. He made up for his lack of offense with his fine throwing arm and glove as well as his expert handling of pitchers.

LIFETIME STATS: BA: .237, HR: 79, RBI: 441, H: 908, SB: 2

#809 Shawon Donnell Dunston

SS, Cubs, Giants, Pirates, Indians, Cardinals, Mets, 1985–2002

The free-swinging Dunston was the first pick in the 1982 amateur draft by the Cubs, and after having some difficulty at first with Chicago in 1985, he rebounded with a fine year in 1986, with 17 homers, the most by a Cubs shortstop since Ernie Banks in 1961. He was named to the All Star team twice with the Cubs. A herniated disc curtailed his effectiveness the next few seasons, and he signed with the Giants in 1996. The next few years, Dunston meandered about the majors as a utility player. His most memorable post season moment was with the Mets in 1999, when, after a 12-pitch at bat, he started the winning Mets rally with a single in the 15th inning in the League Championship Series against the Atlanta Braves.

LIFETIME STATS: BA: .269, HR: 150, RBI: 668, H: 1,597, SB: 212

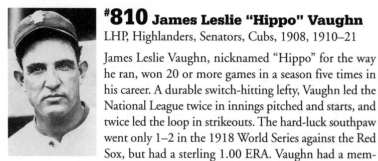

#810 James Leslie "Hippo" Vaughn
LHP, Highlanders, Senators, Cubs, 1908, 1910–21

James Leslie Vaughn, nicknamed "Hippo" for the way he ran, won 20 or more games in a season five times in his career. A durable switch-hitting lefty, Vaughn led the National League twice in innings pitched and starts, and twice led the loop in strikeouts. The hard-luck southpaw went only 1–2 in the 1918 World Series against the Red Sox, but had a sterling 1.00 ERA. Vaughn had a memorable game in 1917 when he and Reds' pitcher Fred Toney were locked in perhaps the best pitching duel in major league history as both were throwing no-hitters after nine complete innings. The Reds got to Vaughn in the top of the 10th on a single, an error and an infield hit off the bat of Jim Thorpe (yes, THAT Jim Thorpe) as the Cubs lost 1–0.

LIFETIME STATS: W: 178, L: 137, SV: 5, ERA: 2.49, SO: 1,416, CG: 215

#811 Juan Milton Romero Samuel
2B-OF, Phillies, Mets, Dodgers, Royals, Reds, Tigers, Blue Jays, 1983–98

Samuel broke in with a bang with the Phillies as he featured both speed and power at the top of the lineup. He was named the Rookie of the Year by the *Sporting News* in 1984, setting a National League record with 701 at bats while compiling a .272 batting average to go along with 15 homers, 69 RBI and a then rookie record of 72 steals. The down side of Samuel's game was the alarming number of strikeouts from a leadoff hitter, 168 in 1984 alone. Samuel, when he made contact, was excellent, as he reached double digits in doubles, triples, and home runs in each of his first four years.

LIFETIME STATS: BA: .259, HR: 161, RBI: 703, H: 1,578, SB: 396

#812 Henry Clement "Heinie" Peitz

C-3B-1B-2B, Cardinals, Reds, Pirates, 1892–1906, 1913

A reliable catcher in the early days of baseball, Henry Clement Peinz was also very versatile and played every infield position but shortstop. He hit a career-high .315 in 1902. He was usually behind the dish when south-paw Ted Breitenstein was pitching for the Reds and the two soon became known as the Pretzel Battery, because of their German ancestry. Despite averaging less than 100 games from 1893 to 1895, Peinz had nine triples in 1893 and 1894, and a career-high 12 three-baggers in 1895, an unusually high count for supposedly slow catchers.

LIFETIME STATS: BA: .271, HR: 16, RBI: 560, H: 1,117, SB: 91

#813 Emil Frederick "Irish" Meusel

OF, Senators, Phillies, Giants, Dodgers, 1914, 1918–27

Emil Meusel was dubbed "Irish" not because he was of Irish descent (he was French) but because he looked Celtic. The older brother of Yankee star Bob Meusel, he came into his own with John McGraw's Giants, with 100 or more RBI years in his first four seasons as the Giants won four straight flags from 1921 to 1924. He was also great in the clutch as he drove in 17 runs in 23 World Series games. He slugged over .500 three times and for all that power Meusel rarely struck out, fanning only 199 times in his entire career, and never more than 33 in a single season.

LIFETIME STATS: BA: .310, HR: 106, RBI: 819, H: 1,521, SB: 113

#814 Jorge Posada
C-DH, Yankees, 1996-2011

Posada was a worthy successor to the likes of Bill Dickey, Yogi Berra and Thurman Munson in the pantheon of great Yankee catchers. Posada was drafted by the Yankees in 1990, and made his way to the big leagues in 1996. He became a regular in 1998. His best season was in 2003, when he hit .281 with 30 homers and 101 RBI. But it was behind the plate where the five-time All Star was most effective. Posada led American League catchers in putouts for three straight years (2001-03). His career fielding percentage of .992 behind the plate is 45th all-time.

LIFETIME STATS: BA: .273, HR: 275, RBI: 1,065, H: 1,664, SB: 20

#815 James Robert "Bob" Horner
3B-1B, Braves, Cardinals, 1978–86, 88

Bob Horner stepped off the campus of Arizona State University and made a big splash in the major leagues with the Braves. After winning numerous college awards for his slugging prowess, he started auspiciously as he homered in his first game against Bert Blyleven and ended the season with the tremendous ratio of one homer per every 14.04 at bats, the most by any Rookie of the Year. Horner, dubbed "Piggy" by some of his less beefy teammates, also had injury problems throughout his career. But when he was right, Horner could slug the baseball; he hit a career-high 35 homers in 1980. He routinely combined with Dale Murphy to provide a lethal one-two punch in the heart of the Braves' batting order.

LIFETIME STATS: BA: .277, HR: 218, RBI: 685, H: 1,047, SB: 14

#816 Frank Joseph Thomas

OF-3B-1B, Pirates, Reds, Cubs, Braves, Mets, Phillies, Astros, 1951–66

Pittsburgh-born Frank Thomas made a hit with the hometown fans in his early years with the Pirates. He belted 30 homers and knocked in 102 runs in his first full season (1953) and because of his blue collar ethic and Eastern European background, the fans loved him as one of their own. Thomas hit 23 or more homers from 1954 to 1958. Thomas became an original Met in 1962, and he found the short left field porch to his liking, clouting 34 homers to lead the team. Thomas had the distinction of playing in the New York Giants' last game in 1957, where he was playing first for the Pirates, and playing the first game for the Mets in left field, both games being played in the Polo Grounds.

LIFETIME STATS: BA: .266, HR: 286, RBI: 962, H: 1,671, SB: 15

#817 Tommy McCarthy

OF, Boston (UA), Braves (NL), Phillies (NL), Browns (AA), Boston (NL), Dodgers, 1884–96. Hall of Fame, 1946

Perhaps the least known member of the Hall of Fame, McCarthy did have some fine seasons in a 13-year career in three major leagues. He came into his own as a player in the 1888 season with the American Association's St. Louis Browns, helping them to a pennant as he played well defensively and swiped 93 bases and led the league with 83 more in 1890. He and Hugh Duffy, while they were helping the Braves win the NL pennants of 1892 and 1893, were called "the Heavenly Twins" for their stalwart outfield play. McCarthy is credited with improving, if not inventing, the hit-and-run play and runner-to-batter signals, and he was very adroit at trapping the ball in the outfield.

LIFETIME STATS: BA: .292, HR: 44, RBI: 735, H: 1,496, SB: 468

#818 James Henry "Jim" Landis

OF, White Sox, A's, Indians, Astros, Tigers, Red Sox, 1957–67

Regarded as one of the best defensive center fielders of his era, Jim Landis won five straight Gold Gloves with the White Sox from 1960 to 1964, and selection to the American League All Star team in 1962. He did have a weak bat, as his .247 lifetime batting average attests, but defensively he had the attitude that there was "no ball he couldn't reach." His career fielding average was an impressive .989, second all time when he retired. He did have a clutch bat in the 1959 World Series, hitting .292 and leading the Chisox with six runs in a losing effort against the Dodgers.

LIFETIME STATS: BA: .247, HR: 93, RBI: 467, H: 1,061, SB: 139

#819 Charles Louis "Deacon" Phillippe

RHP, Louisville (NL), Pirates, 1899–1911

Phillippe, due to his clean-living lifestyle in a rough and tumble era, was dubbed "Deacon" by his peers. He had excellent control: in 2,607 career innings pitched, he only walked 363 batters. That 1.25 walks for every nine innings pitched is the best of any pitcher in the 20th century. Phillippe won over 20 games in his first five years in the National League and was 25–9 in 1903. In the first World Series that year, Phillippe defined the word workhorse as he threw five complete games in the Series, a record that is most unlikely to be broken. He won all of the Pirates' three games, and lost two as Pittsburgh fell to the Red Sox. In 1969 to celebrate baseball's centennial year, Deacon Phillippe was elected the all-time top Pirate right handed pitcher.

LIFETIME STATS: W: 189, L: 109, SV: 12, ERA: 2.59, SO: 929, CG: 242

#820 Carl Frederick Rudolf "Fred," "Bonehead" Merkle

1B, Giants, Dodgers, Cubs, Yankees, 1907–20, 1925–26

Merkle was a very good baseball player, but he is best known for a boner he pulled in a September game in the pennant race of 1908 as he played for the Giants against the Cubs, essentially failing to touch second base at the end of a game. The game went into the record books as a tie and as luck would have it the teams ended the season in a tie, necessitating a playoff game, which, of course, the Cubs won. Merkle was distraught, but he eventually went on to have a fine career as he redeemed himself by helping the Giants to pennants in 1911, 1912 and 1913. He hit a game-winning sacrifice fly in Game Five in 1911, scored five runs in the 1912 Series and hit a homer in Game Four in 1913, all in losing causes. Merkle was also speedy on the base paths as he had 272 career stolen bases, including 11 steals of home.

LIFETIME STATS: BA: .273, HR: 60, RBI: 733, H: 1,580, SB: 272

#**821** Louis Victor "Lou," "Sweet Lou" Piniella

OF-DH, Orioles, Indians, Royals, Yankees, 1964, 1968–84

"Sweet Lou" Piniella first made his mark in 1969, earning Rookie of the Year honors, hitting 21 doubles, six triples, and 11 homers while hitting .282. He hit .301 with a career-best 88 RBI a year later, and two years afterward he was second in the batting race to Rod Carew with an impressive .312 mark. Piniella went to New York in 1974 and the fans loved him for his fiery never-say-die attitude. He hit over .300 five times for the Bombers, and his arm from the outfield was excellent as three times in his career he had 10 or more assists. In 1976, Piniella became the first designated hitter in World Series history, clubbing a double against the Reds.

LIFETIME STATS: BA: .291, HR: 102, RBI: 766, H: 1,705, SB: 32

#822 Gregory Carpenter "Greg," "Gags" Gagne

SS, Twins, Royals, Dodgers, 1983–97

A consistent player who played over 100 games in each of his 13 seasons with three clubs, "Gags" was a clutch performer, especially with the Twins. The Fall River, Massachusetts, native was the "glue" in the infield for the Twins championship teams of 1987 and 1991. Despite committing a league-high 26 errors in 1986, Gagne set a club shortstop record by playing in 47 straight errorless games. Gagne tied an American League record with two inside-the-park homers in one game in October, 1986, and homered twice in the 1987 League Championship Series against the Tigers. Gagne was also instrumental at the plate for the Twins in the Series as he hit another homer, scored five runs, tying for the club lead in that department, and singled in the winning run in Game Seven.

LIFETIME STATS: BA: .254, HR: 111, RBI: 604, H: 1,440, SB: 108

#823 Don Lee "The Blazer" Blasingame

2B, Cardinals, Giants, Reds, Senators, A's, 1955–66

"The Blazer," as he was sometimes called, was a steady player throughout his career with five major league clubs. A great contact hitter, Blasingame would spray the ball to all fields and was an exceptional bunter. Four times in his career, he spoiled no-hitters late in the game, with two coming in August of 1963. Blasingame was extremely hard to double up as he led the league four times in grounding out in the fewest double plays, and hit into only 43 in a career spanning over 5,000 at bats.

LIFETIME STATS: BA: .258, HR: 21, RBI: 308, H: 1,366, SB: 105

#824 Peter Thomas "Pete" Ward

3B-1B-OF, Orioles, White Sox, Yankees, 1962–70

Son of former National Hockey League player Jimmy Ward, this Montreal native had a promising career cut short by injuries. Ward could be a bit erratic in the field as he led AL third baseman in errors in his rookie year, but more than made up for his defensive woes with his clutch hitting, as he beat the Tigers with a homer on Opening Day, 1970. All in all, Ward hit .295 with 22 homers, 84 RBI, and scored 80 runs, as he finished second in the circuit in total bases (289), hits (177), and doubles (34) on the way to being named the Sporting News Rookie of the Year. He had career highs in homers in 1964 including three grand slams, and 94 RBI. His career declined after a 1965 car accident, and he was used primarily as a pinch hitter in his final years, and the clutch Canadian led the AL in that department in 1969, going 17 for 46 for an impressive .370 average.

LIFETIME STATS: BA: .254, HR: 98, RBI: 427, H: 776, SB: 20

#825 Riboberto "Tito," "Parakeet" Fuentes

2B-SS-3B, Giants, Padres, Tigers, A's, 1965–67, 1969–78

The colorful, slick-fielding Fuentes had a fine year with the Giants in 1966, but the following year went into a slump, and was farmed out to Phoenix. In Arizona, Fuentes learned to switch-hit and came back to the big club in 1969, when he hit .295. Fuentes tied the dubious record of getting hit by a pitch three times in the same game, prompting the infamous remark from Tito: "They shouldn't throw at me. I'm the father of five or six kids." Tito led National League second basemen in errors in 1971 and 1972, but then set a league record a year later by committing just six errors in fielding, a sparkling .993. Fuentes had 63 RBI for the Giants in 1973 and four years later he scored 83 runs for Detroit while hitting a career-high .309.

LIFETIME STATS: BA: .268, HR: 45, RBI: 438, H: 1,491, SB: 80

#826 Joseph Anthony "Joe," "Pepi" Pepitone

1B-OF, Yankees, Astros, Cubs, Braves, 1962–73

After playing sparingly but well in 1962, Pepitone was deemed ready to assume the first base duties, and the Yankees traded away veteran Moose Skowron. "Pepi," due to his Italian ancestry and local roots, was an immediate fan favorite and hit .271 while clubbing 27 homers in 1963 to help the Yankees win the AL pennant in 1963. Pepitone continued to hit in 1964, hitting 28 homers and driving in a career best 100 runs as the Yanks won the pennant again, but fell to the Cardinals in the World Series. In 1965, he won his first of three Gold Gloves, but only hit .247. But the Yankees grew tired of the flashy Pepitone's act, so he was sent to Houston in 1970. Stints in Chicago, Atlanta and Japan followed.

LIFETIME STATS: BA: .258, HR: 219, RBI: 721, H: 1,315, SB: 41

#827 Edmund Walter "Eddie," "Steady Eddie," "The Junk Man" Lopat (Lopatynski)

LHP, White Sox, Yankees, Orioles, 1944–55

"Steady Eddie" was a good pitcher, going 50–49 with the second division White Sox in his first four years in the majors, but then was traded to the Yankees, where he was part of a great pitching rotation, helping the Bombers to a record five straight World Championships from 1949 to 1953. Casey Stengel smartly used the junk throwing Lopat after throwing his two fireballers, Allie Reynolds and Vic Raschi to upset the opposition's timing. Lopat went 109–51 from 1948 to 1954. He won 21 games in 1951 and beat the Giants twice in the 1951 Series. "The Junk Man" also was an impressive 4-1 in World Series play in his career with a sterling 2.60 ERA.

LIFETIME STATS: W: 166, L: 112, SV: 3, ERA: 3.21, SO: 859, CG: 164

#828 Richard Leo "Rich" Gedman

C-DH, Red Sox, Astros, Cardinals, 1980–92

A native of Worcester, less than an hour away from Fenway Park, Rich Gedman took over the catching duties, along with Gary Allenson, for the departed free agent Carlton Fisk in 1980, taking over the full-time position in 1984. Gedman was twice an American League All Star, clouting 24 homers and 26 doubles in 1984, and hitting .295 with 80 RBI in 1985. He also knocked in 65 runs in the pennant winning year of 1986, and his fine play behind the plate helped ensure the Red Sox the American League pennant. His offensive statistics declined in the next few years, and he decided to call it a career in 1992 after short stints with Houston and St. Louis.

LIFETIME STATS: BA: .252, HR: 88, RBI: 382, H: 795, SB: 3

#829 John Cornelius "Johnny" Ray

2B, Pirates, Angels, 1981–90

Johnny Ray broke in with the Pirates and in his first full year, and won the 1982 Rookie of the Year Award as the talented switch-hitter led National League second basemen in putouts, assists and total chances while hitting .281 and smashing 30 doubles. Speaking of doubles, Ray tied for the league lead the next two years in that department with 38 each time. In 1986, he made only five errors during the entire season, but was traded to the Angels in 1987. He represented the Halos in his only All Star appearance in 1988.

LIFETIME STATS: BA: .290, HR: 53, RBI: 594, H: 1,502, SB: 80

#830 Charles John "Charlie," "Jolly Cholly" Grimm

1B, A's, Cardinals, Pirates, Cubs, 1916, 1918–36

"Jolly Cholly," so called because of his easy-going demeanor and his love for playing the banjo, had some quality seasons with both the Pirates and Cubs. The constant in Grimm's game was his excellent fielding at first base, as he didn't have an outstanding year with the bat until 1923, hitting .345 while knocking in a career-high 99 runs with Pittsburgh. In 1929, now with Chicago, Grimm hit .298 and had 91 RBI as the Cubs captured the 1929 National League pennant. He hit a robust .389 as the Cubs lost the World Series to Connie Mack's A's.

LIFETIME STATS: BA: .290, HR: 79, RBI: 1,078, H: 2,299, SB: 57

Torriente
C. 43.

#831 Cristobal Torriente

OF, NY Cubans, Chicago American Giants, All Nations, KC Monarchs, Detroit Stars, Cleveland Cubs (Negro Leagues), 1913–28, 1932. Hall of Fame, 2006

Torriente was a powerful slugger who arguably was one of the greatest players ever to come out of Cuba. Though small in stature at only 5'9", "The Cuban Strongboy" proved to be a powerful left-handed swinger and was a terrific bad ball hitter. The talented Cuban possessed a great throwing arm and was an outstanding defensive outfielder. Torriente led the Chicago American Giants to three straight Negro League Championships from 1920 to 1922, hitting a stellar .396 in 1920. He even took a turn on the mound now and then, compiling a 16–5 record. In the 12 years he played in the Cuban League, Torriente hit .352, leading the league in hits and stolen bases three times, and in triples and home runs four times. His career-best batting average was a lusty .402 in 1916.

LIFETIME STATS: BA: .335, HR: 53, H: 774

#832 Thomas Tarlton "Tom" Brown

OF, Baltimore (AA), Columbus (AA), Pittsburgh (AA), Pittsburgh (NL), Indianapolis (NL), Boston (NL), Boston (PL), Boston (AA), Louisville (NL), Browns, Senators, 1882–98

Tom Brown was a journeyman's journeyman, playing for 11 teams in his 17-year career, including three Boston franchises in a row, the Boston Braves of the National

League (1888–89), the Boston Red Stockings of the Player's League (1890) and the Boston franchise in the American Association (1891). In 1891, Brown had his best season as he led the league with 189 hits, 177 runs, 21 triples, and 106 stolen bases. Brown led off a game with a home run 11 times in his career. He then moved to the Colonels of Louisville for the next three seasons, leading the loop in steals in 1893 with 66.

LIFETIME STATS: BA: .265, HR: 64, RBI: 736, H: 1,951, SB: 657

#833 Howard Ellsworth "Smokey Joe" Wood
RHP, Red Sox, Indians, 1908–15, 1917–22

The flame-throwing righty found his groove in 1911 when he won 23 games for fifth-place Boston, including a no-hitter in July against St. Louis. He was dubbed "Smokey Joe" after that. In 1912, Wood enjoyed his finest season, one of the finest any pitcher has ever had, as the right-hander started 36 games, completing 35 with 10 shutouts, a 1.91 ERA, 258 strikeouts, and an eye-popping 34–5 record, winning 16 straight at one point in that fabulous year. His 34 victories are still a Red Sox record and his 10 shutouts tied Cy Young for the team record for a season. The Bosox won the American League pennant and beat the Giants in the World Series. In 1913, Wood broke his right thumb and pitched in pain all year long, going 11–5. He retired in 1916, but made a comeback as an outfielder for the Indians, hitting .296 with five homers and 22 doubles in 119 games.

LIFETIME STATS: W: 116, L: 57, SV: 11, ERA: 2.03, SO: 989, CG: 121. BA: .283, HR: 23, RBI: 325, H: 553, SB: 23

#834 Charles William "Charlie" Moore
C-OF, Brewers, Blue Jays, 1973–87

Moore spent most of his career with the Milwaukee Brewers platooning as catcher and hitting against left-handed pitchers. He did manage to crack the Brewer lineup in the outfield as he was a regular there for the only time in his career. In 1982, Moore, never a potent hitter in the regular season, had the hot bat for the Brewers as he hit an astounding .462 in the American League Championship Series, helping Milwaukee to defeat the California Angels in five games. The right-handed hitter continued his fall heroics in the Series, garnering nine hits in 26 at-bats to the tune of a robust .346 average. Despite Moore's fine hitting, the Brewers lost the World Series that year to the St. Louis Cardinals in seven games. He hit .284 playing regularly in right field the following year.

LIFETIME STATS: BA: .261, HR: 36, RBI: 408, H: 1,052, SB: 51

Would be best to cut a line here

#835 James Kenneth "Jim," "Frenchy" Lefebvre
2B-3B, Dodgers, 1965–72

Lefebvre (pronounced "Luh-FEV-er") was part of the Dodgers' switch-hitting infield along with Wes Parker, Maury Wills and Jim Gilliam. He led the anemic-hitting Dodgers in homers as a rookie in 1965 with 12 as Los Angeles used its pitching prowess to beat the Twins in seven games in the 1965 Fall Classic. Lefebrve homered from both sides of the plate in a 1966 game as he doubled his homer output to 24, while collecting a career-high 74 RBI. Later on that year, he contributed a homer in the 1966 World Series, connecting off Oriole ace Dave McNally.

LIFETIME STATS: BA: .251, HR: 74, RBI: 404, H: 756, SB: 8

#836 Granville Wilbur "Granny" Hamner

SS-2B, Phillies, Indians, A's, 1944–59, 1962

Granville "Granny" Hamner was but a mere lad of 17 when he made his debut with the 1944 Phillies, but it wasn't until 1948 that he became a starter. Between 1949 and 1954, Hamner played at least 150 games a season, and he was selected by Phillies fans as the club's all-time shortstop in 1969. He proved he could hit in the clutch as he hit 30 or more doubles four times in his career. He switched to second base in 1954 and had his best year at the plate, hitting .299 with 13 homers, 89 RBI and 39 doubles.

LIFETIME STATS: BA: .262, HR: 104, RBI: 708, H: 1,529, SB: 35

#837 George Henry "Tioga" Burns

1B-OF, Tigers, A's, Indians, Red Sox, Yankees, 1914–29

Consistent would not be a word to describe "Tioga" George Burns's career as he hit as high as .361, and as low as .224. In his first year with the Tigers, Burns hit a respectable .291 and led the American League in putouts with 1,576, but he also committed a league high 30 errors. He was traded to Philadelphia and hit .352, leading the league with 178 hits, and knocking home 70 runs. He slumped again in 1920, causing Connie Mack to deal him to the Indians, and Burns hit .300 in the World Series as Cleveland won it. Burns was a part-timer in 1921, and hit .361, but was traded to Boston. Cleveland reacquired Burns in 1924, and he responded brilliantly in 1926 as he swatted a then major league record 64 doubles, hit .358, led the loop with 216 hits, drove in 114 runs, and captured the league MVP Award.

LIFETIME STATS: BA: .307, HR: 72, RBI: 951, H: 2,018, SB: 154

#838 Thomas William "Tommy," "Corky" Corcoran

SS-2B, Pittsburgh (PL), Philadelphia (AA), Dodgers, Reds, Giants, 1890–1907

Tommy Corcoran started his career at shortstop, fielding the ball without the benefit of a glove although he made a smooth transition to the leather. An excellent fielder with or without a glove, he set a major league record with the Reds in 1903 with an astounding 14 assists in one game. He led the league in fielding four times, and twice in assists. He is also among the career shortstop leaders in games played and total chances per game. Corcoran was traded to the Giants in 1907, where he played second base.

LIFETIME STATS: BA: .256, HR: 34, RBI: 1,135, H: 2,252, SB: 387

#839 Guy Jackson Hecker

RHP-1B-OF, Louisville (AA), Pirates, 1882–90

The versatile Guy Hecker not only could pitch well, but could hit, and is the only pitcher to ever win a major league batting title, hitting .341 in 1886. In one game alone, Hecker went six for seven, and scored seven times, a record for any player, let alone a pitcher. Three of those hits were inside-the-park homers; the only time in American Association history that any player accomplished that feat. As for his pitching prowess, in 1884, Hecker led the league with 670 2/3 innings pitched, 385 strikeouts, 72 complete games, and won an unbelievable 52 games. Hecker clearly benefited from the 50 foot distance from the pitching rubber to the plate. Those many innings took a toll on his arm but he still remained a threat with the bat.

LIFETIME STATS: W: 175, L: 146, SV: 1, ERA: 2.92, SO: 1,099, CG: 310, BA: .282, HR: 19, RBI: 278, H: 812, SB: 123

#840 James Anthony "Jimmy" Piersall

OF, Red Sox, Indians, Senators, Mets, Angels, 1950, 1952–67

Jimmy Piersall was a talented but high-strung athlete who had major bouts with mental illness, especially early in his career. The illness got out of control in 1953 and the Red Sox ordered Piersall to get counseling. He underwent a series of shock treatments, which somewhat tempered his bizarre behavior. Returning to the field, he was brilliant in the outfield. Piersall led the league thrice in fielding percentage, twice in putouts, and once in double plays, as well as winning Gold Gloves in 1958 and 1961. Piersall made his mark offensively too, as he hit .293 in 1956, leading the AL in doubles with 40, and had 176 hits and 87 RBI.

LIFETIME STATS: BA: .272, HR: 104, RBI: 591, H: 1,604, SB: 115

#841 George Burton Pinkney

3B-2B, Cleveland (NL), Brooklyn (AA), Dodgers, Browns, Louisville (NL), 1884–93

George Pinkney was a steady infielder for a number of teams, most particularly for Brooklyn, who won back-to-back championships in two different leagues, the American Association and the National League, an unprecedented feat. The 5'7" Pinkney was a threat on the bases, stealing 44 or more bases for five years in a row, and totaling 296 thefts for his career. He scored over 100 runs five straight times in his career, leading the league in 1888 with 134. Pinkney also had a keen eye at the plate, leading the AA in drawing walks in 1886 with 70. He also led AA third sackers in fielding in 1887 and 1889.

LIFETIME STATS: BA: .263, HR: 21, RBI: 539, H: 1,212, SB: 296

#**842** Woodson George "Woodie" Held

SS-OF-2B-3B, Yankees, A's, Indians, Senators, Orioles, Angels, White Sox, 1954, 1957–69

Woodie Held was a shortstop with power, a rarity during the time he played. He hit a career-best 29 homers in 1959, and consistently hit 19 or more homers during the bulk of his career in Cleveland. In 1961, Held clouted 23 home runs and had a career-high 78 RBI. This power did come at a cost, however, since Held struck out often, topping the century mark three times in his career. At times, he would get so upset with himself after whiffing, he would throw tantrums.

LIFETIME STATS: BA: .240, HR: 179, RBI: 559, H: 963, SB: 14

#**843** George Hartley McQuinn

1B, Reds, Browns, A's, Yankees, 1936, 1938–48

A six-time All Star, George McQuinn was mired in the Yankee farm system from 1931 to 1936, because Lou Gehrig was playing in New York. He played briefly for the Reds, and then the St. Louis Browns drafted him in 1937. He hit in 34 consecutive games in 1938 on the way to hitting .324 and scoring 100 runs. The following year he hit .316, and scored 101 runs. A slick fielder, McQuinn led American League first basemen in fielding on three occasions and in assists twice. In the 1948 All Star game, when he was back with the Yankees, the smooth-fielding McQuinn set All Star records with 14 putouts in 14 total chances.

LIFETIME STATS: BA: .276, HR: 135, RBI: 794, H: 1,588, SB: 32

#844 Renaldo Antonio "Rennie" Stennett

2B-SS, Pirates, Giants, 1971–81

On September 16, 1975, Rennie Stennett became the first player in the 20th century to get seven hits in a nine inning game, as the Pirates walloped the Cubs, 22–0. Stennett started out his career in the Pirates chain as an outfielder, but moved to second base in 1973. He shone defensively, leading NL second baseman in both putouts and total chances per game that year and again in 1976. He also hit .291 that year while scoring 84 runs. In 1973, he went 59 straight games without an error. A contact hitter, Stennett had his best year at the plate in 1977, where he finished second in the NL batting race to Dave Parker, hitting .336 and stealing a career-best 28 bases.

LIFETIME STATS: BA: .274, HR: 41, RBI: 432, H: 1,239, SB: 75

#845 James Reubin "Jim," "Rawhide" Tabor

3B, Red Sox, Phillies, 1938–44, 1946–47

Defensively, the up side of Jim Tabor was he led American League third basemen in putouts and assists once each and twice in double plays. The down side was he led AL third sackers in errors for five consecutive years. Called "Rawhide" because he backed down from nobody, he once slammed the great Ted Williams against a locker after a minor league game in which Tabor thought Williams wasn't hustling. Tabor had a Fourth of July to remember in 1939 when he hit four homers in a doubleheader against the Philadelphia A's, including two grand slams as he totaled 11 RBI that day. Overall, Tabor was a steady offensive performer with a lifetime batting average of .270.

LIFETIME STATS: BA: .270, HR: 104, RBI: 598, H: 1,021, SB: 69

#846 William Frederick "Billy" Jurges

SS-3B, Cubs, Giants, 1931–47

Billy Jurges was a colorful character who was a talented infielder, especially during the bulk of his career with the Cubs. In 1932, Jurges was enjoying a fine season when he was shot in the ribs and hand by a depressed female fan in a hotel room. In 1935, the fiery Jurges got into a fight during a game with third-string Pirate catcher Walker Stephenson over a remark about the Civil War to which Stephenson, a native North Carolinian, took exception. Jurges had a great year in 1937 as he hit a career-best .298 and led the league in fielding for the third time. After a trade to the Giants, Jurges broke his leg in 1940, but the tough Jurges came back and played three more steady seasons in New York.

LIFETIME STATS: BA: .258, HR: 43, RBI: 656, H: 1,613, SB: 36

#**847** Derrel McKinley "Bud" Harrelson
SS-2B, Mets, Phillies, Rangers, 1965–80

Harrelson was a small package, weighing in at 160 pounds on a good day, but was a spark at shortstop for the Mets as they won an improbable World Series victory over the heavily favored Baltimore Orioles in 1969. He was a daring base runner, stealing home on two occasions. The slick-fielding shortstop was twice an All Star, and won the Gold Glove Award in 1971 after tying the since-broken NL record of 54 straight games without an error at shortstop a year earlier. In 1973, the Mets took on the Big Red Machine in the League Championship Series, a series the Mets would win in five games. Pete Rose was on first base in Game Three at Shea Stadium with the Mets ahead 8–2 in the fifth, when Rose barreled into Harrelson covering second. The smaller Harrelson retaliated, and both benches emptied. The fans, especially in left field where Rose played that day, pelted him with various missiles. Order was finally restored only when Willie Mays, Tom Seaver and Manager Yogi Berra appealed to the riled up fans to calm down. In 1977, Harrelson's batting average fell to an unimpressive .178, but he continued to shine defensively, committing a paltry six errors in 98 games.

LIFETIME STATS: BA: .236, HR: 7, RBI: 267, H: 1,120, SB: 127

#848 Casimir Eugene "Cass" Michaels (Kwietniewski)

2B-SS-3B, White Sox, Senators, Browns, A's, 1943–54

Coming up in 1943 at the tender age of 17 and then known by his given name, Casimir Eugene Kwietniewski, the half Polish–half German infielder decided to Americanize his name to Cass Michaels. Sent down to the minors in 1944, he played well there and was brought up to the White Sox in 1945 to be their regular shortstop until All Star Luke Appleing returned from the service. Michaels' best offensive year was in 1949 when he hit .308 and had 83 RBI while drawing 101 walks. He continued to be a steady performer for three other teams, but had to prematurely call it a career at 28, after suffering blurred vision as a result of being hit by a pitch in 1954.

LIFETIME STATS: BA: .262, HR: 53, RBI: 501, H: 1,142, SB: 64

#849 Frederick C. "Fred," "Sure Shot" Dunlap

2B, Cleveland Spiders (NL), St. Louis (UA), Maroons (NL), Detroit (NL), Pirates, New York (PL), Washington (AA), 1880–91

Dunlop was dubbed "Sure Shot" because of his excellent fielding ability, leading the leagues he played in various categories throughout his career. He had above average range and sure hands, and playing without a glove in those days, he could make the spectacular play with either hand. In 1884, millionaire Henry Lucas formed the Union Association and signed Dunlop away from Cleveland to St. Louis. He led the new league in hitting with a robust .412 batting average (52 points ahead of the second-place hitter), home runs, hits, runs, slugging percentage, and on-base percentage as the Maroons waltzed to the pennant. The next year the Union Association folded, and Dunlop was fined $500 by the National League for jumping leagues. He went to Detroit in 1886, helping the Wolverines to the National League flag.

LIFETIME STATS: BA: .292, HR: 41, RBI: 366, H: 1,159, SB: 85

#850 Aurelio "Radio" Rodriguez

3B, Angels, Senators, Tigers, Padres, Yankees, White Sox, Orioles, 1967–83

A great fielding third baseman, Aurelio Rodriguez won the Gold Glove Award in 1976, breaking Brooks Robinson's hold of 16 straight awards at third base. In 1968, the pitchers dominated in baseball, but Rodriguez had the longest hitting streak in the American League that season at 16 games. Though not considered a power hitter, he managed to hit 19 homers in one season and 15 in another. His impressive fielding average of .987 in 1978 was third highest in major league history for shortstops at the time. In part-time duty with the Yankees in 1981, he hit .346 and then was five for 12 in the 1981 World Series loss to the Los Angeles Dodgers for a .417 average.

LIFETIME STATS: BA: .237, HR: 124, RBI: 648, H: 1,570, SB: 35

#851 Solomon Joseph "Solly" Hemus
SS-2B-3B, Cardinals, Phillies, 1949–59

Solomon Joseph Hemus was a steady infielder for both the Cardinals and Phillies, and was the regular shortstop for the Redbirds from 1951 to 1953. He was masterful at getting on base as he drew a lot of walks for a non-power hitter and he led the league three times in getting hit by pitches, including 20 plunks in 1952. In 1954, he hit a career-high .304. He was named player-manager of the Cardinals in 1959 after playing two and a half years with the Phillies, and used himself primarily as a pinch hitter.

LIFETIME STATS: BA: .273, HR: 51, RBI: 263, H: 736, SB: 21

#852 Bruce Anton Bochte
1B-OF, Angels, Indians, Mariners, A's, 1974–82, 1984–86

The 6'3" lefty swinging Bochte was an impressive hitter and the star of the early Mariners teams in the late 70s and early '80s. He led Seattle in hitting three of the five years he played there. Bochte hit .300 or better twice with the Mariners, including 1979, when he hit .316 with 16 home runs and an even 100 RBI. Bochte was Seattle's player representative during the 1981 strike, and that experience left a bitter taste in his mouth, prompting him to walk away from baseball and move his family to an island in Puget Sound to get away from it all. After a one year hiatus, he returned to the game with the A's in 1984 and played three more seasons, his best in 1985 when he hit 14 homers, while hitting .295.

LIFETIME STATS: BA: .282, HR: 100, RBI: 658, H: 1,478, SB: 43

#853 Russell Earl "Bucky" Dent (O'Dey)

SS, White Sox, Yankees, Rangers, Royals, 1973–84

Forever known in Boston as Bucky "Bleepin'" Dent, he is best known for the three-run homer he hit over Fenway Park's Green Monster off pitcher Mike Torrez, erasing a 2–0 deficit on the way to a 5–4 Yankee playoff win over the Boston Red Sox on October 2, 1978. He topped off 1978 with an MVP performance in the World Series win against the Dodgers, going six for eight in the final four games while hitting a stellar .417. Dent was drafted by the White Sox, where he became the regular shortstop in 1974, and was second in the Rookie of the Year balloting while hitting .275. In 1977, Dent was traded to the Yankees where he made the All Star team in 1980 and 1981. In 1982, he was traded to the Rangers, where he led AL shortstops in fielding for the third time in his career.

LIFETIME STATS: BA: .247, HR: 40, RBI: 423, H: 1,114, SB: 17

#854 Jeffrey Howard "Jeff" Cirillo

1B-2B-3B-SS-OF-DH, Brewers, Rockies, Mariners, Padres, Twins, 1994–present

Cirillo is a good fielding third baseman who is capable of going on hot binges at the plate. A first-round pick by the Brewers in 1991, he got five hits in a loss to the White Sox in 1998. He also collected five safeties in two games in 1999, once in July, when he had a double, homer and three singles to help Milwaukee beat Pittsburgh and in August where he stroked a double and four singles. Cirillo put up some impressive numbers while in Milwaukee, hitting .325 with 15 homers, 83

RBI and 46 doubles in 1996 and again hitting 46 two-baggers the following year. He also hit an impressive .326 in 1999. With Colorado, he hit .326 with 11 homers and so far a career-best 115 RBI and 53 doubles, in 2000.

LIFETIME STATS: BA: .297, HR: 112, RBI: 720, H: 1,587, SB: 63

#855 Antonio Rafael "Tony" Armas
OF-DH, Pirates, A's, Red Sox, Angels, 1976–89

The Venezuelan Armas came up briefly with the Pirates, but made his mark with the A's, and later with the Red Sox. Armas erupted for 35 homers and 109 RBI in 1980. On the down side was his propensity for striking out, as he was a free swinger. He tied for the AL home run lead in the strike-shortened 1981 season with 22, making the All Star team; he was also named the Sporting News American League Player of the Year. He was traded to Boston in 1983 and found Fenway Park to his liking, clouting 36 homers with 107 RBI in his first year in Beantown, and countering that with an even better 43-homer and 123-RBI season in 1984, leading the AL in both categories. Not only could Armas hit, he possessed a tremendous arm in the outfield.

LIFETIME STATS: BA: .252, HR: 251, RBI: 815, H: 1,302, SB: 18

#856 Claudell Washington

OF, A's, Rangers, White Sox, Mets, Braves, Yankees, Angels, 1974–90

Claudell Washington started his career with the Oakland A's and played in the Bay area for the first three years of his career, joining Oakland halfway through the 1974 season, hitting .285 in 73 games. He distinguished himself in Oakland's third straight World Series win over the Dodgers that year, hitting an impressive .571 with four hits in seven at bats in the five-game Series, while playing all three outfield positions. He hit three homers in a game for the White Sox against Detroit in 1979, and did the same for the Mets against the Dodgers the following year, joining Hall of Famers Babe Ruth, Johnny Mize, and six others as the only players to hit three homers in a game in each league. The speedy outfielder was also a base-stealing threat, stealing 40 in 1975, good for second in the league, and 37 the following year.

LIFETIME STATS: BA: .278, HR: 164, RBI: 824, H: 1,884, SB: 312

#857 James Philip "Jimmy," "Pepper" Austin

3B-SS, New York (AL), Browns, 1909–23, 1925–26, 1929

Jimmy "Pepper" Austin was quite the third baseman in his day. In 12 seasons at the hot corner, he led the American League in total chances five times, five times in double plays, and led in other fielding categories throughout his career. Though not a consistent hitter, he had a keen eye at the plate, drawing numerous walks, and stole

244 bases in his career, with a high of 37 in 1913. Austin is the third baseman in the famous picture of Ty Cobb sliding into third with spikes high.

LIFETIME STATS: BA: .246, HR: 13, RBI: 390, H: 1,328, SB: 244

#858 David Brian Cone

RHP, Royals, Mets, Blue Jays, Yankees, Red Sox, 1986–2001, 2003

Coming up originally with his hometown team, Kansas City sent Cone to the Mets in 1987 in what Royals' ownership later said was "the worst trade in [our] history." His first full season was in 1988, when "Coney" went an impressive 20–3 to lead the senior circuit in winning percentage and rank second in earned run average and strikeouts. Cone led the National League in strikeouts for three straight years (1990–92). In 1991, he fanned a then National–League record tying 19 Phillies. In strike-shortened 1994 he was 16-5 and won the Cy Young Award. In 1998 he went 20–7 with the Yankees, and struck out over 200 for the second straight season. In the postseason, Cone was at his best, going 6–1 overall in postseason play for the Yanks. Cone threw a perfect game in 1999 against the Montreal Expos at Yankee Stadium, striking out 10.

LIFETIME STATS: W: 194, L: 126, SV: 1, ERA: 3.46, SO: 2,668, CG: 56

#859 James Robert "Sailor Bob," "Bob the Gob" Shawkey

RHP, Athletics, Yankees, 1913–27

"Sailor Bob" Shawkey, so named because he served in the Navy before he signed a big-league contract, was the ace of the staff for the Yankees in the 1920s. He won 20 or more games in 1919, 1920 and 1922, and also led the league in saves in 1916 (8) and 1919 (5). Shawkey had a 10-game winning streak in 1919 and an 11-game streak in 1920. He struck out 15 Athletics in a game in 1919, which was a Yankee record for 59 years. Shawkey was the winning pitcher in the first game ever played in Yankee Stadium in 1923.

LIFETIME STATS: W: 196, L: 150, SV: 29, ERA: 3.09, SO: 1,360, CG: 197

#860 Edward Francis "Ed" Bressoud

SS, Giants, Red Sox, Mets, Cardinals, 1956–67

Though he was very versatile and could play other positions, Eddie Bressoud was a shortstop for most of his major league career, starting out with the Giants. He was traded to Boston in 1962. A reliable, though not always an everyday player with San Francisco, Bressoud tailored his swing to Boston's friendly wall in left. A right-handed swinger, Bressoud would love pulling the ball over or off the Green Monster. Never before having double-figure years in homers, Bressoud hit 14 in 1962, peaked at 20 in 1963, and then struck 15 in 1964, while hitting a career-high .293 that season. He also cracked 40 doubles twice in Beantown. He finished up as a utility player with the Mets and Cardinals.

LIFETIME STATS: BA: .252, HR: 94, RBI: 365, H: 925, SB: 9

#861 Jorge Ort

2B-DH-OF-3B, White Sox, Indians, Dodgers, Blue Jays, Royals, 1972–87

The Mexican-born Orta signed with the White Sox in 1972 and became the team's regular second baseman in 1973. He quite literally hit it big in 1974 as he hit at a .316 clip, second in the junior circuit, and had five-hit games on three occasions that year. He continued his proficiency at the plate the following year when he batted .304, knocking in a career-high 83 runs. In 1976, he was elected into Mexico's Baseball Hall of Fame. The White Sox moved him around defensively to keep his bat in the lineup, so Orta never again had one defensive position he could work on. He signed on with Cleveland for the 1980 season, hit .291, and he tallied six hits in one game that season as he was named to the AL All Star team.

LIFETIME STATS: BA: .278, HR: 130, RBI: 745, H: 1,619, SB: 79

#862 Leonard Eugene "Gene," "Oopie" Alley

SS-2B, Pirates, 1963–73

A lifetime Pirate, Gene Alley was an excellent fielder and adequate hitter for the Pirates teams of the mid '60s. Nicknamed "Oopie" by Buc announcer Bob Prince, Alley teamed with Hall of Famer Bill Mazeroski to form an airtight middle infield, which set a National League record for double plays in 1966 with 216. Alley also won the Gold Glove that year, as well as the next, and hit a career best .299. The mild-mannered Virginian was a good team player, and manager Danny Murtaugh would use him to bunt or in the hit and run as Alley was an excellent contact hitter. He was selected to the National League All Star team twice.

LIFETIME STATS: BA: .254, HR: 55, RBI: 342, H: 999, SB: 63

#863 Ervin "Pete" Fox
OF, Tigers, Red Sox, 1933–45

Fox was a very dependable outfielder primarily for the Tigers in the 30s. He came up as a pitcher in the Tiger chain, but was convinced to switch to the outfield, which may account for his strong arm from right field. He had a fabulous rookie season in 1933, hitting .288 with a career-best 13 triples. He scored 100 or more runs for three out of four seasons. Fox had a career year in 1935 hitting .321, with a career-high 15 homers, along with 73 RBI, 116 runs scored and 38 doubles. Speaking of two-baggers, Fox stroked a World Series record six doubles in a losing effort in the 1934 World Series against the St. Louis Cardinals. The Tigers got back to the Fall Classic in 1935, and Pete Fox led all Tiger hitters, hitting .385 (10 for 26) as the Tigers won it all.

LIFETIME STATS: BA: .298, HR: 65, RBI: 694, H: 1,678, SB: 158

#864 Douglas Vernon "Doug" DeCinces
3B, Orioles, California Angels, Cardinals, 1973–87

DeCinces had the near-impossible task of replacing Brooks Robinson at third base with the Orioles, and to his credit, he played well enough to at least gain a reputation as a solid fielder and clutch hitter. Traded to California, he finished third in American League MVP voting in 1982 as an Angel. That year, he hit a career-best .301, with 97 RBI, 30 home runs and 173 hits. He hit .316 in the Angels' ALCS loss to Milwaukee in 1982. DeCinces averaged 23 home runs and 86 RBI over 15 seasons.

LIFETIME STATS: BA: .259, HR: 237, RBI: 879, H: 1,505, SB: 58

#865 Abner Frank Dalrymple

OF, Milwaukee (NA), Chicago (NL), Pirates, Milwaukee (AA), 1878–88, 1891

Abner Dalrymple was best known as the speedy lead-off man who played left field for Cap Anson's juggernaut Chicago teams of the 1880s, which won five pennants in seven years. In 1884, Dalrymple hit 22 homers, an almost unheard of total, but the left-handed-hitting out fielder benefited from a short right-field fence, reportedly only 200 feet from home plate. The team boasted a homer total of 142, not to be bested until the legendary 1927 New York Yankees. Dalrymple "only" hit 11 the following year, but it was good enough to lead the league. He also led the circuit in hits in 1880. In 1883, Dalrymple hit four doubles in a game, tying a major league record.

LIFETIME STATS: BA: .288, HR: 43, RBI: 407, H: 1,202, SB: 58

#866 Hubert "Hubie" Brooks

OF-3B-SS, Mets, Expos, Dodgers, Angels, Royals, 1980–94

Hubie Brooks came up to the Mets in September 1980 and quickly became a fan favorite at Shea Stadium. Brooks fulfilled that promise in his first full season, hitting a solid .307, and came in third in the Rookie of the Year vote. In 1984, he hit in 24 straight games, a club record. At the end of that year, the Mets traded Brooks to the Expos, and obtained Hall of Fame catcher Gary Carter in the process. The Expos converted Brooks to a full-time shortstop, and in 1985, he became the first from that position to drive in at least 100 runs since Cub legend Ernie Banks did it in 1960. After two All Star seasons in Montreal and a year in Los Angeles, he returned to the Mets in 1991 and hit 16 more home runs, and even stole home twice that year.

LIFETIME STATS: BA: .269, HR: 149, RBI: 824, H: 1,608, SB: 64

#867 John Joseph "Jack" Barry

SS-2B, A's, Red Sox, 1908–17, 1919

Only a lifetime .243 hitter, Jack Barry had a penchant for playing on pennant winners, four times with Connie Mack's A's, and twice with the Boston Red Sox. Barry seemed to save his hits for when they were most needed, and seemed to make the big defensive play when most crucial also. The prevailing thought in baseball circles was that Joe Tinker and Johnny Evers were the best double play combination in the game. But the A's Connie Mack thought Barry and Eddie Collins were better. The two perfected the first and third cutoff play with runners on first and third.

LIFETIME STATS: BA: .243, HR: 10, RBI: 429, H: 1,009, SB: 153

#868 Jason Dolph Thompson

1B, Tigers, Angels, Pirates, Expos, 1976–86

After a mediocre rookie season, Jason Thompson exploded in 1977 for 31 homers, two completely over the right field roof at Tiger Stadium, and 105 RBI. Traded to the Angels midway through the 1980 season, Thompson ended the season with a combined total of 21 homers and 90 RBI, while hitting .288. Traded to the Pirates during spring training in 1981, Thompson had a rare triple feat the next season: He drove in 101 runs, walked 101 times, and struck out 107 times. He also clouted 31 homers in that season, making him only the eighth player to get 30 or more homers in both leagues. Knee injuries prevented the power-hitting first baseman to continue playing, and after a brief stint with the Expos, he called it a career in 1986 at the young age of 32.

LIFETIME STATS: BA: .261, HR: 208, RBI: 782, H: 1,253, SB: 8

#869 Frederick "Firpo" Marberry

RHP, Senators, Tigers, Giants, 1923–36

Marberry was nicknamed "Firpo" because he resembled Argentinian heavyweight boxer Luis Firpo. Before it was in style, Firpo Marberry was considered the first great reliever. Early in his career with the Senators, he was a starter, and would throw only the fastball. Eventually major league hitters teed off on it. Then manager Bucky Harris moved him to the bullpen, and a new career was born. In 1924, Marberry lead the AL in appearances with 50, 35 out of the bullpen with 15 saves. That helped the Senators win the pennant and the World Series. The year before, without Marberry, the Senators had come in fourth in the AL. (Marberry was the only addition to their roster in 1924). In 1926, he saved a record 22 games, appearing in 64 games, unheard of for a reliever back then. He retired in 1936 having become the first pitcher to record 100 saves, ending up with 101.

LIFETIME STATS: W: 148, L: 88, SV: 101, ERA: 3.63, SO: 822, CG: 86

#870 John "Ellis" Johnny Temple
2B, Reds, Orioles, Indians, Astros, 1952–64

Temple was the Reds' regular second baseman for most of the 1950s. He was a part-time player his first two years, but took over the second baseman's job for good in 1953. That season, he hit .307, with 155 hits and 21 stolen bases. Temple was popular with the fans, and was an All Star for the Reds in 1956, 1957 and 1959. Traded to the Indians the next season, Temple was an All Star again in 1961. He hit .300 or better three times in his career.

LIFETIME STATS: BA: .284, HR: 36, RBI: 395, H: 1,484, SB: 140

#871 Williams James "B.J." Surhoff
C-3B-1B-OF, Brewers, Orioles, Braves, 1987–present

A collegiate star and an Olympian on the 1984 United States team, Surhoff broke in with the Milwaukee Brewers and hit .299 as a rookie catcher, with seven homers. He hit .320 in 1995, good for sixth in the American League. A free agent in 1996, he signed with the Baltimore Orioles and his power numbers shot up to 21 homers in 1996 and 18 in 1997. 1999, however, was his career year for the Birds as

Surhoff hit .308, banged out 207 hits, smashed 28 home runs, had 107 RBI and scored 104 runs while playing the outfield, where he led the league in fielding percentage. He was named to the AL All Star squad that year.

LIFETIME STATS: BA: .281, HR: 175, RBI: 1,069, H: 2,142, SB: 139

#**872** Earl John "Sparky" Adams
2B-3B-SS, Cubs, Pirates, Cardinals, Reds, 1922–34

A speedy little infielder with a sparkling personality, Adams had a good glove and a keen eye at the plate. His strike zone was nearly microscopic as the diminutive Adams stood at only 5'5 1/2". He played every infield position except first base with skill: he logged over 500 games at third and second, and 297 at shortstop, leading the National League in fielding categories various times. Adams was the ideal leadoff hitter, patient and fast. Once he got on, he was a threat to steal as he swiped more than 20 bases four times, and scored more than 90 runs six times in a seven-year stretch. The versatile Adams showed how handy he was in 1927 as he played 60 games at second, 53 at third, and another 40 at shortstop.

LIFETIME STATS: BA: .286, HR: 9, RBI: 394, H: 1,588, SB: 154

#**873** Samuel Washington "Sam" Wise
SS-2B-1B, Detroit (NL), Boston (NL), Washington (NL), Buffalo (PL), Orioles, 1881–91, 1893

Akron, Ohio native Sam Wise was a versatile performer who played 563 games at short and 448 at second in his career. Wise also donned the first baseman's mitt and played the outfield. He was inconsistent early in his career at the plate, hitting a paltry .221 in 1882, then improving to .271 the next year, only to precipitously fall to a dismal .214 in 1884. But his next season he improved again to .283, and never hit below .240 again, peaking in 1887 with a stellar .334 batting average. The lefty-swinging infielder switched uniforms four times in the last four years of his career, starting and ending those four seasons in Washington.

LIFETIME STATS: BA: .272, HR: 49, RBI: 672, H: 1,281, SB: 203

#874 Thomas Joseph "Tommy," "Foghorn," "Noisy Tom" Tucker

1B, Orioles, Boston (NL), Senators, Brooklyn (NL), Browns, Cleveland (NL), 1887–89

Dubbed "Foghorn" and "Noisy Tom" because of his loudness coaching third base, Tucker was a slick-fielding first baseman who led the league twice in fielding. He didn't hit that well in the minors, but once he hit the bigs, he hit a lot better as he topped the .300 mark four times while batting .290 for his career. He didn't hit many homers, but what he lacked in power he made up with speed as he stole a whopping 85 bases as a rookie in 1887. His best year had to be 1889, as he hit an eye popping .372 to lead the league, setting the standard for switch-hitters, and stole 63 bases.

LIFETIME STATS: BA: .290, HR: 42, RBI: 932, H: 1,882, SB: 352

#875 Walter Arthur "Hoot" Evers

OF, Tigers, Red Sox, Giants, Orioles, Indians, 1941, 1946–56

Named after Hoot Gibson, a cowboy star he admired, Evers had his breakout season in 1948 with the Tigers as he hit .314 with 103 RBI. Evers had his best season in 1950 when he hit a career-best .323, hitting 35 doubles, leading the league with 11 triples, and had 103 RBI. He even hit for the cycle in September of that year, something no Tiger would do again in 43 years. The Red Sox obtained him in 1952 to replace the great Ted Williams, who was in Korea. Evers had 14 homers, but broke his finger, limiting his effectiveness, and lowering his hitting to .264. He hung on with three other teams for four more seasons, but did not approach the offensive numbers he posted earlier in his career.

LIFETIME STATS: BA: .278, HR: 98, RBI: 565, H: 1,055, SB: 45

#876 Carlos Obed Baerga

2B-3B, Indians, Mets, Padres, Red Sox, Diamond-backs, Nationals, 1990–2005

The switch-hitting Baerga came up to the Indians in 1990, but it was in 1992 that he established himself as a star. In that season, the Puerto Rican–born second base-man hit 20 home runs with 105 RBI, hitting .312 and collecting 205 hits. In 1993, he put up even bigger numbers, hitting .321 with 21 homers and 114 RBI with another 200 hits. A three-time All Star, Baerga, despite a bad ankle, got three hits in Game Three of the 1995 World Series including a double off the center field wall in the 11th inning that propelled Cleveland to a Game Three win, the first Series game to be played in Jacobs Field, and the first in Cleveland in 41 years.

LIFETIME STATS: BA: .291, HR: 134, RBI: 774, H: 1,583, SB: 59

#877 Stanley Edward "Stan," "Big Stash" Lopata

C , Phillies, Braves, 1948–60

Lopata, a decorated World War II veteran, was the first National League catcher to wear glasses. At the urging of Hall of Famer Rogers Hornsby, he changed his stance at the plate in 1954, going to more of a crouch, and it appeared to pay off as Lopata hit 14 homers in 1954, and averaged 24 home runs a year for the next three years. He was selected to the National League All Star team in 1955 and 1956. He was sent to the Milwaukee Braves where he served as a backup for his last two seasons to the durable Del Crandall, so Lopata only saw limited action.

LIFETIME STATS: BA: .254, HR: 116, RBI: 397, H: 661, SB: 18

#878 Lewis Everett "Deacon" Scott

SS, Red Sox, Yankees, Senators, White Sox, Reds, 1914–26

Before Lou Gehrig and Cal Ripken Jr. came along, there was Everett Scott, who held the pre–Iron Horse record of consecutive games played at 1,307. Not only was he durable, but Scott was a sure-handed fielder, leading the American League's shortstops in fielding for eight straight years from 1916 to 1923 and twice led the loop in double plays, assists and putouts. He proved to be a winner, as he played on six flag winners, and appeared in five World Series with the Red Sox and Yankees, and won four world championships in the process. His best Fall Classic was in 1923 when he hit .318 for the Yankees.

LIFETIME STATS: BA: .249, HR: 20, RBI: 551, H: 1,455, SB: 69

#879 George Maceo "Nig" Cuppy (Koppe)

RHP, Cleveland (N), Cardinals, Braves, Red Sox, 1892–1901

Cuppy was born George Maceo Koppe, but the dark complexioned pitcher came to be known as Nig Cuppy, as many players and sportswriters were more overtly racist in the 19th century. The Cleveland Spiders were tough to beat in the mid 1890s because of the combination of Cuppy and the great Cy Young. Cuppy was 28–13 in his first year with a fine 2.51 ERA. He "slumped" to 17–10 the next season, but the next three years, he averaged 25 wins a season, good for a combined 75–43 record, including eight wins in relief. Cuppy, who was one of the first pitchers to wear a glove, only totaled 19 wins over the next two years, and was traded to the Cardinals, where he posted an 11-8 record.

LIFETIME STATS: W: 162, L: 98, SV: 5, ERA: 3.48, SO: 504, CG: 224

#880 Ralph Orlando "Socks" Seybold

OF, Reds, A's, 1899, 1901–08

Seybold held the home run record for a season when he hit 16 in 1902, before Babe Ruth broke his record with 29 in 1919. The previous season, Socks had a 27-game hitting streak. Although his 16-homer output was the only time Seybold led the league in a "power" category, he led the league in doubles with 45 in 1903, and was consistently among the leaders in homers and RBI during the "dead ball" era. He topped the .300 mark three times, peaking at .343 in 1901. Right-handed all the way, Seybold wasn't considered a great fielder in the outfield, but did have two unassisted double plays in 1907. Injuries curtailed the career of this steady player in 1908 when he was limited to only 48 games, hitting an "un-sox-like" .215 in 130 at bats.

LIFETIME STATS: BA: .294, HR: 51, RBI: 556, H: 1,085, SB: 66

#881 Arthur Frederick "Solly," "Circus Solly" Hofman

OF-2B-SS-1B, Pirates, Cubs, Brooklyn (FL), Buffalo (FL), Yankees, 1903–16

Born Arthur Frederick Hofman, he was dubbed "Circus Solly" for the acrobatic catches he used to make and for being a bit of a "hot dog." The versatile Hofman played every position on the diamond except pitcher and catcher. Hofman was a valuable player and contributed mightily to the success of the early Cubs dynasty of 1906 to 1910. He hit well, and was considered a great defensive player, wherever he played. Hofman once played six positions in six games in 1908. Finally in 1909, manager Frank Chance installed Hofman in center field and he responded by leading the Cubbies in hits and hitting .285. The next year he was even better, hitting a career-best .325 while he led the pennant winning Cubs in triples (16), RBI (86), and steals (29).

LIFETIME STATS: BA: .269, HR: 19, RBI: 495, H: 1,095, SB: 208

#882 Andruw Jones

CF-DH, Braves, Dodgers, Rangers, White Sox, Yankees, 1996-present

A great all-around player, Jones was the defensive anchor for the Braves during their championship years of the 1990s and 2000s. Jones was drafted by the Braves in 1993 and made his big-league debut in August of 1995. By 1997 he was a regular in the Braves' outfield, winning the National League Rookie of the Year award. By 1998, he had won the first of his 10 Gold Glove awards. Jones was also a four-time All-Star. His best year was 2005, when he led the league in home runs with 51 and in RBI with 128. Jones had always been a pretty good post-season player, as well. He has hit .400 or better in five separate post-season series.

LIFETIME STATS: BA: .256, HR: 420, RBI: 1,255, H: 1,887, SB: 152

#883 George "Orator" Shaffer

OF, Hartfords (NA), New York (NA), Philadelphia (NA), Louisville (NL), Indianapolis (NL), Cubs, Cleveland (NL), Buffalo (NL), St. Louis (UA), St. Louis (NL), Athletics, 1874–75, 1877–86, 1890

George Shaffer was nicknamed "Orator," not because he was a skilled speaker, as the sobriquet would suggest, but because he never kept his mouth shut. "Orator" was a fine defensive outfielder, as he led National League outfielders in assists four times in his career. Shaffer jumped to the St. Louis Maroons of the Union Association where he had a fine year, leading the league in doubles with 40, and coming in second in many other offensive categories, among them batting average (.360) and runs (130).

LIFETIME STATS: BA: .283, HR: 10, RBI: 308 (INC.), H: 974, SB: 32

#884 Gordon Craig Reynolds

SS-2B-3B-1B-OF-P, Pirates, Mariners, Astros, 1975–89

Craig Reynolds was drafted by the Pirates and played briefly with the Mariners, but the Houston native played most of his career with the hometown Astros. An excellent bunter, he led the National League in sacrifices three times, one year with an unbelievable 34 bunts in 1981.

Reynolds was the starting shortstop for the expansion 1977 Seattle Mariners and the following year hit a career-high .292 and played in the 1978 All Star Game. He was traded to Houston in 1979. In 1981, he led the league in triples with 12, including a major league record three in a single game. Ever the team player, Reynolds proved his value to the team as a utility player playing third, second and first base, as well as two pitching appearances in lopsided losses to save the Houston bullpen.

LIFETIME STATS: BA: .256, HR: 42, RBI: 377, H: 1,142, SB: 58

#885 Ronald William "Ron" Hassey

C-DH, Indians, Cubs, Yankees, White Sox, A's, Expos, 1978–91

Hassey led all American League backstops in 1980 when he hit .318, and had career bests with 124 hits, and 65 RBI in 130 games. He spent an injury-filled year with the Cubs (knee), and soon was traded to the Yankees. In 1985 Hassey hit a career-high 13 home runs in only 267 at bats as his teammates affectionately called him "Babe." He also hit .296 that year. Between 1984 and 1986, Hassey shuttled between Cubs, White Sox and Yankees. While with the White Sox, Hassey got the reputation of being a reliable backup catcher and pinch-hitter extraordinaire as he was an amazing 10 for 18 for a terrific .556 average.

LIFETIME STATS: BA: .266, HR: 71, RBI: 438, H: 914, SB: 14

#886 John Joseph "Jack" Doyle

1B-C-2B-OF-3B, Columbus (AA), Cleveland (NL), Giants, Baltimore (NL), Washington (NL), Cubs, Senators, Dodgers, Phillies, Yankees, 1889–1905

The well-traveled Doyle was reportedly the first pinch-hitter in major league history when Cleveland Spiders manager Patsy Tebeau asked Doyle to bat for a teammate on June 7, 1892, against Brooklyn. The managerial move worked as Doyle singled and Tebeau continued to use him in that role. Soon, the strategy caught on, and soon pinch-hitting became a common practice throughout the game. Mostly used as a catcher and first baseman, Doyle played 100 or more games at four different positions throughout his 17-year career. He could also hit a bit, as Doyle hit over .300 between 1893 and 1897 and six times overall topped the .300 plateau, with a high of .367 in 1894.

LIFETIME STATS: BA: .299, HR: 26, RBI: 968, H: 1,806, SB: 516

#887 Charles Richard "Charlie," "Smokey" Maxwell

OF-1B, Red Sox, Orioles, Tigers, White Sox, 1950–64

Sundays brought out the best in Maxwell as he had the uncanny ability to hit homers on that day of the week. A total of 40 of his career 148 dingers were hit on that day. Maxwell came into his own with the Tigers in the mid to late '50s. On May 5, 1959, the lefty-swinging Maxwell, who hit 23 career homers against the Yankees, victimized them repeatedly when he hit a homer in the first game of a doubleheader, and erupted for three more in the nightcap on the way to career highs of 31 homers and 95 RBI for Detroit.

LIFETIME STATS: BA: .264, HR: 148, RBI: 532, H: 856, SB: 18

#888 Deron Roger Johnson

1B-3B-DH-OF, Yankees, A's, Reds, Braves, Phillies, Brewers, Red Sox, White Sox, 1960–62, 1964–76

Johnson took his time to make his mark, but make his mark he did for the Reds in 1965 when he exploded for 32 homers and a National League–leading 130 RBI, on the way to being named as the best third baseman in the league by the *Sporting News*. He whacked another 24 homers the following season. While playing for the Phillies in 1971, he erupted for four home runs in four at bats over a span of two games, becoming only the seventh player at the time to accomplish that feat. That same year he hit a career-best 34 dingers. His last good offensive season was in 1975 when he split time with the White Sox and Red Sox, with 19 homers and 75 RBI.

LIFETIME STATS: BA: .244, HR: 245, RBI: 923, H: 1,447, SB: 11

#889 Joseph Franklin "Frank" Demaree

OF, Cubs, Giants, Braves, Cardinals, Browns, 1932–33, 1935–44

Born Joseph Franklin Demaria, Frank Demaree got his first taste of playing as a regular with the Cubs in 1933, and hit .272 in 134 games. Demaree went back to the minors in 1934 where he was named the MVP of the Pacific Coast League. He was back in Chicago in 1935, and stuck, hitting .325, .350 and .324 the next three seasons while collecting 212 hits in 1936 and 199 more in 1937. Demaree appeared in three World Series with the Cubs, who lost them all, but Demaree still holds the Cub record for World Series career homers with three. He was traded to the New York Giants in 1939, and hit .304 and .302 in successive seasons.

LIFETIME STATS: BA: .299, HR: 72, RBI: 591, H: 1,241, SB: 33

#890 Elmer William Valo

OF, A's, Phillies, Dodgers, Indians, Yankees, Senators, Twins, 1940–43, 1946–61

One of the few native Czechoslovakians to play in the big leagues, Elmer Valo had a reputation for hard work, hustle, and the knack for challenging fences. Valo hit over .300 five times in his 20-year career, with a career high of .364 in 1955. In 1949, he cleared the bases twice with bases-loaded triples and the following year hit for the cycle. He moved three times in his career with franchise shifts, including from Philadelphia to Kansas City, from Brooklyn to Los Angeles, and from Washington to the Twin Cities of Minnesota.

LIFETIME STATS: BA: .282, HR: 58, RBI: 601, H: 1,420, SB: 110

#891 Jesse Niles "Tanny", "Powder" Tannehill

LHP-OF, Reds, Pirates, Highlanders, Red Sox, Senators, 1894, 1897–1909, 1911

Jesse Tannehill was an excellent pitcher as well as a good hitter and was the first pitcher ever to win 20 games and hit .300 in the same season. Tannehill was a lifetime .256 hitter and played the outfield and pinch-hit on occasion when he wasn't pitching. In 1898 he went 25–13 for the Pirates, and followed it up with a 24–14 mark on 1899. The next season he really showed his versatility by going 20–6 and hitting .336. After a stint with the Highlanders in New York, Tannehill was traded to the Red Sox in 1904. He won 20 or more games his first two seasons in Beantown and tossed a no-hitter against the White Sox.

LIFETIME STATS: W: 197, L: 116, SV: 7, ERA: 2.79, SO: 940, CG: 263

#892 Nathan "Nate" Colbert

1B-OF, Astros, Padres, Tigers, Expos, A's, 1966, 1968–76

August 1, 1972, is a day that Nate Colbert will always remember. It was on that day that Colbert hit five homers in a doubleheader, tying a record set by Stan Musial 20 years earlier. In addition, Colbert set a major league record driving in an astounding 13 runs that day, accounting for 22 total bases, breaking Stan the Man's mark by one. That year Colbert was the only legitimate threat in the weak Padre lineup, considering he batted in a record 111 of the Padres' measly 488 total runs while hitting a career-best tying 38 home runs. He was a three-time All Star.

LIFETIME STATS: BA: .243, HR: 173, RBI: 520, H: 833, SB: 52

#893 Aaron Lee Ward

2B-3B, Yankees, White Sox, Indians, 1917–28

Aaron Ward was a dependable defensive player for the Yankees during their first pennants in their history in the early 20s. Playing for the Yanks from 1917 through 1926, Ward was a consistent hitter with his high-water mark coming in the Yankees' first pennant year of 1921 when he hit over .300 for the only time in his career (.306). He had a career-high 82 RBI in 1923 and was a clutch hitter in the Bombers' first championship, hitting .417 with 10 for 24 hitting, leading all Yankee regulars in the 1923 World Series win over the crosstown Giants.

LIFETIME STATS: BA: .268, HR: 50, RBI: 446, H: 966, SB: 37

#894 Charles Benjamin "Babe" Adams

RHP, Cardinals, Pirates, 1906–07, 1909–16, 1918–26

Adams pitched most of his career with the Pittsburgh Pirates. Believed to be the very first player blessed with the "Babe" moniker, Adams posted a 12–3 record with a superb 1.11 ERA, both starting and relieving for the 1909 Pirates. Adams was the surprise starter in Game One of the 1909 World Series against the Detroit Tigers. The young right-hander justified the decision by winning the contest, and then followed up with wins in Game Five and the clincher, an 8–0 shutout in Game Seven. Adams was known throughout his career as a control pitcher as he only walked 430 batters in his 19-year career that spanned 2,995 1/3 innings.

LIFETIME STATS: W: 194, L: 140, SV: 15, ERA: 2.76, SO: 1,036, CG: 206

#895 Richard Aldo "Rick" Cerone

C, Indians, Blue Jays, Yankees, Braves, Brewers, Red Sox, Mets, Expos, 1975–92

Cerone was the Blue Jays' regular catcher from 1977 to 1979. But 1979 was the tragic year that Yankee catcher Thurman Munson died, so the Yankees traded for the New Jersey native. Cerone not only became a popular Yankee but he delivered in 1980 helping the Yanks win the AL East as he hit .277 with 14 homers and 85 RBI and was named to the Sporting News AL All Star squad. He also placed seventh in the MVP voting that year. In the strike-shortened 1981 season, Cerone excelled in the playoff win over the Brewers as he homered and singled in the fifth and final game of the best-of-five affair, and played well in the ALCS Series win over the Athletics.

LIFETIME STATS: BA: .245, HR: 59, RBI: 436, H: 998, SB: 6

#896 Rafael Emilio Ramirez

SS, Braves, Astros, 1980–92

Ramirez was a quick, flashy shortstop of the Atlanta Braves from 1981 to 1986, while leading the senior circuit in double plays for four successive seasons. He wasn't too bad with the lumber either at that time: In 1982, Ramirez hit .278 while hitting 10 homers with 52 RBI to go along with 24 doubles and 27 steals. He followed up that fine season with a .297 batting average and 185 hits, both career bests. Ramirez was durable, playing in 150 or more games four times in his career. He made the NL All Star team in 1984.

LIFETIME STATS: BA: .261, HR: 53, RBI: 484, H: 1,432, SB: 112

#**897** Michael Eugene "Mike" LaValliere

C, Phillies, Cardinals, Pirates, White Sox, 1984–95

Winner of the 1976 Most Valuable Player as a teen in the Babe Ruth World Series, Mike LaValliere set a Cardinal record for games caught by a rookie catcher with 108. Though he wasn't a high-average batter, he put the ball in play, and was an excellent bunter. His most important hit was his game-winning single in the 10th inning with two outs that won a crucial game in the 1991 National League Championship Series against the Atlanta Braves, a series Lavalliere's Pirates would lose in seven games. LaValliere was a good defensive catcher, winning the Gold Glove in 1987 and only being charged with 35 passed balls in his 12-year career with four teams.

LIFETIME STATS: BA: .268, HR: 18, RBI: 294, H: 663, SB: 5

#**898** Terry Stephen Puhl

OF, Astros, Royals, 1977–91

Hailing from Saskatchewan, Puhl was a solid and reliable outfielder for the Houston Astros for 14 seasons. He was called up by Houston midway through the 1977 season and hit .301 with an 18-game hitting streak. The following season he was selected to his only National League All Star Game by virtue of his .289 average, his outstanding defensive play, and 32 stolen bases. In 1979, the lefty-hitting contact hitter hit .287, stole 30 more bases, and played 152 games in right field without committing a single error, as he never had more than three errors in a season in his career.

LIFETIME STATS: BA: .280, HR: 62, RBI: 435, H: 1,361, SB: 217

#899 Larry Eugene Hisle

OF-DH, Phillies, Twins, Brewers, 1968–71, 1973–82

Larry Hisle came up in 1968, and in 1969, his first full season, despite striking out 152 times, he struck 20 homers and hit a respectable .266, earning him a berth on the Topps Rookie All Star team. He was traded to Minnesota and his hitting improved to a career high of .314 in 1975. He had his best year in 1977 when he clouted 28 home runs and had a league-high 119 RBI, as he represented the Twins at that year's All Star contest. Hisle signed a lucrative deal with the Milwaukee Brewers in 1978, and had another fine season, with 34 home runs and 115 RBI while hitting .290, and placed third in the American League MVP voting.

LIFETIME STATS: BA: .273, HR: 166, RBI: 674, H: 1,146, SB: 128

#900 James Edward "Diamond" Jim Gentile

1B Dodgers, Orioles, A's, Astros, Indians, 1957–58, 1960–66

Gentile was mired in the Dodger organization for many years behind Gil Hodges. Dealt to the Orioles in 1960, Gentile made the most of his opportunity, hitting .292 with 21 home runs. In 1961, the Yankees' Roger Maris and Mickey Mantle shared the spotlight, but Gentile hit 46 homers and drove in 141 runs, second to Maris's 142, including a new American League–record five grand slams. On May 9 of that year, Gentile hit grand slams in consecutive innings in the same game. Those impressive offensive numbers earned him a third-place finish in the MVP balloting, behind Maris and Mantle. The following year he hit 33 homers on the way to his third straight All Star game appearance.

LIFETIME STATS: BA: .260, HR: 179, RBI: 549, H: 759, SB: 3

#**901** Ted Strong

OF-SS, Indianapolis ABC's, Indianapolis Clowns, Kansas City Monarchs, Indianapolis Athletics (Negro Leagues), 1937–48

Ted Strong was a gifted athlete, who not only played well in the Negro Leagues, but appeared with the famous Harlem Globetrotters in the off-season. The versatile Strong was selected to the East-West Negro All Star Game five times, playing three different positions: shortstop, first base, and outfield. Strong, a switch-hitter, helped the famous Kansas City Monarchs win four pennants in a row in the late thirties and early forties. Already at an advanced age when the color line was broken in 1947 by Jackie Robinson, Strong played in the Texas League for a number of seasons.

LIFETIME STATS: BA: .311

#**902** James Robert "Jim" Lemon

OF, Indians, Senators, Twins, Phillies, White Sox, 1950, 1953–63

After bouncing around the minors and warming the bench for several years, Lemon became a regular in 1956, hitting .271 with 27 homers and 96 RBI. He also led the American League that year with 11 triples. He once hit three homers in a row, an impressive achievement as all three came off of crafty lefty Hall of Famer Whitey Ford. Lemon hit 33 homers in 1959 and also had 100 RBI. He was finally selected to his first and only All Star Game in 1960, coming in second in the league in homers with 38.

LIFETIME STATS: BA: .262, HR: 164, RBI: 529, H: 901, SB: 13

#903 Brian David Harper

C-OF-DH, Angels, Pirates, Cardinals, Tigers, A's, Twins, Brewers, 1979, 1981–95

After playing part-time for five other organizations, Brian Harper finally made his mark with the Minnesota Twins in 1988, hitting .295 as a catcher. The next season he hit a career-high .325 with eight homers and 57 RBI. Harper hit .294 in 1990, including 42 doubles, and then hit over .300 the following three seasons.

LIFETIME STATS: BA: .295, HR: 63, RBI: 428, H: 931, SB: 8

#904 Sam Bankhead

SS-OF-2B-RHP, Birmingham Black Barons, Nashville Elite Giants, Louisville, Pittsburgh Crawfords (Negro Leagues), 1930–50

Bankhead was a versatile star in the Negro Leagues, used at many different positions, including pitching. A seven-time Negro League All Star, Bankhead was known for his strong arm (no doubt from his pitching training) and steady hitting. Bankhead was an important part of the Pittsburgh Crawfords that also featured Judy Johnson, Josh Gibson, and Buck Leonard. The durable Bankhead also played in the Cuban winter league for many seasons, along with many of his contemporaries. Though records are sketchy, the Pittsburgh native hit .342 in 21 games against established major leaguers in his career.

LIFETIME STATS: BA: .284

#905 Michael Cole "Moose" Mussina

RHP, Orioles, Yankees, 1991–2008

Mussina has been "Mr. Consistency" since he broke in with the Orioles in 1991. He has won 10 or more games 15 consecutive years. He has pitched 200 or more innings in 10 of his 17 seasons, and struck out 100 or more batters in 14 of those 17 years.

Mussina has won 19 games twice, 18 games twice and 17 games twice. He averages 34 starts for his career, and has never started fewer than 24 games in a season since he was a rookie. The six-time Gold Glove winner has also been in the top five for the Cy Young Award six times.

LIFETIME STATS: W: 270, L: 153, SV: 0, ERA: 3.68, SO: 2,813, CG: 57

#906 Michael Grant "Mike" Marshall

RHP, Tigers, Pilots, Astros, Expos, Dodgers, Braves, Rangers, Twins, Mets, 1967, 1969–81

Coming up in the Philly chain as a shortstop, Marshall proved to be a defensive liability in that important position, so he switched to the mound in 1962, when Detroit bought him. He was sold to Montreal in 1971, and, aided by a new screwball, saved 23 games that year. The following year he led the National League with 65 appearances, winning 14 games and saving 18 others, with a sterling 1.78 ERA. He was traded to the Dodgers in 1974, and won the Cy Young Award, a first for a reliever. He set a major league record with 106 appearances and pitched an unheard of 208 innings in relief.

LIFETIME STATS: W: 97, L: 112, SV: 188, ERA: 3.14, SO: 880, CG: 3

#907 John Charles "Jack" Rowe
SS-C-OF, Buffalo (NL), Detroit (NL), Pirates, Buffalo (PL), 1879–90

Rowe was a very good fielding shortstop and catcher who played for the Buffalo Bisons in 1879 and throughout the early 1880s. Batting from the left side, Rowe let the league in triples with 11 in 1881, while hitting .333 and having a fine .480 slugging percentage. The Bisons did not field a team in 1886, so Rowe and some of his teammates joined the Detroit Wolverines, where they won the league flag the following year as Rowe hit .318. Rowe, along with teammate and fellow star Deacon White, was sold to Pittsburgh, where the two stars refused to report, opting to buy the Buffalo franchise in the International League and play there. Rowe and White eventually reported to the Pirates, but later helped form the outlaw Players' League, where Rowe finished up his career.

LIFETIME STATS: BA: .286, HR: 28, RBI: 644, H: 1,256, SB: 59

#908 Maurice Wesley "Wes" Parker
1B-OF, Dodgers, 1964–72

Wes Parker was an excellent-fielding first baseman who won six straight Gold Gloves in a nine-year career spent entirely with the Dodgers. Though he didn't have the power of a stereotypical first baseman, Parker was a fine line drive contact hitter who was one of the leading hitters on the weak-hitting Dodger squad of the mid to late 60s and early '70s. Parker became the regular first baseman in 1965. That year he also became one of the four members of the first switch-hitting infield in major league history, joining second baseman Jim Lefebvre, shortstop Maury Wills, and third baseman Jim Gilliam. He finished his major league career tied with four other first basemen for the highest career fielding percentage (.996).

LIFETIME STATS: BA: .267, HR: 64, RBI: 470, H: 1,110, SB: 60

#909 Melvin Lloyd "Mel," "Dusty" Parnell

LHP, Red Sox, 1947–56

Despite the short left-field wall at Fenway Park, southpaw Mel Parnell kept overaggressive hitters off balance with a devastating array of pitches, including a quick breaking slider and better-than-average fastball. Blessed with an effortless delivery, Parnell's first good season came in 1948, when he posted a 15–8 mark, but it was the following year that it all came together for the New Orleans–born lefty. He not only led the league in wins with 25, but also led the AL in innings pitched with 295 and had 27 complete games. He also fashioned a career low 2.77 ERA, also a league best.

LIFETIME STATS: W: 123, L: 75, SV: 10, ERA: 3.50, SO: 732, CG: 113

#910 Gerald Holmes "Gee" Walker

of, Tigers, White Sox, Senators, Indians, Reds, 1931–45

Walker was an exceptional hitter when he came up with the Tigers, hitting .300 or better five times in his first six years. He was also something of a goofball. He once attempted to steal a base while a teammate was being intentionally walked. He was also picked off base twice in one game. Still, in addition to his hitting, he had good speed, making 399 doubles in his career and stealing 20 or more bases five separate years.

LIFETIME STATS: BA: .399, HR: 124, RBI: 997, H: 1,991, SB: 223

#911 Milton Joseph "Milt" Stock
3B- 2B, Giants, Phillies, Cardinals, Dodgers, 1913–26

Stock started out with the Giants and then the Phillies, but came into his own with the St. Louis Cardinals as he bettered the .300 mark four consecutive seasons from 1919 to 1922. The 5'8", 154-pound infielder was then traded to Brooklyn in 1924. Stock had little power, but consistently got his bat on the ball and ran well. He later managed in the minors, including once in Mobile where he managed his future son-in-law, Eddie Stanky. Stanky was a player that Stock eventually traded, proving once again that baseball can be a cruel business.

LIFETIME STATS: BA: .289, HR: 22, RBI: 696, H: 1,806, SB: 155

#912 Loren Dale Mitchell
OF, Indians, Dodgers, 1946–56

Most baseball fans have seen the lefty-swinging Dale Mitchell, in a pinch-hitting role with the 1956 Dodgers, taking a called third strike, ending Don Larsen's perfect World Series game. Mitchell, while checking his swing, claimed to his dying day that the pitch, called strike three by home plate umpire Babe Pinelli, was outside. Ironically, the contact hitting Mitchell was the eighth-toughest man to strike out in major league history, and was an excellent hitter, playing regularly with the Cleveland Indians for most of his career. A lefty hitter and leadoff man, Mitchell hit .316 in his first full season with the Tribe, the first of six .300 batting averages in seven seasons for the spray hitter from Oklahoma. He was an integral part of Cleveland's last world championship in 1948, when he had hit a robust .336 with 204 hits, including 30 doubles.

LIFETIME STATS: BA: .312, HR: 41, RBI: 403, H: 1,244, SB: 45

#**913** Robert "Bobby" Tolan

OF-1B, Cardinals, Reds, Padres, Phillies, Pirates,
1965–70, 1972–77, 1979

Starting out a part-timer with the Cardinals for his first
four seasons, Bobby Tolan was then traded to the Reds,
where he became part of a potent one-two punch at the
top of the Reds' batting order. In his first year with Cincinnati, Tolan hit a career-
best 21 homers, while leading the league's outfielders in putouts. Pete Rose and
Tolan, at various times, started three games with back-to-back home runs. In
1970, the speedy Tolan swiped a league-leading 57 bases while hitting .316. A
torn Achilles tendon suffered in the off-season cost Tolan all of 1971, but he
rebounded with a .283 year in 1972, as the Reds won another pennant.

LIFETIME STATS: BA: .265, HR: 86, RBI: 497, H: 1,121, SB: 193

#**914** Cecil Randolph "Randy," "The Rebel" Hundley

C, Giants, Cubs, Twins, Padres, 1964–77

Randy Hundley was one of the most durable catchers in
major league history as he averaged an unheard-of 153
games behind the plate from 1966 to 1969, with a major
league–high 160 games in 1968. Not only was he durable, but very capable
as he set a since-broken major league record, committing only four errors in
971 chances in 1967. Though not a high-average hitter, as his lifetime mark
of .236 attests, Hundley had the occasional pop as he hit 18 homers and batted in 64, the best power numbers from a Cub catcher since the great Gabby
Hartnett, while hitting .255 for the 1969 Cubs. He, not Johnny Bench, was
the first to popularize catching the thrown pitch with one hand.

LIFETIME STATS: BA: .236, HR: 82, RBI: 381, H: 813, SB: 12

#915 Hugh Melville "Hughie" Critz
2B, Reds, Giants, 1924–35

Hughie Critz had quite a debut with the Reds, getting two hits off the great Grover Cleveland Alexander on the way to a .322 batting average that season. Though never coming close to his first year's hitting prowess, Critz continued to be one of the best fielding second baseman of the '20s and '30s. He led the National League in double plays in 1925 and 1926, and in 1926 led the loop in fielding for the first of four times in his career. The 5'8", 147-pound Critz was sent to the Giants in 1930. Though his offensive numbers continued to dwindle, Critz continued to shine defensively leading the league in fielding and in 1934 led all National League second sackers in double plays.

LIFETIME STATS: BA: .268, HR: 38, RBI: 531, H: 1,591, SB: 97

#916 Franklin Crisostomo "Frank" Taveras
SS, Pirates, Mets, Expos, 1971–72, 1974–82

A speedy shortstop from the Dominican Republic, Taveras started his career with the Pirates and led the National League in steals in 1977 with 70, on the way to swiping an even 300 for his career. Tavares had little power as he only hit two career homers, but he had a respectable .255 batting average. At times, however, he was inconsistent in the field, prompting the Pirates to trade him to the lowly 1979 Mets. Taveras had a good season with the Mets, hitting a career-best .279 while stealing 32 more bases. He reverted to utility roles with the Mets in 1982 and Expos in 1983 before retiring.

LIFETIME STATS: BA: .255, HR: 2, RBI: 214, H: 1029, SB: 300

#**917** William Hayward "Mookie" Wilson

OF, Mets, Blue Jays, 1980-91

Wilson will be forever remembered by Mets (and Red Sox) fans as the batter who hit the slow roller through Bill Buckner's legs that won the pivotal Game Six in the 1986 World Series against Boston. A steady hitter with the Mets, the speedy Wilson stole 58 bases in 1982 and followed it up with 54 and 46 thefts the next two seasons. His best power numbers were in 1984 as Wilson hit a career-high 10 homers and 10 triples with 54 RBI. His best season average was in 1987 when he hit .299. The switch-hitting Wilson was platooned with the young Lenny Dykstra and the disgruntled Wilson was traded to Toronto in 1989. He returned to the Mets as a base coach after his playing days were over.

LIFETIME STATS: BA: .274, HR: 67, RBI: 438, H: 1,397, SB: 327

#**918** Horace Meredith Clarke

2B-SS-DH, Yankees, Padres, 1965–74

The much-maligned Horace Clarke had the misfortune of playing second base during the Yankee decline of the late '60s and early '70s. In truth, he was a pesky, reliable hitter and a solid fielder. After Tony Kubek's premature retirement in 1965, Clarke was one of several Yanks who auditioned for his job, hitting .266, improving to .272 the following year, while stealing 21 bases. He was moved to second base in 1968, but declined to .230, despite stealing another 20 bases. "Hoss" rebounded in 1969, hitting a career-best .285 with 26 doubles and a career-best 33 stolen bases, and was second in the American League with 183 hits. The Virgin Islands native also led league second sackers in assists from 1967 to 1972.

LIFETIME STATS: BA: .256, HR: 27, RBI: 304, H: 1,230, SB: 151

#**919** Gus Edward "Ozark Ike" Zernial
OF, White Sox, A's, Tigers, 1949–59

A free-swinging slugger of the fifties, Gus Zernial hit more home runs (191) between 1951 and 1957 than future Hall of Famers Ted Williams and Willie Mays. He hit 29 homers in 1950 while with the White Sox, but was then traded to the Philadelphia A's. Called "Ozark Ike" after a popular comic strip of the era, the friendly Zernial led the league with 33 homers and 129 RBI in 1951 while with the A's. He also had a career-best 42 homers in 1953, but lost the homer title by one to Cleveland's Al Rosen. Zernial followed the Athletics to Kansas City where he continued to show off his power for two more years. No longer a starter in 1958, he led the league in pinch hits with 15, while playing with the Tigers.

LIFETIME STATS: BA: .265, HR: 237, RBI: 776, H: 1,093, SB: 15

#920 James Anthony "Ripper" Collins

1B-OF, Cardinals, Cubs, Pirates, 1931–38, 1941

Collins supposedly got the nickname "Ripper" as a boy, when he once hit a ball on a fence rail, ripping its cover. But the switch-hitter lived up to his moniker as he hit a league-leading 35 home runs as an integral part of the pennant-winning Gashouse Gang in St. Louis in 1934. Collins led the NL in slugging percentage that year with a .615 mark and had 116 RBI. In 1935, he had 109 RBI. A pitcher flirting with a no-hitter didn't want to see the 5'9" Collins advancing to the plate, as he broke up four no-hitters.

LIFETIME STATS: BA: .296, HR: 135, RBI: 659, H: 1121, SB: 18

#921 Philip Samuel "Phil" Masi

C, Braves, Pirates, White Sox, 1939–52

Phil Masi came on as a pinch runner in Game One of the 1948 World Series in a scoreless pitcher's duel between the Braves' Johnny Sain and Cleveland's fireballer Bob Feller. As Masi danced off second base, Feller whirled and threw to a covering Lou Boudreau and appeared to pick Masi off. Second base umpire Bill Stewart disagreed, however, and ruled Masi safe. Moments later, Masi came on to score the only run of the game as Bob Feller was denied a World Series victory, something he had never done in his storied career. Photographs of the play seemed to back up the Indians, who shook this loss off, and won the World Series anyway. Masi was regarded as an excellent fielding catcher, and had good speed. A four-time All Star, Masi handled the Boston Braves' pitching staff well.

Spending the bulk of his career with the Braves, Masi's best year with the bat was in 1947 when he hit .304.

LIFETIME STATS: BA: .264, HR: 47, RBI: 417, H: 917, SB: 45

#922 Vincent Maurice "Vince" Coleman

OF, Cardinals, Mets, Royals, Mariners, Reds, Tigers, 1985–97

The lightning quick Coleman, dubbed "Vincent Van Go," burst onto the St. Louis scene in 1985 as a highly regarded base stealer, once stealing an unbelievable 145 bases in the minors. Coleman stole 110 bases as a rookie, the third most in the 20th century. He then followed it up with 107 steals in 1986 and 109 more in 1987. The only thing that seemed to stop Coleman was an automatic tarp, as he caught his foot in it before Game Four of the NLCS in 1985 and was injured. The fleet switch-hitter led the league in stolen bases for six consecutive seasons. In 1989, he set a major league record by stealing 50 straight times without being thrown out.

LIFETIME STATS: BA: .264, HR: 28, RBI: 346, H: 1,425, SB: 752

#923 James Edward "Jimmy," "Pee Wee" Key

RHP, Blue Jays, Yankees, Orioles, 1984–98

Key started his career in the Blue Jay bullpen, but with his sharp breaking ball and sinking fastball, became a mainstay of the Toronto pitching staff. Though he was never a 20-game winner, the crafty lefty won a range of

12–17 games for the Blue Jays from 1985 to 1992, when he signed a free-agent pact with the Yankees. His best year in New York, and his career for that matter, was his first year in pinstripes when he went 18-6 and led the league in victories the following year with 17. The soft-spoken Alabaman missed most of 1995 with an injury, but the resilient southpaw came back in 1996 to win 12 games and win Game Six of the World Series.

LIFETIME STATS: W: 186, L: 117, SV: 10, ERA: 3.51, SO: 1,538, CG: 34

#924 Edwin Douglas "Ed," "Ez," "The Poet," "The Glider" Charles
3B, A's, Mets, 1962–69

Charles was nicknamed "The Glider" for his easygoing gait and his third-base prowess. He came up as a 27-year-old rookie with the A's who obtained him from the Milwaukee Braves. Ed was grateful for the opportunity with Kansas City as he had career highs in homers with 17 and batting average with a .288 mark. He hit 15 and 16 homers the next two seasons with the A's, but then dropped to a combined 17 in the next two seasons as Kansas City moved the outfield fences back. He was dispatched to the Mets, where he regained his homer stroke with 15 in 1968 and platooned with Wayne Garrett at third base for the Miracle Mets of 1969. A cerebral man, Charles wrote poetry, including poems about his eight years in the minors in the late '50s and early '60s.

LIFETIME STATS: BA: .263, HR: 86, RBI: 421, H: 917, SB: 86

#925 Ralph Foster "Cy" Perkins

C, A's, Yankees, Tigers, 1915, 1917–31, 1934

Perkins, called "Cy" because of a resemblance to a popular theatrical character, was an excellent defensive catcher in the pre–Mickey Cochrane days of the Philadelphia A's. The strong-armed receiver led the American League in assists three times and in putouts once. He also showed his durability by leading the league in games caught on two occasions. Never regarded as an offensive stalwart, Perkins nevertheless hit .288 with 12 homers and 73 RBI in 1921. In 1925, rookie Mickey Cochrane pinch-hit for him, and Perkins knew that his days as the A's regular catcher were numbered. Ever the team player, Perkins taught the future Hall of Famer the "catching ropes," becoming Cochrane's able-bodied backup for the next six seasons.

LIFETIME STATS: BA: .259, HR: 30, RBI: 409, H: 933, SB: 18

#926 Carroll Walter "Whitey" Lockman

1B-OF, Giants, Cardinals, Orioles, Reds, 1945, 1947–60

Lockman had an auspicious debut, homering in his first major league at bat as an 18-year-old Giant rookie in 1945. Coming up as an outfielder, the lefty-hitting, but righty-throwing Lockman converted to first base, where he played most of his career, primarily with the Giants. In 1949, he hit .301, his career high, and hit over .290 three other times. Lost in the Bobby Thomson home run hoopla in the famous 1951 playoff game with the Dodgers was the big double that Lockman hit in that ninth inning rally, knocking out Dodger ace Don Newcombe, and bringing in Ralph Branca. Branca, of course, was the man whom Bobby Thomson hit a three-run homer off winning the pennant for the 1951 New York Giants. Lockman, over the years, was extremely hard to double up as he only hit into a double play once in every 87 at bats.

LIFETIME STATS: BA: .279, HR: 114, RBI: 563, H: 1,658, SB: 43

#927 Alfredo Claudino Baptist Griffin
SS, Indians, Blue Jays, A's, Dodgers, 1976–93

A durable player, Alfredo Griffin never asked out of the lineup as he played in 392 straight games for the Toronto Blue Jays. He was Co-Rookie of the Year in 1979 with the Twins' John Castino, and after hitting 10 triples in that rookie year, he led the American League with 15 the following year, setting an AL record for triples by a switch-hitter. Griffin was a base-stealing threat as he had 192 career stolen bases.

LIFETIME STATS: BA: .249, HR: 24, RBI: 527, H: 1,688, SB: 192

#928 William Edward "Wid" Conroy
3B-SS-OF, Pirates, Yankees, Senators, 1901–11

Conroy was dubbed "Wid," short for Widow, because of his mother-hen-like concern for younger players in the minors. Conroy was an excellent fielding shortstop and third baseman in his 11-year major league career with three teams. Afflicted with malaria in the minors in 1899, he missed the whole season. The turn of the century brought better luck to Conroy as he was the starting shortstop for the National League–

champion Pittsburgh Pirates in 1902. He signed with the New York High-landers (the early Yankees) in 1903, where he led the league in chances per game twice from his new third-base position. Always a threat to steal, Conroy stole 20 or more bases eight times in his career, with a high of 41 in 1907.

LIFETIME STATS: BA: .248, HR: 22, RBI: 452, H: 1,257, SB: 262

#929 William H. "Yank" Robinson

2B-3B-SS-OF, Detroit (NL), Baltimore (UA), St. Louis (AA), Pittsburgh (PL), Cincinnati (AA), Washington (NL), 1882, 1884–92

Robinson was a 5'6", 170-pound infielder who played mostly second base for five teams in various leagues throughout his 10-year career. Throughout his career he had a keen eye at the plate, three times drawing 100 or more bases on balls, including league-leading totals of 116 and 118 in 1888 and 1889. He hit over .300 for the only time in his career (.305) and hit 32 doubles and had 75 steals in 1887. In 1888, he had 56 steals and had 39 thefts in 1889.

LIFETIME STATS: BA: .241, HR: 15, RBI: 399, H: 825, SB: 272

#930 David "Big Papi" Ortiz

1B-DH, Twins, Red Sox, 1997-present

The imposing Ortiz was one of the foundations of the Red Sox championship runs in both 2004 and 2007. He debuted with the Minnesota Twins in 1997 but his stint with the Twins was unproductive, and he was released by Minnesota in 2002. The Red Sox signed him as a free agent just prior to the 2003 season. In Boston, Ortiz blossomed. He hit 31 home runs as a DH, and drove in 101 runs that first year. The next year, he was even better, leading the Sox to an astonishing 4-3 win over the Yankees in the ALCS and then helping the Red Sox gain their first World Championship since 1918. Ortiz was the MVP of the ALCS. In 2007, it was more of the same, as he batted .333 in the Sox sweep of Colorado.

LIFETIME STATS: BA: .283, HR: 378, RBI: 1,288, H: 1,760, SB: 11

#931 Benjamin Michael "Benny" Kauff

OF, Yankees, Indianapolis (FL), Brooklyn (FL), Giants, 1912, 1914–20

Benny Kauff was called "The Ty Cobb of the Federal League." After only 11 at bats and five games with the Yankees in 1912, Kauff jumped to Indianapolis of the Federal League, where he had a career year, leading the league in hitting with a .370 average, in hits with 211, doubles with 44, runs with 120 and stolen bases with 75. He followed that up with a .342 year, and led the Federal League in stolen bases again with 55. He and his brother were also accused of running a stolen car ring in 1921. The good news for Kauff was he was acquitted of the charges; the bad news was that he was thrown out of baseball anyway.

LIFETIME STATS: BA: .311, HR: 49, RBI: 454, H: 961, SB: 234

#932 William Adolph "Bill," "Wamby" Wambsganss

2B-SS-3B, Indians, Red Sox, A's, 1914–26

Wambsganss was the regular second baseman with the Indians from 1915 to 1923. He was regarded as an average hitter, with little power, but a great fielder. He helped lead the Tribe to the American League pennant and later a World Series win over the Brooklyn Dodgers in 1920. "Wamby," of course, made the only unassisted triple in World Series history. It was in Game Five with the Series tied at two games apiece. Wambsganss's play was amazing, but what was strange was that Brooklyn manager Wilbert Robinson called for a hit-and-run with runners on first and second with nobody out.

LIFETIME STATS: BA: .259, HR: 7, RBI: 520, H: 1,359, SB: 140

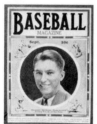

#**933** Melvin Leroy "Mel," "Chief," "Wimpy" Harder
RHP, Indians, 1928–47

Mel Harder pitched well for the Indians for 20 years, winning more games for the Tribe than any other pitcher except Hall of Famer Bob Feller. Only Walter Johnson and Ted Lyons appeared in more games with one club than the bespectacled right-hander. Joe DiMaggio once said that Harder was one of the toughest pitchers for him to solve. Harder won 20 or more games in successive seasons (1934–35), and appeared in four All Star games. The Cleveland right-hander was also among the leaders in major pitching categories, especially form 1932 to 1935, as he tied for the league lead in shutouts with six (1934), while his ERA was second lowest in the league.

LIFETIME STATS: W: 223, L: 186, SV: 23, ERA: 3.80, SO: 1,160, CG: 181

#934 David Arthur "Dave," "Kong" Kingman

OF-1B-DH-3B, Giants, Mets, Padres, Angels, Yankees, Cubs, A's, 1971–86

Dave Kingman came up with the Giants in July 1971 and showed his tremendous power early as he hit 17 homers before being sent to the disabled list. He was regarded as a poor defensive player, and as prodigious and often as his homers were, he struck out often, eclipsing the century mark in whiffs 13 times in his well-traveled career. After hitting 36 and 37 homers with the Mets in 1975 and 1976, he was sent to the Cubs. His finest year in the Windy City was in 1979 when "Kong" erupted for a league-leading 48 homers and hitting a career-high .288, while also leading the circuit with a slugging percentage of .613. The 6'6" Kingman led the NL in home runs in 1982 as well, hitting 37 for the Mets. Strangely enough, despite his high homer totals, Kingman topped 100 RBI only twice.

LIFETIME STATS: BA: .236, HR: 442, RBI: 1,210, H: 1,575, SB: 85

#935 Ralph "Red" Kress

SS-1B-3B-OF, Browns, White Sox, Senators, Tigers, Giants, 1927–36, 1938–40, 1946

Kress became the Browns' regular shortstop in 1928 and hit a respectable .273 while leading the league in errors and putouts. During the next three seasons, Kress put together his best years in his career. Back then, in the pre–A-Rod days of baseball, it was rare for shortstops to put up big offensive numbers, but in 1929 Kress had 107 RBI, hitting .305. The following year, he hit 16 homers with 112 RBI and a .313 average. In 1931, he clouted another 16 home runs, with 114 RBI while hitting .311. He continued to have off and on seasons defensively, however, as in 1929 he led the league in fielding, while in 1930, he led the American League in errors.

LIFETIME STATS: BA: .286, HR: 89, RBI: 799, H: 1,454, SB: 47

#**936** Lyndall Dale "Lindy," "Preach" McDaniel

RHP, Cardinals, Cubs, Giants, Yankees, Royals, 1955–75

Lindy McDaniel, named after the famous aviator Charles Lindbergh, began his career as a starter with the Cardinals, without any minor league experience. His second full year with St. Louis, McDaniel posted a 15–9 mark with a 3.49. He became a reliever in 1959, leading the league in saves and winning 13 games in relief. After pitching for the Cubs and Giants, he was traded to the Yankees, where, at one point, he retired 32 straight hitters and had a career-best 29 saves in 1970. McDaniel, an ordained minister, was known as "Preach." McDaniel also led the American League in relief wins in 1973 with 12.

LIFETIME STATS: W: 141, L: 119, SV: 172, ERA: 3.45, SO: 1,361, CG: 18

#**937** Albert Henry "Al" Bridwell

SS-2B-3B-OF-1B, Reds, Braves, Giants, Cubs, St. Louis (FL), 1905–15

Bridwell was regarded as one of the top fielding short-stops of his era. His best years came with the New York Giants, where he hit a career-high .294 with 32 stolen bases in 1909. But Bridwell got his most famous "hit" in the infamous "Merkle Boner" game in 1908, against the rival Cubs. With runners on first and third, Bridwell hit the ball through the infield, seemingly the game winner. The Giants and their fans celebrated their "victory," but in the pandemonium that followed, Fred Merkle, the runner on first, didn't touch second. Cub Johnny Evers noticed it, retrieved the ball and touched second, for the force play on Merkle. So instead of a game-winning hit and a hero's welcome, Al Bridwell's clutch at bat became merely a force out. Bridwell even said later that he regretted getting that hit, so he could have spared Fred Merkle the humiliation.

LIFETIME STATS: BA: .255, HR: 2, RBI: 238, H: 1,064, SB: 136

#938 John Francis "Honest John" Morrill

1B-3B-2B-SS, Braves, Washington (NL), Boston (PL), 1876–90

John Francis Morrill was dubbed "Honest John" because of his straightforward answer when asked how the Braves won the 1883 pennant. Morrill stated, "Good pitching and catching, and lucky hitting won for us. When the season started, I thought we would finish fourth or fifth." A Boston native, Morrill played in front of the hometown fans for 14 of his 15 years in the major leagues. He hit over .300 twice, with his high-water mark coming in 1883 when he hit .319, with 16 triples. The right-handed hitter also was the player-manager of Boston from 1882 to 1889, winning 348 and losing 334, capturing the aforementioned pennant in 1883 and coming in second the following season.

LIFETIME STATS: BA: .260, HR: 43, RBI: 643, H: 1,275, SB: 61

#939 Walter Scott "Steve" Brodie

OF, Braves, Cardinals, Baltimore (NL), Pirates, Orioles, Giants, 1890–99, 1901–02

Brodie was a consistent left-hand-hitting outfielder who started his career in Boston and St. Louis, but flourished when he got to Baltimore. He hit .361 for part of the 1893 season and then hit .366 and .348, with over 100 RBI in helping Baltimore win the National League pennants from 1894 to 1896. Brodie led the league in fielding from his center-field position in 1897, and proved to be durable as he played in 727 consecutive games between 1891 and 1897, establishing a 19th-century record for endurance. Bride was also a base-stealing threat as he stole 25 or more bases seven times in his career.

LIFETIME STATS: BA: .303, HR: 25, RBI: 900, H: 1,726, SB: 289

#940 Donn Alvin "Clink" Clendenon

1B, Pirates, Expos, Mets, Cardinals, 1961–72

A gifted athlete coming out of college, Clendenon weighed offers from the NFL's Cleveland Browns and the Harlem Globetrotters before settling on baseball. Though frequently a strikeout victim, setting a then record of 163 in 1968, Clendenon hit for power, peaking in 1966 with 28 homers and 98 RBI. He was regarded as an adroit fielder at first base as he led the league in double plays five times. In June 1969 he was traded by the Expos to the Mets. Clendenon hit 12 homers in 200 at bats as the Mets won it all in 1969. In the five-game Series, Clendenon struck three homers and hit .357 in the Series, and was named the MVP.

LIFETIME STATS: BA: .274, HR: 159, RBI: 682, H: 1,273, SB: 90

#941 Christopher Andrew "Chris," "Spuds" Sabo

3B-DH-OF, Reds, Orioles, White Sox, Cardinals, 1988–96

Sabo broke in with the Reds in 1988, and hit .271 with 40 doubles and 46 stolen bases, and won the Rookie of the Year Award. Sabo led the National League in fielding twice and was selected as an All Star three times. Sabo made the most of his only World Series, when, in 1990, he led the Reds to a shocking sweep of the favored Athletics by hitting a gaudy .562 with two homers and five RBI. Flourishing under the tutelage of Manager Lou Piniella, Sabo had his best season the following year with 26 homers, 88 RBI and a .301 average.

LIFETIME STATS: BA: .268, HR: 116, RBI: 426, H: 898, SB: 120

#942 John "Jack" Picus Quinn

RHP, Yankees, Braves, Baltimore (FL), White Sox, Red Sox, A's, Dodgers, Reds, 1909–15, 1918–33

John Quinn Picus changed the order of his middle and last names, and was still pitching at the age of 50 after playing in the big leagues for 23 years. After stints with the Yankees and Boston Braves, Quinn jumped to the renegade Federal League, and went going 26–14 with 28 complete games. After being out of baseball for two years, Quinn resurfaced with Chicago and then returned to New York where he posted an 18–10 record. From there he pitched for the Red Sox, posting sub-.500 seasons. Quinn became the oldest man to hit a home run at 47 in 1930, and lead the league in saves, at age 49. After he hit the big 4–0, Quinn fashioned a 109–97 mark, a record since broken by knuckleballer Phil Niekro.

LIFETIME STATS: W: 247, L: 218, SV: 57, ERA: 3.29, SO: 1,329, CG: 242

#943 Kalvoski "Kal" Daniels

OF, Reds, Dodgers, Cubs, 1986–92

Kal Daniels broke in with the Reds in 1986 and spent four of his seven years there. The lefty-swinging Georgian hit .320 in 74 games with 15 stolen bases in 1986, and followed it up the next year with a .334 campaign with 26 homers, 64 RBI and 26 steals. In 1988, he continued to put up steady numbers, hitting 18 homers and knocking home 64, with a career-best 27 stolen bases. He played for the Dodgers next and had his biggest power year, stroking 27 homers and knocking in 94, both career highs, while hitting .296. His offensive production steadily declined the next two years in Los Angeles, and Daniels spent the last year in his brief career with the Cubs in 1992, hitting .250 in just 108 at bats.

LIFETIME STATS: BA: .285, HR: 104, RBI: 360, H: 666, SB: 87

#944 James Francis "Shanty" Hogan

C, Braves, Giants, Senators, 1925–37

Hogan was nicknamed "Shanty" because someone thought the 6'1", 240-pound catcher looked like a small hut or shanty. Regardless of his appearance, Hogan was a solid hitter and catcher throughout his career. He led NL catchers in fielding one year, and hit .300 or better in four of his five seasons with the New York Giants. Hogan hit a high of .339 in 1930 after hitting .333 two years before. After being dealt to the Boston Braves in 1933, Hogan never was a regular again, but managed to hit a fine .301 in 1935 for Beantown, in 163 at bats. He finished up his career in Washington, appearing in only 40 games the next two seasons.

LIFETIME STATS: BA: .295, HR: 61, RBI: 474, H: 939, SB: 6

#945 Jim Thome

1B-DH-3B, Indians, Phillies, White Sox, Dodgers, Twins, 1991-present

Thome is the latest member of the 600-home run club, having hit a total of 604 in his 21 seasons. Thome was drafted by the Cleveland Indians and made his big-league debut in 1991. His first full year was 1995 when he recorded 142 hits, 29 doubles and 25 home runs. It was the first of 10 consecutive seasons in which Thome would hit 25 or more home runs. In 2003, Thome led the league with 47 home runs, and finished in the top five in homers in eight other seasons. In 2002, Thome led the league in slugging percentage, with a .677 mark, and also was in the top 10 sluggers nine other times. A five-time All-Star, Thome was in the top 10 of MVP voting after three seasons: 1997, 2001 and 2002. Thome is not just a big slugger. He is a discerning batter, having led the league in walks three times and is the active leader in Major League Baseball with 1,725.

LIFETIME STATS: BA: .277, HR: 604, RBI: 1,674, H: 2,287, SB: 19

#946 Martin Glenn "Marty" Barrett

2B, Red Sox, Padres, 1982–91

Marty Barrett became the starting second baseman for the Red Sox in 1984, and he put up some solid seasons from 1984 to 1988. In 1984, the steady Barrett hit a career-high .303, and led all American League second basemen in fielding. Barrett was an ideal number-two hitter. Three years in a row, 1986–88, he led the league in sacrifice hits. A very intelligent, heady player, he thrice in his career pulled the hidden-ball trick. He helped the Red Sox to the 1986 pennant and starred in that year's postseason by collecting a record 24 hits in 14 games, winning the MVP of the League Championship Series and hitting a robust .433 in the World Series.

LIFETIME STATS: BA: .278, HR: 18, RBI: 314, H: 938, SB: 57

#947 James Edward "Jim" Hegan

C, Indians, Tigers, Phillies, Giants, Cubs, 1941–42, 1946–60

An excellent handler of pitchers in his day, Hegan caught three no-hitters with the Indians, for Don Black in 1947, Bob Lemon in 1948 and Bob Feller in 1951. He was prized for his skill in calling games behind the plate. Hegan homered in the 1948 World Series to help the Indians defeat the Boston Braves. He was named to the All Star team five times.

LIFETIME STATS: BA: .228, HR: 92, RBI: 525, H: 1,087, SB: 15

#948 Ezra Ballou Sutton

3B-SS, Phillies, Braves, 1876–88

"Uncle Ezra," a fan favorite in Boston for the Braves, was an integral part of the Braves' 1877, 1878, and 1883 championships. He hit over .300 three years in a row (1883–85), his best mark being a .346 average in 1884 as he led the league in hits with 162. Sutton had some historic firsts in his career, both positive and negative. On the positive side, he hit the first professional home run in the National League (and the second later in the game). He also scored a record six runs in one contest. On the negative side, Sutton made the very first error in the history of the National League.

LIFETIME STATS: BA: .294, HR: 25, RBI: 671, H: 1,574, SB: 69

#**949** Michael Jay "Mike" Andrews

2B, Red Sox, White Sox, A's, 1966–73

Andrews came up to the Red Sox in 1966 and became the regular second baseman of the 1967 "Impossible Dream" team, hitting .263 that year. He improved to .271 in 1968, but his best offensive season was in 1969 when he added power to his game, clouting 15 homers with 59 RBI while hitting a career-best .293. Andrews landed in Oakland in 1973. Despite having a fine reputation as a fielder, Andrews made two errors in Game Two of the World Series against the Mets, prompting eccentric A's owner Charlie Finley to coerce Andrews into signing a document stating that he was medically unable to play, in effect putting him on the disabled list for the rest of the Series. The fans, his teammates, and eventually Commissioner Bowie Kuhn intervened, reinstating Andrews for the rest of the Series. When Andrews was introduced to the Mets crowd for Game Three, he was given a standing ovation. The A's won that World Series in seven games, and Andrews retired from baseball.

LIFETIME STATS: BA: .258, HR: 66, RBI: 316, H: 803, SB: 18

#**950** Todd Helton

1B, Rockies, 1997-present

A five-time All-Star, Helton is one of the great all-around players who a majority of fans are unaware of, probably because he plays in Colorado. But Helton is good. Helton was the 2000 batting champion with a gaudy .372 average, and has finished in the top five hitters in seven other years. The 2000 season was also the year in which Helton led the league in hits (216), slugging percentage

(.698), RBI (147) and doubles (59). But Helton is more than just a good hitter. He has also won three Gold Glove Awards, and has never been lower than fifth in the National League in fielding percentage. Helton led the league in on-base percentage twice, and was in the top five in six other seasons.

LIFETIME STATS: BA: .323, HR: 347, RBI: 1,308, H: 2,363, SB: 36

#**951** Alonza Benjamin "Al" Bumbry
OF-DH, Orioles, Padres, 1972–85

Not only a star on the diamond, Bumbry was also a standout on the battlefield, as he won the Bronze Star while serving in Vietnam. After he got back in 1973, Bumbry was the Rookie of the Year, hitting .337 and blasting 11 triples to share the league lead with Rod Carew. The durable Bumbry was the Orioles' leadoff hitter from 1974 to 1984, and only missed part of the 1978 season with an injury. Bumbry stole 20 or more bases five times in his career, peaking in 1980 with 44. He is still the all-time top base stealer in Oriole history, with 252 lifetime thefts. While with the O's, Bumbry played on four division winners, two pennant winners and a World Series champion. He was traded to San Diego, but retired after one year there.

LIFETIME STATS: BA: .281, HR: 54, RBI: 402, H: 1,422, SB: 254

#952 John Elmer "Jack," "Happy Jack" Stivetts

RHP-OF, St. Louis (AA), Braves, Cleveland (NL), 1889–99

But for three points, "Happy Jack" Stivetts could have been a 200-game winner and a .300 hitter. He started out with St. Louis of the American Association and won an astounding 60 games for them in two years, leading the league in strikeouts with 259 and walks with 232 in 1891. He jumped leagues and pitched for Boston in the National League, where he was 35–16 while completing 45 games as the Braves won the pennant. He had two more 20-win seasons, winning 27 in 1894 and 22 in 1896. When he wasn't on the mound, the Pennsylvania native played the outfield, and hit over .300 four times, with a career-best .367 in 1897.

LIFETIME STATS: BA: .297, HR: 35, RBI: 357, H: 592, SB: 31. W: 203, L: 132, SV: 4, ERA: 3.74, SO: 1,223, CG: 278

#953 Vance Aaron Law

3B-SS-2B, Pirates, White Sox, Expos, Cubs, A's, 1980–89, 1991

The son of Pirate pitching ace Vern Law, Vance signed and started off with the Pirates in 1980, but played sparingly, and was sent to the Chicago White Sox. He had a strong 1984 season in the Windy City, when he erupted for 17 homers with 59 RBI, while playing third base on a regular basis. On May 8 and 9 of that year, he played errorless ball at third base for all 25 innings of the longest game in American League history against the Brewers. He was dealt to the Expos, and showed his versatility playing many other positions, including the outfield. Law signed a free-agent contract with the Cubs in 1988 and made the All Star team, while hitting a career-high .293, hitting 11 homers and a career-best 78 RBI.

LIFETIME STATS: BA: .256, HR: 71, RBI: 442, H: 972, SB: 34

#**954** Lee Louis "The Italian Stallion" Mazzilli

OF-1B, Mets, Rangers, Yankees, Pirates, Blue Jays, 1976–89

Blessed with matinee-idol good looks, "The Italian Stallion" was a popular draw for the Mets from 1976 to 1981, and the switch-hitter hit 16, 15, and 16 homers, and averaged 72 RBI from 1978 to 1980, being named to the NL All Star team in 1979. The fleet-footed Mazzilli also stole 20 or more bases three times with the Mets, swiping 41 in 1980. He was traded to Texas, where injuries affected his game. He was eventually dealt back to the National League, and became a valuable reserve for the rest of his career. He was an excellent pinch hitter, leading the league in at bats in that role in 1985 with 72 and reaching base 62 times for an impressive .425 on-base percentage.

LIFETIME STATS: BA: .259, HR: 93, RBI: 460, H: 1,068, SB: 197

#955 Eugene "Spider" Benson

OF, Bacharach Giants, Pittsburgh Crawfords, Newark Eagles, Philadelphia Stars (Negro Leagues), 1934–48

Many baseball fans credit the great Willie Mays with inventing the basket catch in the fifties, but in fact it was Gene "Spider" Benson who may have popularized the crowd-pleasing technique two decades earlier. The 5'8" Benson was a speedy player who covered a lot of ground in center field, and participated in two Negro All Star Games, one in 1940, and the other in 1946. As was the custom with many other players in the Negro Leagues, Benson played winter ball in Cuba and Venezuela. Incomplete statistics show that his career batting average was over .300, with a career high of .370 in 1945.

LIFETIME STATS: BA: .310

#956 Gerald Peter "Jerry" Remy

2B, Angels, Red Sox, 1975–84

Jerry Remy started out his career with the California Angels and played a steady second base for them for three seasons. He was a base-stealing threat as he stole 34, 35 and 41 bases in his seasons with the Halos. Remy, a Fall River, Massachusetts native, was then traded to nearby Boston, and loved the familiar surroundings as he hit .278, with a career-high 24 doubles and 30 stolen bases, and was selected to the AL All Star squad. An excellent bunter and team player, Remy led the Sox in sacrifices for seven of his 10 seasons.

LIFETIME STATS: BA: .275, HR: 7, RBI: 329, H: 1,226, SB: 208

#957 George Ernest "The Bull" Uhle

RHP, Indians, Tigers, Giants, Yankees, Indians, 1919–34, 1936

Whoever said that pitchers can't hit never saw George "The Bull" Uhle. He had a lifetime .289 average and in one 1921 game collected six RBI. Uhle's best season was in 1923 as he was an impressive 26–16, leading the league in wins (by five) and in complete games with 29, and even had time to hit an amazing .361. He had another stellar year in 1926 when he went 27–11. The durable right-hander arguably may have been the inventor of the slider, which Uhle used very effectively throughout his 17–year career. While with the Tigers in 1929, Uhle pitched 20 innings against the White Sox before being removed for a pinch runner.

LIFETIME STATS: W: 200, L: 166, SV: 25, ERA: 3.99, SO: 1,135, CG: 232

#958 Walter William "Walt" Weiss

SS, A's, Marlins, Rockies, Braves, 1987–2000

Walt Weiss was known for his fine defensive play at short-stop and for his knack for getting into the postseason, a feat he accomplished seven times in his 14-year career. The switch-hitting Weiss was named American League Rookie of the Year in 1988 in his first full year with Oakland, and hit .333 with two doubles in a playoff sweep of the Boston Red Sox in ALCS. He then played for the Marlins and the Rockies, before signing a free-agent contract with the Atlanta Braves, and was voted the National League's starting shortstop in the 1998 All Star game.

LIFETIME STATS: BA: .258, HR: 25, RBI: 386, H: 1,207, SB: 96

#959 Jose "The Black Diamond" Mendez

RHP-2B-3B-SS-OF, Cuban Stars, All-Nations, Kansas City Monarchs, 1908–26. Hall of Fame, 2006

Mendez began his career as a fastball pitcher in the Cuban Leagues. In 1908, pitching for the Cuban Stars, he went 44–2. A majority of these teams were semipro squads, but Mendez dominated teams, whatever the caliber.

In 1910, he was 18–2 in the Cuban Winter League; and in 1913, he was 10–0. New York Giants manager John McGraw said at the time that he would pay the Stars $50,000 for Mendez. Of course, McGraw knew the black-skinned Mendez would never be allowed to play for his team, at least not in that era.

Mendez pitched in Cuba for most of his career, and he was possibly the first Cuban baseball legend. He would often be recruited to pitch against Major League stars. He was 8–7 in these exhibitions in his career, defeating Jack Coombs and Hall of Famer Eddie Plank in separate games in 1909 and splitting with another legend, Christy Mathewson, the next season.

LIFETIME STATS: NOT AVAILABLE

#960 Salvatore Anthony "Sal," "The Barber" Maglie

RHP, Giants, Indians, Dodgers, Yankees, Cardinals, 1945, 1950–58

Sal Maglie started his career as a 28-year-old rookie in 1945, but jumped to the renegade Mexican League. Maglie returned, only to have Major League Baseball bar him from playing. Maglie was reinstated with the Giants for the 1950 season. He started out in the bullpen, and was an emergency starter, going an impressive 18–4 and tying for the league lead with five shutouts in just 16 starts. Maglie went 23–6 in 1951, leading the Giants to the 1951 flag, and 18–8 in 1952. Dubbed "The Barber," he routinely brushed back or shaved opposition batters, claiming that he "owned the plate."

LIFETIME STATS: W: 119, L: 62, SV: 14, ERA: 3.15, SO: 862, CG: 93

#**961** Ronald John "Ron" Oester
2B, Reds, 1978–90

Ron Oester (rhymes with coaster) was a very good defensive shortstop in the minors, but with Dave Concepcion firmly entrenched at that position for the Reds, he had to learn a different position. And learn he did, playing a terrific second base for most of his career, all with his hometown team, the Cincinnati Reds. Oester proved to be durable between the 1982 and 1986, when he played in 150 games or more each year, but that streak ended with a broken leg suffered in mid-1987. He had little power, but what he couldn't provide in that department, he more than made up with his glove. Oester did hit 11 homers in 1983, his only year in double figures in that department, and his highest batting average as a starter was .295 in 1985. He retired a world champion after the 1990 season, hitting .299 in part-time duty.

LIFETIME STATS: BA: .265, HR: 42, RBI: 344, H: 1,118, SB: 40

#962 Ruppert Sanderson Jones

OF, Royals, Mariners, Yankees, Padres, Tigers, Angels, 1976–87

The left-handed Ruppert Jones was the first player chosen in the 1976 expansion draft by the newly formed Seattle Mariners. Jones rewarded the Mariners by hitting a career-best 24 homers and knocking home 76, representing the M's in the All Star game. In 1979, Jones hit .267 with 21 homers and a career-high 78 RBI while scoring 109 runs. Jones showed his speed around the horn, by swiping a personal-best 33 bases that season. Jones was a fan favorite in the Kingdome, even after he left the team, as the fans used to chant "Rupe!! Rupe!!" when he played there. After a stint with the Yankees, he was traded to the Padres, and made his second and last All Star team in the process, before going on the disabled list with a foot injury.

LIFETIME STATS: BA: .250, HR: 147, RBI: 579, H: 1,103, SB: 143

#963 Charles F. "Heinie" Wagner

SS-2B, Giants, Red Sox, 1902, 1906–13, 1915–16, 1918

Wagner was one of two players to play for the Red Sox in all four championship seasons in the 1910s. (The more heralded Harry Hooper was the other.) He started out in 1902 with the Giants, but didn't play much and was sent down to the minors. He resurfaced with Boston in 1906. Wagner was considered an excellent infielder as he led American League shortstops three times in total chances, a testament to his excellent range. Wagner's best year was the World Championship year of 1912, when he hit .274, scored 75 runs, socked 25 doubles and stole 21 bases, the last of four times he would steal 20 or more in a season. When Babe Ruth came on the Boston scene in 1914, it was Wagner who got the job of keeping tabs on the fun-loving Babe.

LIFETIME STATS: BA: .250, HR: 10, RBI: 343, H: 834, SB: 144

#964 Jeffrey James "Jeff," "The Terminator" Reardon

RHP, Mets, Expos, Twins, Red Sox, Braves, Reds, Yankees, 1979–94

Jeff Reardon, called "The Terminator" for the way he would end games, started out his career as a starter in the Mets' farm system. He was traded to the Expos for Ellis Valentine, one of the worst deals in Mets history. Reardon flourished north of the border as he averaged 23 saves per year his first three years there. Then he really came into his own, saving a league-leading 41 in 1985 and winning Fireman of the Year. In 1987, he was traded again, this time to the Twins, and Reardon helped the Twins immediately, second in the league for saves as the Twins won their first World Championship. After the 1989 season, when he saved 31 more games, he declared for free agency and signed with his home-state team, the Red Sox, where he continued to pitch well with 21, 40 and 27 saves over the next three seasons.

LIFETIME STATS: W: 73, L: 77, SV: 367, ERA: 3.16, SO: 877, CG: 0

#965 Julio Louis "Juice" Cruz

2B- DH, Mariners, White Sox, 1977–86

Julio Cruz took over at second base full-time for the Mariners in 1978. That year he only hit .235, but stole an incredible 59 bases. He improved his hitting to .271 the following year and also stole another 49 bases. The next three years, Cruz stole 40 or more bases every season, at one time stealing 32 in a row. He was also quite a fielder: In 1981 he flawlessly fielded a record 18 chances in a nine-inning game. Cruz was traded to the White Sox midseason in 1983 and helped them to the postseason. He swiped 57 bases with Seattle and Chicago that year, and hit .252. Cruz also hit .333 in the ALCS that season in a losing cause against the Orioles.

LIFETIME STATS: BA: .237, HR: 23, RBI: 279, H: 916, SB: 343

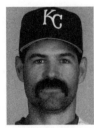

#966 Jeffrey Wayne "Jeff" King

3B-1B-2B, Pirates, Royals, 1989–99

Jeff King started his career with the Pirates, and toiled in obscurity for the first four years. In 1993, he started to make better contact, and hit .295 with 98 RBI. That RBI total was 33 better than his previous high the year before. That year he also led National League third-sackers in assists. King in 1995 hit two homers in the same inning, and repeated this feat the following year, when he exploded for 30 homers (almost twice his previous high). He also added 111 RBI, another vast improvement in that department. King hit .271 that year. He was then traded to Kansas City, where his batting average fell to a dismal .238, but he continued putting up the power numbers, hitting 28 more home runs and knocking in a career-high 112 runs.

LIFETIME STATS: BA: .256, HR: 154, RBI: 709, H: 1,091, SB: 75

#967 Michael Andreas "Mike," "Iron Mike" Kreevich

OF, Cubs, White Sox, A's, Browns, Senators, 1931, 1935–45

Kreevich was signed by the Cubs and played briefly there, but it was playing for the team on the other side of town, the White Sox, that made him comfortable. Kreevich enjoyed a fine rookie season in 1936, hitting .307 and scoring 99 runs. The following year, he led the league in triples with 16, hit .302 and tied a major league record when he hit four doubles in a late-season game. Kreevich was considered an excellent defensive player and had a terrific arm as he threw out a league-leading 18 base runners in 1939. He hit over .300 three times in his career, and just missed that hallowed mark one other time, hitting .297. Kreevich also shares the dubious record of grounding out into a double play four times in one game (along with Goose Goslin and Joe Torre).

LIFETIME STATS: BA: .283, HR: 45, RBI: 514, H: 1,321, SB: 115

#968 William Edward "Eddie" Robinson

1B, Indians, Senators, White Sox, A's, Yankees, Tigers, Orioles, 1942, 1946–57

Robinson was the first baseman on the last Cleveland Indian championship team of 1948, hitting 16 homers with 83 RBI. The left-handed batter was then traded to Washington where he spent 1949 and part of 1950 before going to the White Sox and emerging as a star. A two-time All Star in Chicago, Robinson hit 29 homers in cavernous Comiskey Park in 1951 and drove in a career-high 117 runs. His next stop was with Philadelphia, and he was selected as an All Star again, with 22 homers and 102 RBI, his last big power year.

LIFETIME STATS: BA: .268, HR: 172, RBI: 723, H: 1,146, SB: 10

#969 Ivan DeJesus

SS, Dodgers, Cubs, Phillies, Cardinals, Yankees, Giants, Tigers, 1974–88

DeJesus first became a starter with the Chicago Cubs in 1977, hitting .266 with 24 stolen bases. He led the National League in runs scored the following year with 104 and stole 41 more bases. His 44 steals in 1980 set a Cub record for a shortstop. DeJesus was excellent defensively as his league-best 595 assists in 1977 set a Cubs' record that still stands. Only an average hitter, DeJesus surprised everyone by becoming the 11th Cub in history to hit for the cycle in 1980. The Cubs traded him to the Phillies in what many believe to be one of the best deals the Cubs ever made. Coming over from Philadelphia was shortstop Larry Bowa and a then-unknown second base-man named Ryne Sandberg.

LIFETIME STATS: BA: .254, HR: 21, RBI: 324, H: 1,167, SB: 194

#970 Samuel Charles "Sammy" White

C, Red Sox, Braves, Phillies, 1951–59, 1961–62

Sammy White had a tryout with the Minneapolis Lakers of the NBA, but signed instead with the Red Sox, and was their dependable starting catcher for most of the fifties. A fine defensive catcher, White had the ability to "frame" pitches well, sometimes making borderline pitches seem like strikes to the umpire. He proved to be very durable too, catching 100 or more games for the Sox between 1952 and 1959. In 1952, he hit a ninth-inning grand slam to win a game in Fenway Park against the Browns and Satchel Paige. White also had the distinction of being the only player in the modern era to score three runs in a single inning as the Red Sox erupted for a 17-run inning against the Tigers in a 23–3 win in 1953.

LIFETIME STATS: BA: .262, HR: 66, RBI: 421, H: 916, SB: 14

#971 William Russell "Bill," "Billy Bull" Johnson

3B, Yankees, Cardinals, 1943, 1946–53

Johnson broke in with the Yankees in 1943, and hit .280, but duty beckoned and Johnson missed the next two seasons, serving in the military during World War II. Johnson became the Bombers' starting third baseman in 1947, when he had his finest offensive season, hitting .285 and coming in fifth in the league with 95 RBI while being selected for his only All Star game. He set a record in the World Series that year as he hit three triples in seven games in a win over the Dodgers, and led the Yankees in runs with eight. In 1948, Johnson hit a career-best .294 and led American League third baseman in total chances per game. He was traded to the Cardinals in 1951 and in his last season as a starter, led NL third baseman in fielding and hit a career-high 14 homers.

LIFETIME STATS: BA: .271, HR: 61, RBI: 487, H: 882, SB: 13

#972 Ernest Gordon "Babe," "Blimp" Phelps

C, Senators, Cubs, Dodgers, Pirates, 1931, 1933–42

Phelps started out in 1931 with the Senators, came back in 1933 with the Cubs, and starting catching regularly with the Dodgers of 1936. Called "Blimp" because of his 6'2", 225-pound frame, he hit an impressive .367 that year, second in the league by six points to future Hall of Famer Paul Waner. Phelps, who was also called "the Grounded Blimp" because of his refusal to fly, hit over .300 twice more in his Dodger career. The lefty-hitting Phelps was traded to the Pirates, and finished his career there as a backup catcher, hitting .284.

LIFETIME STATS: BA: .310, HR: 54, RBI: 345, H: 657, SB: 9

#973 John Anthony Franco

LHP, Reds, Mets, Astros, 1984–2005

Franco broke into the majors with the Reds, pitching only 54 games in relief and registering his first four saves. In 1985, Franco won 11 games in a row and fashioned a 12–3 record out of the Red bullpen. In 1986, Franco was the Reds' closer as he saved 29 and was selected for the first of four times to the National League All Star team. The following year, he started a streak of 30 saves or more for the next five seasons. In 1988, he led the league in saves. Traded to the Mets in 1990, Franco became the first Met to lead the league in saves, with 33. He won the Rolaids Fireman of the Year Award for the second time. (He also won it in 1988.) Franco's two best years with the Mets were when he saved 36 and 38 in 1997 and

1998. Franco has the most saves of any southpaw in history with 424, and is the active leader in that department. He is also second all-time to Lee Smith, who recorded 486 career saves.

LIFETIME STATS: W: 90, L: 87, SV: 424, ERA: 2.89, SO: 975, CG: 0

#**974** Trevor Hoffman
RHP, Marlins, Padres, Brewers, 1993-2010

Hoffman went against the grain for most of his 18-year career: A relief specialist who got people out, not by blowing a fastball past batters, but by changing speeds. Hoffman was drafted by the Reds, and in 1993 taken by the Florida Marlins in the expansion draft. He debuted that year. He has never been a starter, coming out of the bullpen all 18 seasons. Hoffman pitched 1,089 innings without ever being on the mound at the beginning of a game. Hoffman's 601 saves are second all-time in Major League Baseball history. He led the National League in saves twice, in 1998 and 2008, and had 30 or more saves in 14 seasons. The seven-time All-Star also finished second in voting for the Cy Young Award twice.

LIFETIME STATS: BA: .248, HR: 56, RBI: 381, H: 988, SB: 69

#**975** U.L. Washington
SS-2B, Royals, Expos, Pirates, 1977–87

A product of the famous Royals Baseball Academy, Washington was a great base runner and played excellent defense. He was in double figures with steals for six of the eight years he was with Kansas City, peaking with 40 thefts in 1983. He was also known for chewing a toothpick while batting. In a 1979 game, the switch-hitter homered from both sides of the plate. He also proved to be clutch in the pick while batting. In a 1979 game, the switch-hitter homered from both sides of the plate. He also proved to be clutch in the postseason when he drove in the game-winning run in Game Two of the ALCS against the Yankees as the Royals swept New York. He had his best season with the bat in 1982, as he hit 10 homers and recorded a .286 batting average.

LIFETIME STATS: BA: .251, HR: 27, RBI: 255, H: 703, SB: 132

#976 Frederick Charles "Fred" Snodgrass

OF-1B, Giants, Braves, 1908–16

Snodgrass played with the Giants for most of his career, becoming their regular centerfielder in 1910, and was a member of the Giants' pennant-winning teams of 1911 to 1913. His best offensive year was in 1910, when he hit .321, the only time he hit over .300 as a starter. Snodgrass was also speedy on the bases as he stole 25 or more bases five times, swiping a career high of 51 in 1911, then followed it up by stealing 43 in 1912. The sure-handed outfielder, ironically, is known for a famous error he made in the 1912 World Series that led to the Red Sox defeating the Giants. In the deciding game, the Giants were leading 2–1 as the Red Sox batted in the bottom of the 10th. Pinch hitter Clyde Engle lifted an easy fly to Snodgrass in center, but the usually dependable centerfielder dropped it as Engle went to second. Engle eventually came on to score, and Boston won the championship. Manager John McGraw, who could be extremely strict on mental errors, forgave his center fielder.

LIFETIME STATS: BA: .275, HR: 11, RBI: 351, H: 852, SB: 215

#977 Alexander "Alex" Johnson

OF-DH, Phillies, Cardinals, Reds, Angels, Indians, Rangers, Yankees, Tigers, 1964–76

Known as a great hitter, Johnson was often a headache to several major league teams with his apparent lack of hustle and surly attitude. In 1964, the right-hander hit .303 in 109 at-bats with the Phillies. After two seasons in St. Louis, he was traded to the Reds, he hit .312 in 1968 and winning the Comeback Player of the Year Award, and .315 in 1969. Johnson then was traded to the American League Angels, where he led his new league in hitting with a .329 average, just nosing out Boston's Carl Yastrzemski for his only batting championship. Johnson was known to be belligerent with the press and with his fellow Angels. He was fined a whopping 29 times and even suspended for lack of effort, something he even later admitted saying he was "just paid to hit."

LIFETIME STATS: BA: .288, HR: 78, RBI: 525, H: 1,331, SB: 113

#978 Edward Cunningham "Eddie," "Kid" Foster

3B-2B, Yankees, Senators, Red Sox, Browns, 1910, 1912–23

Known as "Kid," the speedy Foster was fifth in the AL in doubles with 34 in his first full season in 1912, and stole 20 or more bases six times in his 13-season career. The durable infielder led the American League in at bats on four occasions and had his best season in 1912 when he hit a steady .285. Always a good contact hitter, the diminutive Foster broke up the great Eddie Plank's no-hitter in 1917 with a double as Plank needed just one out to complete his masterpiece.

LIFETIME STATS: BA: .264, HR: 6, RBI: 451, H: 1,490, SB: 195

#**979** John Joseph "Honest John" Anderson

OF-1B, Dodgers, Senators, Milwaukee (AL), Browns, Yankees, Senators, White Sox, 1894–99, 1901–08

Anderson stole 20 or more bases 10 ten times in his career, and led the league with 39 in 1906. He achieved double figures in triples five times with an impressive 22 in 1898, leading the league. He also hit nine homers that season, an impressive number in the "dead ball" era, and led the league in slugging with a .494 mark. In 1901, while with Milwaukee in the American League's opening season, Anderson hit a career-best .330 with a career-high 99 RBI. The switch-hitting Norwegian retired in 1908 with 338 career stolen bases.

LIFETIME STATS: BA: .290, HR: 49, RBI: 976, H: 1,841, SB: 338

#**980** Amos Aaron Strunk

OF, A's, Red Sox, White Sox, 1908–24

Strunk was a fine defensive outfielder with sure hands and speedy feet. He used those feet to steal 20 or more bases four times in his career, with a high of 29 in 1912. He also developed a knack for scoring from second on a sacrifice bunt, often catching the defense napping as he used his good speed to take the extra base. A member of the early A's dynasty, Strunk was traded to the Red Sox in 1918, and then to the White Sox as he hit a career-high .332 for Chicago in 1921. In 1923, he was a stalwart pinch hitter for the White Sox as he led the American League with 12 pinch hits.

LIFETIME STATS: BA: .284, HR: 15, RBI: 530, H: 1,418, SB: 185

#981 George Cutshaw

2B, Dodgers, Pirates, Tigers, 1912–23

Cutshaw was considered the best defensive second baseman in the 1910s, and the fielding statistics from that era bear that out. Cutshaw led the National League in putouts from 1913 to 1916 and again in 1918, and in assists from 1914 to 1916 and 1918. In addition, he led the loop in double plays in 1913 and 1914. The 5'9", 160-pound second baseman set a new fielding record that stood for 23 years, when he fielded .980 in 1919. At times, Cutshaw could also help his team offensively, too, as in 1915 he went six-for-six in one game (all singles). Cutshaw stole 20 or more bases seven times in his career, his highest output being 39 in 1913. He also had seasons of 36 and 34.

LIFETIME STATS: BA: .265, HR: 25, RBI: 653, H: 1,487, SB: 271

#982 Kenneth Jerry Adair

2B-SS, Orioles, White Sox, Red Sox, Royals, 1958–70

Jerry Adair was a terrific defensive second baseman who came up with the Orioles to stay in 1961. He set a league record in 1964 with an outstanding .994 fielding percentage, committing only five errors. He followed that up with another sterling performance in the field in 1965, handling 458 straight chances without making a single error. His best offensive output was in 1962 when the right-hand hitting Oklahoman hit .284 with 11 homers and 29 doubles, all career highs.

LIFETIME STATS: BA: .254, HR: 57, RBI: 366, H: 1,022, SB: 29

#**983** Willie Clay Upshaw

1B-DH, Blue Jays, Indians, 1978, 1980–88

The first cousin of NFL star lineman Gene Upshaw, Willie Upshaw had some fine seasons with the Blue Jay teams of the 80s. He really came into his own in 1983, when he hit 27 homers and had 104 RBI while hitting an impressive .306. Spotting a vulnerability to inside fastballs, American League pitchers starting busting Upshaw inside, and he had difficulty adjusting, resulting in a drastic decline in offensive production. Toronto dealt him to Cleveland, where Upshaw spent his last season hitting .245 with 11 home runs.

LIFETIME STATS: BA: .262, HR: 123, RBI: 528, H: 1,103, SB: 88

#**984** Thomas Andrew "Tom," "Bruno" Brunansky

OF, Angels, Twins, Cardinals, Red Sox, Brewers, 1981–94

Brunansky was signed by the Angels and played there sparingly as a rookie in 1981. Dealt to the Twins the following year, Brunansky became a mainstay in the Twin Cities, playing well there for seven seasons, including the 1987 World Championship year. "Bruno" had 20 or more homers six times in Minnesota, with season highs of 32 twice. Selected as an All Star in 1985, Brunansky twice led AL outfielders in double plays. He was magnificent in the 1987 ALCS against the Detroit Tigers, slugging 1.000 as he tore up Tiger pitching with two homers and four doubles.

LIFETIME STATS: BA: .245, HR: 271, RBI: 919, H: 1,543, SB: 69

#985 Walter Wayne "Wally" Backman
2B-3B, Mets, Twins, Pirates, Phillies, Mariners, 1980–93

Backman came up with the Mets in 1980, and the switch-hitter topped .300 three times for them in his first nine seasons. In 1986, Backman helped the Mets win the pennant and the World Series as he hit .320; though he had little power, he was a terrific hit and run man as he often made contact, rarely striking out. He hit .333 in the World Series against the Red Sox, and scored the winning run in Game Seven.

LIFETIME STATS: BA: .275, HR: 10, RBI: 240, H: 893, SB: 117

#986 Walter Franklin "Walt," "Wally" Judnich
OF-1B, Browns, Indians, Pirates, 1940–42, 946–49

Judnich had the misfortune of playing center field in the Yankee farm system in the mid to late 1930s, with future Hall of Famer Joe DiMaggio playing ahead of him in New York. Judnich finally got his break when the Yanks traded him to the St. Louis Browns, where he started his career in 1940. In his first season, the left-handed hitter clouted 24 homers with 89 RBI, both career highs, and a .303 batting average. Judnich, like many others, lost three prime years when he was in the military during World War II, coming back in 1946, but slipping to .262 with 15 homers. Always considered to have a better-than-average arm, Judnich led American League outfielders in fielding three times in his abbreviated career.

LIFETIME STATS: BA: .281, HR: 90, RBI: 420, H: 782, SB: 20

#987 Spike Dee Owen

SS-1B-2B-3B, Mariners, Red Sox, Expos, Yankees, Angels, 1983–95

Spike Dee Owen (his real name) was a good fielding, no-hit player who twice led National League shortstops in fielding. While in the American League with his original team, the Mariners, and the Red Sox in 1986, Owen led league shortstops in double plays and total chances. The Red Sox, in their pennant drive year of 1986, picked up Owen. Owen, uncharacteristically, came alive with the bat in that year's ALCS against the Angels, hitting a gaudy .429, then as an encore hit .300 in the World Series against the Mets. He was sent to the Montreal Expos in 1989 where he shone defensively for four seasons.

LIFETIME STATS: BA: .246, HR: 46, RBI: 439, H: 1,211, SB: 82

#988 Louis "Lou" Criger

C, Cleveland (NL), Cardinals, Red Sox, Browns, Yankees, 1896–1910, 1912

Criger, though not a great hitter, was nonetheless considered one of the best defensive catchers of his era. All-time-wins leader Cy Young certainly thought so, as Criger caught the great Young in Cleveland and St. Louis, and when Young jumped to Boston, in 1901, he insisted that Criger go with him. Criger also had a strong accurate arm, as the great Ty Cobb rarely ran on him. Twelve years after his career ended, rumors began to circulate that Criger was offered $12,000 to throw the 1903 World Series. Criger admitted that he was approached by a gambler, but refused his offer, telling no one except Young.

LIFETIME STATS: BA: .221, HR: 11, RBI: 342, H: 709, SB: 58

#989 Glenn Earle Davis

1B-DH, Astros, Orioles, 1984–93

Davis was one of the better sluggers in the National League in the '80s despite playing half of his team's games in the spacious Houston Astrodome. He was selected to the National League All Star team twice and became the first Astro to hit 30 or more homers three times, peaking with 34 circuit clouts in 1989. His lethal bat was a big reason why the Astros won the NL West in 1986, as the right-hand-hitting Davis had a career-best 101 RBI with 31 homers. In Game One of the NLCS against the Mets, he hit a homer for the only run of the game.

LIFETIME STATS: BA: .259, HR: 190, RBI: 603, H: 965, SB: 28

#990 Ben Taylor

1B, Chicago American Giants, Indianapolis ABC's, St. Louis Giants, Bacharach Giants, Washington Potomacs, Harrisburg Giants, Baltimore Black Sox, Baltimore Stars, Brooklyn Eagles, Washington Black Senators, New York Cubans (Negro Leagues), 1913–40. Hall of Fame, 2006

Ben Taylor was a well-traveled Negro League player, donning the uniform of eleven teams in his 28-year career. The youngest of four baseball-playing brothers, Taylor was considered to be one of the top first basemen of his era, primarily in the first part of the century. He had his best years with the Indianapolis ABC's between 1915 and 1922, all while being managed by his brother, C. I. Taylor. The left-hand-hitting Taylor had a Negro League World Series to remember in 1916 as he went 11-for-18, a lusty .611 mark, while stealing three bases in five games. In 1921, he hit a robust .421, and followed that up with a

.362 campaign the following year. Defensively, he was also smooth around the bag.

LIFETIME STATS: BA: .335

#**991** Gregory Scott "Gregg" Jefferies

3B-2B-DH-1B-OF, Mets, Royals, Cardinals, Phillies, Angels, Tigers, 1987–2000

The switch-hitting Jefferies came up with much promise with the Mets and because of his .321 hitting in late 1988, became the regular third baseman there, helping the Mets win the NL East that year, and hitting .333 in the NLCS. After a brief stint in Kansas City, Jeffries was traded to St. Louis. As a Cardinal, Jefferies resurrected his career, hitting .342 and .325 in his two seasons in Missouri. He also hit 16 homers and had 83 RBI with 46 stolen bases in his initial season with the Redbirds. Jefferies stole 10 or more bases nine times in his career.

LIFETIME STATS: BA: .289, HR: 126, RBI: 663, H: 1,593, SB: 196

#**992** Leon Joseph "Bip" Roberts

2B-OF-3B, Padres, Reds, Royals, Indians, Tigers, A's, 1986, 1988–98

Roberts came to the big leagues with the Padres as a great contact hitter with a lot of speed. He regularly led off for San Diego in 1990, and hit an impressive .309 with 46 steals, all the while playing second, third, or the outfield with equal dexterity. Bothered by injuries in 1992, he still hit .323, stole 44 bases, and tied a league record by making 10 consecutive base hits. He also had 34 doubles that year, and was named to the NL All Star team. Always a threat to steal, Roberts stole 20 or more bases seven times in his career.

LIFETIME STATS: BA: .294, HR: 30, RBI: 352, H: 1,220, SB: 264

#993 John Frank "Buck" Freeman

OF-1B, Washington (AA), Washington (NL), Braves, Red Sox, 1891, 1898–1907

Freeman was one of the best power hitters of the "dead ball" era. The lefty-hitter and thrower, he was Babe Ruth before Babe Ruth, as he was a converted southpaw pitcher who had outstanding power for his time. In his first full season, Freeman led the National League with 25 homers, only two homers shy of the then record held by Ned Williamson, and a total not approached until the Babe himself broke Williamson's record when he hit 29 in 1919. While with the Red Sox, Freeman came in second in homers twice and again led the league with 13 in 1903, as he became the first player to lead both leagues in homers. Freeman also led the American League in RBI in 1902 and 1903.

LIFETIME STATS: BA: .293, HR: 82, RBI: 713, H: 1,235, SB: 92

#994 Damaso Domingo Garcia

2B, Yankees, Blue Jays, Braves, Expos, 1978–86, 1988–89

After a short stint with the Yankees, Garcia was signed by Toronto and spent seven successful seasons there. He became the first Blue Jay ever to amass 1,000 hits. In 1982, he hit a career-high .310 and stole an astounding 54 bases. (His previous high had been 13.) He followed that up with a .307 season with another 31 stolen bases, and stole 46, 28 and nine bases more the next three seasons on the way to an impressive career total of 203 thefts. In 1986, Garcia tied a major league record when he stroked four doubles in one game against his original Yankee team. A two-time All Star, Garcia was traded to Atlanta, but he hit a puny .117 in limited action there, and finished up his career with the Expos.

LIFETIME STATS: BA: .283, HR: 36, RBI: 323, H: 1,108, SB: 203

#995 John Good "Long John" Reilly

1B-OF, Reds, Cincinnati (AA), 1880, 1883–91

Hailing from Cincinnati, the lanky (6'3", 178 pounds) Reilly played his entire career in his hometown. Reilly was one of the game's first sluggers as he tied for the league lead with 11 homers in 1884, and led the circuit with 13 homers and 103 RBI in 1888. That 1888 season was a banner year for Reilly as the smooth-fielding first baseman also swiped an amazing 82 bases that summer, and led the league in slugging with a .501 average. Right-handed all the way, Reilly led the National League in 1890 with 26 triples, on the way to a career total of 139. He retired after the 1891 season, where he hit .242, his lowest mark in a fine, though brief, 10-year career.

LIFETIME STATS: BA: .289, HR: 69, RBI: 740, H: 1,352, SB: 245

#996 Alfonso "Chico" Carrasquel
SS-3B-2B, White Sox, Indians, A's, Orioles, 1950–59

Carrasquel was originally signed by the Brooklyn Dodgers. The Dodgers had a shortstop already, by the name of Pee Wee Reese, so they traded the Caracas, Venezuela, native to the White Sox, where Carrasquel played for six of his 10 big-league seasons. As a rookie in 1950, he hit .282 and had a 24-game hitting streak, and the following year was named the American League's starting shortstop, outdistancing the reigning AL MVP Phil Rizzuto. Carrasquel would be named to the All Star team three other times in his career with Chicago. In 1954, he led AL shortstops in double plays, scoring 106 runs while hitting a career-best 12 home runs.

LIFETIME STATS: BA: .258, HR: 55, RBI: 474, H: 1,199, SB: 31

#997 George Alexander "Twinkletoes" Selkirk
OF, Yankees, 1934–42

Selkirk had the unenviable task of following Babe Ruth as the Yankees' right fielder, and even wore number 3 before it was retired, but finally won over the Yankee fans with his solid play. Nicknamed "Twinkletoes" because of the way he ran on the balls of his feet, the lefty-swinging Canadian hit over .300 five times in his nine year career, all with the Yankees. He also had two 100-RBI seasons, with 107 in 1936 and 101 in 1939, and appeared in six World Series in his career. In his very first World Series in 1936, Selkirk hit .333 with two homers and a triple, slugging a terrific .667 while scoring six runs.

LIFETIME STATS: BA: .290, HR: 108, RBI: 576, H: 810, SB: 49

#998 Mervin Weldon "Merv" Rettenmund

OF-DH, Orioles, Reds, Padres, Angels, 1968–80

Super athlete Rettenmund was also drafted by the Dallas Cowboys out of Ball State, where he starred as a halfback. He eventually chose baseball instead, signing with the Baltimore Orioles, and was named The Sporting News Minor League Player of the Year. Promoted to the O's in 1968, the right-hand-hitting Rettenmund led the team in hitting for his first two full seasons, with .322 and .318 marks in 1970 and 1971. He hit in double figures in home runs for the only times in his career also, with 18 in 1970 and 11 in 1971. He was traded to the Reds, where he continued to struggle at the plate. From there he went to San Diego, where he was an excellent pinch hitter, leading the league in pinch-hits with 21 and in pinch-hit at bats with 67. At the time, the 21 pinch-hit total was the eighth-best total in major league history.

LIFETIME STATS: BA: .271, HR: 66, RBI: 329, H: 693, SB: 68

#999 Roberto Conrado Kelly

OF, Yankees, Reds, Braves, Expos, Dodgers, Twins, Mariners, Rangers, 1987–2000

Roberto Kelly became a starter for New York 1989, hitting .302 and stealing 35 bases. His power numbers increased in 1990 as Kelly hit 15 homers with 61 RBI while pilfering 42 bases, a career high. In 1991, stroked a career-best 20 homers and 69 RBI, and made the All Star team the next year. He was then traded to the Reds, and Kelly made the National League All Star team for the first and only time, hitting .319. But, after playing two seasons in Cincinnati, Kelly had to keep his suitcase packed as he journeyed throughout the majors with six other teams, before coming back to the Yankees in a limited role in 2000.

LIFETIME STATS: BA: .290, HR: 124, RBI: 585, H: 1,390, SB: 235

#**1000** Richard Fremont "Rich" Dauer

2B-3B, Orioles, 1976–85

Dauer had some big shoes to fill when he broke in with the Orioles in 1976 with the departure of Bobby Grich. A .257 lifetime hitter, Dauer was superb defensively. In 1978, he set a major league record by playing in 86 consecutive errorless games, while going error-free for 425 chances. In Game Seven of the 1979 World Series against the Pirates, Dauer, rarely a power threat, smashed a homer, giving the Orioles the lead, an advantage that was short-lived as the Pirates came back and won the championship that year. The right-handed-hitting Dauer's best batting average was in 1980 when he hit .284.

LIFETIME STATS: BA: .257, HR: 43, RBI: 372, H: 984, SB: 6

Player Index

A

Aaron, Henry Louis "The Hammer," 25
Adair, Kenneth Jerry, 628
Adams, Charles Benjamin "Babe," 579
Adams, Earl John "Sparky," 567
Adcock, Joe, 271
Agee, Tommie Lee, 477
Alexander, Grover Cleveland "Pete," 28
Allen, John Thomas "Johnny," 514
Allen, Newton Henry "Newt," 466
Allen, Richard Anthony "Dick," 131
Alley, Leonard Eugene "Gene," "Oopie,"
    561
Allison, William Robert "Bob," 441
Alomar, Roberto "Robby," "Bobby," 160
Alou, Felipe Rojas, 363
Alou, Mateo Rojas "Matty," 457
Anderson, Brady Kevin, 448
Anderson, John Joseph "Honest John," 627
Andrews, Michael Jay "Mike," 609
Anson, Adrian Constantine "Cap,"
    "Pop," 79
Aparicio, Luis Ernesto "Little Louie," 140
Appling, Lucius Benjamin "Luke," "Old
Aches and Pains," 128
Armas, Antonio Rafael "Tony," 557
Ashburn, Don Richard "Richie," 202
Ashby, Alan Dean, 429
Austin, James Philip "Jimmy," "Pepper," 558
Avila, Roberto Francisco "Bobby," 407

B

Backman, Walter Wayne "Wally," 630
Baerga, Carlos Obed, 569
Bagwell, Jeffrey Robert "Jeff," 123
Bailey, Lonas Edgar "Ed," Jr., 328
Baines, Harold, 296
Baker, John B. "Dusty," Jr., 373
Baker, John Franklin "Home Run," 95
Bancroft, Dave "Beauty," 272
Bando, Salvatore Leonard "Sal," 171
Bankhead, Sam, 584
Banks, Ernest "Mr. Cub," 70
Barfield, Jesse Lee, 448
Barrett, James Erigena "Jimmy," 484
Barrett, Martin Glenn "Marty," 607
Barry, John Joseph "Jack," 564
Bartell, Dick, 320
Bassler, John Landis "Johnny," 359
Battey, Earl Jesse, Jr., 392
Bauer, Henry Albert "Hank," 516
Baylor, Don, 298
Beaumont, Clarence Howeth "Ginger," 340
Beckert, Glenn Alfred, 405
Beckley, Jacob Peter "Jake," 398
Belanger, Mark Henry, 419
Bell, David Gus "Buddy," 215
Bell, David Russell "Gus," Jr., 394
Bell, George Antonio, 411
Bell, James Thomas "Cool Papa," 80
Bell, Jay Stuart, 248